To the memory of Huicmuse, Sotoatijeium,
Pixpixuecas, and all the other Indians I came to
know through the pages of the mission records

CHIEF MARIN

CHIEF MARIN

LEADER, REBEL, AND LEGEND

BETTY GOERKE

Foreword by Greg Sarris

HEYDAY BOOKS · *Berkeley, California*

The publisher is grateful to the Federated Indians of Graton Rancheria
for their generous support.

Library of Congress Cataloging-in-Publication Data

Goerke, Betty.
Chief Marin : leader, rebel, and legend / Betty Goerke; foreword by Greg Sarris.
p. cm.
Includes bibliographical references and index.
ISBN-13: 978-1-59714-053-9 (pbk. : alk. paper)
1. Marin, Chief, ca. 1780-1839. 2. Miwok Indians--Biography. 3. Miwok Indians--
History. 4. Miwok Indians--Missions. 5. San Rafael Mission (Marin County, Calif.)--
History. 6. Marin County (Calif.)--History. I. Title.
E99.M69M374 2007
979.4004'9741330092--dc22
[B]
2006032665

Cover Art: Gambling scene by Louis Choris courtesy of The Bancroft Library, University
of California, Berkeley. Photo of Mt. Tamalpais by Fraser Muirhead.
Cover and Interior Design: Victoria Kuskowski
Printing and Binding: McNaughton & Gunn, Saline, MI

Orders, inquiries, and correspondence should be addressed to:
Heyday Books
P. O. Box 9145, Berkeley, CA 94709
(510) 549-3564, Fax (510) 549-1889
www.heydaybooks.com

Printed in the United States of America

10 9 8 7 6 5 4 3 2 1

CONTENTS

APPENDICES

FOREWORD

GREG SARRIS

There was a man who could turn into a fly. He had songs for this purpose. My grandmother's niece, who told me this story, said the man would lie next to a log and then leave his body. He could travel great distances. People hired him to find lost friends and relatives. Once a woman from Tomales Bay disappeared, and her husband gave this old man the woman's shawl in order that he might know her scent. The husband was jealous; he suspected his wife had run off with another man. The wife, a big woman with striking tattoos, had in fact gone to pick herbs—which was where she was found, deep in the hills above the bay, at the bottom of a ravine with a broken ankle, her basket of fresh mountain balm leaves spilled all around her. "Bring a litter; you will have to pack her out," the old man told the ashamed husband.

I thought of the story—and the old man—as I read Betty Goerke's book. Not that Betty Goerke is a fly or, for that matter, a person who could turn into a fly. Those things about her I wouldn't know. But I was reminded of people and places I had heard about from old-timers, and, further, I often learned something new about them—a name I could connect to a particular character in a story, for instance; maybe a village where one of my ancestors originated—and in that way Betty's scrupulous research into the life of Chief Marin, the Coast Miwok leader after whom a county was named, became for me a kind of magical creature, or text if you must, locating lost friends and relatives. Oh, to hear the names of Coast Miwok nations, such as Huimen, Omiomi, and Aguasto; and the names of villages: Anamas, Livaneglua, Naique, Nanaguani, Alaguali, Olompali, and Petaluma, just to name a few; and the people: Ysidra and Ysidro, Otilia and Otilio, Elzeario, Juana, Rafaela, Jose Calistro, Sebastian, Juan Evangelista, Camilo, Quintino (after whom Point San Quentin and the present-day prison is named), Salvador, Tom Smith, and Bill Smith.

The book, though, is not just something wondrous for me. As Betty Goerke sketches the life story of Chief Marin, she effectively remaps Marin and southern Sonoma counties, providing Indian and non-Indian alike a rich historical tapestry of the region's native people and their against-all-odds survival, a tapestry that has heretofore been ignored or forgotten. We read about the life ways of indigenous people who, for thousands of years, maintained a sustainable relationship with the natural world, and their adaptation and resistance to colonizing forces; these topics should appeal to readers, Indian and non-Indian, far beyond the territory. Certainly one method of indigenous resistance is silence. No doubt Coast Miwok people edited much of what they told the mission padres, and Betty Goerke culls much of her information from the mission records. Nonetheless, what *was* recorded testifies to a rich and complicated people in place and time, enough so that the story herein can help us think about ourselves here and now and know better what once might have been lost in the land we call home.

I can't stop thinking about the man who could turn into a fly. Again, according to my grandmother's niece, he had lived in Sebastopol, which is in southern Pomo territory, prompting me to have assumed he was southern Pomo. My tribe, the Federated Indians of the Graton Rancheria, is comprised of Coast Miwok and southern Pomo descendants. We are intermarried and our stories go back and forth between different families. I discovered in this book that the man who could turn into a fly was not southern Pomo. Well, not on his father's side. His father was from Alaguali, the Coast Miwok village just below Tolay Lake, the place notorious for powerful medicine. Did this man learn the tricks of his trade, so to speak, at his father's village, where medicine men and women convened from near and far? In any event, I know this man's great-granddaughters—they are my cousins—and I will have to tell them where their great-grandfather came from. The stories go round and round, on and on...

ACKNOWLEDGMENTS

This book would never have been completed without the enthusiasm, dedication, and sense of fun of numerous anthropology students at College of Marin. My deep appreciation and thanks go to these students, some of whom remained engaged in research for the book long after they had left the college. Two former students in particular have been of great help: Robert Rausch and Alicia Allen. Rausch registered archaeological sites discovered during our research for this work, hiked many miles to gauge the time it took to walk from one Indian village to another, took photographs for me, and searched for materials at the Bancroft and the Marin Civic Center Libraries. Over the years, Alicia has spent her days off from work joining me at the Bancroft Library, the San Francisco Mission, and the Chancery Archives. Her aid has been absolutely invaluable in helping to translate Spanish letters between priests and the military as well as many entries in the mission documents.

Other key translation help was provided by Samantha Aguilar, Sylvia Buenaventura, and Sandra Aguerrebere. Many of the students who were essential in the transcription of the San Rafael mission records came once a week to my home, where we worked together around my dining room table. In addition to the women mentioned above, I am indebted to Nancy Miller, who also worked on the mission records during three school vacations while at College of Marin and U.C. Berkeley, and to Mariah Josefovsky, Marvin Collins, Michelle Royall, Teresa Rodriquez, Mary K. Temple, Sue Missimer, Robin Heard, Daniel Arquette, and Anne Olney. Mary Haring was valuable in many aspects of the book, providing computer skills and an uncanny ability to remember native names, which helped to make connections in the mission records. Mary also read and commented on an early version of the manuscript.

In the 1980s, author Cary James, a former student, showed me the phenomenon of the sun rising between the two peaks of Mount Diablo during the equinox, which led to my search for solstice events, first photographed in Marin County by Robert Rausch in 1995.

The maps were prepared by former student Rick Waterman, and the artwork of archaeological artifacts was drawn by students Lucille Bennett, Aimee Hurley, and Erik Beadle.

Students who helped with library research include Nancy Miller, Wynn Richards, Lori Stevens, Dilwara Fletcher, Mair Vidal, Susan Scott, Jean Laurie, Nadine Smith, Marti Rutishauser, Robin Hadley, and Robert Rausch. Thanks, too, to the archaeology students who worked at the Alto Mound in the 1970s, including Nancy Perkins (my assistant), Katy Jo Sebastian, Dulce Shafer, Jean Gettier Gilman, and Lucille Bennett, and to those who carried out site surveys: Robert Rausch, David and Erin Blackwolf, Rick Waterman, Patrick Bryant, Marti Rutishauser, and students in the archaeological field classes.

Tribal members Greg Sarris, Gene Buvelot, Kathleen Smith, Verna Smith, Patricia Cummings, Jeanne Billy, Jeannette Anglin, and Rita Elgin Carrillo shared their histories; Miwok Archaeological Preserve of Marin (MAPOM) board members—particularly Sylvia Thalman, Ralph and Lisa Shanks, and the late Don Thieler—provided encouragement and expertise.

Randall Milliken's transcription of the San Francisco mission records were invaluable, as was his carefully researched book *A Time of Little Choice,* a must-read for anyone who wants to understand the mission period.

I am indebted to a number of people, many of whom have become my good friends, for heightening my awareness of the Marin environment: to Elizabeth Terwilliger, for teaching four-year-olds and their mothers about birds; to four women—Remmy Kingsley, Nona Dennis, Virginia Havel, and Kathy Cuneo, all of Natural Science Education Resource—who taught me about ecology; to Bob Stewart, who patiently taught me the differences in bird songs and opened my eyes to butterflies; and most recently to David Herlocker and Merle Sundove, who kept my interest in these matters alive.

My great appreciation also goes to Dr. Jeffrey Burns of the Chancery Archives, Archdiocese of San Francisco, who went the extra mile to assist me with the records at the Archives; to the staff at the Bancroft Library at the University of California at Berkeley; to Jocelyn Moss of the Marin Historical Society and the California Room at the Civic Center Library; to Laurie Thompson at the California Room; to Joyce Crews of the Mill Valley Library; and to the staff at the Santa Barbara Mission Archives Library.

The following priests were helpful in sharing the records in their respective churches: Father Maurice McCormick of Mission Dolores, Father Paul Rossi and Monsignor Richard Knapp of St. Raphael Parish, and Father Robert K. White of Church of the Assumption, Tomales.

Skillful photographers whose work appears in this book include Alonso Chattan and Christina Noble of College of Marin; Marvin Collins; J. Fraser Muirhead, M.D.; Doreen Smith; John Niebauer, M.D.; and David Blackwolf. Naturalists

Wilma Follette, Virginia Havel, Bob Stewart, and David Herlocker answered many questions, as did Jeff Fentriss, Nancy Valente, Miley Holman, Richard Ambro, Jack Estes, Dewey Livingston, Phyllis Faber, Chuck Oldenburg, Dr. Douglas Long of the California Academy of Sciences, Breck Parkman, Tom Origer, Sally Washburn, Leigh Jordan, Glenn Farris, Frank Ross, Gay Pollock Lynch, Julie Haring, Janice Goucher, Bill Mulloy, and Charles Kennard.

I am indebted to Veronika Grahammer, of the Staatliches Museum für Völkerkunde, Munich, Germany; Henry Kammler, of the Museum der Weltkulturen, Frankfurt, Germany; and Elena Okladnovika, of the Peter the Great Museum of Anthropology and Ethnography (Kunstkamera), who assisted me in photographing objects in their museums in St. Petersburg, Russia.

Those who read and commented on various sections of the book included archaeologist and author Randall Milliken; journalist Paul Peterzell; tribal chairman Greg Sarris, of the Federated Indians of Graton Rancheria; College of Marin faculty colleagues Ted Bright, Leah Shellada, and Nancy Siedler; anthropology instructors Leslie Fleming of Merritt College and Sue Sperling of Chabot College; former students Rowena Forrest and Marvin Collins; as well as Katharine Goerke, Mindy Ariowitsch, and Diane Bright.

Mary Renaud of U.C. Press had the most difficult task of helping me cut the book by one third, and did this over many months with great skill, humor, and patience.

The team at Heyday Books in their sunny aerie in Berkeley shepherded the book through its various stages with seeming ease. Heartfelt thanks to Malcolm Margolin, publisher of Heyday, who long ago read what became Chapters 1 and 5 of this book and encouraged me to continue, and to Jeannine Gendar, editor, for her thoughtful questions and good advice. And my appreciation goes to the rest of the team who worked so hard to make it a professional production: Lisa K. Manwill, Diane Lee, Rebecca LeGates, Lorraine Rath, Wendy Rockett, Lillian Fleer, and Heyday affiliates Victoria Kuskowski and Sarah Neidhardt.

My son Jon provided computer expertise, and my husband Jon was a helpmate in every sense of the word: reading the entire manuscript in many of its various drafts; assisting with charts and diagrams; taking photographs in Russia, Germany, and California; and fixing problems with the computer without ever kicking it.

INTRODUCTION

In Marin County, California, few people are aware that the area is named after a Coast Miwok Indian. The rare extant stories about this Native American depict a colorful, clever, defiant, and even diabolical man, yet he is largely unknown and unsung. The first published account of "Chief Marin" appeared in 1850, at the time of California statehood, when Mariano Vallejo, the former Mexican commandante general, proposed "Marin" as the name for the county north of San Francisco. Vallejo wrote of a chief who had been captured by the Spanish military and taken to the San Francisco presidio, only to escape in a tule boat and continue harassing Spanish soldiers north of the Golden Gate. Years later, according to Vallejo, Chief Marin was caught a second time, after hiding on the islands off San Rafael, and it was at that point he finally came to accept a life in the mission. Other stories of Marin's exploits began appearing in the American press in the 1860s, helping to give the story of his life a mythological cast.

In the 1880s, historian Hubert H. Bancroft threw cold water on the stories of Marin's exploits, writing in his multivolume *History of California* that such tales were unsupported and that the remembrances of Vallejo and his contemporaries were a "strange mixture of fact and fancy." In a 1940 article, Dorothy H. Huggins looked at numerous sources and essentially supported Bancroft's hypothesis. The famous U.C. Berkeley anthropologist Alfred Kroeber, known as the man who befriended the "wild" Indian Ishi, doubted that Marin had ever been a chief and suggested instead that he had been the headman of a village group and nothing more. None of these experts understood the man Marin because they had seen neither his mission records nor other documents about him.

It is not surprising, then, that the popular press and textbooks showed little interest in Chief Marin or in his Coast Miwok people, and thus they failed to describe the complexity, variety, and creativity of California Indian culture from his time and place. Until the 1990s, textbooks one-sidedly emphasized how the mission system had benefited Native Americans and avoided mentioning how the mission experience had disrupted Indian culture and had hastened the deaths of many, causing some to run away and others to rebel and resist those who intruded on their territory. From the 1940s through the 1960s, articles about the local Indians in Marin County's newspaper, the *Independent Journal,* spoke of Indians' rudimentary technology and "weird" customs, showing the authors' ignorance of Indian culture and lack of respect for the Coast Miwok.

Today, however, there is great interest in accurately and sensitively portraying the Native American past and in telling the story of Marin and the Coast Miwok using valuable information in previously ignored old documents. This book aims to pull Marin out of the shadows of history and to illustrate the vibrancy of his Coast Miwok tribe, relying on the cowhide-bound, handwritten mission ledgers that were meticulously kept by the priests. The entries in these ledgers, scratched with quill pens, recorded the births, marriages, and deaths of the Coast Miwok who entered the missions. The entries are often difficult to read, blurred by too much ink or obscured by a priest's bad handwriting, but they pull aside the curtain to give us a glimpse of what life may have been like for mission Indians. Unpublished letters between the military officers and priests, as well as documents preserved by General Vallejo himself, open the curtain a little wider. Fortunately, the reminiscences of two Coast Miwok who were interviewed by anthropologist Isabel Kelly in 1931 and 1932 reveal the Indian point of view that is missing from many of these sources and provide valuable details concerning ceremonies and spiritual life. One of these Coast Miwok, Tom Smith, was a ninety-year-old religious leader; the other, Maria Copa, was a sixty-year-old relative of Chief Marin.

Marin did not join the mission until he was a young adult. Having spent his first twenty years in a traditional native community, he then abruptly faced a different reality in the mission, with its harsh and puzzling regulations decreed by priests and soldiers. When the mission system was eventually disbanded, he had to adjust to yet another group of power brokers: white settlers bent on taking Indian land for themselves. Trained in ancestral ways of solving problems, Marin had to negotiate in disparate worlds that competed for his loyalty. As a young man, he confronted the dilemmas many other Indian leaders faced throughout California at that time: whether or not to join the mission, and, after becoming a member of the mission community, when to defy mission regulations and when to accommodate for survival.

In thinking about Chief Marin, I kept coming back to the landscape in which he grew up, wondering how he must have experienced the sounds, colors, and smells of the San Francisco Bay area before Spanish arrival. Knowing the setting, particularly the locations of villages in his home area of what is today southern Marin County, helps us to picture his early pre-mission years, which would have been enriched by colorful ceremonies, the daily activities of hunting and fishing, and the nightly sharing of tribal lore.

Although there are some gaps in our knowledge of Marin's whereabouts during his lifetime, we can nonetheless assemble a coherent narrative from the available records, starting just six years before his birth, when Captain Ayala piloted the first Spanish ship through the Golden Gate into San Francisco Bay and the officers and crew made contact with the Coast Miwok. At Mission Dolores, in 1801, the twenty-year-old Huicmuse, Marin's original name, was baptized as "Marino." (I use that baptismal name throughout the book, except when quoting nonmission figures, who usually referred to him as Marin.) Other nonmission accounts expose Marin's conflicts with the military and the priests, his skills as a boatman, his participation on an expedition with the captain of the San Francisco presidio, and his mysterious relationship with another Coast Miwok who was court-martialed and shot.

Marin is significant. All existing sources have considered him to be a historical figure of some importance. He was witness to a time of cataclysmic change, and he was a survivor, buffeted by events largely out of his control. Through one man's experience, we can follow the journey of the Coast Miwok people from a peaceful existence in their native villages to the desperate times when white settlers stole both their land and their livelihood. But this tragic story does not have an entirely tragic ending, for even after the arrival of the Americans, when the Indians were devalued and belittled, they were not destroyed. Their modern struggle to win federal recognition for their tribe—a goal accomplished in the year 2000—is a testament to their strength and identity as Indians.

THE NATURAL WORLD OF THE COAST MIWOK

At the time of Marino's birth, about 1780, the Native American villages in what is now Marin County were still intact, and no Indian from this area had yet entered the San Francisco mission, established by the Spaniards four years earlier. The natural world into which Marino was born, then, was the world in which his parents and earlier ancestors had lived—a landscape whose sounds, colors, fragrances, and plant and animal life had shaped the Coast Miwok culture and worldview for generations.

If modern Californians could be transported back to an Indian trail in 1780, the first thing they would notice would be the stillness. The enormous shadow gliding silently on the trail in front of them might be cast by a noiseless condor, with its nine-foot wingspan. Without today's background noise, they could hear the sliding of a garter snake along a dirt path, the rustlings of a field mouse in an open clearing, and each "shag step" of the spotted towhee as it searched for food in the fallen leaves. Even at a distance, they could hear the sounds of ducks jostling for position near the shore or harbor seals barking when the herring were running.

Today, at dawn in late May, Californians can still savor a few of the once-common natural sounds. As darkness recedes, the robin hesitantly starts its song, which five minutes later becomes a long series of triplets announcing its presence and territory. In another five to ten minutes, the awakening California towhee calls its repetitive one-note "teek," sounding like an alarm clock that won't turn off. A few minutes later, a Bewick's wren begins its own variations on a theme, proclaiming that it is also awake and looking for a mate. One can hear these sounds because the streets are not yet singing the song of tires on pavement. But in the eighteenth century, an Indian hunter patiently waiting for a bird to walk into a trap or a Coast Miwok woman quietly weaving a basket outside her home could have heard even the whir of butterfly wings. And some of the quieter noises might have even seemed frightening: the careful movements of a coyote or a mountain lion at dawn in the grasslands, the awkward ramblings of a grizzly in the underbrush.

No wonder Native Americans were so aware of their environment—they could hear it. Imagine living an entire day hearing only the sounds of natural life; John Muir expressed this experience as living "in" rather than "on" the environment.[1] Surely the Coast Miwok took for granted this full sense of their surroundings before the gunshots, ship bells, and jingling spurs of Spanish soldiers intruded into their world.

The vivid color palette of the landscape in Coast Miwok territory varied with the seasons. All year round, the different hues of the bay reflected cloud cover, fog, or clear sunny skies. Following the first rains, the hills, covered in native perennial bunchgrasses, were a grayish silver-green, the color varying only slightly as the grasses dried out in the summer (unlike today's "green and golden" grasslands). Patches of vibrant green covered much of the land, thanks to forests of evergreen oak, Douglas fir, and redwood, which provided color even during the dry summers. Green pickleweed at the bay shore's edge became red in the fall.

Beginning in early spring, butterflies of solid soft creams and yellows, as well as multicolored ones with vibrant orange, shades of blue, and spots and wing edges of contrasting colors, filled the oak woodland and riparian environments. The whites and yellows of early flowers such as milkmaids, footsteps-of-spring, and suncups shared the canvas with the reddish pink of shooting stars and flowering currant, giving way as the season progressed to the yellows and oranges of monkeyflowers, buttercups, Indian paintbrush, and California poppies. The great fields of early spring flowers on Ring Mountain in Tiburon today hint at what must have been a common sight to the Coast Miwok: swaths of colorful orange poppies and goldfields, blue lupine, violet-tinted fields of blue-eyed grass, yellow tidytips with white edges, and, in early May, the striking purple shades of blue delphinium. (Figures 1a, 1b, and 2)

The scents of the natural environment may have been less vivid than the colors. The plants and trees that produce the powerful fragrances we associate with the San Francisco Bay Area today—wisteria, rose, narcissus, mock orange, jasmine, stephanotis, eucalyptus—had not yet been introduced into the landscape. Rather, the fragrances of the Coast Miwok world came from buckeye flowers, California bay leaves and bark, ground iris, California rose, angelica, marsh mint, wallflower, and sages such as pitcher sage, mugwort, and California sagebrush. Of course, there were also the odors of controlled burnings of grasslands, smoky cooking fires, cut herbs and grasses, caught fish, shellfish, dead animals, drying and rotting foliage and fruit, and the first fall rains.[2]

The weather in this part of the Bay Area in the 1780s was similar to today's, with seasons marked by dry periods from late spring to early fall and rains from late fall to early spring. Proximity to the summer fogs of the Golden Gate and the coast can make Marin mornings cool and windy until the fog lifts in the warmer afternoons. On such summer days, temperatures can range from the high 50s (F) on the coast to 80 degrees or more inland. In winter, temperatures can be cold enough to cover the top of Mount Tamalpais, at a height of 2,604 feet, with an occasional snowfall.

Mount Tamalpais has a strong effect on rainfall, with most precipitation occurring on the mountain's eastern side. In a 1931 interview, Maria Copa, a Coast Miwok raised in Nicasio, told anthropologist Isabel Kelly how rain could be predicted: "When [the sky] is bright red in the east in the morning—like blood—then it is going to rain. But if it gets red in the west, in the evening they say the *utecos* [ghosts, dead people] are burning seeds and that it will not rain." Times of drought were not unknown. Tom Smith, an elderly Coast Miwok of the Bodega tribe who also spoke with Kelly in the 1930s, shared his traditional way of bringing rain: "Go down to the beach and burn kelp in a fire."[3]

The Coast Miwok surely experienced the frequent earthquakes that have shaken the Bay Area for centuries. After the Spaniards arrived, for example, an 1808 quake was so powerful that it toppled statues at Mission Dolores in San Francisco, and an 1812 quake generated a tidal wave that covered the "ground of the plaza." Tom Smith claimed that earthquakes were caused by a man "lying under the ground, face down, arms outstretched before him. Moves his fingers and makes earth move....We give him money, beads, silver; throw in a big fire. Do this after an earthquake."[4]

The Coast Miwok territory in Marino's day featured vast forests of redwoods, oaks nestled in valleys at edges of creeks, and hillsides covered with edible plants. The Indians sought out redwoods for shade on hot summer days and used redwood bark to cover the outsides of their homes. Perhaps the towering size of these majestic trees and their dark understory hinted at the sinister: the Coast Miwok people of Nicasio and Tomales Bay had a story about the "little folk" who lived in the redwoods and could "make people crazy."[5]

Oaks were the most important trees for the Coast Miwok and their neighbors. Essential to the tribes' survival, the usually plentiful acorns provided carbohydrates, fats, fiber, and protein in the Indian diet. They were also easily stored, offering food year round. Preparing acorns was laborious, however, for tannins had to be removed by leaching in streams before the acorns could be ground into meal for cooking. Buckeyes, which required even more extensive leaching to remove their poisonous content, became the emergency staple when the acorn crop failed. But neither oaks nor buckeyes were available for all to harvest: Tom Smith recalled that trees near a village were owned by individuals and that each tree was identified with a pattern made by stripping the bark. At a man's death, his children and widow inherited his trees.[6]

The smaller and less plentiful nut of the California laurel (also known as California bay or pepperwood) was edible without leaching, and its leaves served as medicine for headaches and stomachaches. Elderberry trees provided shoots for flutes. This tree, with its musical associations, figures in a number of Miwok tales collected by ethnologist C. Hart Merriam in the early 1900s, including stories about the acquisition of fire and the origin of humans.[7]

Meadows and hillsides, some with shoulder-high grasses, provided the most reliable foods: a rich variety of seeds, clover and mallow greens, wild onion and soaproot bulbs, hazelnuts, currants, blackberries, and manzanita berries. The Coast Miwok ate the gathered foodstuffs raw, or prepared them by cooking or grinding. Later, gold-seeking Americans who observed Native Americans collecting seeds and digging for precious bulbs and tubers neither understood nor appreciated their efforts and referred to them derisively as "digger Indians."

Native Americans effectively used almost every living thing around them for food, medicine, clothing, and housing or for constructing tools, baskets, fish traps, and cordage. Many plants had more than one use. Tule, for example, was extremely versatile: the Coast Miwok ate the roots and used other parts of the plant as covers for houses and granaries, as material for women's skirts, and as absorbent material in infants' cradleboards and in sanitary napkins.[8] Perhaps the most ingenious use of this plant was in the construction of boats so dependable and maneuverable that the Spaniards relied on tule crafts paddled by Indians to transport them around the bay.

In place of pottery, most California Native Americans used baskets woven from plant materials, typically willow for the warp and sedge for the woof. They wove into the design the contrasting colors of other plants, such as redbud, bulrush, and hazel. Basketmakers also used plant dyes: yellow from the flowers of buttercup and the leaves of cow parsnip, black from the juice of poison oak or California blackberry.

Many plants also served as medicines. The Coast Miwok brewed roots or leaves as therapeutic teas and crushed other plants to make poultices. Frederick William Beechey, visiting California in the 1820s, observed that Native Americans who lived outside the mission system were healthier, and he attributed this to their use of medicinal herbs. In the 1930s, Tom Smith and Maria Copa recalled that earlier generations of Indians had a wealth of local herbs available and could prescribe angelica and buckwheat for colds; coyote brush and wild cucumber for swelling; larkspur, mugwort, blue-eyed grass, and hedge nettle for stomachaches; monkeyflower and yarrow leaves for sores; buckwheat for spitting blood; elder for fevers; and blue-eyed grass for menstrual problems and abortions. Tom Smith warned that iris root was poison—"everyone knows that"—but added that if it was made into a weak tea, it could be helpful for stomachaches.[9]

Ecologists today are impressed with how successfully the Indians managed their environment. They pruned selected wild plants to eliminate knobs and lateral branches, resulting in the hundreds of straight rhizomes and branches needed for basketry, musical instruments, and arrows. They were also careful to leave a portion of their food sources for future use. They gathered seeds with seed beaters and baskets to ensure that they would take only the seeds that were ripe at the time, leaving others to generate the next season's crop.[10] Many tribes throughout California, including the neighboring Pomo (though perhaps not the Coast Miwok), used controlled burning to increase forage for game, to stimulate seed production, and to regenerate soil. This hazardous practice was apparently widespread, prompting Governor Arrillaga in 1783 to send an order to all the Spanish missions prohibiting such burns.

Game fulfilled many needs: food, clothing for everyday wear and for rituals, musical instruments such as flutes and whistles, and tools for various purposes. Fur was used for warm blankets, and bird feathers were used for costumes in dance rituals and ceremonies. Some animals, however, such as the coyote, an important figure in Native American life, were considered too powerful to be used for food or clothing.

Deer and elk, found in great numbers throughout Coast Miwok territory, were by far the most valuable mammalian food source. Steven Richardson, describing his youth in the 1840s, wrote that on an "ordinary jaunt from Sausalito to San Rafael, I would see enough elk, deer, bear and antelope to fill a good-sized railway train." Large herds of elk were not uncommon; Richardson described the thousand head of elk seen on Point Reyes in the "deep grass...bordering on Drake's Bay and Limantour Bay." Incredibly, two to three thousand elk were observed swimming between Mare Island and the mainland in northern San Pablo Bay in the early 1840s.[11]

The Indians used all parts of the animals they hunted and the plants they harvested. When they killed a deer, for example, tanned deerskin became clothing, and sinews were used in bows. Tines of antlers became implements for flaking stone tools, ribs served as sweat scrapers, and scapulas were notched and may have become fiber strippers. Cannon bones were used as awls in basketmaking, anklebones were handy as gaming pieces, and hoofs tied together made a nice sound for rattles and for ornaments on dance costumes. Just as oaks and buckeyes were considered private property, hunting grounds for deer and other small mammals were owned by individuals and inherited by one's children.[12]

The landscape was replete with grizzly bears. These fearsome predators, not as reclusive as mountain lions, were a constant threat to the Indian community. California has been described as a "grizzly Eden" inhabited by up to ten thousand bears. One of the earliest explorers in the San Francisco area, Pedro Fages, in 1770 and 1772 observed that the Indians "seemed in many places to be unable to compete with the bears for mastery of the land,"[13] and numerous others wrote of Indians being killed by ferocious grizzlies.

The smaller black bear, which varies in color from brown and cinnamon to black, also roamed the Marin peninsula. Prodigious eaters, both black bears and grizzlies searched for acorns and blackberries in some of the same areas frequented by the Indians. Observers warned that when the acorn harvest was poor, the black bear was very dangerous. As swimmers, black bears were even a danger to those in boats on the San Francisco Bay in the 1820s. Auguste Bernard Duhaut-Cilly reported that a bear swimming to Angel Island tried to climb aboard a long boat and was killed by soldiers just as it "was getting its claws on the boat."[14]

Although Tom Smith described men cooking bear meat, Maria Copa reported that "old people never ate bear....Hunter used to believe bear talked—said 'Don't bother me, don't try to kill me.' Bear stopped. Never used to bother people long ago." However, she also recalled that "one time a bear chased my grandmother," possibly on the road from San Rafael to San Lucas.[15]

Early European visitors all reported coyotes, bobcats, and wolves as well as bears. As Charles A. Lauff remembered, "In the early days the Bear Valley country [Point Reyes] was alive with large brown and black bear, and it was worth a person's life to pass through that country on foot." He described mountain lions, bobcats, and coyotes who "roamed the hill like jackrabbits on the prairie." Two large white wolves were observed stalking deer in San Rafael in the 1820s, and wolves were still a menace in Tennessee Valley between Sausalito and Mill Valley in the 1840s.[16]

The Coast Miwok hunted small mammals for meat, and they also sewed the skins of rabbits, field mice, and wood rats into warm blankets. In a typical blanket, forty rabbit skins were made into four-inch-wide strips and then twisted on cordage for a water-repellant blanket or wrap.[17]

Larger seagoing mammals were sometimes fair game to the Indians. Spouting whales were sighted in San Pablo Bay in the 1770s, although, according to Tom Smith, the Coast Miwok did not eat beached whales "except for a piece of each side of the jaw." Still-plentiful harbor seals resided in Bolinas Lagoon, on Yerba Buena Island, and elsewhere in San Francisco Bay; and sea lions covered the rocks near the entrance to the bay.[18]

Otter bones have been found in archaeological sites in Marin County; these animals could have been used both as food and as a source of warm capes. The great numbers of otters in the ocean and in San Francisco Bay proved irresistible to the Russians, who secretly sent Alaskan natives to the bay to bring otter skins back to the Russian settlement at Colony Ross in Mendocino County. By the 1820s, the otter population was reportedly dwindling fast, although as many as a hundred were seen in San Quentin Bay in 1830, and Richardson asserted that they still "swarmed" in San Francisco Bay in the 1840s.[19]

The year-long supply of rockfish from the ocean and the bay, plus the seasonal migration of salmon and steelhead, provided variety to the Coast Miwok diet and supplied necessary protein and lipids when acorn stocks were low. During the winter, the Indians trapped salmon in all the major creeks and caught sturgeon in the bay in nets made of lupine. These resources were so important that preferred fishing areas were privately owned and sometimes marked by sticks.[20]

Indians gathered mussels, clams, and oysters from the extensive salt marshes and mudflats around San Pablo Bay, San Francisco Bay, Bolinas Lagoon, Tomales Bay, and Bodega Bay. The heaps of shellfish remains, most now crushed into tiny pieces, at almost every ancient Indian mound in the area testify to the importance of these foods to the Coast Miwok. Smith claimed that clam beds, like fishing areas, were privately owned but that others could pay to use them.[21]

The Coast Miwok did not usually eat small birds, but many types of birds were prized both for their spiritual power and for their feathers, which were used in ceremonial clothing. Some feathers, such as those of the red-shafted flicker and the brown pelican, were owned by tribal leaders.[22] Flickers were easily netted near trees in open grasslands while they fed on grasshoppers, crickets, and ants; and the raucous acorn woodpecker, another source of feathers, could be trapped at its nesting hole.

Tom Smith said that eagle tail and wing feathers were so highly prized that "someone might come to see you and try to steal the feathers." He claimed that feathers were pulled out of a live bird, which was then released. Smith did not say whether he was referring to bald or golden eagles; both species resided in Coast Miwok territory. In some California tribes, eagle nests were owned by families, and everyone knew the locations in tribal territory.[23]

Revered by the Coast Miwok, condors played an important part in the Native American ceremonial cycle. These striking birds, with black body feathers and white wing linings, have a large, orange, bald head and a nine-foot wingspan. They were last seen in Coast Miwok territory in 1847, when more than a dozen were observed in Fairfax.[24] The Indians would entice a condor with an offering of deer meat into which was placed a gorget that would effectively choke the bird as it consumed the meat. They then fashioned the condor's feathers into stunning cloaks, aprons, and headdresses.[25]

Feathers and skins of pelicans were also part of Indian costumes, as were feathers from crows, ravens, turkey vultures, spotted owls, and great horned owls. But Copa's grandmother and other elders were apparently afraid of owls. When Copa imitated an owl's call for Kelly, she said that when you hear that sound, "then you know it is bringing sickness."[26]

The Coast Miwok sought quail for both eggs and feathers. Since quail feed and nest on the ground, catching them with traps or nets was relatively simple. A Russian visitor to California from 1817 to 1819 commented that flocks of quail could number between two and three hundred birds and that the birds lived close to settlements. Richardson remembered their abundance in Marin County in 1850: "In an early morning I have seen whole valleys a veritable moving mass of these birds. They were never molested except by predatory animals....Around every hacienda there was sure to collect an immense flock of quail...as tame as barn yard fowls."[27]

The meadowlark, a handsome, robin-sized bird, with a yellow throat and belly and a black V on its chest, has a beautiful, distinctive song. But Maria Copa considered the chattering meadowlark dangerous, and she related the story of a *maien,* a female leader, who became angry at the insults of a meadowlark and subsequently died. Copa also reported that a meadowlark had insulted a Pomo man in Spanish: "That bird talks any language," she asserted. In 1910, Merriam noted that other tribes in central California believed that meadowlarks were "bad birds....They say he talks too much and is a gossip and they do not like him."[28]

In Marino's day, San Francisco and San Pablo bays were substantially larger than they are today, and Coast Miwok territory included wide expanses of marshy areas, lagoons, and ponds, stretching from the Golden Gate to the northern shore of San Pablo Bay and extending through the inland areas around river systems in southern Sonoma County and the bays of Tomales and Bodega.[29] (Appendix J, Map II) Marshes and lagoons were inviting homes and migration stopover spots for ducks, geese, swans, and other waterfowl. In the early 1800s, San Francisco priests mentioned that the Indians at Mission Dolores preferred "hunting for ducks and fishing...[at] night because the ocean is quiet and the ducks are more together in the lagoons and estuaries."[30] The Coast Miwok used duck decoys to lure waterfowl into handwoven nets.[31] Duck feathers, particularly those of the mallard, decorated belts, caps, arrows, and baskets. Richardson recalled:

> As for waterfowl, the flight of the shore birds, mostly of species now extinct, fairly blackened the air as you rode along the margin of the bay. In the winter,

myriads of geese, swan and wild duck descended from the north, filling the air with their clamor and covering the waterways, bays, marshes, and ponds. I have seen times when the whole shore line of the Bay of San Francisco seemed a solid packed mass of ducks for several hundred yards out from the bank. It never occurred to me as one of the most remote possibilities that they would ever become comparatively rare.[32]

————

This rich and varied landscape into which Marino was born and in which he lived much of his early life was not to last. Throughout the eighteenth and nineteenth centuries, an influx of Spanish, Mexican, and U.S. settlers and gold seekers would inexorably alter the Coast Miwok territory by cutting down trees, clearing land for cattle, introducing grasses, and killing game at an alarming rate. Many of the oaks, streams, wild plants, animals, and birds would be lost. A Wintu woman perhaps best expressed the Indians' ties to the land and their views of the changes that began in the early eighteenth century during Marino's lifetime:

The white people never cared for land or deer or bear. When we Indians kill meat we eat it all up. When we dig roots we make little holes. When we build houses we make little holes. When we burn grass for grasshoppers we don't ruin things. We shake down acorns and pine nuts. We don't chop down the trees. We use only dead wood. But the white people plow up the ground, pull up the trees, kill everything....The spirit of the land hates them.[33]

2

MARINO'S VILLAGE:
ARCHAEOLOGICAL EVIDENCE

The archaeological record is a particularly important source of information about how the Coast Miwok lived. Archaeological surveys and excavations reveal the distribution of villages and campsites and the preferred environments for these settlements. They also help us understand the antiquity of these native sites, the continuity and stability of the tribes, and the range of their material possessions.

Overall, what was once Coast Miwok territory—today's Marin County and southern Sonoma County—contains more than 850 ancient Indian sites. Located primarily on water—on creeks that empty into San Francisco Bay, Richardson Bay, or San Pablo Bay, or situated farther west on Tomales or Bodega Bay—these Indian sites took advantage of prime gathering areas, sources of fresh water, and protection from the winds. Many were small seasonal hunting or gathering locations; some were marked only by carved stationary rocks. Others were the sites of larger, more permanent villages (which the Spaniards called *rancherias*), typically composed of five to ten dwellings housing at least thirty to sixty inhabitants.[1] Most villages also included a semi-underground communal house where inhabitants gathered (known variously as a round house, dance house, or assembly house) and a smaller sweathouse.

HUIMEN VILLAGE SITES

Thanks to the record of Marino's baptism at Mission Dolores, we know that his home territory was in southern Marin and that he was a member of the Huimen tribe, a branch of the Coast Miwok.[2] The land of the Huimen covered all of the

Richardson Bay area and the communities that surrounded it, including what we know today as Sausalito, Mill Valley, Belvedere, and Tiburon.

We do not know how much farther north the Huimen territory extended or how fluid and distinct the boundaries may have been. Randall Milliken has identified the tribal area just to the north as belonging to the Aguasto people, who were centered around San Rafael and Point San Pedro, in valleys to the north such as Miller Creek and Gallinas Creek, and in valleys to the west, including upper San Anselmo Creek.[3] It is uncertain, then, whether the drainage of Corte Madera Creek was in Huimen or Aguasto tribal territory. Most of the area that now makes up lowland Corte Madera, Larkspur, and Greenbrae was covered with an extensive marsh, intersected by waterways that twisted and turned toward the bay and that were filled with little islands whose size depended on the changing tidal waters. (See Figure 20) This land was rich in tule and bird life and would have been a desirable location for any tribe.

In southern Marin, most of the village sites were leveled by the construction of roads and houses between 1900 and 1950, before they could be thoroughly excavated and studied with modern techniques such as scientific dating. But archaeologists have collected some important evidence over the years. For example, Nels Nelson, a young archaeologist from the University of California at Berkeley, surveyed many of the Indian sites on the bay shore between 1907 and 1909, when they were still recognizable. Although by this time it was already impossible to make out the separate features of a village, Nelson's descriptions of the sizes and depths of these sites and the number of burials and types of artifacts found in each location remain an invaluable source of cultural information. In addition, archaeologists have been able to establish when the sites were occupied by studying the styles of specific artifacts, particularly shell beads, whose shapes changed over time.

Unfortunately, other diggers had been literally destroying these ancient villages for many years. These diggers (commonly referred to as "pothunters," even though the Coast Miwok had no pots) usually arrived on weekends with their wheelbarrows,[4] dug indiscriminately in the Indian mounds, carried away the soil for gardens, and disturbed burial sites in search of arrowheads and other artifacts. Whereas some of the pothunters were genuinely interested in the past and kept notes of what they found, they were seemingly unaware that they were destroying precious evidence and making it impossible to interpret the past. Some may have assumed, incorrectly, that there were no Coast Miwok left to care about burial places being disturbed. Such pothunting is illegal today, as county, state, and federal laws protect Indian sites from such disrespectful digging.[5]

Although archaeological evidence suggests that additional rancherias were occupied during Marino's lifetime, the San Francisco mission records mention only three Huimen villages—Anamas, Livaneglua, and Naique. The priests who noted these names did not locate them precisely, except to say that Naique was across from Angel Island and that Anamas was the port of the Huimen people.

WAS ANAMAS MARINO'S VILLAGE?

Our only clue for identifying Marino's home village comes from Nelson's 1907–1909 survey. Concerning the largest mound in Mill Valley, Nelson wrote: "It is said that big chief Marin, after whom the county was named, was born on this spot."[6] Although he registered more than two hundred sites in Marin and southern Sonoma County, this was Nelson's only reference to the name of a specific Indian. Fortunately, we know the name of this village, because it was identified by surveyors in 1835 and again in the 1870s as the rancheria Anamas. Unfortunately, we do not know the source of Nelson's information. Neither Spanish documents nor the accounts of early settlers contain any evidence concerning Marino's birthplace. An elderly descendant of one of the first settlers in the area, who had grown up near the mound, knew of no connection between that location and "chief Marin."[7] Thus, Nelson's comment, made sixty-eight years after Marino's death, cannot be verified.

In 1834, Marino himself was part of a team from the San Rafael mission that was sent out to survey mission lands. Their records noted the name "Animas," whose location would, of course, have been well known to Marino. The original map of this survey is missing, but a copy in Hubert Howe Bancroft's *History of California* shows the word "Animas" stretching all the way from the hills that divide Corte Madera from Mill Valley to near the marsh and adjacent to the Tiburon peninsula—too large an area to allow us to pinpoint the location. Although it would have been logical for Anamas, which was mentioned as the San Rafael mission boundary in 1822 and 1828, to have been on the north side of the hills that separate Corte Madera from Mill Valley, the historical evidence points to the Mill Valley location.

The rancheria Anamas was also identified in the 1835 survey that defined the first land grant in Marin County, made to John Reed. This grant included eastern Mill Valley, the Tiburon peninsula, and a part of Corte Madera, to the marsh. The survey team included Nereo, a Coast Miwok and Marino's friend, though not a Huimen. Field notes for the survey mention a *cañada* (a dell or ravine) that had at its entrance "the house of the owner Don Juan Reed, a brook with a willow thicket, and the remains of a rancheria called Anamas."[8] Later surveys and a court record of the 1870s also refer to this rancheria as Anamas.[9] This village on Richardson Bay may seem an unlikely place for what the priests called a tribal port, but the tule boats of the Coast Miwok were small and did not draw much water, so any site on the bay or on creeks adjacent to the bay could have served this function.

When Nelson arrived to investigate, the mound was still 20 feet high, 450 feet long, and 200 feet wide, making it one of the larger mounds that he located in Huimen tribal territory.[10] Using the best archaeological methods of the time, Nelson dug a small trench at both ends of the mound and uncovered burials and stone tools.

But he was not the first excavator. Neighbors had been digging haphazardly in the mound for years. One of the earliest individuals who removed significant parts of the mound was Henry Fontine's father, who took his son with him in the early 1900s as he collected the soil and put it in his horse-drawn cart to sell.[11] This dark soil, known as "midden," contained shellfish fragments; charcoal; animal bones; objects of bone, stone, and shell; and occasionally human remains. Used as cover for tennis courts, driveways, and paths in the years before the widespread use of concrete and asphalt, this soil can be seen today scattered far from the mound itself. Other neighborhood excavators in the 1930s and 1940s included two young boys who respectfully labeled and saved each artifact they found[12] and a youngster who used skulls from the mound for target practice.[13] Over the years, as foundations were dug for homes and houses were remodeled, more artifacts were uncovered.

The types of artifacts recovered by archaeologists and pothunters indicate that the Indians utilized local materials such as sandstone, soapstone, and chert to make tools and charmstones. Olivella shells, the major source for beads, came from the Bolinas area, and the brittle, glasslike obsidian used for knives and arrowheads was obtained through trade with the Wappo tribe. The sheets of mica used for constructing pendants could have come from a location as close as the Tiburon peninsula.[14] Because these artifacts were removed from their original context, however, archaeologists cannot construct a meaningful picture of Indian life at this mound.[15]

The Mill Valley mound would have been an ideal site for a rancheria: it was close to a marsh, bordered by a creek, and adjacent to Richardson Bay with its bountiful stocks of fish, shellfish, and waterfowl. (Figure 21) Its Huimen residents could have covered their conical homes with redwood bark from nearby stands of redwood. To its north and south lay hillsides rich in oaks, vegetation, and game; and the old Indian trail from Sausalito to San Rafael passed right by the site.[16] As a child, Marino could have walked or navigated his tule boat to visit kinfolk at nearby villages on Richardson Bay or hiked into Tennessee Valley, Alto Valley, and Tamalpais Valley for seasonal foods and game.

Just a fifteen-minute walk away was another village in the Alto area of Mill

Valley. Both of these sites were thus on the edge of the marsh and on the same trail leading to San Rafael. The style of olivella beads found at the Alto mound indicates that it may have also been occupied during Marino's lifetime.[17] It too was heavily pothunted, and the top of the mound was removed for construction of a subdivision in 1950.[18]

Near the Mill Valley mound, other villages with artifacts probably contemporaneous with Marino are within sight of each other across Highway 101 and have been excavated professionally.[19] The largest of these, at Silva Island, is one of the oldest (five thousand years old) and deepest mound in Marin County.[20] A female figurine of baked clay links this site culturally and temporally with another Huimen village in Sausalito as well as with Coast Miwok–speaking villages farther north in Ignacio and Novato.[21] The time span represented by the artifacts recovered at Silva Island indicates that it was a desirable location for a long time, with objects from the earliest known period in the county as well as the mission period.

THE LOCATION OF LIVANEGLUA

In 1907, Coast Miwok individuals identified Livaneglua, the home village of the first Huimen people to enter Mission Dolores, as being "at or near Sausalito."[22] We do not know whether Livaneglua was the large site in what is now downtown Sausalito, another large site within today's neighboring Marin City, or one of the smaller sites found on Sausalito creeks that empty into the bay. Trade beads, gifts of the Spaniards to the Indians, were found at the downtown Sausalito site, indicating that it was occupied during Marino's lifetime.[23]

Living in this general Sausalito area, the Huimen people could have easily trapped waterfowl in the lagoons nearby. They could have walked two hours to Rodeo Lagoon, adjacent to the ocean, either camping there for a few days or returning the same day, laden with ducks from the lagoon or with game from the Gerbode and Rodeo valleys. The neighboring Marin City area also offered easy access to food sources: the marsh was at the foot of the rise on which the village was located, and a ninety-minute walk to the ocean through Tennessee Valley would have provided opportunities for hunting game and birds.

THE LOCATION OF NAIQUE

Naique, the third village associated with the Huimen tribe, could have been as close to Angel Island as Belvedere or Tiburon, or farther away in Sausalito, but there are no definitive clues to its location. Most of the sites in Belvedere and Tiburon were damaged by construction projects and the building of the railroad yard and tracks in the 1880s. Nevertheless, there are two village sites in the immediate vicinity that may have been contemporaneous with Marino, based on artifacts uncovered by archaeologists and residents from the 1920s to the 1940s.[24] The high quality and variety of these artifacts suggest that even in the past these were wealthy neighborhoods.

One of these sites is on the border between Tiburon and Belvedere, on a quiet, shallow bay with a view of Mount Tamalpais, and the other is at the northeastern end of Belvedere. The first was effectively destroyed in 1938, when much of the artifact-laden soil was moved to allow construction of the lagoon road and was then used as fill to enclose Belvedere lagoon.[25] The excavated burials revealed a surprising number of artifacts associated with particular individuals: in one case, there were ninety abalone shell ornaments; in others, eighty black soapstone beads, antler earplugs decorated with olivella and with abalone beads fixed with asphaltum, and deer bones inlaid with olivella and abalone beads.

The second site in Belvedere was disturbed when a golf course was built, and then further damaged when homes replaced the golf course. The discovery of trade beads in the 1920s suggests possible activity or occupancy during Marino's time.[26] Burial sites of high-status persons were found here, too; one individual was buried with eight bear claws, and others were adorned with eleven obsidian spear points, seventy-six abalone shell pendants, and nearly four hundred slivers of red ochre–stained obsidian. There was even a canine burial with olivella shell beads. The pothunters who uncovered artifacts at these two sites worked at night, under the glare of car headlights, believing as they dug through the soil upended by contractors' shovels and machines that they were saving evidence of the past.[27]

Either of these sites would have been in an ideal location for a village; even in the 1920s, it was easy to catch fish off Belvedere, and there were oysters on the rocks on the island's west side, and migrating ducks favored the lagoon as a resting place.[28]

SACRED SITES

In addition to these possible village sites, Marin County also contains many locations that were sacred to the Indians. Some of the sacred sites are known, some are surmised, and some we may never discover or recognize. Archaeologist Tom King interpreted one of these sites, a cemetery in Tiburon excavated in the 1960s, as evidence that the Indian community living there had not been egalitarian: he noted the disparity between styles of burial for various individuals and differences in both the quality and the quantity of artifacts buried with them.[29] In another area of Tiburon, an elderly pothunter recalled a collection of burials consisting solely of pregnant women and women with tiny infants, which had been exposed sometime between

1920 and 1940. No archaeologist had an opportunity to study or evaluate the rationale for this unusual cemetery.

Perhaps the best-known sacred site in the Huimen tribal area is Ring Mountain, on the Tiburon peninsula. (Appendix J, Map II) In more than twenty-five locations on the mountain, carved designs known as petroglyphs are visible on rock surfaces of chlorite schist. They appear as engraved circles with raised centers, some in groups of up to three circles.[30] Many of the petroglyphs are difficult to see unless light chances to illuminate them at the right angle, which is how a geologist, Salem Rice, first noticed them in the 1970s. Similar engraved rocks have been recorded in other parts of Coast Miwok territory, in both Marin and southern Sonoma Counties. One spectacular large boulder of green schist in southeastern Sonoma County is unusual in that it contains not only engraved circles, but cupules, parallel lines, a grid, and a rectangle. Many, but not all, petroglyph sites are at an elevation high enough to provide a commanding view of the surrounding hills, mountains, or water.

While archaeology can describe and compare sites, catalog the artifacts found at the sites, and estimate the date the sites were occupied, it cannot reveal to us the life and soul of the village, exemplified by family and kinship ties, ceremonies, religious beliefs, and the efforts of elders to share tribal lore with the young. For this cultural information, we need the first- and secondhand descriptions given by Indians themselves.

---------------------------------- 3 ----------------------------------

CULTURE OF THE COAST MIWOK

KEEPING TRADITIONS ALIVE

During winter evenings, a young Marino and his family would have typically assembled with others of their village around a flickering fire in the large communal round house, listening as elders recited the tribe's sacred narratives, described the creation of the world, and spoke of supernatural figures with miraculous powers.[1] These gatherings kept alive the oft-repeated stories of the families and ancestors of the Coast Miwok and reminded children how they were connected to the natural world, guaranteeing that tribal beliefs, customs, and memories would be passed to future generations.[2] Such repetition as an aid to remembering, whether through storytelling or song, was common among all peoples who had an oral rather than a written tradition.[3]

Such events were recalled by a seventy-year-old white man who had spent his boyhood, from age six to sixteen, living in central California in a Yokuts tribal village,[4] where the custom of nightly storytelling was similar to that of the Coast Miwok. Sixty years after young Thomas Jefferson Mayfield left the tribe, he could still vividly recall the power of these nighttime events:

> After the evening meal they would all lie around the fire on the ground through the long evening and tell stories and sing until as late as ten or eleven o'clock. This was the finest part of their lives. Here was the real family circle. The long evenings were spent about the fires in the most pleasant way imaginable. Every night was a bonfire party. The old sages would tell stories about their own experiences when they were young, or about the history of their

tribe, or just simple stories they may have made up. We youngsters would sit around with our mouths and eyes and ears open and listen until we had to go to bed....As the evening wore on, and various individuals grew tired or sleepy, they would wander off to bed. We would go inside and lie down on the tule mattresses next to the walls of the house with our feet to the fire and cover up with a rabbit skin blanket, or whatever the weather demanded.[5]

A Maidu Indian woman, Maym Hannah Gallagher, who lived north of the Yokuts, reminisced:

A long time ago, when I was a little girl, I used to go around with my grand-mothers and grandfather....When it got dark, we all used to sleep in a little house, built Indian style. The children would all be bedded down and my late grandfather would tell tales of Coyote. He would say to us, "Listen well." Afterwards, with his elderberry flute, he used to sing Indian songs. "All of you listen very closely," he would say to us. "I am talking in the ancient manner." Then he would talk and tell us many things of long ago...[6]

Maria Copa recalled her grandmother sharing similar tales: "My grandmother used to tell them to me; some were so long I went to sleep. She used to tell them every night in winter; she said the nights in summer were too short."[7]

Many of the tales told how supernatural beings helped to shape the world. Chief among these beings was Coyote the trickster, a prominent character in Native American lore throughout North America. Malcolm Margolin has described Coyote as both "good and evil, crafty and foolish, godlike and scroungy...prankster and the dupe....He dies, is dismembered, decays, and then is pulled back together again to continue his journey."[8] Tom Smith explained this many-sided individual:

Coyote our god....Four months every winter [we] tell stories about him. Coyote made some wooden people, a man and a woman. He kept them close to his house for four days, with the man lying close to his wife. He kept them four days, and they became people. They became my people and the Tomales people. He also made mud people; these may be the Sebastopol peo-ple....Coyote talked as he made these people. Sometimes they answered him; sometimes they didn't.[9]

The concept of Coyote describes a supernatural being who was nonetheless part human, a "divinity called Coyote-man." As explained by C. Hart Merriam, who interviewed Miwok people before 1910, animals, rocks, and celestial phenomena existed originally as the "First People" and took their present form before Indians were created by Coyote-man.[10] The Coast Miwok explained that Coyote used feathers to create people. An elderly woman raised in Nicasio told Merriam that Coyote-man took feathers to the top of Sonoma Peak and that when the wind blew them away, they became people. Another old woman from San Rafael said that Coyote-man placed bundles of feathers in four different directions, and each bundle became tribal people who spoke a different language, such as the people at Santa Rosa, Sonoma, San Rafael, and south of San Francisco Bay.[11]

Many other powers were ascribed to Coyote-man. According to Smith, when Coyote made the low tide, he made it too low. The fish that were small survived in ponds, but other fish and whales died, so Coyote changed the tide to allow sea life to survive. Coyote was also responsible for thunder and produced fog by smoking at his home off the coast. Another of Smith's tales describes how Coyote acquired fire by sending the hummingbird *(kulupi)* to catch it along the coast "past Tomales"; the bird's red throat is visible evidence today of his important deed.[12]

The nighttime narratives also acted as morality tales: children were taught proper behavior and laughed at the escapades of Coyote when he became too boastful or acted foolishly. Coyote's rank behavior, such as farting and dealing with his uncontrollable penis, which often got him into trouble, were part of Coyote lore in California but were not included in Miwok tales reported by Merriam, Smith, and Copa. In one of Copa's narratives, Coyote's greed got the best of him, a common theme for this character. In that tale, blackbirds appealed to Coyote's foolhardy nature by throwing oak galls in the water to make it appear that the water was full of blackbirds for him to catch and eat. Following their calls and songs to jump in, Coyote plunged in—and promptly drowned. Yet, true to all of Coyote's adventures, he managed to recover for another escapade.[13]

When Native Americans in California and other western states told stories of Coyote, it was traditional to have Coyote and other animals speak in an amusing way. The use of high voices or unusual speech patterns—a lisp, the addition of extra vowels or consonants, replacing standard letter sounds with others—helped listeners distinguish which animal was talking. For example, according to Ishi, a member of the Yahi tribe of northern central California, Coyote spoke with a lisp and replaced the sounds of "l" and "r" with the sound of "n."[14]

The importance of storytelling cannot be exaggerated; it was the richly textured fabric in which children, grandparents, and members of the village were woven together. Moreover, it provided a common reference for people of associated rancherias; even when details differed, the narrative was recognizable to all. Younger children might fall asleep before the stories were completed, but they would hear them many times and understand them on different levels as they matured. Essie Parrish, a famous Pomo basketmaker and doctor, told her children: "Remember the stories; that's how we'll know what we did."[15]

CELEBRATING LIFE'S CHANGES WITH RITUAL

The tribes of central California believed that one should follow prescribed rituals when participating in life-altering events such as birth, tribal initiation, marriage, and death. These rituals were often woven into the nightly stories so that young people could understand what was expected of them.

Among the Coast Miwok, proper behavior after childbirth required that both parents observe food restrictions. The father could not hunt deer, and it was "bad luck to go out. He…stayed around and worked.…[Otherwise] he might see a snake or another animal." The mother avoided eating meat and fish. Copa said that during childbirth the woman was "steamed" on a bed of hot rocks covered with grasses, but Smith disagreed, recalling that she would simply lie next to the fire pit. He added that the baby was nursed until it began to walk.[16]

After the birth of a couple's fourth child, a newborn could be killed by a female doctor, although Kelly described this as an act "held more in theory than in practice." The practice was not unique, however: many nomadic hunting and gathering groups around the world have practiced similar infanticide when overpopulation threatened the survival of family, village, or tribe. And, in fact, some tribes within the Pomo group who practiced infanticide did not consider a newborn baby "alive" until after a naming ceremony or comparable event.[17]

Children also had rites to follow. Young boys, for example, were initiated into the tribe between the ages of five and seven. At that age, Marino was still living in a traditional village and would have participated in such a ritual. Tom Smith remembered how scared he was when he was initiated with twelve others in front of the members of his tribe in the round house. Before the young boys performed tribal dances and songs in these ceremonies, women danced with clay effigies a foot high, said to represent the dead. The naked boys were placed on the ground near the fire pit, covered only with feather blankets. As Smith described it: "Lay down, close to fire; scared…feet to fire.…Boys very quiet. Pretend they are dead." The ceremony stretched over four nights. A *walipo* doctor, feared as both a curer and a poisoner, held each young boy over a fire on the first and fourth nights. Eventually, the boys were dressed in clamshell necklaces, abalone shell "tiaras," feather "horns," and newly prepared pelican skins. They danced while adult singers and dancers wearing clamshell beads and abalone shells accompanied them. When the initiation dance ended, the boys were "thrown out the smoke hole by walipo" and caught on the roof by an assistant.[18]

With the arrival of a young girl's first menstrual period, Copa said, she was "steamed" on a bed of hot rocks. Proper behavior during this time included using a scratching stick ("if a woman scratched her head with anything except a special bone or stick, her hair would fall out"), burning one's tule menstrual pads, not washing one's face and hands, and not eating fresh meat. According to Smith, a helper— the *kitca-onik-tai'i* (blood-face-man)—remained outside the hut in which the young woman was sequestered, gave her medicine, sang, and reassured her. When the girl's confinement ended, she bathed in cold water, and a dance was held in her honor. Also at puberty, the girl was given a facial tattoo; the dye was the charcoal of poison oak, the punctures made with a sharp bone.[19]

A woman having her menstrual period stayed in a special hut, the *wilak-kotca,* and both she and her husband followed food restrictions such as avoiding meat. During these times, women eschewed weaving, and female doctors put aside their practice. Once when Smith was planning to make poison, he went to his grandmother's house. But when she saw him coming, she held up her hand to indicate that she was *wilak,* and he stayed away because "wilak...spoils any kind of doctoring thing."[20]

Of course, marriage had its own traditions. According to priests from the San Francisco and San Jose missions, tribal customs were still being observed in the missions;[21] for example, a male suitor had to ask a girl's parents for permission to wed their daughter. If they agreed, he gave them a present, and the young people were considered married. Tom Smith explained that in a traditional village the groom was also required to seek permission from both the village headman and the bride's grandparents, after which he presented the bride's parents with meat from a black bear that he had killed. A dance was then held to confirm the marriage. Although the young couple could live with either set of parents, they usually lived with the husband's family; in any case, in-laws were addressed respectfully, with more formal speech. Although a man could openly choose to have more than one wife, even a different one at each of four rancherias, a woman, according to Copa, was more likely to keep any co-spouse secret, to avoid making her husband jealous and causing a fight.[22]

Not everyone married. Among many North American Indian tribes, certain males were transvestites and performed chores typically associated with women's work in their cultures. The Coast Miwok also recognized this transgender status: Smith noted that a male could be "half man, half woman....Sometime dresses like a man, sometimes like a woman. Never marries." Copa commented: "These people who were half women made baskets and did women's work....There was a boy who played with the girls all the time. He played with mud dolls. My mother said he was a real boy, not half girl." Transgendered males (known as *putcu-tai'i*) often played an important role in making intricate feather belts and boys' pelican coats, although their roles were not the same in all tribes. For example, among the Yurok in northern California, they were "shamans [doctors] and esteemed as such"; among the Yokuts in central California, they had the "privilege and obligation" of handling the dead, which included preparing a body for burial or cremation and leading the annual mourning ceremony. In some areas, these individuals married same-sex partners.[23]

When a Coast Miwok Indian died, both Smith and Copa related, the body was cremated, and most of the deceased's property was burned. Smith explained: "When a person dies, don't bury him. After [the body is] burned, pick up the bones and bury them….Every rancheria had a burning ground…called *wuki-yomi* (fire-home)….If you have no wood, you have to bury the dead person." After a death, mourners wailed, cut their hair, wore long shell necklaces, and never mentioned the name of the deceased again. Copa reported that an old Coast Miwok custom included scattering "seeds in the hills and crying and singing" after the burial. She recalled that the dead were thought to travel to the west to be with Coyote. "In the early days," Smith said, "people didn't die. [Then] Coyote wanted to hear people crying after somebody died. He like to listen to the noise. I don't remember who was the first to die."[24]

FOLLOWING THE RELIGIOUS CALENDAR

The lives of the Coast Miwok revolved around a spiritual calendar, with special ceremonies held variously in the round house, in a smaller women's dance house, in a brush-enclosed clearing, or in the sweathouses of smaller rancherias. These activities helped to maintain a proper balance between the people and the world of animals and spirits.

Just as storytelling reinforced the belief system of the tribe, the elaborate spiritual ceremonies with dancing, singing, and colorful costuming reaffirmed individuals' connections with each other and with their tribal neighbors. Tom Smith observed: "Used to dance because they wanted to have a good time. If someone was sick, [they] danced to cure them. If nobody sick, danced anyway." According to Kelly, they danced to ensure luck in hunting "bear, deer, and salmon…to harvest,…to install a new chief,…to recognize a new doctor and select a new maien [female chief], and to mark the end of the boys' initiation."[25] Many dances included curing; others followed the killing of game. Special dances or ceremonies were dedicated specifically to birds of prey such as condors, eagles, Cooper's hawks, and falcons as well as to pelicans, quails, American goldfinches, flickers, and robins.[26]

Each dance was characterized by a unique schedule, ritual, costume, and number of participants.[27] Two secret societies sponsored some of the dances, their members having already been trained in "the use of costumes and regalia, dance steps, and songs" and "a special language known as society talk."[28] The membership of one of the secret societies was open to both women and men, while the other, for women only, had its own smaller dance house. Villagers from other rancherias were sometimes invited to these ceremonies with "invitation sticks," distributed four days before the event. Some dances took place over four nights and two important dances each lasted six to eight days. Hospitality for the visitors, including food, was an expected part of the ceremony. Guests also brought food to share.

Those dances and rituals held at night inside the round house must have been particularly dramatic. In the flickering firelight, dancers and singers displayed painted bodies resplendent with jewelry of bone and shell; some wore pelican coats and headdresses decorated with beads or feathers. Accompanied by a foot drum, the participants played bone flutes and whistles, shook rattles of cocoons filled with pebbles, and hit split-stick clappers on their hands or thighs. Sometimes clowns and ventriloquists would stand outside on the roof and call down, sounding as if they were in the round house. With the smoky firelight, the colorful dancers, and the endlessly repeated melodies, the effect must have been mesmerizing, mysterious, and frightening as well as entertaining and reassuring.

Smith's family considered a dance that was performed after the killing of a bear to be a "little dangerous," and they told him to stay away from it.[29] The bear's head was removed from its body, placed on a pole, and then cooked and eaten by the hunter's family; the bones of its skull were buried. Following this, the hunter honored the bear by throwing beads into the fire, after which dancers circled the flames wearing headless bearskins and carrying short canes. The bear was then cooked in the fire and shared with others.

The eagle ceremony, however, did not celebrate the killing of a bird; rather, it was performed before eaglets were caught and again after they were fed and released. The ceremony lasted for four days, with the participants sleeping at night.

For the condor, a nighttime celebration lasted until dawn the next day. A powerful female leader known as the *hoipu kulele* directed this dance; according to Smith, she was the "woman chief" and the "boss" for this dance only.[30] Before the dance began, two human effigies were constructed of tule, attached to a painted pole outside the round house, and shot at with bows and arrows.[31] Male dancers wearing back-aprons of condor feathers were accompanied by a drummer and singers of both sexes with painted faces, wearing hairnets decorated with clamshells. The dancers stepped into a fire in which an offering of acorn mush had been poured.

Another type of dance was more mysterious. It was known as a *suya* dance, which Copa described as "kind of a fit....Women used to start this dance in the hills, when they were gathering seeds. Got kind of crazy. With their hair hanging down in the face and blood coming out of the mouth." Tom Smith was "afraid" of this dance, which could produce visions and unconsciousness, causing dancers to appear drunk and to fall down. It seems likely that the suya dance, which was held in the summer "when the grass gets dry," was associated with ingesting one of the datura plants. Copa was concerned that Tom Smith not learn that she was sharing information about hallucinogens in her interviews with Isabel Kelly, but both Copa and Smith discussed two plants thought to be species of datura. One, *monoi* (probably *Datura stramonium,* also called jimsonweed), was described by Copa as a "sort of Indian opium. Makes those who use it see visions." Smith said that dancers who took this substance were "as happy as could be."[32]

CURING AND POISONING

Many of the important ceremonial dances featured curing as part of their observances. These dances, which could last four days and nights, were performed by different specialists (Smith noted at least five) who were called to treat childbirth, a girl's first menses, broken bones, snakebite, or poisoning. The prescribed cure depended on the type of doctor and might consist of singing and dancing, sucking an object out of the patient's body, drinking herbs, and using objects of power in the doctor's medicine kit, such as rattles of cocoons, a split clapper stick, obsidian blades, feathers, quartz crystals, animal bones, or assorted sticks and stones. Smith remembered singing doctors and recorded a curing song of only two lines, in which the first line was sung twenty-two times before the second line was heard. He believed that a sucking doctor, who could remove a harmful object, was "stronger than just a singing doctor": "The doctor says 'It is here; I see it'...He has a small cup of water for rinsing his mouth before he sucks. Uses his own cup. Sucks out blood; spits it out. Sometimes he gets a small snake, the length of a finger. The doctor buries the stuff [that has been removed from the patient]."[33]

Central California tribal members greatly feared being poisoned. According to Margolin, tribes believed that some illnesses were caused by a "physical object... which had been magically shot into the body by an enemy or [by] a shaman who had been hired for the deed." A person with enemies faced a constant threat of being poisoned, because an enemy could pay a poison doctor with clamshell money to do the job. If the threat became reality, the poisoned individual turned to a doctor to help counteract the poison. Tom Smith reported that there was "lots of poisoning, from Bodega to Santa Rosa to Healdsburg. Give you medicine. Make you get sick, cold, feel poorly. Some doctors could cure poisoning....Sometimes the family of a patient who died killed the doctor. Did it secretly."[34]

Maria Copa claimed that her mother had been poisoned by a man who touched her with a stick. Her mother had been carrying Copa's younger sister on her back, and the poisoned stick touched the baby, who subsequently died. He "hit my mother and baby—pretended he was playing....Baby cried little while then closed her eyes—died in a couple days. My mother sick for a month...skin all peeled off....She was treated by a doctor."[35] People took threats of poisoning so seriously that they hid their nail parings, their hair trimmings, and even their feces to prevent a potential poisoner from using them.

RESPECTING POWERFUL PLACES AND TIMES

Members of the Coast Miwok tribe today say that poisoners often met on Mount Tamalpais, and, according to a story about Marino, most Miwok avoided the mountain. In a history of Marin County published in 1880, an "old timer" relates a tale about a surveying expedition that included Marino and others from his tribe. These Coast Miwok refused to accompany the surveyor to the top of Mount Tamalpais to collect data, saying that the mountain "was inhabited by evil spirits." When the surveyor reached the top, he created a crosslike structure with dead tree limbs, which could be observed from below. In response, Marino hiked up the mountain by himself, allegedly to show his bravery, and hung his red shirt on one of the tree limbs, so that it could be seen from the foot of the mountain.[36]

To the Indians, mountains were clearly places of power inhabited by the supernatural. Besides Mount Tamalpais, other high spots such as Sonoma Mountain, Mount Diablo, Mount St. Helena, and Mount Konocti are featured in the Miwok sacred narratives collected by Merriam. Miwok from the Sierra region believed that three sacred figures—Falcon, Condor, and Coyote-man—once met on Mount Diablo, east of San Francisco Bay, to discuss how to create humans. The creation story told by an elderly Coast Miwok woman from Nicasio described Coyote-man on top of Sonoma Mountain, whereas the tradition of the Clear Lake Miwok pictured Falcon resting on Mount Konocti before he and Coyote-man were involved in creating humans.[37] Even among the Coast Miwok, the location of the mountain where a rock giant lived differed: the Nicasio/San Rafael version had his home on

Mount Tamalpais, whereas Smith, from Bodega Bay, said that the giant lived on Mount St. Helena.

On certain mountains, one could find prized materials such as quartz crystals and obsidian. The crystals were used by doctors, who carried them in their sacred bundles, and the locations of quarries from which crystals were taken may have been places of power known only to a few. One known quarry in Coast Miwok territory is at a high elevation and has a commanding view of the bay and Mount Diablo, which may have enhanced its supernatural powers.

Observing the natural world in relation to such high places helped many groups of California Indians to mark the solstices. Although existing information about Coast Miwok observances is sketchy, we do know that some forty California tribes, including the Pomo and the Ohlone, recognized these occasions. Many of these tribes assigned the tabulation of the sun's movement to one or more older men. For the Pomo, the head of a secret society, the *yomta,* traced the summer and winter solstices as well as the yearly calendar: "The yomta kept track of the solstices by observing over what part of a certain hill the sun rose. At the time of a solstice it was said that the sun rose four times over the same spot." In 1812, at Mission San Jose, a priest noted that one Indian group was interested in the winter solstice: "They adored the sun when it receded towards the South Pole. They thought it was angry, and they held dances in its honor and offered it seeds etc. until they knew it was about to return to them."[38]

Smith and Copa could still recall some of the Coast Miwok words for the stars, constellations, and eclipses, but they had forgotten much other astronomical lore. For example, Tom Smith knew that there were words in his language for the "long-sun," or the longest day in the summer, as well as for the shortest day. But he did not know the month of the summer solstice, claiming that "the old people never paid any attention; it was in the summer time." (It is also possible that Smith considered this information too sacred to share with Kelly or, just as likely, that the older men who had been in charge of such observations might have died in the missions before passing on their knowledge to others.) Smith knew that there were names for the different positions of the sun but could not recollect what they were. Copa recognized the Milky Way but could not remember the old word for it.[39]

Solstice observances are associated with pictographs and mountains in the East Bay and with various mountains and rock alignments in other areas, particularly San Diego.[40] In Coast Miwok territory, solstices could be marked by the sun's position in relation to specific views of mountains, such as Mount Diablo, and to petroglyphs or rock alignments. Not all summer solstice mornings are clear of fog, but three times in the past eight years this author has observed that the summer solstice sun rose over a rock that cast its shadow that day directly upon a petroglyph rock. At another petroglyph site, the summer solstice sun rose between the two peaks of Mount Diablo. The winter solstice sun can also be seen from two southern Marin archaeological sites. Yet another sacred site is at Tolay Lake, now a Sonoma County regional park. Since the 1870s, archaeologists and former landowners have uncovered a unique collection of approximately one thousand shaped stones, known as charmstones, in an area that was a former lake bed. Many of the plummet-shaped charmstones are clearly phallic, and some of them were made of non-local materials. Although the function and meaning of so many charmstones is not clear, one early settler in the 1850s noticed that Indians would gather there in the fall and have "some kind of a powwow."[41] Greg Sarris, current tribal chairman of the Coast Miwok and the southern Pomo, suggests that this was a locale where "...doctors from different tribes convened for sacred ceremonies and the exchange of ritual objects and songs for the purpose of healing."[42]

Sarris helps us understand the full extent of sacred areas when he describes an imaginary map of Bodega Bay: "There would be so many [such] places and connecting lines...that the map would finally look like a tightly woven, intricately designed Miwok basket. The patterns would circle around, endless, beautiful, so that the map would, in the end, designate the territory in its entirety as sacred."[43]

MEN AND WOMEN LEADING THE TRIBE

The most powerful figures in a major Coast Miwok village were a nonhereditary headman, known as the *hoipu,* and two female leaders. The most important of the two women was the *maien,* whom Smith referred to as a "woman chief." He asserted that the "maien bosses everyone, even hoipu." Kelly summarized the apparent primacy of the maien using quotations from Copa and Smith: "Some dancers won't mind the hoipu, but they do [mind] the maien....Maien did all the work....She was just like hoipu....Maien knows more than a man; she knows [everything]....Overrules hoipu....Maien tells hoipu to watch the people; she is taking a rest."[44]

The hoipu occasionally mediated disputes within the tribe; acted as a go-between in marriage arrangements; prepared the bed of hot rocks for a girl at first menstruation, at the request of the maien; and made speeches. He gave these speeches every night, telling the people to be good, Copa said, although she noted, "They were mean just the same." The maien gave similar speeches requesting that people behave, but she spoke only inside the sweathouse.[45]

Any father, "just a common man," could propose his young son for the job of hoipu. Once selected, four older women were in charge of training the young man in speechmaking and other leadership skills. As Smith explained, "The old men know what is going on, but let the women do it all. Women know a little more than men. They have more sense." The young man slept either at home or at the house of the current hoipu. When he felt that he was ready for the job, he informed the women. But a new hoipu could not be initiated until the death of his predecessor. Smith recalled: "One of the old women gets the poison man to kill the old hoipu. The boy [the new hoipu] gets the necessary money [to pay the poisoner] from his father...but does not pay the full amount until the old man dies. Sometimes the old hoipu gave up the job and then didn't have to be poisoned." As for a new maien, "the old people, the old maien, and the old hoipu selected the girls to be trained as maien," and, fortunately, her predecessor did not have to die.[46]

Copa and Smith recalled that females among the Coast Miwok had more power than the soon-to-arrive Spanish and Mexican authorities ever recognized. Because of their cultural bias and their own patriarchal societies, Spaniards and Mexicans found what they expected to find and quickly recognized only male Native American leaders, therefore depriving female leaders of their traditional roles and obligations.

Other forms of status and social stratification also existed among the Coast Miwok. Smith's descriptions of individuals who owned prized feathers and of families who owned prime hunting and gathering spots (see Chapter 1) as well as archaeological evidence recovered from Indian burial sites (see Chapter 2) all point to a society that was not strictly egalitarian. Receiving payment for doctoring, poisoning, making ceremonial regalia, and allowing others to use preferred hunting and gathering areas made some families richer than others. Those with more wealth proudly wore their strings of olivella or clamshell beads, evidence of high status in the tribe. This level of social stratification, however, was not comparable to that of the Yurok tribe in northern California, where a small group of elites flaunted their status by talking in a special way, wearing distinctive clothing, and demanding respect from lower-status people, who could be fined for lack of deference. Apparently, many California tribes had a class structure that was "characterized by elites or nobility, commoners, poor, and sometimes with a fourth class of slaves or vagabonds."[47] Neither Smith nor Copa mentioned these particular distinctions in regard to the Coast Miwok, however.

DAILY ACTIVITIES AND MATERIAL CULTURE

Unlike most Europeans, Indians considered their material world to be a part of their spiritual world. Every aspect of Native American life, from hunting and fishing to the construction of stone tools and the weaving of mats, was imbued with prescribed behavior and respect for the natural world and its materials. When fishing, Tom Smith explained, Coast Miwok asked the salmon spirit for help to keep the "fish from being frightened of you." Before a hunt, hunters avoided sexual relations for four days, ate acorn mush and atole, rubbed angelica leaves on their bodies, and sang special songs. When eating mud hens, Smith shared, one should "throw the bones into the fire. Otherwise you won't have any more luck. You won't get nothing. All kinds of animal bones thrown in the fire for good luck."[48]

Practicing land management (see Chapter 1), their activities depended on the season, with intense periods of activity occurring when certain foods were available and needed to be harvested, processed, and stored; these times alternated with leisurely periods for preparing objects of beauty and function. Deer, crab, and shellfish were available all year long, but staples such as acorns had to be collected in the fall and either leached or stored in a granary for later use. After leaching and pulverizing by pounding, the acorns could be baked in an underground oven for bread or cooked with a hot stone in a watertight basket for mush. In the spring, the Indians collected clover and seeds for pinole, placed them in the sun to dry, and later parched them with coals before breaking them up with a mortar. Their winter diet included acorn bread, pinole, salmon, seaweed, mud hens, and geese.[49]

Many chores were assigned according to gender. In addition to hunting and fishing, and preparing the tools for these activities, men's chores included gathering mussels, preparing nets and rope, crafting beads out of stones and shells, and constructing pelican feather coats. Women wove most of the baskets (although men did occasionally make large storage baskets and cradles), constructed duck decoys, gathered seeds, and prepared acorns for flour. Among the children, elders taught boys how to make shell beads in the sweathouse. Young girls learned how to gather seeds and acorns; later they were taught basketmaking. Both girls and boys became proficient at the delicate task of trapping small birds.[50]

Some activities were shared, for instance a husband shot or choked the pelicans for his wife's pelican skin cloak (as distinct from pelican feather coats), and she prepared the garment for wearing. Old men or transgendered males made feathered belts, and women occasionally sewed the decorative beads onto them.[51] Women also assisted men in beadmaking by drilling the holes. Women gathered wild tobacco, and men dried it; and both males and females made their own wooden pipes. Some tasks, such as making rabbit skin blankets, were performed by both sexes.[52]

Most of the ritual clothing, baskets, and beads were made by specialists, who needed both skill and time to produce these items, for which they were paid in clamshell beads. The skills of the basketmakers were particularly impressive and demonstrate the conceptual ability of the female artisans who wove the patterns without a drawing. The men who could flake the impressively large, flat obsidian blades without breaking them were also skilled artisans.[53]

Hunting Skills

Native Americans were renowned for their ingenious hunting and trapping methods. In 1826 and 1827, Frederick William Beechey observed how the Indians caught waterfowl: they attached a net to poles on either side of a stream and placed duck decoys in the water; as the birds arrived, the net was quickly raised, catching ducks and geese in flight. As for killing deer, the Russian Otto von Kotzebue, in his 1824 trek between San Rafael and Fort Ross, reported seeing Indian hunters tracking deer, wearing headdresses made from deer heads. Imitating the movements of the deer so as not to frighten them, these Indians were able to get close enough to dispatch their arrows successfully.[54]

Weaving Baskets

The Coast Miwok managed to imbue even their utilitarian objects with beauty, a talent particularly noticeable in their baskets, which are known throughout the world. The coiled and twined baskets of the Coast Miwok are described as "some of the most elaborate and beautiful...in all California."[55] The designs are in black (of bulrush root, and perhaps bracken fern root) on a light brown surface of sedge root, and some of the more colorful are decorated with shells, pendants, or acorn woodpecker and quail feathers. The baskets shown in Figures 5a, 5b, 6a, 6b, and 6c, with shell decoration, were likely made as gifts or ceremonial objects, not intended for everyday chores.

Working with Stone

Although the styles changed over the centuries, Coast Miwok stone work remained a time-consuming process. It took many days to form boulders into stone mortars, creating shapes that were both functional and aesthetically pleasing. These mortars were used for grinding seeds and minerals or pounding acorns. Some were enormous: one from the Point Reyes area weighed 98 pounds; another, from Bodega, in the possession of tribal elder Gene Buvelot, weighs an astonishing 118 pounds and measures 9½ inches high, 20 inches wide, and 7 inches deep. According to Copa, stone mortars that were too heavy to carry from one grinding location to another were left behind and buried.[56] Other shaped stone work included charmstones and cylindrical stones worn around the neck or hung under the arm. One of the uses of these objects was for good luck, particularly in hunting and fishing. (Figures 18f and 18g)

Making Beads

When the Spaniards first arrived, beads made of Washington clamshells were the currency in the Bay Area, although olivella shell beads had been used earlier. Besides being worn as jewelry, shell beads were applied to baskets, hairnets, and hair and ear ornaments. Beads and cylinders of magnesite were even more valuable (Smith called them "our gold"), but they were not available locally and had to be obtained in trade from Napa County.[57]

Working with Feathers

Native Californians placed a high value on hats, belts, coats, and blankets, many containing hundreds of feathers. Besides their use in baskets, feathers were also incorporated into earrings, hairpins, wristlets, and boas up to five meters long. (Figures 9–11c) The Indians used whole bird skins for pelican capes and condor capes, but their more detailed use of single feathers is particularly striking and beautiful. Drawings made by artist Louis Choris at Mission Dolores in 1816 give us an idea of how the intricately crafted feather items were worn and used. (Figures 9 and 12b)

Feather headdresses and belts, in particular, required remarkable skill and materials. Perhaps the best known of northern California headdresses are the dance-associated headbands made from the colorful orange-red wing and tail feathers of the red-shafted flicker. The band was constructed so that part of it lay against the forehead, secured by ties, while the ends flapped freely as the dancer moved.[58] (Figures 9, 10a, 10b, and 10c) A typical headband might contain the feathers of at least 25 individual flickers, but some bands used feathers from 60 to 150 birds. At Mission Dolores in 1806, the German naturalist Georg von Langsdorff saw a headband containing 450 flicker tail feathers; because it used only the two middle tail feathers of each bird, it required at least 225 flickers.[59] (Figure 10c)

Other headdresses worn on top of the head incorporated tail feathers from birds such as ducks, owls, pelicans, magpies, gulls, vultures, ravens, and crows. Sir Francis Drake observed these "topknot" pieces in 1579 when they were worn by Indians accompanying an individual assumed to be "the king." They were drawn in the early 1800s by three visiting artists: Georg von Langsdorff at the San Jose Mission, Louis Choris at Mission Dolores, and Mikhail Tikhonovich Tikhanov at Bodega Bay.[60] (Figures 17c, 8, 12b, and 7) One headdress collected by the Russians incorporated feathers from fifty magpies; another, a woman's topknot, used one hundred gull feathers. In this type of headdress, the feathers were attached to a cord, which was then wound around a hoop made of willow or hazel shoot.[61]

Ceremonial feather belts with alternating patterns of feathers from red woodpecker scalps, olivella shell beads, and feathers of the greenish-purple iridescent scalps of mallard ducks were the most valued items of central California, worn, said Smith, "when you wanted to look fancy." (Figures 13a, 13b, and 13c) The Russian

Dmitry Zavalishin, who had received such a belt from either a Coast Miwok or a Pomo, commented that it "had been passed from generation to generation in one tribe, from one chief to the next, as one of the symbols of their esteem, and it had not lost any of its freshness, despite long use." These belts were up to 6 feet long and 3¼ inches to 4¾ inches wide. They were constructed on cordage, with the feathers woven in as the work progressed.[62] As many as 125 red woodpecker caps were used in a single belt, primarily from acorn woodpeckers.[63] The larger pileated woodpecker may also have been used for its prominent red head and crest.

The central California Indians created warm feather blankets. In 1814, Langsdorff described a blanket made of duck and goose feathers bound "closely together in a string-like fashion, which strings are afterwards joined tight, making a dress of a feather-fur appearance." Another blanket was composed of a staggering five hundred mallard tail feathers.[64]

MAKING PEACE AND AVOIDING WAR

The Coast Miwok barely acknowledged warfare. Tom Smith, from the Bodega area, did not recall any fights or wars. Margolin writes that "native Californians were by and large peaceful—or at least they valued peace.…The quarrelsomeness and suspicion between neighboring groups often led to skirmishes; yet war for its own sake was rarely practiced in California.…Most Californians saw warfare as an evil to be avoided."[65] Perhaps the frequent ceremonies that involved more than one rancheria kept most friction at bay, along with the fear of sorcery. Lacking a tribal chieftain for a number of rancherias, it would have been difficult to carry out any concentrated attack on another tribe because, for the most part, each rancheria was politically autonomous and there was no overarching government. Large-scale warfare like that practiced in southeastern California by the Mohave was absent, but skirmishes between mission and nonmission Indians did occur, and acts of cruelty were sometimes inflicted on enemies.

The Russian P. Kostromitonov learned the words for a war song of the Bodega Miwok when he was at Colony Ross in the 1830s. (See Appendix C) F. P. Wrangell, speaking of the Native Americans at the Russian colony and Bodega, also discussed warfare but did not distinguish between the Bodega Miwok and the Pomo: "In their warfare, fearlessness is respected; captured enemies are not killed, but exchanged after the end of the battle."[66]

Maria Copa said that the tools of war were the bow, arrow, and spear and that men fought without armor, "except for a few beads across the chest." Choris labeled a picture of Indians dancing at Mission Dolores "A War Dance." It is unclear whether this European's interpretation was based on fact, however. Neither Copa nor Smith spoke of a war dance for the Coast Miwok, and records of the nearest Miwok neighbors, the Pomo, contain few references to warfare. When confrontations did occur between Pomo groups, they were typically over trespassing. They could include "surprise attacks on villages and…formal battles…with emphasis on hurling insults and dodging missiles. There were no hand-to-hand engagements." Alfred Kroeber commented that "on the whole, there is little doubt, [the Pomo were] peaceably inclined," an assessment that is supported today in the words of Otis Parrish, a Pomo: "We are not warriors…we are a loving people."[67]

4

EARLY CONTACT WITH EUROPEANS

The clanking of a noisy anchor chain dropping into the water. The calling of the hours in a strange tongue. The deep ringing of a ship's bell. These unfamiliar sounds may have alerted the Huimen people that a Spanish ship had arrived off their shore, an arrival that would change their lives forever. The Indians, ever sensitive to the predations of bears, mountain lions, coyotes, and foxes, and to the soft rustlings of mice, deer, and elk, must have been aware that a large foreign vessel had dropped anchor in their tribal waters that night.

This ship, the *San Carlos,* had sailed into what is now known as San Francisco Bay on August 5, 1775, after a journey up the coast from Baja California with a stopover in Monterey. The fifty-eight-foot ship, with its square mainsail and mizzenmast carrying the fore-and-aft spanker, likely resembled a Spanish packet or an English snow. (Figure 22a) The thirty men aboard included the captain, the sailing master, a priest, officers, a surgeon, and a cook as well as the sailors, who were described as being "petty criminals and unfortunate fishermen from the Mexican coast, who had been impressed into service."[1]

Although the ship's men had spotted what seemed to be signal fires during the trip and wondered whether the Native Americans might have been announcing the ship's presence to one another, they had encountered no hostility. They had no reason, then, to proceed quietly that night, although they were well equipped with cannon and muskets to defend themselves. On this clear night, lit by a half moon, they were driven by gale-force southwesterly winds around Lime Point, at the narrowest part of the Golden Gate, as they looked for their longboat, which had been sent out at sunset to find good anchorage for the ship. The winds had died down by

34

ten-thirty that evening, when the *San Carlos* dropped anchor in Richardson Bay, off what is today Sausalito.

Even if the Indians had slept through the night and had not heard the ship's arrival, they were alerted to its presence at half past six o'clock the next morning, when its crew hailed the appearance of the missing longboat. By that time, the dawn chorus of insistently chirping California towhees and singing robins had been in full voice for about an hour. More than likely, the Indians were lighting morning fires to ward off the night's chill, hungry children were crying, and fishermen were launching their reed boats to take advantage of the calm morning waters following the previous evening's wind.

It probably was not a typical foggy summer morning—reportedly, the weather was near perfect during the entire forty-four days the Spanish ship was in this part of San Francisco Bay. Juan Manuel de Ayala, captain of the *San Carlos,* wrote that the "climate, though cold, is altogether healthful and it is free from such troublesome daily fogs as there are at Monterey, since these scarcely come to its mouth, and inside there are very clear days."[2] Therefore the ship and its many sails could have been seen clearly from land at night and at dawn, both by Indian fishermen and by scouts on the bluffs above the little sandy beach at Whaler's Cove.

The men in the longboat rowed northwest into Richardson Bay and had their first view of a Huimen village. Although the crew members on the *San Carlos* were armed with deadly weaponry, they were nevertheless more cautious than the Indians, positioning themselves out of the range of arrows in case the indigenous population proved to be unfriendly. One of the Spaniards' greatest advantages was that they had a general idea of what to expect: that the local people would fancy glass trinkets; that the local language would differ from the languages they had heard in Mexico; and that the native peoples could be lifesavers, supplying food if Spanish rations ran short. They were already familiar with many Indian customs, such as the preparation of food, the use of sweathouses, and the wearing of animal skins and shell necklaces.

In contrast, the Coast Miwok knew next to nothing about the Spaniards and might have been expected to look upon the newcomers with awe and fear, considering them mysterious, unpredictable, and incomprehensible. Instead, the Indians' response was one of courtesy, friendliness, and curiosity.

Although the *San Carlos* may have been the first foreign ship in San Francisco Bay, it was not the first foreign ship to land on Coast Miwok soil. Other known sightings had occurred in 1579, when Sir Francis Drake landed at Point Reyes and remained for five weeks; and in 1595, when Sebastian Rodriquez Cermeño's ship was wrecked off the same coast. Indians may also have seen one of Sebastian Vizcaíno's ships off Tomales Point in 1603. Notwithstanding the years that had elapsed since these early visits, the memory of those long-ago events may well have been part of the oral history of these Native Americans, told around their nightly campfires over the years. So although these new visitors from the *San Carlos* were strangers, they were not necessarily feared.

Additional reports of unusually dressed strangers with horses could have reached the Coast Miwok from the neighboring Ohlone[3] and Bay Miwok tribes, as early as 1769, when an expedition led by Captain Gaspar de Portolá explored the southern part of the San Francisco peninsula on horseback. The next year, an expedition led by Lt. Pedro Fages reached El Cerrito, in the East Bay. Fages returned again in March 1772, passing through what we know as Oakland, Alameda, and Richmond to reach the Carquinez Strait in the north.[4] All of these expeditions communicated with the Indians of the area and, in some cases, avoided starvation because the Native Americans gave them gifts of food.

CONTACT BETWEEN THE COAST MIWOK AND THE SPANIARDS

The journal of Father Vicente Santa María, the priest on the *San Carlos,* provides an account of Indian and Spanish contact during the forty-four days of the ship's visit. He found the Indians endlessly fascinating and described them with respect, admiration, humor, and pathos. Even though his priestly eighteenth-century outlook included an intolerance for "idolatry" and an overly optimistic view of the Indians' veneration of Christian symbols, he lacked the Eurocentric outlook of his countrymen.

In Santa María's account, the initial contact with the Huimen people began early that first morning. While searching for better anchorage, the Spaniards in the longboat saw a village less than a mile northwest of the *San Carlos*'s position. The inhabitants "were not dumbfounded…though naturally apprehensive." Rather than running away, the Indians "left their huts and stood scattered at the shore's edge." One individual, probably the headman, made a speech, "raising his voice…with much gesticulation." Because the Spaniards were in the longboat, the Huimen had to shout to be heard. Others tried to encourage the longboat to land, even "throwing their arrows to the ground and coming in front of them to show their innocence of treacherous dissimulation."[5]

> The Indians, guessing that our men were somewhat suspicious, tried at once to make their intentions clear. They took a rod decorated with feathers and with it made signs to our men that they wished to make them a present of it;

but since this met with no success they decided on a better plan, which was to draw back, all of them, and leave the gift stuck in the sand of the shore near its margin.[6]

Throughout that first day, some of the Huimen men tried repeatedly to entice the new arrivals to come ashore. Three Indians, their bare bodies painted silver, descended a hill on the northwest, carrying their bows and arrows. One of them, "with high and rapid utterance and animated gestures, made a long harangue."[7] All three traversed back and forth, apparently hoping that the visitors would land near them. Offshore, the Spaniards in the longboat continued their search for a better anchorage. When they approached a steep rock face, the Indians hid from them in the oak trees.

In the afternoon, Santa María noticed a group of Huimen approaching on a hill closer to the ship. Two of their group were carrying rods, which he believed designated their superior status. Again, one Indian made a welcoming speech, and the men indicated that they wanted the Spaniards to come ashore.

In the early evening, when the longboat went out again, some Huimen approached the shore. Others were seen "carrying something heavy," which they left on the shore. When they departed, the curious captain directed the longboat to go ashore, where he found food and woven clothing:

> A basketful of pinole…some bunches of strings of woven hair, some of flat strips of tule, rather like aprons [grass skirts] and a sort of hairnet for the head, made of their hair, in design and shape best described as like a horse's girth, though neater and decorated at intervals with very small white snail shells. Limited though it was, we did not hold this unexpectedly friendly gift of little value; nor would it have been seemly in us to be contemptuous of a present that showed the good will of those who humbly offered it.[8]

Not to be outdone, a few Spaniards returned the following day in a small boat and left a present of glass beads and earrings, which they placed in one of the Huimen baskets. When Santa María received the captain's permission to meet the Native Americans on shore, nine Huimen men without weapons came to greet the priest, the two sailing masters, and the surgeon with great dignity. The visitors were offered a string of shells separated with black knots,[9] and they were led to more gifts of food.

Santa María described the nine as three older men, two of whom had cataracts, and six young men of "good presence and fine stature," noting that the young men were respectful of their elders, keeping their eyes downcast and not moving unless directed to do so. One young man had stripes of blue body paint across his shoulders as well as from his lower lip to his waist. Some had in their hair a "four toothed wooden comb and bound up the end in a net of cord and very small feathers that were dyed a deep red; and in the middle of the coiffure was tied a sort of ribbon, sometimes black, sometimes blue."[10]

Although the priest remarked that the Indians did not seem curious or surprised at the Europeans' dress, the contrast could not have been more striking. The priest in his full-sleeved, cowled gray robe, held together with a twisted rope around his waist, was probably wearing thick-soled brown sandals. "Swarthy and bandanna'd" sailors were barefoot, whereas others, such as the surgeon, wore stockings and shoes. Unless they were costumed for a special occasion, the Indian males were most likely naked, given the summer weather, although they might have worn body paint, dressed hair, and feathered caps. In spite of these differences, the Indians comported themselves well, although one of them could not resist touching the whiskers of the priest, "as if in surprise that I had not shaved." The Huimen, not familiar with how earrings were worn, gestured to their guests to show them; and the priest, the surgeon, and two sailing masters placed the earrings in the ears of the delighted Indians.[11]

The next day saw more contact, as the surgeon and a sailing master came ashore and met nineteen Huimen men, who again offered gifts. One of the Huimen draped a black and white feathered boa over the cap and shoulders of the second sailing master. (Figure 11c) But a more significant communication came on the following day, August 9. Early that morning, the Indians had again implored the Spanish crew to leave their ship and visit, but when dancing on shore drew no response, they gave up. When the longboat returned from exploring the bay, however, Santa María, the surgeon, and five sailors used it to leave the ship and head for land.

There were no longer any Indian guides on shore, so the group from the *San Carlos* made their way up the hillside with some trepidation. They found a village one league away, on the shore of a rather large round cove, where they were welcomed warmly by the men. As they approached the huts, however "all the men stood forward as if in defense of their women and children."[12] Santa María recognized some of the men from earlier encounters, but others, including those he believed to be the leaders, were not there, suggesting that men from more than one village had previously greeted the ship. In the shadows at that time of evening, the women of the village were difficult to see, but the priest did notice that they were wearing clothing made of otter pelts and deerskin.

The Spanish visitors were entertained at a feast put on by the Indians, but first Father Santa María gave a speech. When he began to sing the Alabado, a hymn of praise, he was unable to get beyond the words *"pura concepción"* before his hosts interrupted him to offer food. After eating, Santa María taught the headman how to cross himself. Gifts were exchanged; offering a small piece of chocolate as a present, a sailor received in return a sweet-tasting food made from a seed. The evening ended when, "as [the Indians] saw that the moon was rising, they made signs to us to withdraw."[13]

Four days later, Santa María was again on land. He and one sailor climbed to a ridge, pursuing the Huimen who had been observing them. Reaching the ridge, the priest found six men, three of them armed, and encouraged them to stay by offering gifts. All went smoothly until he opened his snuffbox, at which they became frightened and ran away.

Later that day, the *San Carlos* hoisted anchor and moved to a new location just off Angel Island, in the cove now named after Captain Ayala. Here it remained anchored for most of its sojourn. Further contact with Native Americans occurred primarily on the ship, and once on the island itself.

Before the first tule boat came out to visit, Santa María was on Angel Island, looking for a stream to quench his thirst, when he found a rock with a cleft containing what he interpreted as evidence of idolatry. The priest observed arrows stuck in the ground, along with three decorated rods a yard and a half high, ornamented on top with small pieces of hairnets and white feathers and topped by black and red-dyed feathers. Believing that the feathers represented worship of the sun, Santa María burned what he could.

On August 23, five Huimen came out from the mainland in two tule boats and boarded the *San Carlos*. Santa María described the Indians' delight in seeing the rigging; discovering the stock of lambs, hens, and pigeons; and hearing the sound of the ship's bell, which was rung for them. During these visits, the Huimen showed that they remembered the names of the Spaniards they had met previously, which delighted Santa María. He and other crew members continued to teach the Huimen new words, even chanting a hymn of praise, which the Indians "followed so distinctly that it was astonishing with what facility they pronounced the Spanish."[14]

The next morning, August 24, the Huimen returned. After greeting them, Santa María went to his room to say his morning prayers. The Indians, impatient that he was not on deck with them, came to his quarters. The "chieftain…came up to where I was reciting my prayers and, placing himself at my side on his kneecaps, began to imitate me in my manner of praying, so that I could not keep from laughing; and seeing that if the Indian should continue I would not get on with my duty, I made signs to him to go back down and wait for me there. He obeyed at once."[15] The Huimen left, and Santa María realized that he had probably offended them.

That same day, two tule boats arrived at the *San Carlos* with men from a different language group, the Huchiun (Ohlone) of the East Bay. Native Americans throughout this region shared common patterns of polite behavior, and the Huchiun were no different: in greeting the Spaniards, they clearly identified and deferred to their own leaders, made speeches, and shared food. From their first day in Richardson Bay, the Spanish crew had observed the importance of speeches by men who seemed to be leaders and who were attempting to communicate appropriately, respectfully, and forcefully with the visitors.

The Huchiun headman who boarded the *San Carlos* on August 24 gave a formal speech, introduced his men by rank, and offered pinole, making sure that everyone on board had a chance to taste it. Santa María believed that the Huchiun had gone to some trouble to dress, covering their bodies in designs made with red ochre and charcoal. "Some had adorned their heads with a tuft of red-dyed feathers, and others with a garland of them mixed with black ones. Their chests were covered with a sort of woven jacket made with ash-colored feathers." According to Ayala, the visitors particularly fancied the biscuits and learned to ask for them in Spanish.[16]

A poignant incident occurred when the Huchiun left the *San Carlos* and went ashore on Angel Island. Suspecting that the Indians might take some items that the crew had left on the shore, the captain sent the dugout after them. Instead, the Huchiun performed one generous act after another: helping the crew beach their dugout, trying to put a tree in the dugout when they thought the Spaniards wanted it, and helping some of the sailors carry water casks to the dugout, which then returned to the ship. Seeing these Indians still on the shore of the island, Santa María paddled out in the redwood dugout and remained there alone with them for a time.

> They all crowded around me and, sitting by me, began to sing, with an accompaniment of two rattles that they had brought with them. As they finished the song all of them were shedding tears, which I wondered at for not knowing the reason. When they were through singing they handed me the rattles and by signs asked me also to sing. I took the rattles and, to please them, began to sing to them the "Alabado"...to which they were most attentive and indicated that it pleased them.[17]

The rattles the Huchiun brought with them could have been cocoons filled with pebbles, deer hooves tied together with cordage or strips of deerskin, or a dry branch split at one end, which gives a sharp sound when hit at the cut end. Santa María's musical offering, the Alabado, was a hymn of praise.[18]

By this time, Father Santa María was convinced that the Native Americans were interested in the church and would be good converts. He encouraged the Huchiun to kiss his statue of St. Francis, and "they did so with so much veneration, to all appearances, and willingness that they stole my heart and the hearts of all who observed them."[19]

When the Huchiun men returned the next day, the two groups made attempts to learn each other's language, and Santa María expressed his admiration of the Indians' linguistic skills. One man, Jausos, corrected a fellow Indian's Spanish pronunciation; another, Mutuc, was recognized by Santa María as being "noticeably clever, so perceptive that he not only grasped at once what we said to him in Spanish, and repeated it exactly, but also, as if well versed in our language, he showed how the Spanish terms we asked about were expressed in his."[20] Modern linguists have been impressed with the great number of native languages that were spoken in the Americas, more than one hundred in California alone.[21] As a result of marriages and trade between tribes, a great number of Native Americans could speak more than one language, which may help to explain the ease with which they learned Spanish.

Visits from other rancherias continued. Numerous headmen and their small parties arrived in tule boats, without weapons, to meet the Spanish visitors, to determine the intentions and customs of the newcomers, and to observe their material possessions. The Indian leaders followed the practice of making speeches before they boarded the *San Carlos*. Santa María mentioned only once that there was tension between men of two rancherias, dissipated, he believed, because the Spaniards treated them all as equals.[22]

THE *SAN CARLOS* DEPARTS

As the *San Carlos* began its return trip on September 7, Captain Ayala, observing that the seas and wind at the Golden Gate looked threatening, put in at Horseshoe Cove, east of Lime Point on the mainland. But as the ship moved toward land, it hit some submerged rocks, and the crew had to spend ten days at the cove repairing the rudder. During this layover, Huimen Indians from yet another rancheria came to visit. Later, the priest, the surgeon, and one sailor walked to this village.

As they approached the rancheria, all the men and women came out to greet them. The headman placed his arms around the priest's shoulders and guided him to the "assembly house."[23] The Spaniards were treated to pinole and water, and they all amused one another as the Indians taught the guests how to pronounce the names of their hosts.

As they left, Father Santa María wrote, the headman "comported himself so politely that he came out with one arm around me and the other around the surgeon and went with us a part of the way, until, taking leave of us he went back to his rancheria....What is certain is that they themselves seem to be asking a start at entering within the fold of our Catholic religion."[24]

Two months after the ship *San Carlos* left the Marin coast, Father Santa María wrote to the warden of his college:

> Y'r Reverence is to know that these are most extremely skillful, bold Indians, and exceedingly clever fellows, from what we learned of them in the forty-four days we spent at this harbor. Thus when they first came to our ship, they called us all by name; and at the time they took leave of us, their farewell was to say, "Santamaria Vicente Father, Love God"—it is to be noted that the latter had been taught to them during the many times I met with them. I managed to stay in two villages when they received me and those with me with great pleasure....[They] so charmed me that had I been able I would have remained with them, even all by myself.[25]

Another observer, the first sailing master, Canizares, conveyed to Captain Ayala particular praise for a very large rancheria of four hundred people near the Carquinez Strait, which he had visited four times during his survey of San Pablo Bay. "I have marked upon them a civilized bearing and, what is more, among the women much modesty and circumspection." The sailing master also remarked on the native boats, which were made of "rushes so curiously worked and woven together that I was astonished at seeing what these Indians had made. The boats carry four men each, going fishing, each man using a double bladed paddle, with which they get along so nimbly that, as I found out, they went faster than the longboat."[26] (Figure 14b)

In November, Captain Ayala wrote to his superior to describe the "fine harbour" at San Francisco:

> To these many good things is added the best of all: the heathen all round this harbour are always so friendly and so docile that I had Indians aboard several times with great pleasure, and the crew often visited them on land. In fact, from the first day to the last they were so constant in their behavior that it behove me to make them presents of earrings, glass beads, and pilot bread, which last they learned to ask for in our language clearly. Beyond question

such amity was a great help to us. For it let us carry out with little fear the exploration with which I was charged.[27]

Just five years later, the man we know as Marino was born in the Richardson Bay area. His parents might well have had direct contact with these early Spanish visitors or might at least have viewed the ship from the shore. Even if one or both of his parents had initially been out on a collecting expedition on the ocean at Rodeo Lagoon, or farther north at Bolinas, the news would have spread quickly, and they would have had time to return in order to see this spectacle for themselves.

5

MISSION DOLORES:
HUICMUSE BECOMES MARINO

In the fall of 1775, only six months after Captain Ayala and Father Santa María had left the San Francisco Bay Area, the Spaniards returned, reconnoitering likely locations for a military presidio and for a mission church with quarters for the priests. The following June, seventy-five people, accompanied by 286 head of cattle, left Monterey for the San Francisco peninsula. The group included two priests, fourteen soldiers, seven families of settlers (with children), thirteen Indians who would act as servants, and an Indian interpreter.[1]

After pitching tents in the area where the San Francisco mission stands today, some of the party left to work at the site chosen for the presidio, almost an hour away on a trail over loose sandy hills and scrub vegetation. When the ship *San Carlos* returned in August, its crew helped to construct simple buildings of "timber, stakes and mud with tule thatched roofs" for the presidio's chapel, storehouse, guardhouse, and dwellings for the families.[2]

The location chosen for the mission, milder in climate and less windy than the presidio site, was near the Ohlone village of the Yelamu tribe.[3] These Ohlone generously offered food to the newcomers, and both sides were initially friendly and supportive. Just six weeks after the Spaniards set up their tents, however, another Ohlone group, the Ssalsons, attacked the villages of the Yelamu, causing them to scatter to the East Bay and the Marin peninsula in their tule boats. Although the Yelamu eventually returned, the Spanish forces were determined to assert control, causing relations between the Yelamu and the Spaniards to sour and resulting in a series of skirmishes, the death of one Indian, and the flogging of others.

This new mission, San Francisco de Asís, popularly known as Mission Dolores, was the latest and most northerly of a string of such settlements that had originated at San Diego in 1769. The mission system was the outgrowth of the political, economic, and religious ambitions of the Spanish government, which was trying to protect its territory from British and Russian incursions. In order to flourish, this system needed forts and soldiers at the various presidios, which by 1776 had been built at San Diego, Santa Barbara, Monterey, and San Francisco. In addition to keeping out the British and the Russians, the military supported the priests in their conflicts with the Indians.

Ironically, it was the Indians who helped to make the whole system possible, by serving as a source of free labor for growing food, for constructing and maintaining mission buildings, and for performing various chores such as carpentry, iron working, and weaving. The priests had the additional responsibility of "civilizing" the Indians and supplanting their native religion with Catholicism. Once introduced into this system and baptized as Christians, the Indians lost their freedom. They were forced to remain at the missions and were punished, often by whipping, if they tried to escape or if they failed to follow the priests' rules.

THE LURE OF THE MISSIONS

The process of converting Native Americans to Catholicism was not an overnight success. One of the priests at the San Francisco mission, Francisco Palou, admitted that the first converts had been attracted to Catholicism only by "presents and other inducements,"[4] which they likely shared with their non-Christian relatives. By the end of 1777, thirty-two young men and women, some of them children of tribal leaders, had become part of the mission community through baptism. These initial converts came from the San Francisco peninsula and, shortly thereafter, from East Bay tribes.

One important inducement to joining the mission was the visible material wealth of the Europeans: metal tools, bells, and guns; and domestic livestock such as horses, cattle, and sheep. Both the priests and the Californios (non-native residents of California) spoke of the treasures the priests had offered Indians to entice them into the mission. For instance, the priests commonly gave them beads, which were significant status objects in Native American communities. This new acquisition of wealth by some of the poorer families threatened to destabilize the tribal hierarchy.

The seeming promise of a constant food supply was further incentive to joining the mission, especially during droughts or poor acorn harvests when starvation loomed. Since the missions maintained a storable surplus of agricultural products, the Native Americans who lived there could eat three meals a day. According to

José de Jesús Vallejo: "A greater part of the Indians were abandoning their savage life rather more animated by the desire to better their social condition than by being impelled by religious sentiments....During dry years when there was a scarcity of acorns, the number of Indians...was greater than the number who came...in years in which the forests and fields yielded an abundance of harvest."[5] In addition, the Spaniards cultivated and provided new fruits and vegetables previously unknown to the Native Americans.

The Indians, whose own culture included a rich spiritual life, may also have been attracted to the spirituality of the Catholic church, enhanced by the ceremonial pomp of mass, complete with priests in colorful brocaded vestments and a gilded altar, which visually supported their perception of the church's piety, power, and wealth. Indians who lived in the mission were encouraged to think of their non-Christian relatives as *bestias* (beasts).[6] Along with priestly assurances about the benefits of Christianity and the dangers of the devil—a presence clearly understandable to a Native American population who believed in sorcerers—there was enticement enough to participate in a new life at the San Francisco mission. Nevertheless, the Californios wrote emphatically that the Indian population was not "genuinely converted."[7]

The Coast Miwok, in particular, did not flock to the new mission in great numbers, despite the extremely cordial relations that had existed between the Huimen tribe and Father Santa María during the 1775 visit of the *San Carlos*. Not until 1783, six years after the mission was established, did the first Coast Miwok couple, Juluio and Olomojoia, Huimen from Livaneglua (Sausalito), bring their children to Mission Dolores for baptism. We do not know whether they believed that baptism conferred spiritual advantages to their children or whether they hoped for gifts such as beads, which would enhance their own social status. However, less than a year later, they returned to baptize the child of Juluio's co-wife; and in 1784, Juluio and Olomojoia themselves came to be baptized and married at the mission. Between 1783 and 1800, 148 Coast Miwok were baptized at Mission Dolores; this number represented a scant 13.4 percent of the baptisms that took place among the Coast Miwok and members of the various San Francisco peninsula tribes at that mission.[8] Most of these baptized Coast Miwok individuals were southern Huimen from Richardson Bay, whom Father Santa María had visited in 1775, but there were also smaller numbers of Guaulen from Bolinas and Aguasto from San Rafael.[9]

MARINO'S ARRIVAL AT THE MISSION

In the winter of 1801, something impelled another young Huimen couple, known as Huicmuse and Mottiqui, to leave their native village in what is now Marin County for the restrictive life at Mission Dolores. Had that winter been particularly difficult for the southern Coast Miwok peoples? Had the fall acorn harvest been too poor to feed them all? Had the heavy winter winds torn up the woven tule *kótchas* in which they slept, or had the rains flooded those rancherias not on high ground? What did the mission offer that their village lacked? The records do not explain the reasons, but they do show that a large number of Indians from Huimen villages entered the mission in 1801.

The young couple, later to be baptized Marino and Marina, had certainly learned from their relatives and from other Coast Miwok about the wondrous Spanish possessions and about the gifts given to their people by these bearded strangers. But they also had a realistic picture of life at the mission, based on the accounts of runaways who had escaped and returned home. In 1795, when Huicmuse and Mottiqui were fourteen and still living in their tribal village, one-quarter of the Native Americans at Mission Dolores had fled a scene of unrest, abuse, illness, and death; the young people must have listened intently to the reasons these runaways had forsaken the mission life and then opted not to go there themselves.

Nevertheless, by 1801 the Coast Miwok had begun returning to the mission. With the loss of so many people from the local tribal area, it would have been difficult, if not impossible, for Huicmuse and Mottiqui to continue their traditional yearly schedule of rituals and social festivities in the villages. They may have chosen to leave their homes and join their relatives and fellow villagers at the mission in order to maintain their religious calendar and ties of kinship and friendship; certainly life in the villages would have been lonely and meaningless without family members. Some of the new Coast Miwok converts may also have hoped to protect themselves against the strange diseases that seemed to be on the rise back in their villages, illnesses that apparently did not fell the Spanish priests and soldiers. Others may have found Catholicism acceptable, after questioning their traditional religious practices, which had in the past contributed to their sense of well-being.

Huicmuse and Mottiqui, both twenty years old when they crossed the Golden Gate in a tule boat to join other Coast Miwok at Mission Dolores, would not have arrived empty-handed. They would surely have brought with them their carefully made and frequently used tools: Mottiqui's bone awl for making baskets, her digging stick, her gathering baskets for seeds and acorns, Huicmuse's kit for preparing stone tools (his favorite hammerstone for breaking pieces of chert and obsidian to the right size, his flaker for sharpening an edge), and his fishing gear. Their possessions probably also included valuable clothing such as rabbit skin blankets to ward off the chill, necklaces made of shell beads, and perhaps baskets that had been made as gifts and ceremonial regalia such as feather costumes, items that were too precious to leave behind in their village.

Beaching their tule boat, they would have walked to the mission and encountered a different world: a cacophony of non-Miwok languages; former tribal enemies nearby; new rules and regulations based on assigned chores; a time schedule completely foreign to people who planned their activities more by the season than by the hour of day; new codes of proper behavior; unusual punishments for natural acts; a new faith, including a powerful devil; and bewildering new illnesses without the chance to purify oneself in the sweathouse and without access to traditional doctors for treatment. Beyond that, they were now entering a linear world of rectangular dwellings, workshops, and storehouses on straight streets, completely unlike their circular world of round family homes, sweathouses, and ceremonial houses on winding paths.

The ordered world of the mission had by then grown from the original chapel and priests' quarters to an active village, including an open plaza, a church, adobe houses for some of the Indian families, separate dormitories for single men and women, barracks for soldiers, a kitchen, a dispensary, workshops, magazines for storing goods and food produced at the mission, and an orchard. The most impressive structure was the church, where baptisms and marriages took place. Its adobe walls were four feet thick, with large redwood logs supporting the roof. It was "covered with tile, the floor was covered with brick, [and there were]…five doors with locks and also five windows of which three were of glass and two of glazed linen."[10] Although there were no seats, the painted ceiling, the gold leaf altars, the chalice, and the chanting and singing during mass combined to make the church and its ceremonies an attractive spectacle for the native newcomers.[11]

In their first days at the mission, Huicmuse and Mottiqui would have heard not only their own Coast Miwok language, spoken by just a small percentage of the population, but also a confusing mix of Spanish and at least three nonrelated Indian languages. At that time, the majority of Indians at the mission conversed in an Ohlone dialect spoken in the East Bay and on the San Francisco peninsula. Huicmuse and Mottiqui were probably familiar with this language, since the Huchiuns in the East Bay, though not always friendly, were likely trading partners of the Huimen, and marriages between the two groups occurred at the mission. Bay Miwok, spoken by tribes who lived in the hills east of Oakland, was also heard at the mission, but it differed greatly from the Coast Miwok language. By 1810, however, Coast Miwok would become the predominant Indian language spoken at Mission Dolores.[12]

Huicmuse and Mottiqui spent their first weeks at Mission Dolores as catechumens, learning the catechism of proper prayers and responses taught to them by an interpreter, most likely the eighteen-year-old Jacinto, a fellow Huimen who came from Anamas, Marino's reported birthplace.[13] Approximately two weeks later, on

March 7, 1801, Huicmuse and Mottiqui were baptized as Marino and Marina and then married. In the mission records, Marino's name is listed first in the group of eleven Huimen baptized that day, suggesting that he was the leader of the group. Jacinto was a godparent for the baptisms of both Marino and Marina and a formal witness at their marriage.

Thereafter, in the early mission records, Huicmuse is referred to primarily as Marino, although the names Marino and Marin are used interchangeably in later records. At the time of his baptism, Marino received an identifying number, #2182, indicating that 2,181 individuals had been baptized at the mission before him. This number and his name appear in the mission record books kept by the priests to document the baptisms, marriages, and deaths of the baptized Indians, who were known as neophytes.

By 1817, a total of 1,699 Coast Miwok people had been baptized at Mission Dolores. One hundred sixty of them were from the Huimen tribe.[14]

MISSION HOUSING AND WORK

The mission's permanent adobe houses, which had dirt floors and tile roofs, could not accommodate all of the 651 neophytes who lived at Mission Dolores in the year 1800.[15] As newcomers, Marino and Marina at first were not eligible to live in these adobe houses. Most likely, they took their belongings to an area where they could join other Huimen newcomers, perhaps in the village of conical tule huts on the edge of the plaza near the orchard.[16]

In 1792, British visitors George Vancouver and Archibald Menzies, a botanist, described the Indian huts in the mission village as 9 to 12 feet high and 6 to 7 feet in diameter. Vancouver noted the construction in detail:

> Using willow stakes the upper ends of which being small and pliable are brought nearly to join at the top,…and these being securely fastened, give the upper part or roof somewhat of a flattish appearance. Thinner twigs… are horizontally interwoven between the uprights, forming a piece of basket work about 10 or 12 feet high; at the top a small aperture is left, which allows the smoke of the fire made in the centre of the hut to escape, and admits most of the light they receive.…The whole is covered over with a thick thatch of dried grass and rushes.[17]

He also found the huts "abominably infested with every kind of filth and nastiness."[18] These unsanitary conditions may have developed because the priests prohibited the periodic burning and moving of huts, a traditional practice that had performed a useful cleansing function in the Indians' home villages.

As a married woman, Marina was not locked up at night in the women's dormitory (referred to as a nunnery by more than one foreign visitor). But if Marino left the mission for any length of time, this dormitory, reserved for Indian widows, single women, and girls as young as nine years old, would have been her temporary home. The goal was to prevent any sexual activity between these females and male Indians, soldiers, settlers, and, in some cases, the priests themselves. The priests were clearly disturbed by the sexuality they observed. Many of them described the most common vice among the neophytes as "unchastity," "fornication," or some other euphemism for sexual activity.

Foreign visitors, gathering their information from the priests, mentioned other reasons for this nightly incarceration: Vancouver claimed that it prevented the Indians from attacking the mission or missionaries; and Louis Choris reported that it was a response to "jealous" husbands who wanted their wives protected when they were away.[19] Indian girls and women were forbidden to leave the courtyard without permission, even during the day. In fact, the priests guarded their single doorway to the outer world.[20]

During his visit in 1816, Choris learned that 250 women were sleeping in the crowded dormitory. At the nearby Mission Santa Clara, Otto von Kotzebue, a captain in the Russian navy, described the women's dormitory in 1824 as a large windowless building that "resembled a prison for state criminals....These dungeons are opened two or three times a-day, but only to allow the prisoners to pass to and from the church. I have occasionally seen the poor girls rushing out eagerly to breathe the fresh air, and driven immediately into the church like a flock of sheep, by an old ragged Spaniard armed with a stick."[21]

Jean François de Galaup, Comte de la Pérouse, a French visitor to the Carmel mission in 1786, remarked that the Indians were treated like slaves, and Kotzebue believed that their situation was even worse than that faced by Negro slaves. In the American South, slave widows and children were not as a rule physically separated from their families on a daily basis, although they could be sold to another owner. Female slaves in the South were, however, often raped by white overseers and plantation owners. Placing Indian women in a dormitory at least nominally protected them from such injustices. Single men also had a locked dormitory to which they were expected to return at night. Although a priest was given the keys every night, there were slip-ups in which an individual of the opposite sex was locked in the "wrong" dormitory; if caught, the individual was whipped.[22]

The smooth functioning of the mission relied heavily on the hard work of neophytes of both sexes. Women in the dormitories prepared wool for weaving on looms made by other Indians; their labor helped to provide the clothing worn by both men and women. (Figures 12a and 12b) Women also ground corn, which was "the most laborious employment" at the mission. Men were typically employed as "weavers, tanners, shoemakers, bricklayers, carpenters, and blacksmiths."[23] At the San Jose mission, each Indian weaver had a quota to fulfill: those who made serapes had to complete nine in a week, and those producing blankets, thirty a week.[24] Men also herded cattle and sheep at large ranches nearby and farmed crops from out-stations at other locations. Soldiers escorted those who worked on crews away from the mission, as depicted in a Choris watercolor (Figure 23). Precise rules and hours for work, morning mass, and meals governed their existence; infractions were met by punishments unfamiliar to the Indians: stocks, fetters, shackles, whipping, and caning.

Marino was fortunate to have a special skill that set him apart and gave him a sense of freedom that others lacked: the Californio Antonio María Osio wrote that Marino carried letters for the priests in his tule boat and that he had taught the commandante of the San Francisco presidio, Luis Argüello, to read the tides.[25] (This would prove to be only one of the key connections between Marino and this important military figure.) Even though the Spanish soldiers at San Francisco built launches in 1809, they continued to use the tule boats of the native peoples regularly and must have relied on the navigational skills of Indian boatmen to guide all their boats. Serving as a boatman meant that Marino would have spent less time at the San Francisco mission than the other neophytes, and this may have been one of the reasons for his survival.

PRIESTLY AUTHORITY

Religious needs at Mission Dolores were overseen by two or more priests, who remained for varying lengths of time before being sent to other missions. Most of the fathers clearly believed that they were doing the best they could for the native population by using baptism to place the Indians into the hands of God, by feeding them, and by teaching them the skills necessary to work in a European-style agri-cultural society.

But not all the San Francisco priests approached their work in the same way, and they often differed dramatically in personality. Father Vicente Santa María, for example, made every effort to learn the language of the Indians he first met dur-ing the visit of the *San Carlos* and those he encountered later at various missions where he was sent. Many others, however, were not interested in the language and culture of their Indian charges. One visitor, the naturalist Adelbert von Chamisso, wrote in 1816: "The contempt which the missionaries have for the people to whom they are sent seems to us, considering their pious occupation, a very unfortunate circumstance. None of them appears to have troubled himself about [the Indians'] history, customs, religions or languages."[26] Ten years later, Captain Beechey commented:

> It is greatly to be regretted that…the priests do not interest themselves a little more in the education of their converts, the first step to which would be in making themselves acquainted with the Indian language. Many of the Indians surpass their pastors in this respect and can speak the Spanish language, while scarcely one of the padres can make themselves understood by the Indians. They have besides, in general, a lamentable contempt for the intellect of these simple people, and think them incapable of improvement beyond a certain point.[27]

Some priests treated the Indians harshly: Father Martin de Landaeta would not let them visit their relatives; Father Antonio Danti was temperamental, caned Indian workers, and ordered whippings.[28] At the San Jose mission, Father Durán punished wrongdoers "every Sunday after mass with a dozen or more lashes at the church door, after which the culprit was sent to kiss the padre's hand in sign of submission."[29] Father José Ramón Abella, however, showed compassion by appealing to Governor Pablo Vicente Solá to release six Indians who had been imprisoned in the presidio for a year and whose "only crime had been running away."[30]

Other priests were adventurous and often left their flocks to go on expeditions: Father Abella accompanied the military on two trips up the Sacramento and San Joaquin rivers, and Father Blas Ordaz joined Captain Luis Argüello on an expedition in 1821 (described in Chapter 7). Father Ordaz's adventurous nature also expressed itself in his reported "fondness for women [which] involved him occasionally in scandal."[31]

Foreign guests such as sea captains, military officers, ships' doctors, and naturalists, who disembarked at San Francisco from Russia, Germany, France, England, and the United States, had mixed impressions of the role of mission priests. Some visitors had little sympathy for the padres' attitude toward the Indians, whereas others supported what they described as the priests' difficult task of taming a wild land and people.

Complaints about the priests' intolerance, not only toward the Indians' native religion but toward other religions as well, were voiced by both English and Russian visitors, who found the fathers' comments bigoted and offensive. Dmitry Zavalishin, visiting in the early 1820s, reported that Father Esténega locked him and his companions in a room at the mission and refused to let them out until they had "agreed there was a purgatory, which obliged us of course to force the door."[32]

Foreign guests frequently derided the priests for crying poor while concealing from outside eyes an impressive store of foodstuffs (necessarily provided by the Indians' labor) as well as supplies and trading goods. The Russian Shishmarev, after negotiating with the clergy at San Francisco, saw them as avaricious: "The priests, who are great spongers, not only ask but demand, and they feel that we are obliged to give them presents." Eusebio Galindo, a former soldier who had been with the San Francisco company in 1828, reminisced in 1877 that the "poor Indians worked for their missions, but they never had any other benefits than the meager bites that merely kept them alive and a few rags to half cover their nudity. The net proceeds went to Mexico, Spain or Rome. It was never known what the priests did with those funds [the "Pious Fund" monies dispensed by Spain for the support of the missions]. The poor Indians never saw a cent of those funds."[33]

In 1824, Captain Kotzebue observed:

> I am convinced that the system of instruction and discipline adopted by the monks has certainly tended to degrade these step-children of Nature. If to raise them to the rank of intellectual beings had been really the object in view, rather than making them the mock professors of a religion they are incapable of understanding, they should have taught [them] the arts of agriculture and architecture, and the method of breeding cattle; they should have been made proprietors of the land they cultivated, and should have freely enjoyed its produce.[34]

Vancouver was more sympathetic to the priests and disdainful of the Indians. He asserted that the Indians were "certainly a race of the most miserable beings possessing the faculty of human reason…their faces ugly, presenting a dull, heavy and stupid countenance, devoid of sensibility or the least expression." P. E. Botta, an Italian scientist visiting California, denigrated the Indians' intellect, claiming that on their faces one could see "indolence and stupidity.…[The] Californians are an inferior race of men"—even as he praised their music, their basketmaking, and their feather work.[35] It is hard to imagine that these Indians were the same people whose hospitality, warmth, curiosity, intelligence, and communication skills were lauded by Captain Ayala and Father Santa María in 1775.

In 1823 and 1824, the Russian visitor Achille Schabelski contradicted Vancouver's description of the Indians as "savages entirely deprived of intelligence," commenting that this "judgment was probably suggested to [Vancouver] by the priests, who hoped to hold [the Indians] under an absolute guardianship.…A more impartial observation showed us that these Indians are capable not only of all the aspects of agricultural work, but in time would even become artisans, and it is to them that

California is indebted for what little is produced."[36]

The visitors who were more sympathetic to the Indians recognized the sorrow and despair of the neophytes. What passed for "indolence" may well have been suffering caused by one of the debilitating illnesses ravaging the neophyte population, or even mourning for a newly deceased relative. Others may not have wanted to work at tasks that seemed pointless or that kept them from pursuing what their culture deemed essential for survival: gathering food according to the seasons, performing religious ceremonies associated with the daily round of activities, and using the sweathouse for purification. The combined psychological impact of losing their freedom, the underpinnings of their culture, and their traditional support system must have been devastating. The neophytes' doleful appearance may have led to the disparaging remarks made by visitors who had little understanding of what the Indians had lost.

An additional burden for the neophytes was that the priests and their superiors held them to standards that the clergy would never have tried to enforce back home in Spain. In discussing the situation at the Carmel mission during the 1770s, Malcolm Margolin noted that the missionaries

> would be expected to gather together several hundred Indians of various, often hostile, groups (people whose languages they didn't speak and whose customs they neither understood nor respected), draw them by whatever measures they could into the mission, and teach them to live by Spanish codes and morals. [Further,] the aspect of European civilization they were trying to reproduce was not Spanish village life, which would have been difficult enough. Indeed the behavior that the monks were demanding of their new subjects—chastity among the unmarried, long hours of prayer, obedience to superiors, etc.—was far in excess of what was expected of European villagers.[37]

Any misstep in carrying out the priests' plan for the mission was blamed on the Indians and not on the unrealistic goals of the Franciscan order or the actions of the priests themselves.

According to Richard Carrico, the priests believed that Satan was active in California and that his work was evident whenever individual neophytes disobeyed their orders or united against them. Attributing such defiance to the devious "work of the devil" conveniently absolved the priests from responsibility when the Indians complained of injustices. Carrico noted that "according to Catholic dogma, the Devil preceded Christianity to the godless shores of the New World, by hundreds of years."[38] Thus, the church claimed to be competing with a force of many years' duration, giving the priests a feeling of urgency and zeal as well as a rationalization for their presence in California. This zeal may have led the fathers to treat the Native Americans more strictly than they would have treated peasants in rural Spain.

Nonetheless, the idea of the devil may also have helped to sell Christianity to the Indians. In 1932, two Coast Miwok, Maria Copa and Tom Smith, told anthropologist Isabel Kelly about the existence of poison doctors (walipo), who wore horns and a tail made out of tule. Copa said, "I think it is the devil; looked just like a real person. Real people dressed as walipo."[39] Was Copa's depiction the result of incorporating Native American beliefs into Catholic doctrine? Perhaps the Spanish clerics' fear of the devil resonated with the native peoples' fear of poisoners and convinced the Indians that the priests could protect them and counteract the power of both the devil and native poisoners.[40]

INDIAN ALCALDES AT THE MISSION

Although the priests were firmly in control, the neophytes also had to deal with Indian overseers known as *alcaldes*. In the early days of the missions, this role was intended as a way for Native Americans to govern themselves. But the plan backfired when a disagreement arose between the alcaldes and the missionaries, with the alcaldes accusing a priest of murdering Indians at Santa Clara. Subsequently, the position was reduced to that of a subordinate who took his orders from the priests and was not permitted to charge priests with malfeasance.[41] Nevertheless, it remained an important office in the neophyte community; wearing clothing such as pants and shoes marked an alcalde's status. The plan was to elect alcaldes annually, but the missionaries apparently controlled the nominations and terms of appointment.

At Mission Dolores, those who became alcaldes apparently were not those who had been the religious leaders, doctors, or headmen of their native villages. The priests seemed almost unaware of the existence of traditional leaders. At San Francisco, they reported: "Among these Indians little distinction of persons is observed....Those who are held in a little higher esteem are those who are more skilled in fishing and hunting." Priests at the San Jose mission showed only a little more understanding of leadership roles: "They recognize no distinctions nor grades among themselves. In war alone they obey the most valiant....In superstitious practices they obey the soothsayers and wizards."[42]

Alcaldes were expected to oversee chores and maintain discipline among the neophytes. In numerous instances, they had to control Indians who were traditional enemies, making even-handedness difficult. The priests were supposed to order the physical punishments the alcaldes meted out, but testimony from the neophytes suggests that the alcaldes made some decisions on their own. Moreover, alcaldes were not always subservient to the priests and, once they learned how the power structure worked, were in a position to cause havoc for both the clergy and the military.[43]

BAPTISMS AND MARRIAGES

Baptism and marriage are two of the most important sacraments of the church. Priests carefully recorded the baptismal ceremonies and the weddings of Indian converts. In addition to the primary participants, these rituals typically included other neophytes: a same-sex godparent for a baptism, and three witnesses for a marriage. Frequently, a man and woman were baptized and married on the same day, as Marino and Marina were. Parents were not necessarily baptized on the same day as their children, however; the adult baptisms often occurred three days to three weeks later, which implies both immediate baptism for children and a period of instruction for the parents.[44]

When Beechey visited four northern California missions in the 1820s, he observed that Indians were instructed for a "few days" before baptism by another Indian who could speak their language and who taught them how to cross themselves and to say the Lord's Prayer in Spanish, along with "certain passages in the Roman litany." If these newcomers to the faith refused to be converted, "it is the practice to imprison them for a few days, and then to allow them to breathe a little fresh air in a walk round the mission, to observe the happy mode of life of their converted countrymen; after which they are again shut up, and thus they continue to be incarcerated until they declare their readiness to renounce the religion of their forefathers."[45]

Marriages were recorded in a separate book, repeating the baptism number, tribal organization, and parents if known. Because of the high death rate at the mission, most marriages did not last very long. Sixteen months after Marina's marriage to Marino, she died of an unspecified illness. Two months later, he married Doda, the sixteen-year-old daughter of a *capitán* (leader) of the Huchiuns, from the East Bay. When Doda died nine years later, in August 1811, however, her death record contained no mention of a husband.[46] This omission could simply reflect a busy priest's lack of attention to detail, but it is a puzzling breach in otherwise careful record-keeping. Marino may have been absent from the mission at the time of Doda's death, either on a pass or as a runaway, but he was there five months before her death, officiating as a witness at the marriage of two Omiomi, Coast Miwok from the Novato area.[47]

Not until five years later, in August 1816, did Marino marry again, this time to Sotoatijeium, a twenty-four-year-old Coast Miwok woman from Olompali. She had been baptized as Juana, along with her mother, Martina, the day before the marriage. Martina had another child, by the unbaptized Telemele, capitán at Olompali, but we do not know whether this influential Coast Miwok leader was also Juana's father.[48] If he was, we might interpret Marino's marriages to Doda and Juana, both daughters of tribal leaders, as evidence of his high status in the Indian community.

Bancroft described mass pairings and marriages of neophytes at many of the missions: men and women stood in opposing lines, and each male moved down the line until he made his choice. Unless a man admitted to a prior sexual liaison with one of the young women in the line, he was free to choose whomever he wanted. The young woman could refuse, however, and then the man would choose another.[49] It is not likely that Marino participated in such a lineup in his marriages to Doda or Juana. Marino and Juana's wedding occurred during a period when groups of twelve to twenty Coast Miwok were married on the same day, but Marino and Juana were the only couple wed on August 28, 1816.

According to Randall Milliken, marriages in mission and pre-mission days were typically between men and women from adjacent villages within the same tribe or neighboring tribes, and less commonly between individuals from tribes who lived more than twenty miles apart. Those few brides and grooms who originally lived more than twenty-five miles apart are assumed to have come from high-status families.[50] The distance from Marino's Huimen territory to Juana's Olompali was approximately nineteen miles as the crow flies. Their wedding might have represented the joining of high-status people through marriage, but it could also have been an artifact of living in the mission, with few surviving Huimen or neighboring Aguasto and Guaulen available.

Indians who served as witnesses at weddings, godparents at baptisms, or interpreters at either event enjoyed a special status at the mission. The men had jobs around the mission church rather than in the fields, and dressed in pants and shoes, since they were officiating in church ceremonies; we do not know whether the women's dress distinguished them in any way. Like house slaves in the American antebellum South, Native Americans in California who had church-related positions had more privileges, such as easier work and better clothing. They probably all spoke Spanish and were considered by the priests to be more reliable and trustworthy than others, although this judgment sometimes proved to be misplaced. As the priests were to learn, status as an alcalde or a mission assistant did not prevent an Indian from running away or revolting; instead, it put the individual in a position of leadership, which could be used against the church.

The first reference to Marino serving in such an official capacity appears only one year after he was baptized, when he assisted Jacinto at a wedding in April 1802.

Marino's additional contributions to the church's functions as either witness or god-parent are few (1804, 1806, 1811, and 1816), but the official record helps to track his presence as well as his stature (see Appendix B). If he was helping Jacinto in 1802, that fact implies that he had already learned sufficient Spanish to participate, but it does not explain why he was only an occasional and not a frequent participant in this capacity. He may have been working on mission affairs at a distance, or he may even have been a fugitive.

EVERYDAY LIFE FOR INDIANS AT THE MISSION

Between 1813 and 1815, priests at the various missions responded to a questionnaire about Indian customs at each location. This unusual document offers anthropological evidence of the characteristics of a subject people. The accuracy of the answers, of course, depended on the priests' power of observation, their degree of insight, and their knowledge and appreciation of the complexity of Indian culture. Their interpretations of Indian life must have been heavily influenced by their training at religious colleges and by their application of European norms; nevertheless, the responses provide a wealth of detail about such topics as "family life, personal virtues and retention of ancestral customs."[51]

At Mission Dolores, the priests reported that the Indians ate their own ground seeds "whenever they wish[ed]" and that the mission provided three meals a day: "horse-beans, peas, wheat, barley, corn and meat." But numerous authors have suggested that the mission diet did not provide sufficient calories. Foreign visitors in 1792 and 1806 described an unimpressive two-acre garden that included some vegetables, herbs, and young fruit trees not yet bearing any fruit. By 1817 or 1818, however, a French naval officer, Lt. Camille de Roquefeuil, wrote of a garden that was then producing an "abundance of...cabbage, onions...pears, apples and some other fruits." The storehouses for corn and peas impressed Langsdorff, who also noted that ships from Mexico occasionally brought supplies, including such luxuries as "wine, brandy, sugar, chocolate and cocoa." These items were most likely for the priests and their guests, whereas the "iron tools,...kitchen utensils, and implements for husbandry" seen by Langsdorff could benefit both the clergy and the neophytes.[52]

Choris noted in 1816 that "in their free time...[the Indians] work in gardens that are given to them; they raise therein onions, garlic, cantaloupe, watermelon, pumpkins, and fruit trees. The products belong to them and they can dispose of them as they see fit."[53] Indians could also obtain traditional foods when they had permission to hunt for ducks and fish, gather shellfish, and collect acorns for meal.

When asked about the neophytes' attire, the priests at Mission Dolores emphasized the Indians' preference for nudity and their dislike of mission clothing. At

Mission San Jose, the priest reported that "only when it is exceedingly cold, do they cover their bodies with deerskins or other similar things, coarse and unfinished," although foreign observers in the Bay Area noted cleverly constructed garments and blankets of rabbit skins. Langsdorff in 1806 described women's cold-weather attire of otter skins as well as twisted strips of otters' pelts, sewn together, similar in construction to duck- and goose-feather garments, both of which were made double-layered, providing "excellent protection against the cold."[54]

Two scenes painted by Choris in 1816 illustrate Indian clothing, jewelry, and hairstyles at nonceremonial events (Figures 12a, 12b, and 14a). In Choris's sketches for his paintings, the men's breechcloths of mission blanket material are tucked under a belt both in front and in back; the women's blankets are worn over their shoulders. Their hair is either worn short with a ponytail on top or worn long, and their heads are occasionally encircled by material resembling a sweatband. Choris's drawings do not show the shirts or skirts worn by the women or the pants and shoes worn by the alcaldes. As K. T. Khlebnikov reported: "Artisans and servants of the priests are dressed in suits made of frieze; but laborers ordinarily have woolen blankets with which they wrap themselves."[55] These coarse woolen blankets the neophytes wore came to be known as mission blankets.

When they weren't working for the mission, the Native Americans often found an outlet in gambling. Many visitors wrote of the Indians' keen interest in games of chance, even to the extent of gambling away their clothes or their wives. The most popular game consisted of hiding a piece of wood in one hand and then holding out both hands and having the opponent guess which hand held the wood (see Figure 12a). The Russian V. M. Golovnin observed the fun in these contests and the attempts to distract opponents by making noises, singing, and making funny faces. The Indians also picked up card games played by the Spaniards.[56]

Native Americans' musical skills elicited many positive comments from the priests and, in some cases, rave reviews from foreign visitors. Botta wrote that the Indians' "tribal songs are generally melancholic, and the same goes for their tunes; nor are they devoid of charm. Rather I shall say that it seems to me that the most outstanding trait of these Indians is their inclination for music. In the missions they learn soon and easily to play the violin, the cello, etc. and to sing together in such a manner that they can perform the music for the Mass of a very complicated harmony, certainly better than the peasants of our lands would be able to do after years of study."[57]

Most of the missions reported that the Indians played traditional instruments such as flutes, whistles, clappers, and drums. The fathers in missions just north of Monterey did not mention such instruments, but it is evident from ethnographic interviews and other sources that the Coast Miwok did indeed use them.[58] Mass on Sundays and holidays at many of the California missions included music. At Mission Dolores, children played violins, bass viols, drums, trumpets, and tabors (small drums, hung from the neck and played with one hand). According to Choris, the drums had such an effect that when they began to beat, the worshippers fell "to the ground as if they were half dead. None dares to move; all remained stretched upon the ground without making the slightest movement until the end of the service."[59]

A San Francisco priest reported: "Only at their dances do [the Indians] sing. To me it seems they sing but three or four stanzas of four lines on a single night, for they repeat them. Some tunes are lively and others quite sad. They keep good time, for they have acquainted themselves with the songs of the birds."[60] This comment may refer to the neophytes' ability to identify birds by their songs, a distinctive musical skill that helped them to recognize the bird species in a specific area, particularly when gathering colored feathers for ceremonial clothing. The padre's comment might also have suggested that the Indians learned how to keep time from the birds, as if they were incapable of doing so without help.

Foreign visitors recorded their observations of the Indian ceremonies that were allowed on select Christian feast days at Mission Dolores, usually in the plaza in front of the church. During these periods, one observer wrote, the Indians "seemed to us to emerge from their habitual apathy. "[61] Choris's watercolors of body painting and clothing provide exquisite detail of the participants' costuming. (Figures 8 and 9) He also provided a description of dancing following a mass:

> On Sunday, when the service is ended, the Indians gather in the cemetery, which is in front of the mission house, and dance. Half of the men adorn themselves with feathers and with girdles ornamented with feathers and with bits of shell that pass for money among them, or they paint their bodies with regular lines of black, red, and white....The men commonly dance six or eight together, all making the same movements and all armed with spears. Their music consists of clapping the hands, singing, and the sound made by striking split sticks together which has a charm for their ears; this is finally followed by a horrible yell that greatly resembles the sound of a cough accompanied by a whistling noise. The women dance among themselves, but without making violent movements.[62]

UNREST AND RESISTANCE AT THE MISSION

The picture of Indian life painted at some missions today is of a bland but happy spiritual existence, which contrasts greatly with the historical record of the missions as stark and unhappy places for indigenous people. Fear of punishment was ever present, even during mass. In 1826, F. W. Beechey wrote that at high mass at the San Jose mission, where Coast Miwok were also residents, he observed guards equipped "with whips, canes and goads [prods with pointed ends] to preserve silence, maintain order and…to keep the congregation" on their knees. He noted that the goad was a "better" tool of discipline than the whip because it could "reach a long way and inflict a sharp puncture without making any noise."[63] Many missions today also fail to describe the vibrant past and culture that the Indians were forced to abandon when they entered the missions.[64] As early as 1795, the mass exodus of 280 neophytes from Mission Dolores reflected their unhappiness with the constant labor demanded by the padres and the harsh punishments and loss of freedom.

A military inquiry investigating the cause of the 1795 exodus questioned neophytes, soldiers, and priests, and brought to light many abuses. The neophytes testified that they had been whipped, caned, and placed in stocks by both alcaldes and the priests. Timoteo, who had run away, complained that the alcalde Luis had whipped him when he did not feel well; Claudio accused the alcalde Valeriano of making him work when he was sick and "clubbing him every time he turned around." Claudio had been feuding with Valeriano's brother-in-law and believed that his punishment was the result of that argument. Magin had been placed "in the stocks when he was sick on orders from the alcalde." Father Antonio had ordered Otolon whipped because he "was not looking out for his wife."[65]

A man who eventually became Marino's father-in-law, Prospero Chichis, testified that he had been "stretched out and beaten" on the orders of Father Danti, for the crime of going out at night to hunt ducks. Father Danti was blamed again when Tiburico testified that he had been whipped on five occasions because he was crying, after the death of both his wife and his daughter. Whipping was also the punishment for running away, for stealing stock, for robbing, and for armed resistance. For example, an Indian who threw a stone at a soldier was given twenty-five lashes.[66]

In response to such treatment, some neophytes in California rebelled, killing priests at the San Diego and Santa Cruz missions and poisoning them at Missions San Miguel and San Antonio de Padua. Occasionally, Indians from one mission would join those at another to plan and execute a rebellion. However, according to José Fernandez, a former soldier in the San Francisco company, neophyte schemes against the mission and the military were frequently thwarted when a priest heard of plans during confession or when women directly informed the priests of the plots.[67]

Strife among the Indians themselves also undermined the cooperation necessary for carrying out revolts. There were many, often lethal, fights between members of different language groups as well as confrontations between members of the same tribe. In one conflict over a woman, Jacobo was accused of beating to death Evacio, a Coast Miwok of the Aguasto tribe. Jacobo was defended by Lt. José María Estudillo, who argued during the trial that Indian and Spanish cultures differed, because the Indians did not know the morals of Christianity. Saved from the death penalty, Jacobo and his two accomplices, Apolinario and Toribio, were flogged and given ten-year prison sentences.[68]

Complaints about the administration of the mission system abounded: Californios, soldiers, and European visitors denounced the priests' poor attitude and shortsightedness toward the Indians. (Years later, Juan Bautista Alvarado, a former governor of California, complained that the priests had "stripped" the Indians of their "pride"; he went so far as to describe the padres as "men of the cassock who had a grey costume, a grey hood but a black soul.")[69] Others, however, noting the hard work of the priests, blamed the Indians. Except for the testimony of runaways explaining why they had fled, the neophytes expressed their anger primarily through their actions. One neophyte at San Jose, angered at Father Durán, took off his shirt and blanket—gifts and symbols of being a Christian—and threw them on the floor, declaring: "Take your Christianity. I don't want it anymore."[70]

RUNAWAYS

Twice a year, some of the Indians received passes that allowed them to return to their native villages for a brief period. Kotzebue observed:

> This short time is the happiest period of their existence; and I myself have seen them going home in crowds, with loud rejoicings. The sick, who cannot undertake the journey, at least accompany their happy countrymen to the shore where they embark, and there sit for days together, mournfully gazing on the distant summits of the mountains which surround their homes; they often sit in this situation for several days, without taking any food, so much does the sight of their lost home affect these new Christians.[71]

Chamisso told a similar tale of a couple from Mission Dolores, both invalids, who were unable to accompany their relatives to their homeland. They remained on the beach, not returning to the mission, even though they were without clothes and lacked protection from the rain. "Their glances remained fixed on those blue mountains; they saw their fatherland and they comforted their hearts, as they had not been able to reach it." Choris noted that passes to leave were given only to "those Indians upon whose return [the priests] believe they can rely"—but, he added, "it often happens that few of these return."[72]

Indians who left the mission without passes were considered runaways—and a great number of neophytes did escape their virtual enslavement over the years. According to some estimates, about 10 percent of all the neophytes fled, although the number of runaways varied widely from year to year in response to conditions at the mission.[73] The numbers would have been higher if the punishment when captured had not been so great, or if more of the Indians had been physically or emotionally healthy enough to try escaping. Kotzebue felt that they would all run away "if they were not deterred by their fears of the soldiers, who catch them, and bring them back to the Mission as criminals."[74]

La Pérouse, in Monterey in 1786, put the runaway's situation clearly:

> The moment an Indian is baptized, the effect is the same as if he had pronounced a vow for life. If he escapes to reside with his relations in the independent villages, he is summoned three times to return; if he refuses, the missionaries apply to the governor, who sends soldiers to seize him in the midst of his family and conduct him to the mission, where he is condemned to receive a certain number of lashes with the whip.[75]

The priests used force in dealing with runaways not only because successful escapes would entice others to flee, thereby depleting the workforce, but also because souls could be lost. They believed that once the Indians had accepted baptism, they had made an agreement or "contract" with the church and had Christian obligations to fulfill. Seeing themselves as engaged in an active holy war with the devil, the padres expected the Christian converts to perform their part as soldiers in this war.[76] As Milliken explains, "Day in and day out throughout the mission era, ambivalent native villagers along the mission-tribal frontier struggled with a choice—find a place in the new mission system, or resist its attractions. The decision to reject mission life could be made a thousand times, but the decision to join a mission community could be made only once."[77]

Runaways tended to escape to their native villages and to avoid rancherias in which they were not known or which were considered the home of traditional enemies. In 1806, as Langsdorff noted: "No sooner is any one missed than search is made after him....On account of the enmity which subsists among the different tribes, he can never take refuge in any other [tribe]....It is scarcely possible for him to evade the researches of those who are sent in pursuit of him." According to Beechey, this "animosity between the wild and converted Indians is of great importance to the mission, as it checks desertions."[78]

Sent out to bring back runaways, the priests or soldiers tried to explain to the village headmen that they were interested only in the runaways and were willing to let the inhabitants remain in their village. In reality, however, nonmission Indians were sometimes killed in the course of recapturing neophytes, and in some cases others were taken to the presidio.

Runaways were the bane of the mission establishment, much as runaway black slaves were in the American South. Although no money had passed hands at the mission, the priests felt that they had "purchased" Indian souls for God through the act of baptism and needed to retrieve and punish them. Both black slaves and Native American runaways were looking for freedom. Both served a master without pay, toiled at jobs not of their choosing, and suffered punishment for disobedience. When Indians ran away, they were often running to their homeland, something the slaves could not do. But for both, the dangers of running away were similar, and they could not count on the outside population for protection.

When Indian runaways were caught, they were either returned to the mission and forced to wear a long iron bar attached to one ankle or sent to the presidio and placed in the dark and cramped confines of the jail. In 1792, the jail consisted of two small rooms no larger than 5.5 by 4.1 feet. A prisoner could be incarcerated for a year or more in rooms that would have been particularly cold and damp during winter rains and summer fogs. The only warmth in the winter came on sunny days when the prisoners were allowed to sit outside.[79] Those confined here were whipped, shackled, and put in stocks, joining other prisoners who had defied authority by stealing clothing or church supplies, killing livestock, murdering, or fomenting rebellion. Prisoners were also forced to work at the presidio, a benefit for the military that may have accounted for the lengthy incarceration of runaways.

MARINO'S REBELLION AND CAPTURE

Apparently, Marino himself was a runaway for a time. His name does not appear in the Mission Dolores records from March 1811 to July 1816, indicating that he fled sometime during this period. We do not know what prompted his rebellion, but he was surely aware of the repercussions of being apprehended. According to the Mexican general Mariano Vallejo, "Chief Marin" was captured in 1815 or 1816 and taken to the San Francisco presidio jail, only to escape again. Vallejo's account, which clearly contains inaccuracies, is the only surviving record of these events. It is not verifiable and has been doubted by some historians,[80] but much of it is consistent with mission records.

General Vallejo, our source for reports on some of Marino's activities, was raised in Monterey, where he joined the military in 1823 and rose rapidly through the ranks. He was transferred to San Francisco in 1831 to become the commandante of the San Francisco company. In 1836, he was promoted to commandante general of northern California and eventually headquartered in Sonoma.[81] In later years, he penned two versions of Marino's 1815–1816 capture and escape. The first version was written for an 1849–1850 California Senate report, in which Vallejo justified naming a county after Marino. The second version, an elaboration of the first, appeared in 1875 in Vallejo's five-volume history of California, titled *Historical and Personal Memoirs Relating to Alta California,* which the historian H. H. Bancroft described as an "extensive...fascinating...useful aid," but also, like the writings of other Californios, as a "strange mixture of fact and fancy."[82]

In the first version, Vallejo refers to Marino as "Marín" and describes him as a

great chief of the tribe Licatiut, and the other tribes...[of Marin] and Sonoma.... In the year 1815 or 1816 a military expedition proceeded to explore the country north of the bay of San Francisco, and on returning by the Petaluma valley an engagement ensued with Marín, in which he was made prisoner and conducted to the station of San Francisco, from which he escaped, and again reaching Petaluma, he united his scattered forces, and thenceforth dedicated his most strenuous efforts to harass the troops in their hostile incursions into that part of the country.[83]

The second and more detailed version reports that Marín led six hundred Indian warriors in the Petaluma Valley in an attack against the Spaniards, who were commanded by Captain José Argüello and accompanied by the priest Blas Ordaz. The Indians fled in the face of the Spanish firepower, but Argüello captured Marín and took him to the San Francisco presidio. Vallejo continues:

During the first weeks of his incarceration at the presidio, Marín gave signs of being reconciled to his fate, and it seemed that the words of Reverend Father Ramón Abella were making a deep impression upon his soul. By this artifice he succeeded in persuading the Christians that he had taken a liking to them. As Father Abella was very insistent that the door be opened for him, and that he be not left shut up in the dark jail in which he had been placed, Don José Argüello gave in to the entreaties of the missionary and granted Marín permission to stroll about in the vicinity of the presidio. Scarcely did the latter find himself at liberty than he stole a horse with a saddle and a bridle, crossed the bay on a balsa raft and went to rejoin his tribe...and was the cause of the retarded condition in which the territory lying to the north remained for so long.[84]

Vallejo had no firsthand knowledge of this story, since he was a boy of eight at the time. But he may have learned about it later in Monterey as a teenager, when he was secretary to Captain Luis Argüello, commandante of the San Francisco company, who became acting governor of California at Monterey in 1822. By the time Vallejo was stationed in San Francisco and Sonoma, Marino was at the San Rafael mission, and they knew each other there.

Vallejo's 1875 account contains several glaring inaccuracies. Neither Captain José Argüello nor Father Blas Ordaz was assigned to San Francisco at the time, and the commandante in 1815 was not José Argüello, who had left the area in 1806, but his son, Luis Argüello. Either Vallejo's date was incorrect or he had confused the two Argüello family members. Vallejo also had a tendency to exaggerate the number of Indians when describing clashes with the military. For example, it is unlikely that Marino led a band of six hundred Coast Miwok, since the Coast Miwok group was in fact composed of smaller tribes, each with a headman; we have no record of a "chief" for a large group of Coast Miwok tribes or for their Pomo or Ohlone neighbors. In addition, Vallejo was obviously unaware that Marino had been a neophyte in San Francisco and therefore already knew Father Abella, having served under him as a witness and godfather. This previous acquaintance, coupled with Marino's persuasive powers and knowledge of Spanish, no doubt helped him convince the priest to let him roam free in the presidio, setting the stage for his daring escape.

Vallejo's story cannot be corroborated because extant presidio records do not give prisoners' names and often did not list the names of soldiers and officers who went out on expeditions.[85] We do know, however, that the jail was very busy during this period. A letter from Argüello to the governor reports that six runaways had been caught in Bodega in December 1815 and brought back to San Francisco, "where they're working like the others."[86] According to other reports, between October 1815 and May 1816, thirty-six prisoners were brought in for murder or running away, thirty were released, and thirty-two others escaped, most of them while trying to put out fires.[87] This heavy prison traffic may explain why Marino was able to make his escape undetected.

It is possible, as Vallejo claimed, that Marino headed to the Petaluma area, where many nonmission Coast Miwok were living.[88] He presumably avoided the nearby but abandoned Huimen rancherias. If he had already formed a relationship with his future wife Juana at this time, he would have been safe at Olompali, and perhaps at even more northerly villages such as Petaluma.

But Marino could not have remained in the north causing trouble for very long, because he was back at the mission in July 1816. From the mission records, we know that in that month Marino was in *"el monte,"* a mountainous or forested area, where he baptized a dying woman. Her husband was from Petaluma, suggesting that the mountainous area could have been either Mount Burdell, adjacent to Olompali and south of Petaluma, or Sonoma Mountain, northeast of Petaluma, both in Coast Miwok territory. Marino, acting as a priest and familiar with the ritual when he baptized the woman, gave her the baptismal name of Samuela.

Shortly thereafter, he brought Samuela's daughter, Juliana, to Mission Dolores for baptism,[89] thus ensuring his reacceptance at the mission, an important political decision on his part. Father Abella, who had not wanted to treat Marino like an ordinary prisoner before his escape from the presidio, must have welcomed him. Just a month later, Marino appeared to be fully accepted as a participant in church rituals, acting as a godparent to the baby daughter of a fellow Huimen man.

Then, on August 28, at Mission Dolores, Marino married Juana, who was three to four months pregnant. If we assume that Marino was the father of her baby, we can deduce that he was in Coast Miwok territory three to four months before their marriage, even before he baptized Samuela. From March to September of that year, there was an unprecedented influx of Coast Miwok to the mission from Olompali, Petaluma, and West Marin; and Marino may have chosen to return to the mission in order to maintain his relationship with these surviving Coast Miwok.

At the time of Marino's return, Captain Luis Argüello was looking for boatmen at the San Francisco presidio. Argüello's request in September 1815 for twenty oarsmen had not been satisfied by Fathers Abella and Sainz, who claimed that no good boatmen were available because potential candidates were all suffering from syphilis.[90] Thus Marino's skills had become more valuable than ever, and Argüello may have had a hand in overlooking his transgressions, perhaps even encouraging Marino to return without imposing another jail sentence. Marino was still at Mission Dolores in July 1817, participating in a wedding ceremony as a fourth witness with the same three Huimen men who had been witnesses at his own wedding.[91]

ILLNESS AND DEATH AT THE MISSION

The poor health of the neophytes cast a pall over every event at the San Francisco mission. The San Francisco and Santa Clara missions had "among the highest continually sustained death rates anywhere,"[92] and the victims were disproportionally women and infants.

Death touched Marino in January 1817, when Juana gave birth to a baby boy, Melchior, who contracted an undiagnosed illness and died just five days later.[93] We do not know whether Melchior's godparents, Ceciliano and his wife, Justina, took part in the mourning afterward or even how the baby's death was mourned. Marino and Juana never had another child.

The despair and grief caused by these too-frequent deaths must have been crushing to the Indian community. In addition, many of the priests did not seem to understand or appreciate the significance of the Indian rituals of mourning and lamenting, which were in fact common to many cultures around the world. A priest at Mission San Jose observed that "they have no other ceremony than to cry much with shouts and wailings"; at Mission Dolores, "they grieve much and yell quite a bit,…cut their hair, disfigure their faces, bedaub themselves, and there are some old women who repeatedly strike their breast with a stone who not rarely bring death among themselves." Other priests described the mourners' rituals more sensitively: scattering beads and seeds on the dead "in token of their love for the deceased," cutting the hair of the family members, throwing ashes on the survivors, weeping, refraining from eating, never again mentioning the name of the deceased, and smearing pitch on the faces of the older women.[94]

In contrast, the mission death records contain no mention of any ritual at death. These dry accounts include only a list of the deceased, the date of death, and, if the priest knew or had time to note it, the name of the spouse or the parents. Occasionally, the cause of death was also included.

European diseases to which the Indians had no immunity exacted a heavy toll on the neophyte community, as did more commonplace illnesses whose effects were amplified by overcrowding and unsanitary conditions. There were also epidemics of unspecified or unknown diseases, which swept through the mission population and into the surrounding countryside.

When Marino's first wife, Marina, died in July 1802, just a year and four months after their marriage, the cause of her death was not recorded. But it may have been what the priests called *peste,* an illness mentioned in many death records beginning just two weeks later and reaching epidemic proportions soon thereafter. Reported symptoms indicate that the disease was neither flu nor plague, but the description of debilitating headache, stricture of the throat, pneumonia with pain in the side, high fever, and cough suggest diphtheria; other possible diagnoses include pneumonia, scarlet fever, tuberculosis, or a number of different diseases that struck at the same time.[95] At least twenty-three Coast Miwok died, with the majority coming from Marino's tribal group. Many of them did not die at the mission, however; they fled Mission Dolores in August, carrying the disease with them, and their September deaths in their tribal villages were not reported until December.

It was a natural reaction to escape the mission during an epidemic, but the consequences were disastrous for the Indians' home territories. When neophytes ran away or returned home with a pass, they unknowingly spread peste, measles, syphilis, and other diseases to more distant populations, including nonmission Indians. We do not know the number of nonmission Indians felled by these diseases, however, because the priests recorded only the deaths of those who had been baptized.

Just four years after the widespread deaths from peste, an epidemic of measles at Mission Dolores killed more than three hundred Indians during a terrifying three-month period in spring 1806. One-quarter of the Indian population at the mission died at this time, including almost half of the women and seventy-one children.[96] Knowledge of this tragedy among nonmission natives may account for why so few Coast Miwok moved to the mission in 1806 and 1807.

Priests, military officials, and foreign visitors all stressed the havoc that sexually transmitted syphilis wreaked on both the Spanish and the Indian communities. This disabling and lethal disease played a major role not only in the physical decline of the population but also, according to Sherburne F. Cook, in its moral and social disintegration. "Once introduced, its spread was an easy matter," he wrote. "The relations of the soldiers with the Indian women were notorious, despite the most energetic efforts of both officers and clergy to prevent immorality."[97]

Writing in the 1930s, Cook summarized the situation at all the missions: "Perhaps there were some who were able to avoid the infection, but this must have been rare in communities so generally unsanitary, so crowded, and so characterized by sexual promiscuity as the mission....The mass effect of venereal disease upon the population must have been tremendous and must have made itself felt in a multitude of ways."[98] Certainly, with resistance down because of concomitant infection with syphilis, the Indians were also less capable of fighting off the other diseases to which they were exposed.

Father Vicente de Sarría despaired of those who had not been exposed to syphilis marrying those who had it, leading him to claim that "at some of the missions for a person to marry was tantamount to dispatching the same to the cemetery." Even the priests acquired syphilis. As reported by the Indian Lorenzo Asisara, Father Gil y Taboada at Mission Santa Cruz was a man of "very amorous nature....He used to embrace and kiss the Indian women and had carnal contact with them until he contracted a venereal disease and developed buboes."[99]

In 1806, Langsdorff described symptoms of syphilis that included inflammation and swelling at the corners of the eyes as well as "spots upon the neck, with many other horrible and disgusting deformities, consumption and death." Today we know that pregnant women in the early stages of syphilis are more likely to pass it on to their infants than women in the later stages. If the infants survive, they may mature more slowly, have many medical problems, and be mentally retarded. The third, deadly stage of syphilis has numerous debilitating and painful symptoms depending on which part of the body is involved—very often the heart and brain.[100]

The behavioral symptoms associated with late-stage syphilis might even help to explain the pejorative comments about mission Indians made by Botta and Vancouver. In this tertiary stage, the symptoms include poor concentration, memory deterioration, fatigue, lethargy, unkempt and dirty appearance, depression, and a sad-looking face. Perhaps this is why Father Abella of the San Francisco mission noted the feelings of fear and despair among those afflicted.[101]

Deaths among the Coast Miwok neophytes from all these causes increased from approximately 116 in 1815 to 161 in 1816, prompting Father Abella to write to the governor that the only "way for the Indians to survive is to dispatch them to the hills; but this isn't possible, because then what good are the missions?"[102] This revealing statement, in which Abella judged the mission system itself to be more important than the health of his neophytes, was tempered by what in effect was a compromise: providing passes for the Coast Miwok to go to their homeland.

In 1817, the priests at Mission Dolores recorded 127 more deaths among the Coast Miwok. Of the approximately 1,699 Coast Miwok who had entered the mission since 1783, only 485 had survived by December 1817. The Coast Miwok tribes of central and southern Marin were especially hard hit. Of all those who had been baptized, just 11 percent of the Huimen, 19 percent of the Guaulen, and 20 percent of the Aguasto were still alive.[103] The surviving sixteen Huimen included Marino and three children of Quilajuque (baptized as Juan Antonio),[104] one of whom was Cayetana, the only female Huimen survivor. All of these Huimen were to gain prominence during the ensuing years.

6

EARLY SAN RAFAEL MISSION

At Mission Dolores, Indians continued to die in horrifying numbers throughout 1817. Demoralized and desperate, some Coast Miwok fled. Others were given passes to return to their homeland, in the hope that better weather would improve their health. But when reports of another twenty-nine deaths on the Marin peninsula reached the priests, it was clear that a different solution had to be found.

Governor Pablo Vicente de Solá decided to send priests to the area, both to administer last rites for those near death and to build a hospital mission, an *asistencia,* north of the Golden Gate at San Rafael. Constructing this new mission, he reasoned, would also help to put some distance between the Coast Miwok and the soldiers at the San Francisco presidio, whom Father Abella blamed for the spread of syphilis among the Indians.[1] In addition, a northern mission would allow the Spaniards to keep a closer eye on the Russians, who had built several settlements on the coast—Port Rumianstev at Bodega Bay in 1811, and Fort Ross a year later near the Kashaya Pomo village of Metini. (Collectively, these Russian enclaves became known as Colony Ross, which eventually included a hunting settlement on the Farallon Islands as well as three Russian ranches settled after 1833.)[2]

Thus in December 1817, during the rainy season, more than two hundred Coast Miwok, accompanied by five soldiers and two priests, set out for their home territory. They came from both Mission Dolores and Mission San Jose, which was also experiencing a high death rate. The cold and stormy month of December was an unusual time to ferry sick people across the bay, but the situation may have been so critical that the padres thought it best to act before spring. Transported and aided by skillful boatmen such as Marino, the Indians traveled in open launches and tule boats. Their goal was the San Rafael Bay, formed by the San Quentin peninsula on the south and Point San Pedro on the north.

We do not know whether they faced this relocation with eagerness, joy, trepidation, or resignation. The back-and-forth chatter among some of the Indians must have become animated as they rounded the San Quentin peninsula and began to see such familiar landmarks as the clamming areas of Point San Pedro, the islands (later to be named after Marino) off the mouth of San Rafael Creek, favorite stands of oak, and grazing elk and deer. Others, however, may have been too sick or demoralized to experience joy or relief. They were not, after all, returning home to resume their former lifestyle or to resettle in their rancherias; they were moving to a hospital outstation, to what would become the San Rafael mission. Nevertheless, the psychological benefit of returning to familiar territory and avoiding conflicts with non–Coast Miwok peoples at the San Francisco and San Jose missions must have been great.

The boats made their way to the mouth of San Rafael Creek through the marshlands, surely disrupting the feeding of mallards and ruddy ducks. The protected San Rafael Bay and the calm waters and narrow channel of the creek made for an easy landing on the northern bank, perhaps at the spot where a known trail climbed up the hill to an area above the marsh. Those in tule boats, which had a low draft, may have been able to paddle closer to the mission site, a place the Coast Miwok called Nanaguani, before disembarking.

As the travelers stepped onto dry land, their activities likely attracted not only Coast Miwok neophytes who had been sent there earlier for their health but also nonmission Indians and runaways. Indians from Coast Miwok rancherias as far away as Tomales Bay had come to San Rafael for the first celebration of mass, and they too may have been part of the welcoming party. (A gathering of five thousand, however, as later claimed by Juan Garcia, son of a Spanish soldier, seems improbable.)[3]

As a working boatman, Marino undoubtedly made numerous trips back and forth between San Francisco and San Rafael, bringing those who would make up the core group at the new mission. Two hundred and forty Coast Miwok had chosen or had been selected to leave the two older missions.[4] At the time Mission San Rafael was founded, 750 individuals who spoke Coast Miwok were still alive at the San Francisco and San Jose missions, which means that only 24 percent of the known Coast Miwok mission population relocated to San Rafael. We do not know how many of these individuals had a choice in the matter.[5]

One of the few surviving Huimen tribal members at Mission Dolores, Teodorico, either chose to remain at San Francisco or was asked to stay. He apparently held an important position there, perhaps as assistant to Father Tomás Esténega, and he may have been reluctant to relinquish his status. But other Huimen people who transferred to the new asistencia, such as Marino and José María (Teodorico's half-brother), quickly began to assume leadership roles at San Rafael that might have been unavailable to them in San Francisco. This original core group at San Rafael was unique in that it included Indians who were familiar with mission life and its routine, who all spoke the same language, and who knew how personal power was exercised at the mission. The healthier individuals among them would soon begin to participate in running the mission, acting as godparents, witnesses, and alcaldes. These leaders would also set the tone both for the neophytes' compliance with the priests and the military and for their defiance of the Spanish authorities.

Two priests—Father Abella of San Francisco and Father Luis Gil y Taboada of Santa Ines—accompanied the Native Americans, although only one would be permanently assigned to the San Rafael mission. Father Durán of San Jose and Prefect Vicente Francisco de Sarría, a member of the church hierarchy, arrived on December 13. All four priests participated in vespers that evening and helped to plant the cross. The following day, a Sunday, in a covered, three-sided brush enclosure, twenty-six Coast Miwok children were baptized at the first mass, which was said in two languages and sung with music.[6] Marino participated as a godparent for this first mass, signifying that he had once again been accepted by the priests.

Father Gil, who had asked to be relieved of his priestly responsibilities because of poor health only a year earlier, had volunteered to assume responsibility for the asistencia, a job he perceived as a dangerous assignment. Writing to Captain Luis Argüello at the San Francisco presidio four months after the mission was founded, he mentioned that he could not ignore those who were dying at the Tomales rancheria and asserted that he had been willing to "sacrifice" himself by going to San Rafael even at the "cost of my own blood and life."[7]

The priest who truly put his stamp on the new mission, however, was Father Juan Amorós, who replaced Father Gil in the summer of 1819 and remained at San Rafael until he died in July 1832. Many extolled the sterling qualities of Father Amorós. His letters reveal him to be a hard-working man of humor, honesty, kindness, and humility, although he was known to be wily in his dealings with the Russians. He had his detractors, too: at another mission, Amorós had been accused of having a woman in his room. But the priest Sainz de Lucio, who defended Amorós's character in a letter to Governor Solá, explained that children had also been present in the room and begged Solá not to discuss this further "even with the prefect."[8]

In his notes in the mission records, Father Amorós added important and intimate details about the Native Americans under his protection, and he appeared to care deeply about them. The letters he wrote to Argüello, the commandante at the San

Francisco presidio and later the governor, are essential sources for understanding life at the mission.

OTHER EUROPEANS IN COAST MIWOK TERRITORY

The founders of the San Rafael mission were not the first Europeans to venture into Coast Miwok territory. (Chapter 4 describes early sightings of foreign ships beginning in the late sixteenth century as well as the extensive visit of Captain Ayala, Father Santa María, and the crew of the *San Carlos* in 1775.) Most of the visitors between 1775 and 1793, both Spanish and English, stopped on the coast at Tomales Bay or Bodega Bay.[9] They found that the Indians treated them graciously, offering gifts of food, jewelry, and, in one case, precious feather work.[10]

Inland expeditions were rare. In 1793, Lt. Felipe de Goycoechea and a band of soldiers on horseback, led by an Indian guide, traveled overland from Sausalito through Huimen territory. They encountered no Indians until they reached Bolinas. Continuing on to Bodega Bay to reconnoiter with the Spaniard Juan Bautista Matute, Goycoechea met Coast Miwok groups at Olema, at other sites on both sides of Tomales Bay, and at Bodega Bay. Although he found the Indians friendly, he discovered that some were fearful of their Coast Miwok neighbors: "they preserve little harmony amongst themselves, even at short distances those of some settlements do not go to others because of fear."[11] Goycoechea's horses fascinated the Indians; at their request, Goycoechea remained a little longer at Bodega Bay before returning to San Francisco, so that the inhabitants of neighboring villages could see the animals.

Spanish priests from Mission Dolores rarely spent time in Coast Miwok lands, but Father Fortuni was in southern Marin in 1809 and baptized a baby in a rancheria of the Huimen people; in 1811, the priests traveled farther north and baptized individuals in an Alagauli village on the shore of San Pablo Bay.[12] Between 1810 and 1814, the Spanish officer Gabriel Moraga also passed through the area to investigate Russian activity at Bodega and Fort Ross; he met a Coast Miwok capitán (Ióllo) at Bodega in 1810. Two other soldiers, Sergeant José Sánchez and Corporal Herrera, dressed as Indians, spied on the Russians. Native Alaskans, working for the Russians, were also in Coast Miwok lands. Brought in by American and Russian ships, they were engaged in the lucrative business of catching otters from skin boats *(baidarkas)* along both the ocean coast and the bay shore of Huimen territory, where they were observed in 1809 portaging their baidarkas in Tennessee Valley.[13]

The Coast Miwok, then, had been aware of foreign intruders long before the San Rafael mission was established. But these visitors had been few and far between, and, except for those Russians who settled at Colony Ross, they were usually just passing through. The permanent Spanish settlement with a mission, including all its rules and regulations, would prove to have a much greater influence on the Indians' lives than the Russian colony. Nevertheless, the local nonmission Indians apparently accepted the presence of the new asistencia, perhaps finding its attractions similar to those that had drawn Marino and Marina to Mission Dolores in 1801.

NANAGUANI

The mission was established in the Aguasto tribal area known to the Native Americans as Nanaguani,[14] which was situated on a rise and was thus protected from the flooding of San Rafael Creek as well as from unusually high tides. Just north of Nanaguani was the 710-foot San Rafael Hill, which acted as a buffer against the prevailing winds.

The Aguasto had used the large adjacent marsh as a source of abundant waterbirds, ducks, and fish as well as willows for basketmaking and tule for boats. Clams and mussels, harvested from nearby beds, were important staples in the Coast Miwok diet. The Point San Pedro area was also rich in shrimp (which, Maria Copa reported, were "caught with fingers and eaten raw"),[15] as well as flounder and perch.

Nanaguani may have been part of an important trade network, since it was situated at the junction of trails from three directions. The roads from Bolinas and Olema/Tomales to the west (representing the Guaulen, Olema, and Tamal peoples, respectively) met both the Olompali trail from the north and the trail from the southern Huimen villages of Livaneglua, Naique, and Anamas. From Nanaguani, the Aguasto could look east and observe who might be coming into the slough in a tule boat. Another northern trail led to other Coast Miwok settlements north of San Rafael, past Petaluma up to Licatiut territory in southern Sonoma, and east to villages north of San Pablo Bay. Larger villages on major trails served as trading centers, where the Aguasto could exchange shells from the coast and quartz crystals from Mount Tamalpais and Fairfax for magnesite and obsidian from non–Coast Miwok speakers such as the Pomo and Wappo, who were living in what we know today as Sonoma and Napa counties.[16]

By 1817, however, the population of the Nanaguani area had undoubtedly dwindled. In earlier years, all of the Huimen people from the southern part of the Marin peninsula had either left their villages for the San Francisco or San Jose missions or had died. The only remaining occupants of Nanaguani and other Aguasto sites in early December of that year may have been runaways and Indians sent there for health reasons by the priests.

BUILDING THE MISSION

When building commenced at the mission site itself, the Indians were directed to construct one low and extended adobe building containing a chapel, a women's dormitory, a dispensary, and separate rooms for priests and visitors, rather than erecting separate buildings around a courtyard as had been done at other missions. Bancroft estimated that this original adobe building was 87 feet long, 42 feet wide, and 18 feet high.[17] By 1819, the mission complex had been enlarged to include a kitchen, another women's dormitory, a carpenters' shop, a house for the *mayordomo* (chief overseer or supervisor), and a tack room.

This asistencia was relatively poor and remained so for many years. In 1818, in the first year's inventory, Father Gil noted that the ceremonial clothing was "used or very used." A cape was added in 1820, along with a church bell, a silver chalice, a golden ciborium, and a tabernacle on loan. (The last two items were containers for the consecrated bread and wine used in communion.)[18]

According to a Russian visitor, M. N. Vasilyev, the early community in December 1820 included "a church, a house for the padres, storehouses, workshops…[and] a building where the women and children lived [while] the other Indians are in huts thatched with rushes—just like they usually live in the hills." Tile roofs were eventually added to the adobe buildings, and San Rafael began to resemble other California missions, with a dormitory for boys and single men and houses for Indian families. (Figure 28a) When the church was finally completed in 1824, Father Amorós drew a picture of the exterior of the new building in the margin of a baptism entry (Figure 27a); the interior was relatively simple, with a dirt floor and wooden benches.[19]

Many of the Native Americans were housed in five structures that had workshops on the lower floors and dormitories on the upper floors.[20] (See Figure 28b for a diagram of where these buildings may have been, and the original footprint of the 1824 mission church compared with church today.) An Indian cemetery, which has never been moved, was established near today's mission library and rectory. An orchard of pear and apple trees and a vineyard were planted east of the mission.

Overall, San Rafael was a much smaller establishment than the missions at San Francisco and San Jose and employed only one priest. It lacked a presidio for soldiers and their families, and its complement of soldiers was small, usually only one or two, although as many as five were sometimes stationed there when requested by the priest. In contrast to San Francisco, there was no deepwater port to welcome ships from Mexico or foreign lands, no opportunity to exchange European goods and enjoy new companionship, no fandangos and flirtations between visitors and soldiers' daughters, and no dinners and jollity to be enjoyed by the priest at a presidio. Visitors to San Rafael, both foreign and clergy, stayed but a few days at most; the foreigners were usually Russians.

Although the mission complex was relatively small, an 1828 description claimed that the mission lands extended from Bodega and Tomales in the west to the *rinconada* (the neck of the Tiburon peninsula). (Appendix J, Map II) The northern boundary was in the San Antonio Valley, and the southern border was listed as "Annamas called San Pedro Alcantara" in the "Corte Madera."[21] (San Pedro Alcantara was a wood-cutting area in today's Mill Valley, not the location of another major wood source in Larkspur with an almost identical name, Corte Madera San Pablo Alcantara.)

THE MISSION POPULATION

The population of the mission began to increase immediately after its founding. During the first two months, almost all the baptisms were of infants and children whose parents were not themselves baptized. These parents came from many different villages, a majority arriving from west Marin and from as far away as the mouth of Tomales Bay. From the mission's founding in December 1817 to the end of the next year, 212 baptisms were recorded, and the population climbed to 386 and then to 590 by December 1820.[22]

Father Amorós did not stay at San Rafael, waiting for the Indians to come to him. In their zeal for converts, both he and his predecessor traveled from San Rafael to the Tomales-Point Reyes area in November of 1819 and 1820, seeking Indians who were too sick or incapacitated to come to the mission, even baptizing them in bed when necessary. Amorós also took a newborn baby back to the mission to baptize her before she died; the baby's unbaptized mother, unable to breastfeed her newborn, granted him "permission" to take the baby to San Rafael so that the child could be baptized in order to "be a member of God's heaven."[23]

Meeting many aged and infirm Coast Miwok in the Tomales Bay region, Amorós was "afraid they were about to die in the winter, [so] I talked to them about being Christians"[24] and baptized them where they lived. Subsequently, he was criticized by Father José Altimira for not giving these new converts more instruction, but in at least two cases someone remained behind to instruct them, and Amorós wrote in the baptismal record that he had talked to them for three to four hours and had given them "a half of a tortilla,"[25] a reference to the bread offered at communion. The baptismal records seem to indicate that many of these new converts, even a few eighty-year-olds, made it to the mission months later for a second ceremony in the chapel or church: in the margin of the original baptismal record, a new date was added in tiny writing.[26] In 1820, Amorós planned to have those who were the least disabled "carried to the asistencia," and he wrote of his success: "This week two were brought, carried by their sons, also Christians."[27]

When the need arose, Amorós made special trips to baptize individuals who were near death. He journeyed to the home of Ygnacio, a sheepherder, in 1820 to baptize Ygnacio's mother, who was "gravely sick"; to Tomales Bay to baptize Pio, who had been mortally injured and lay in a tule boat; and to the Petaluma neighborhood in 1819 and again in 1821 to baptize first Francisco de Borja and then Anselmo, who had been attacked by bears.[28]

The mission population had surged as more northerly Coast Miwok—the Petaluma and Licatiut peoples—joined the mission, particularly in 1820 and 1821. They were followed by non–Coast Miwok peoples from southern Pomo-speaking villages such as Livantolomi and Gaulomi in 1821 and 1822 and by the Wappo-speaking Guilucs in 1822 and 1823. By 1823, the mission boasted 895 members, 456 male and 439 female. The highest reported population figures were from 1827, with 1,051 Native Americans.[29] (Appendix D)

The mission population statistics reported by both Gil and Amorós may be inflated, because they were based on the number of people baptized. For example, many of those baptized individuals, particularly the elderly, remained in their villages and never went to live at the mission; and some Coast Miwok had become permanent runaways, enjoying a life with the Russians at Colony Ross. On the other hand, deaths were underreported: many who died at the time of their baptisms were not included in the death records, especially if they died in their villages. In the end, many of these deaths were reported neither by neighbors nor by Gil or Amorós.[30] Also, the deaths of some who had been baptized in San Francisco or San Jose appeared only in the records of the mission with which they were originally affiliated and not in the locations where they died.[31]

Fifty couples were married during the first year of the San Rafael mission. As at other missions, marriage was the only way for a female to escape the women's dormitory with its rigid rules. Although some older widows lived with their married children,[32] younger widows and widowers usually married soon after the death of a spouse. Following a familiar mission pattern, most couples were married and baptized on the same day and given similar names, such as Celestino and Celestina, Agapito and Agapita, and Damian and Damiana.

Some married women did not have children, and some men never married.[33] Among the southern Pomo who were baptized at the mission, two adult males— Zacarios from Luppuyomi and Antolin from Jauyomi/Gualomi—were described by the priest as hermaphrodites.[34] We do not know whether Amorós used the term to refer to individuals who had both male and female genitalia (a rare biological condition) or whether he referred to transvestites or transgendered individuals (see Chapter 3).

DAILY LIFE

With only one priest and a few soldiers, Mission San Rafael relied more heavily than other missions on the skills of the neophytes, both for religious tasks and for the day-to-day chores that kept the mission functioning. In the church, the sacristans Francisco, Justino, Acisclo, Juan de Dios, and Elzeario assisted the priest, and interpreters helped to teach church doctrine to the catechumen. These interpreters also assisted at marriages and worked with Amorós to translate Catholic prayers into Coast Miwok. (See Appendix C)

The neophytes were called to prayer by the ringing of a deep bell, which, according to Kotzebue in 1824, was hung between two upright posts. By 1833, the mission had acquired three additional bells of different sizes and pitches.[35] Church ceremonies were enlivened by a seven-member string orchestra that included a violin played by Elzeario, Maria Copa's grandfather; after Teodorico came to San Rafael from Mission Dolores in 1832, he also joined the small orchestra, playing the cello. The church at San Rafael owned an organ, and, since Amorós could sing a mass, services may have featured choral music. Those Indians who came to San Rafael from Mission San Jose had already been exposed to the musical instruction of the talented Father Durán, who taught the neophytes to sing Gregorian chants and melodies with two-, three-, and four-part harmony.[36]

Juan Garcia, recollecting the time his father was stationed in San Rafael, painted an idealized picture of Sundays and feast days at the mission. He told of Indians who would come "for miles around and attend mass in the mission church…[bringing] venison, clams and hides" in exchange for "provisions…from the mission store house. It was not an uncommon sight to see 2,000 Indians gathered around the mission on Sundays." On Easter Sunday in 1819, he reported, the priest led a procession to the church, including two hundred children, some of whom were to be confirmed, that was watched by "several thousand" Indians who had come for mass and the horseracing festivities and feasting that followed. (Although there may have been colorful processions with crowds of people watching and participating in various years, nothing in the 1819 baptismal records or the annual report on the mission supports Garcia's claim of two hundred children being involved.)[37]

It was apparent, however, that not everyone was participating fully in the religious life of the mission. The mission records indicate that only a small proportion of the Indians went to confession or received communion. From 1824 through 1828,

Amorós heard yearly confession from only 21 percent of the neophytes, whereas 66 percent of the neophytes at the San Carlos mission went to confession during the same years. As for communion, fewer than 2 percent of adults took communion in San Rafael during the years 1824 to 1828.[38] Steven Hackel notes that priests could deny communion to those they deemed unfit; and he also suggests that some neophytes may not have known enough of the catechism to receive communion, while other Indians may have purposely rejected it.[39] In addition, since Amorós was the only priest assigned to San Rafael after 1818, which had three to four times as many neophytes as the San Carlos mission, his workload may have prevented him from offering confession and communion to more neophytes, especially among those Indians who lived in western Marin villages and could not travel to the mission for Easter, when confession and communion typically took place.[40]

Only men were designated as witnesses at weddings. Because many of these witnesses were described in the marriage records by the jobs they performed—ironworkers, carpenters, cooks, nurses, weavers, and nurserymen, for example—we have a picture of their everyday occupations. Because Indian women were not marriage witnesses, we know less about their chores.

Not everyone was confined to the mission village; some chores required Indians to leave for varying lengths of time. Alcaldes oversaw work in the fields, and they also accompanied Amorós on his visits to rancherias. The alcalde Geronimo apparently went on baptizing excursions by himself. Boatmen also left the mission for trips of more than a day's duration, carrying small gifts of fruit or fish to Captain Argüello at the San Francisco presidio, bringing back food from Father Durán at Mission San Jose or brandy from Captain Argüello for Amorós (who commented, "I put it to good use"), transporting soldiers and guests, taking Amorós to dinner with Argüello at the presidio, and carrying mail from the mission to the presidio. It is said that the boatmen placed the mail on their heads so that it would not get wet. The boatmen's labors were not insignificant: presidio account books in 1822 credited San Rafael with five hundred dollars for the work of the Indian boatmen.[41]

Stockmen and vaqueros spent weeks, perhaps months, away from the mission. Their ability to maintain and increase the herds of cattle and horses and flocks of sheep—which provided not only food but also hides, tallow, and wool that could be used or traded for other material goods—was essential for the mission's survival.[42] There were not enough soldiers to supervise them, so these men enjoyed a great deal of independence and freedom. During the dry period (approximately May to October), cattle and horses were kept close to the mission. For the rest of the year, the cattle grazed in valleys throughout today's northern San Rafael, Novato,

Olompali, and Nicasio; horses grazed as far north as San Antonio Creek, which lies on today's boundary between Marin and Sonoma counties. Coast Miwok vaqueros such as Porfirio and Tiberio had primary responsibility for tending these growing herds, which by 1823 included one thousand head of cattle and two hundred horses.[43] The sheepherder called Ygnacio may have worked in the area north of San Rafael that carries his name today.

The vaqueros were particularly privileged: after Prefect Sarría's January 1818 decision limiting the Indians' access to modes of transportation such as horses, they were the only neophytes allowed to ride horseback. Vaqueros were also distinguished by their clothing: hat, shirt, trousers, jacket, shoes, and boots.[44] Dmitry Zavalishin, a Russian visiting California in 1824, noted that the vaqueros were fluent in Spanish. Their job was "guarding the herd," he reported, adding that they "were also important in that they were mission police...and in this capacity were hated by the Indians as executors of sentences, instruments of their punishment and coercion, and spies for the missionaries." Yet he also pointed out that their "devotion...was sometimes only a clever ruse; during an uprising at mission Santa Cruz, the missionaries were betrayed by the vaqueros and were put to agonizing deaths."[45]

The neophytes assigned to agricultural work were more restricted and may have left the mission only during the day. European crops grown on mission lands included wheat (the predominant crop), barley, corn, beans, fava beans, and peas. Not all years were productive, however. In response to a plea from Amorós in 1822, Father Durán of San Jose agreed to help San Rafael by sending supplies of corn, beans, and lard. In 1829, the crop was "a very light one" spoiled by rats, locusts etc....; and in 1830, Amorós wrote of a poor harvest because of "Egyptian plagues, ducks 'mice' all reasons to try our patience." The total harvest at San Rafael in 1828 was lower than at either the San Francisco or the Sonoma mission and less than half of what Mission San Jose was producing.[46] It is not clear how free the Coast Miwok living at the San Rafael mission were to go clamming, hunt game, or gather acorns, seeds, and tubers, but Father Amorós's more relaxed style of governing no doubt allowed and encouraged such activities, particularly during periods of drought, plagues, and poor harvests.

The mission grew enough grapes that General Vallejo appropriated some of the stocks for his own vineyard in Sonoma in the 1840s. The indigenous grape, *Vitus californica*, was not palatable, but an import known as the Mission grape—most likely a true *Vitus vinifera*, a black grape from Spain—had been brought to California in 1779. Indians picked the grapes, as depicted in an 1825 wall painting at Mission San Fernando. They then crushed the grapes, either by placing them in a cowhide bag and stomping on them or by trampling them with their washed feet on cattle hides, as seen at Mission Purísma Concepción. The neophytes wore clean loincloths and tied pieces of cloth around their wrists and hands to prevent their sweat from dripping into the must.[47]

HEALTH OF THE NONMISSION INDIANS

In the early days of Mission San Rafael, a good number of unbaptized Coast Miwok continued to live in the Tomales and Petaluma areas, their lives touched only minimally by the mission's presence. Some of these individuals provide a striking picture of how native people adjusted to handicaps such as blindness or paralysis, or simply to the vagaries of old age, while continuing to lead productive lives. When Amorós was baptizing in the Tomales region in 1819, for example, he encountered forty-year-old Vitala, who was blind. She agreed to go to the mission for the formal rite of baptism, but only if she could then return to her village to take care of her partially paralyzed husband, Vital, who was still able to fish from his tule boat.[48]

In 1819 and 1820, Amorós also met a surprising number of Coast Miwok elders in Tomales. Of thirty-one elders whose ages ranged from sixty to more than eighty, four were blind, and two were both blind and deaf. A similar pattern of longevity was found in southern Pomo rancherias, where forty-three Pomos aged sixty to ninety were baptized between 1824 and 1836.[49]

It is clear that the Indian lifestyle permitted longevity, which was fostered by the support of family and community and by the use of native medicinal plants and traditional healers. At the missions, in contrast, traditional healing practices were frowned upon, and it was more difficult to acquire medicinal plants. Among mission residents, elders were some of the first to perish, along with children, and their loss must have been keenly felt, for they were the repositories of family and tribal history, sacred traditions, and environmental knowledge.

NATIVE AMERICAN LEADERSHIP

Native Americans who were alcaldes, vaqueros, or boatmen, and who thus had more freedom, responsibilities, and privileges than the other neophytes, became de facto power brokers in the Indian community. The capitáns of various Indian rancherias were also a force to be reckoned with as they entered the mission system, supported by their own people who were baptized along with them. In addition, Indians who participated in church activities, such as interpreters, sacristans, godparents, and witnesses, had an advantage, if only because they understood Spanish and had a firsthand view of how the system worked (and of how to work the system). Individuals who filled such leadership roles were usually assigned less onerous duties and granted other marks of status such as special clothing. The priests must have needed these leaders and thus were willing to risk having them in positions of authority. Perhaps they also hoped to keep them busy with duties and privileges rather than leaving them free to foment trouble.

Marino and Juana as Godparents

In the celebration of the first mass at San Rafael, on December 14, 1817, Marino was a prominent figure. He was the only local Indian godparent at the first baptisms that day, sponsoring three male children; soldiers and an Indian from the San Carlos mission sponsored the others. When more children were baptized two days later, Marino was the only male godparent. From the first day, the priests identified him in the records as "married to Juana," although she did not act as a godmother until February 1818, when she participated in the baptism of five female Indians.[50]

Marino and Juana usually served as godparents individually, on different days, rather than as a couple on the same day, indicating that each played an important role in his or her own right. Of the two, Juana was a godparent more often; on some days, she sponsored every female baptized for that day. On July 11, 1818, for example, she was godmother to eighteen women and two girls. Marino and Juana did sometimes serve jointly, however; once, in 1822, they discovered a sickly newborn boy in the countryside and carried him to the mission for baptism. The child, Mathias, died three days later.[51]

After the first two years at San Rafael, Marino was rarely listed as a godparent, except when he sponsored the sons of other leaders, his nephew Basilio, and a three-year-old from Olompali who was his namesake.[52] Juana's role as godparent may have continued longer than Marino's because she was from northern Marin, as were most of the newly arrived neophytes. She had a close relationship with the wives of leaders, acting as their godmother soon after their arrival at the mission and later as the godmother of their female offspring. After 1820, Marino and Juana were only infrequently listed as godparents, although they continued to serve in this role for select Coast Miwok families such as those of José María and María Josepha, and Nereo and Nerea. This ongoing relationship implies that the parents had some latitude in choosing the godparents and that the presence of Marino or Juana was important to these leaders and their spouses.

Marino as an Alcalde

The most significant role an Indian could assume at the San Rafael mission was that of alcalde, the overseer of all the Indians at the mission, who reported directly to the priest. At the San Carlos mission, Father Amorós had held elections for this post: "These Indians [have been] elected, they are capable of some jobs, and I will prepare them, and then they will be elected formally by law." It is not clear whether Amorós restricted the list of candidates. At the large mission of San Luis Rey, north of San Diego, the Indian Pablo Tac reported that the priests appointed the seven alcaldes from among those who could speak Spanish "more than the others and were better than the others in their customs." He also said that they carried rods, which were a "symbol that they could judge others."[53] The rods may have been a holdover from earlier traditions: both Drake's men in 1579 and Father Santa María in 1775 noted the use of the rod as a symbol of rank among the Coast Miwok.[54]

In the 1870s, former governor Juan Bautista Alvarado wrote that the alcaldes were tools of the priests. He argued that the padres "had an organized police force selected from amongst the oldest neophytes and the oldest married catechumens, who had families and enjoyed a good moral reputation. These individuals, who were given the title of 'alcaldes' and were implicitly trusted by the missionaries, were protected and instructed...[so] that the Indians might be kept aware that their guards or jailers were on the alert."[55] Yet alcaldes were also leaders of resistance at a number of missions. Besides speaking Spanish, the alcaldes must have also understood something of the Spanish civil, religious, and military structure at the missions—no mean feat, given that their cultural background was so antithetical to that of the Spaniards.

Not until Father Amorós arrived at San Rafael in the summer of 1819 was an alcalde mentioned in the records—and it was Marino. Other alcaldes were also named, but in these early days Marino was elevated above them to *alcalde primero* or *alcalde mayor* (the first, or major, alcalde). Marino's status increased again when he was named mayordomo, an honor first mentioned in February 1820.[56] This title referred to a civil post usually held by a member of the *gente de razon* (a term used for non-Indians such as soldiers and settlers) and indicates the high regard in which Amorós held Marino, who was then thirty-nine years old. In 1819, Amorós recorded the building of a tile-roofed residence for the mayordomo, tangible proof of Marino's status.[57]

Marino's tenure as a high-status person was quite short-lived, however. By March 12, 1820, and in all subsequent baptismal entries that list Juana as a godmother, she is no longer described as the wife of the mayordomo or the alcalde primero, but only as the "wife of Marino." Thereafter, there is no mention of an alcalde primero or mayordomo, and the mission records never again refer to Marino as an alcalde. Further, a baptismal record from July 1820 indicates that the previous *alcalde segundo* (the alcalde second in rank), José María, had been elevated to the position of alcalde and was identified as the *llavero* (keeper of the keys, or housekeeper).[58] Marino's change in status could have had many causes, one of which might have been his absence from the mission much of the time: his name appears in the mission documents only a few times from 1821 to 1823, not at all during 1824, once in 1825, and then not again until June 1832. (The following chapters discuss possible reasons for his absence.)

Other Indian Leaders

José María, the man who supplanted Marino as alcalde, was another Huimen, originally from the village of Livaneglua (also spelled Lihuangelua) in the Sausalito area. He would have known Marino well, not only from their shared experiences in a Huimen village but also from their time together at Mission Dolores. José María came from a well-placed family. His father, Quilajuque, had four or five wives[59] and nine children, at least three of whom became leaders at the mission. José María was a widower twice over when he married María Josepha in the first marriage ceremony performed at San Rafael in February 1818. Whatever the cause of Marino's seeming demotion and José María's elevation, it did not disturb their special relationship; Marino served as godparent to their only child in 1823.

When José María died at the mission in 1825, Father Amorós honored him in an unusual fashion: the alcalde was buried with his habit (*habito*, special clothing denoting his status) and the ciborium (*copon*, a utensil for the Eucharist). Such a burial was a surprising recognition for José María's services, since he was not a priest. Amorós explained his decision by noting that José María "was the capitán of this land."[60]

Another alcalde mentioned frequently in this early period was Geronimo, a member of the Tamal tribe. He had been baptized at Mission Dolores in April 1808, at age twenty-four, on the same date as José María. These two alcaldes would have been in the same catechism class and might have arrived at San Francisco together.[61]

In addition to his duties as alcalde, Geronimo was a frequent witness at weddings, a godparent at baptisms beginning in 1819, an interpreter, and a nurse. In the spring of 1824, he was sent out into the countryside to convert unbaptized Indians and look for runaways. During his travels, he ran into trouble and was killed by other Indians near Livantolomi, a Pomo village in southern Sonoma, near Sebastopol. Some of his bones were recovered a month later and buried at San Rafael by Father Amorós, who printed Geronimo's name in large letters in the death records.[62]

The powerful capitáns of the different tribes continued as leaders throughout the history of the San Rafael mission. Some assumed numerous responsibilities: for example, Toribio, a Coast Miwok capitán of the Licatiut, was also an alcalde and an interpreter, helping to translate for the Pomo and Wappo, two non-Coast Miwok groups.[63] Two Coast Miwok brothers from the Bolinas area, Justino and the alcalde

Nereo, also played many roles. At various times, Justino was an interpreter, a sacristan, a godparent, a nurse, and a witness at weddings; his brother was not only an alcalde but also a witness, an interpreter, and a nurse who helped to care for those whom Amorós described as the "the nuns," apparently a reference to the women who were sequestered in the all-female dormitory.[64] The two brothers married their wives on the same day as José María's wedding, in the first marriage ceremonies performed at San Rafael. The influence of these two brothers extended over many years, and their wives, Justina and Nerea, also participated in mission affairs.

The Network of Influence

Which members of the Coast Miwok tribe exercised authority at the mission? The complicated web of influence and relationships can be traced through the mission records documenting the marriages that linked important families and listing those who assisted at rites of marriage and baptism. Just as Marino and Juana supported the families of José María and Nereo, so did the brothers Justino and Nereo support another Coast Miwok, Pacifico, who was the son of the capitán Telemele (baptized Nemenciano) of Olompali.[65]

Another Huimen of great significance was Quilajuque, baptized Juan Antonio at San Francisco in 1814.[66] He was the father of at least three important children, including José María, the alcalde described earlier, and of Teodorico, who had been a witness at the wedding of Marino and Juana and who had remained in San Francisco when the San Rafael mission was established. Teodorico later became one of the claimants to Indian land in Nicasio in the 1830s. A third child, Cayetana, became the wife of Jacome, the leader of Olompali, and later the wife of his successor.

Other important Coast Miwok individuals at the mission included Juana's mother (Marino's mother-in-law), Martina. Her first Christian marriage took place in her fifties, when she wed the widower Nemencino Telemele, the capitán of Olompali. This was not a new relationship: he was acknowledged in the San Francisco records as the father of Martina's daughter Francisca, born in 1813, before Martina entered the San Francisco mission.[67] Before her marriage, Martina may have lived in the women's dormitory at San Rafael or possibly with Juana and Marino.

It is interesting to note that Martina's Indian name, Chonchonmaen, ends in the suffix -maen, which was the title for a female tribal leader among the Coast Miwok (see Chapter 3), suggesting that she was an important person. Similarly, the Indian name of the daughter of the Bodega capitán was Xisemaen.[68] This speculation may be problematic, however. Of the twenty-three females at the San Rafael mission whose Indian names ended with -maen or -mayen, one was a Wappo Indian, and two were only nine and eleven years old. Although such young children were considered adults in the mission system, it is difficult to believe that they could have been seen as powerful in Indian society at that age. At San Francisco, four other Coast Miwok females besides Martina had names ending in -*maen,* and one was a six-month-old.

The wives of alcaldes, capitáns, vaqueros, and a carpenter were all influential women at the mission who often acted as godmothers. In 1932, Isabel Kelly wrote to her professor, Edward Winslow Gifford, of her surprise at what she was hearing about women in her interviews with elderly Coast Miwok members: "The amazing thing about the ceremonial make-up as I see it is the extremely prominent role played by women. The head of the secret society is a woman; and women are said to have more 'power' than men."[69] It seems doubtful that the Spanish priests, with their patriarchal background, could have recognized or appreciated the key role of women in Coast Miwok culture. Since the priests allowed only males to serve as marriage witnesses, it is difficult to trace or recognize influential women except through their husbands.

At Mission Dolores, the priests clearly identified several women as troublemakers. In June 1817, Father Abella complained to the governor about two individuals at Livantolomi: a neophyte from Mission Dolores and a woman who was "encouraging the nonmission Indians to fight" the soldiers.[70] In that same year, Abella thanked the governor for releasing a number of Indians from the presidio, among them the Coast Miwok Raymundo, who had been imprisoned with five others for "forgetting to return to the mission when they go for walks." The priest believed that Raymundo's wife, Raymunda, also of the Tamal/Libantone tribe, was actually "at fault" and mentioned that it would have been better if she had not been baptized.[71] Nevertheless, at San Rafael, Raymunda joined Juana as a godmother as early as April 1818, just fifteen months after the priest at Mission Dolores had complained about her, and she continued to act as a godmother until two years before her death, in 1838. She was the only woman in the San Rafael accounts to have her occupation listed (she was a cook).[72] She provides an interesting example of a troublemaker who became a valued participant in mission activities.

TROUBLE AT THE MISSION

Although Indian alcaldes and capitáns had some influence in running mission affairs, the real control remained in the hands of the Spanish priests, supported by a small military force. Over the years, Father Amorós, and before him Father Gil, requested that the San Francisco presidio send as many as five additional soldiers to the San Rafael mission for short periods. Gil wanted support when he visited the sick in the Tomales Bay area, whereas Amorós typically wanted soldiers to help find and return runaways to the mission or take them to the presidio. Once, Amorós wanted a soldier to "help run off a few old Christian rebels who are damaging our cattle, horses and crops."[73] Both priests believed in the healing power of their religion to dispel conflicts, but obstacles continued to arise. Longstanding tribal irritations and suspicions remained and led to both inter- and intratribal strife: inhabitants of rancherias attacked runaways who sought refuge with them, nonmission Indians kidnapped neophytes, and the military pursued both runaways and those with legitimate passes who refused to return.

Tribal Relationships

Old rivalries and distrust among the Indians themselves were still rampant after the mission system was established in northern California, and in some cases even after the missions were disbanded. These entrenched differences often prevented Indians from making common cause against the Spanish military or vindictive priests. General Vallejo recognized the necessity of fostering such hostilities among the Indians and bragged in later years of his policy that aimed to "divide and conquer," allowing the military to control and subjugate the native population.[74]

Coast Miwok rancherias often feuded with one another over problems common in some form to all societies: reacting to personal slights; cheating at games; violating property rights when fishing, clamming, or gathering acorns; suspecting neighbors of sorcery or ill will. In the 1930s, Maria Copa, a Coast Miwok, described an earlier time this way: "Tomales didn't like Nicasio people—Nicasio don't like Healdsburg—Petaluma didn't like Marshall. Bodega don't like San Rafael." In Copa's list, only Healdsburg is a non-Miwok group.[75]

Problems between the Coast Miwok and the southern Pomo rancheria Livantolomi surfaced even before the founding of the San Rafael mission. In June 1817, Father Abella asked Governor Solá to send Luis Argüello on a seven- to eight-day expedition against this rancheria, where a San Francisco neophyte and a woman were reportedly urging resistance against the Spanish military. According to Abella, even the Indians who lived in the vicinity of Livantolomi were afraid of the rancheria's inhabitants, who were also known by "another name around here: wild ones." He continued: "Our *neofitos* are also afraid of them, and I don't dare send them to hunt for deer, because they say the wild gentiles [unbaptized Indians] come very close to their lands at night, and they are afraid they will be hit by an arrow."[76]

Solá answered the next day, saying that he had no objections to Argüello going to Livantolomi and picking up the runaway neophytes in the village. Apparently, Sergeant José Sánchez and a force of ten soldiers were sent out to respond to the threat in Livantolomi. But instead of bringing the runaways back to the mission, the Spanish military killed two neophytes, Santiago and Sulpico, on June 19.[77]

Nine months later, five armed Livantolomi "spies" went to the *milpa* (the cultivated fields) of the newly established San Rafael asistencia but were scared away by a vaquero. In response, Father Gil requested that soldiers be sent to the Pomo village in the hope that "we will make them see that they need to put aside the hatred of their fellow man, because we are all brothers, created by God for heaven. In this way we would be able to easily conquer the next rancherias. We will also succeed in calming the nerves of our neophytes who are panic stricken when simply hearing the name Lihuantuleyomi [Livantolomi]."[78]

In spite of these calming words, Pomo neighbors continued to be a problem. In 1823, Father José Altimira, on an expedition to found a new mission at Sonoma, camped in the Petaluma plain in the "company of eight or ten Petaluma Indians [Coast Miwok] who were wandering around there hiding from the fury of the Indians from the rancheria of Libantiloyomi [Livantolomi]."[79] A year later, the San Rafael alcalde Geronimo was killed by nonmission Indians in this same area.

Such hostilities aside, the Coast Miwok and the southern Pomo must have had a history of peaceful contact and trade, because each group had goods the other lacked and needed. In the 1930s, Tom Smith recalled that the Coast Miwok went to the Pomo area of Healdsburg for basket material, and Maria Copa indicated that they went even farther afield, to Lake County, for obsidian.[80] Similarly, the Pomo from the Healdsburg area came to coastal Marin to fish and clam. Evidently, however, their trading relationship did not mitigate their wariness.

Runaways and Herrera's Imprisonment

Notwithstanding these conflicts, three Pomo capitáns, including Elizeo from Livantolomi,[81] entered the San Rafael mission in 1822, where the neophytes were predominantly Coast Miwok. But when the Pomo Indians received passes and went to visit their home villages, all of them refused to return to the mission. Father Amorós dispatched Corporal José Herrera to the San Francisco presidio in an effort to convince Captain Luis Argüello (now governor of California) that the San Rafael mission needed two more soldiers in order to bring back the runaways.[82]

Neophytes from the Wappo-speaking Guiluc group were also refusing to return to the mission. The Guilucs posed a serious problem because the unbaptized among them were killing Christian Indians who had been discovered in their villages, and some neophytes had joined in raiding and burning villages. With the additional soldiers requested by Corporal Herrera, the plan was to have a military patrol swing through both Pomo Livantolomi and Wappo-speaking Guiluc villages looking for runaway neophytes. Amorós particularly wanted these converts returned in time for Easter week.

Herrera set out on a six-day expedition from San Rafael in late February or early March. When the Spaniards marched out to confront the rebellious Guilucs, they met strong resistance. But the military firepower proved overwhelming. In the ensuing fight, the nonmission Indians suffered the most: six were killed and eight were wounded. Herrera returned with forty Guiluc captives, including unbaptized Indians as well as the twenty-five neophytes who had been his initial target. All thirteen adult male prisoners, including three capitáns, were taken to the San Francisco presidio. Presumably, the remaining captives were women and children, who were taken to the San Rafael mission.[83]

Reporting to his superior, Amorós expressed his hope that "God [will] light their way so they become more docile." A month later, however, he decided not to leave it all up to God and requested four more soldiers to round up additional Guiluc runaways. When Herrera returned from this new expedition with more captives, Amorós wrote that the Guilucs were now quiet, the heathens were "happy" to be baptized, and the "old capitán Magma" had been instrumental in bringing them in. Because of his cooperation, the sixty-year-old capitán was not taken to the presidio; instead, both he and his daughter were baptized in April at San Rafael.[84]

As for the runaway Indians from Livantolomi, neither praise nor threats had brought them back. Amorós wanted to pursue them as soon as possible, requesting four more soldiers from Argüello for a force that would include some neophytes. But a disturbing event involving Corporal Herrera occurred during an expedition to Livantolomi led by Second Lt. Santiago Argüello, the governor's brother. In October 1823, Luis Argüello was notified by acting commandante Ignacio Martínez that Corporal Herrera was to be imprisoned immediately upon his return from the expedition.[85]

Amorós did not hear about the charges against Herrera until the following month, when Santiago Argüello told him that Herrera had done things "which destroy men." Although he believed that Herrera had some good qualities, Amorós realized at that point that Herrera should "not set foot in this area again."[86]

What kind of atrocity Herrera had committed was never explained. A Russian visitor in the early 1820s, Achille Schabelski, described how the military sometimes rounded up Indians and forcibly brought them to the missions. Using neophytes to scout out an area, the soldiers moved in at night, firing their muskets and surprising the villagers. When the confused Indians left their huts, the soldiers lassoed them. "As soon as an Indian is caught, he is dragged to the ground and the soldier rides at a great gallop [dragging him] so that the Indian is weakened by the loss of blood from his wounds. He is then bound and turned over to the Indian allies." Schabelski noted that this "did not at all conform to the principles of Christianity." Golovnin, in California from 1817 to 1819, also observed the lassoing of Native Americans, noting that it was similar to the methods used in catching wild horses, bulls, and bears, with a tragic consequence: "when lassoing the Indians, they frequently kill them."[87]

Herrera's incarceration must have been a personal blow to Amorós; they both had been assigned to the San Rafael mission in July 1818 and had relied on each other. Herrera and Marino had also known each other from the time of the first mass at the mission, when they both participated as godparents. In addition, it must have been strange for the Indians imprisoned at the presidio to share their confinement with the very man who had put them in jail. Although there is no extant record of a trial, Herrera was still at the jail in February 1824, when he was reported to be sick. He was officially discharged in March 1824, after which his name disappears from written accounts.

In spite of Herrera's actions, Santiago Argüello was able to assure the runaways at Livantolomi of a warm welcome if they returned to San Rafael, and the soldier Dolores Cantúa and six others were sent on horseback in November to bring them back before the rainy season.[88] Gradually, these and other Pomo people began entering the mission again, and on the day after Easter the following spring, forty-four new converts were baptized.

COAST MIWOK WITH THE RUSSIANS

Some of the Coast Miwok chose to escape the obligations and punishments at the San Rafael mission by fleeing north to the Russians at Colony Ross. The advantages of reaching such a haven more than compensated for the hazards of traveling through non-Christian villages and Pomo territory. According to V. P. Tarakanoff, a hunter for the Russian-American Company, the Indians were paid both for their work at New Albion and for any provisions they brought in, such as "fish, fowl, game, berries or roots." One of the chiefs told Tarakanoff that the Spaniards were "bad men who took his kinsmen captive and made them work like cattle in the fields." Without a permanent priest at Fort Ross, the Indians were not forced to attend church. At least one Coast Miwok woman, Talia Unutiaca, had married a Russian before she was later baptized at San Rafael.[89]

This avenue of access to Russian territory caused tension between the San Rafael mission and its neighbors to the north. Father Amorós sent out a force of a few soldiers and neophytes to retrieve and harass those who had fled to Colony Ross. Achille Shelikhov, manager of Fort Ross, complained to the agent of the Russian-American Company in November 1825 about the military activity and about Amorós pestering him to send the Indians back to the mission, which he was reluctant to do:

"The chief of the Bodega Indians known to you as Valenila has asked me not to return his band of Indians to the Spaniards, saying they belong to the Russians and in no way see themselves as subject to the Spanish, and that although some of them have been christened and have lived for a little while with the Spanish, they were all captured perfidiously at Little Bodega in Russian dwellings."[90] Valenila was most likely the Indian who had been baptized as Tadeo at San Rafael in August 1819[91] and had apparently fled the mission. Previously, in 1810 or 1811, Chief Ióllo (Figure 7), Valenila's predecessor, had given the Russians permission to use Bodega Bay, for which he had received "an Italian-style cape, a coat, trousers, shirts, arms, three hatchets, five hoes, sugar, three files and beads."[92]

The Russians provided damning accounts of Spanish attempts to prevent the Coast Miwok from moving northward. N. K. Khlebnikov learned that Lt. José María Estudillo planned a northerly expedition "to catch Indians for the mission, [and] with regard to taking Indian prisoners, he said he always tried to capture *toions* [leaders], and by so doing, could obtain as many people as needed, avoiding bloodshed unless absolutely necessary." Achille Schabelski, who traveled through San Rafael on his way to Fort Ross, saw "several tents of unhappy fugitives from Mission San Rafael, who, taking me for a Spaniard, fled to the mountains." At the Russian River, he encountered other Indians bringing back runaways, led by the "chief of their tribe." (Schabelski was probably referring to a capitán of one of the many Coast Miwok tribes.) While these Indians showed him the way to Fort Ross, he "had the occasion of seeing how [the mission Indians] hunted the native peoples from whom they differ only by their cruelty and the knowledge of some superficial ceremonies of the Catholic religion."[93]

When the Russian admiral Otto von Kotzebue reached Colony Ross via San Rafael in 1824, he too contrasted the treatment of Native Americans at the mission and at Fort Ross. The Indians at Fort Ross were being paid for their work, inter-married with the Russians and Aleuts, and were left alone by the Greek Orthodox Church. He noted that the Indians at the Russian outpost were "much more cheer-ful and contented than at the mission, where a deep melancholy always clouds their faces, and their eyes are constantly fixed upon the ground; but this difference is only the natural result of the different treatment they experience."[94]

Father Amorós grew increasingly concerned about both the runaways and the Russian presence. He wanted Argüello to act and warned him in 1823 about the activities of the administrator at Fort Ross, who had made two excursions in a dug-out canoe, one to Point Reyes and the other upstream from Bodega. Explaining that the Russians had found a "copious" silver mine, Amorós asked for more soldiers and suggested that "we should not delay the conquest of that area....If the Russians go in, there will not be any guarantees for our empire."[95]

A NEW MISSION IN SONOMA

Other problems took precedence, however. In 1821, Mexico was successful in its rebellion against Spain, and the new Mexican government became responsible for managing California and its missions. The priests were expected to sign papers signifying their loyalty to the new government, and some were refusing. Trouble was also brewing within the priesthood at San Francisco, San Jose, and San Rafael over a local issue. In 1823, with the support of Governor Argüello, Father José Altimira of Mission Dolores set out to found a new mission, San Francisco de Soláno, in Sonoma. He also initiated simultaneous maneuvers to close the missions in both San Francisco and San Rafael.

Father Amorós pleaded with Governor Argüello in May and June to keep his San Rafael mission intact, emphasizing that the mission was peaceful and that the neophytes were healthy and producing plenty of food. He also reminded the governor how hard it was to find and keep Indian converts with the Russian settlement as a neighbor. Amorós then threatened to resign rather than be forced to move east to a new mission.[96] Nevertheless, with the support of the governor and without waiting for the approval of religious superiors, Altimira and Lt. Ignacio Martínez took possession of some of the San Rafael mission's goods in August and left with sixty neophytes, who were to help build the new mission.

The Franciscan prefect, Vicente Francisco de Sarría, refused to support Altimira's attempts to close the San Rafael mission and opposed transferring Indians away from San Rafael. He told Argüello that under the new Mexican regime the Indians were "free citizens and equal to white men,... [and] forcing them to leave their birthplace and their lands, their houses, and the padre whom they love" was a "great wrong." Altimira, on the defensive, attacked both Amorós and Father Durán at the San Jose mission, accusing them of organizing "raids for converts [and] forcefully seizing and killing those who resisted"—charges that may have referred to Herrera's actions with the Guiluc and Livantolomi people.[97]

Despite Argüello's power and Altimira's boldness, Amorós eventually won the day, and the San Rafael mission remained open. But the conflict between the priests must have affected both the Indians who went to Sonoma and those who remained behind in San Rafael. Amorós's distress, the increased presence of the military, a different priest issuing orders, and the transfer of some of the neophytes must have been confusing to many of the Indians, signaling a lack of authority on Amorós's part.

The new mission in Sonoma was originally populated with Indians who had been at the missions in San Francisco and San Jose and who spoke Coast Miwok, Patwin, and Wappo languages.[98] Not surprisingly, all did not proceed smoothly. Father Altimira's personality generated immediate conflict. By fall, the Indians had destroyed some of the new construction, and Altimira was complaining about their insubordination, rebellion, and escape attempts. Altimira turned to Argüello, hoping that he would put his foot down—*hacer un alarde de autoridad*—and force the Indians to tend to their duties.[99]

A Russian visitor, Zakahar Tchitchinoff, noticed the tense atmosphere at the Sonoma mission: "Both the priest and soldiers beat [the Indians] when they did not move fast." In September, Altimira complained loudly about Celso, who was in charge of boats at the mission. Celso, either misunderstanding or disagreeing with Altimira's instructions about the proper length of oars, cut an oar to a length that displeased Altimira and received fifty lashes. Angered, Celso escaped, taking horses with him and telling Altimira that he and others were going to Monterey to complain about the beatings.[100]

The antagonistic relationship between Altimira and the Indians came to a head when the Indians burned some of the Sonoma mission buildings in 1826. The priest retreated to San Rafael with a few neophytes. Amorós, known for his kindly and humble manner, probably received Altimira graciously, despite their conflicts. The authorities reassigned Altimira to missions in the south later that year. In a surprising move two years later, Father Altimira locked the door of the San Buenaventura mission, left his flock without a missionary, and fled California "stealthfully" with another priest on an American boat, amid rumors that he had departed with some of the mission's wealth. Although there was an investigation of the rumors, Bancroft concluded that "the truth can never be known."[101]

1a · Farewell-to-spring at Ring Mountain, Tiburon. Photo by Fraser Muirhead.

1b · Goldfields and tidytips at Chimney Rock, Pt. Reyes Peninsula, Marin County.
Photo by Fraser Muirhead.

2 *(in rows from left to right)* · a. Spring wildflowers: California poppy, blue-eyed grass (roots used to induce menstruation and abortion), iris (roots for poison, leaves for medicine), tidytips, and goldfields (seeds used in pinole). b. Datura, a hallucinogen. c. Tobacco. d. Sedge, for basketry. e. Tule, for making mats and boats. f. Willow, for basketry. Photos by Fraser Muirhead (a.) and Doreen Smith (b.-f.).

3a · Mt. Tamalpais, seen from Ring Mountain, Tiburon. Photo by Fraser Muirhead.

3b · Mt. Diablo, seen from the hills above Fairfax, Marin County. Photo by David Blackwolf.

4a · Tolay Lake, Sonoma County. The green area is the drying lake bed in the summer. Photo by Jon Goerke.

4b · Summer solstice sunrise in Marin County. Photo by Robert Rausch.

5a · Coast Miwok basket with diagonal patterns of olivella shell disc beads, abalone pendants, and a clamshell rim. Photo by Jon and Betty Goerke. From the collection of the Staatliches Museum für Völkerkunde, Munich, Germany, #142.

5b · Basket decorated with clamshell, olivella, and abalone beads. Photo by Jon and Betty Goerke. From the collection of the Peter the Great Museum of Anthropology and Ethnography (Kunstkamera), Russian Academy of Sciences, St. Petersburg, Russia, #MAE 570-103.

6a · Coast Miwok basket, with patterns of olivella disc beads, abalone and European glass trade bead pendants, and clamshell beads on the rim. Photo by Jon and Betty Goerke. Courtesy of the Museum der Weltkulturen, Frankfurt, Germany, #E 172.

6b & c · Coast Miwok or Ohlone (Costanoan) basket, side and bottom view, with patterns of olivella beads and with clamshell beads on the rim. Photos by Jon and Betty Goerke. From the collection of the Staatliches Museum für Völkerkunde, Munich, Germany, #143.

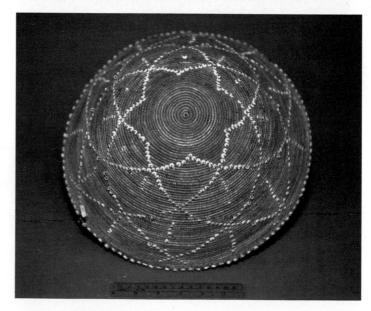

7 · Interior of Chief Ióllo's hut in Bodega, featuring his wife, whose cropped hair suggests he has just died. Note also the tattooed necklace on his wife, and the feather topknot hat and string of beads held by one of the two attendants. Artist Mikhail Tikhonovich Tikhanov, 1818. Courtesy of the Scientific Research Museum, Russian Academy of Fine Arts, St. Petersburg, Russia.

8 · Mission Indians dancing in front of Mission Dolores, 1816. Note the two priests on the left and the ceremonial regalia of the Indians. Artist Louis Choris. Courtesy of The Bancroft Library, University of California, Berkeley.

9 · Detail of Indians in ceremonial regalia for a dance at Mission Dolores, 1816. *Left:* Worn vertically on the head, a flicker-feather headband with feather puffs and a feather and bone hairpin; at the waist are more feathers and a belt. *Right:* At the waist, a front and back apron made with crow or raven feathers; at the neck, a feather boa; on the head, a flicker-feather headband, feathered topknot, and hairpins with flicker feathers. Artist Louis Choris. Courtesy of The Bancroft Library, University of California, Berkeley.

10a · Flicker tail feathers.

10b · Close-up of flicker-feather headband.

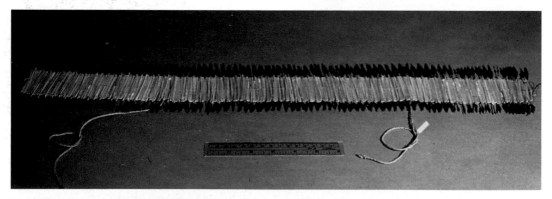

10c · Flicker-feather headband consisting of the two longest tail feathers from 225 flickers.

Photos on this page by Jon and Betty Goerke. From the collection of
the Staatliches Museum für Völkerkunde, Munich, Germany, #368.

11a · Topknot headdress of encircled crow feathers and standing magpie feathers. Photo by Jon and Betty Goerke. Courtesy of the Museum der Weltkulturen, Frankfurt, Germany, #E-169.

11b · Abalone necklace. Photo by Jon and Betty Goerke. From the collection of the Peter the Great Museum of Anthropology and Ethnography (Kunstkamera), Russian Academy of Sciences, St. Petersburg, Russia, #MAE 570-22.

11c · Boa of feathers five meters long. From the collection of the Peter the Great Museum of Anthropology and Ethnography (Kunstkamera), Russian Academy of Sciences, St. Petersburg, Russia, #MAE 570-10.

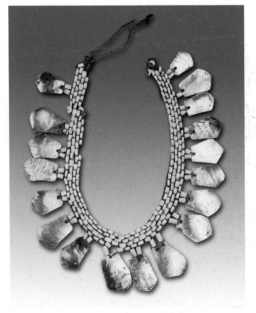

11d · Abalone necklace. From the collection of the Peter the Great Museum of Anthropology and Ethnography (Kunstkamera), Russian Academy of Sciences, St. Petersburg, Russia, #MAE 570-22.

GAMBLING AT MISSION DOLORES, 1816.

12a · Note the similarity of the necklace with the one in Figure 7. Artist Louis Choris. From the collection of Sean Galvin.

12b · Note that one gambler has a string of beads as part of his winnings. Note also the feather topknot, the tattoos on the nursing mother, and the abalone necklace worn by a female observer. Artist Louis Choris. Courtesy of The Bancroft Library, University of California, Berkeley.

13a & b · Coiled belt of olivella shells, red woodpecker scalps, and iridescent green mallard feathers. *Below:* A close-up of the first of four shell patterns in the belt above. Photos by Jon and Betty Goerke. Courtesy of Museum the der Weltkulturen, Frankfurt, Germany, #E 168.

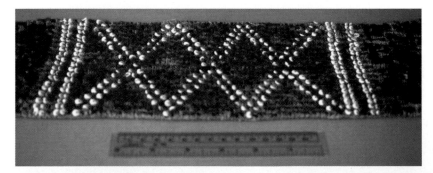

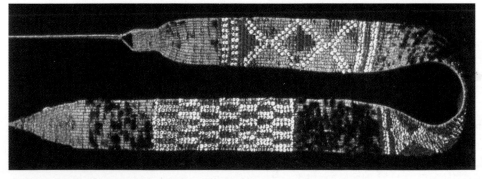

13c · A different belt, showing the same, common pattern as the belt above. From the collection of the Peter the Great Museum of Anthropology and Ethnography (Kunstkamera), Russian Academy of Sciences, St. Petersburg, Russia, #MAE 570-12.

14a · The two figures in the front are Coast Miwok. Note the face tattoos of the female on the left. Artist Louis Choris. Courtesy of The Bancroft Library, University of California, Berkeley.

14b · Three neophytes in a tule boat. The middle figure in the blanket may be trying to keep something dry on his head, possibly mail. Artist Louis Choris. Courtesy of The Bancroft Library, University of California, Berkeley.

15a · Ayala Cove on Angel Island, close to Ayala's 1775 anchorage, where he was visited by Indians from the East Bay and Marin County. Photo by David Blackwolf.

15b · View along the route of the 1821 expedition, which went through low valleys west of Chico and then westward over the Coast Ranges. Photo by Betty and Jon Goerke.

16a · View from Ring Mountain toward the Richmond–San Rafael Bridge, the Marin islands, and the San Rafael coastline. Photo by Jon Goerke.

16b · View from San Pedro Road to the Marin islands, with the Richmond–San Rafael Bridge in the background. Photo by Jon Goerke.

17a · Maria Copa at Nicasio, 1932, at the time of her interviews with Isabel Kelly. Photo by Isabel Kelly. Courtesy of the Phoebe Apperson Hearst Museum of Anthropology and the Regents of the University of California.

17b · Tom Smith in his sixties, before being interviewed by Isabel Kelly, ca. 1900. Photo by Eugene R. Prince. Courtesy of the Phoebe Apperson Hearst Museum of Anthropology and the Regents of the University of California.

17c · *Dance of Indians at Mission San Jose*, 1806. Artist G. H. von Langsdorff. Courtesy of The Bancroft Library, University of California, Berkeley..

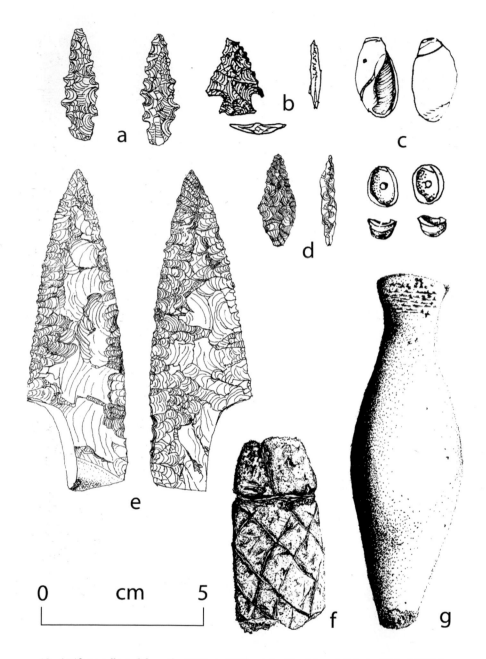

18 · Artifacts collected from the 1930s to 1970s at the Alto Mound (Marin 12) in Mill Valley (unless otherwise noted). a. Serrated obsidian point. b. Obsidian corner-notched point. c. Olivella shell and beads. d. Obsidian projectile point, found in Sausalito, Marin 2. e. Obsidian biface, found in Sausalito, Marin 2. f. Charmstone, phallic style. g. Charmstone, fishtail style. Drawings by Aimee Hurley (a., e.), Lucille Bennett (b., c.), and Erik Beadle (d.,f., g.).

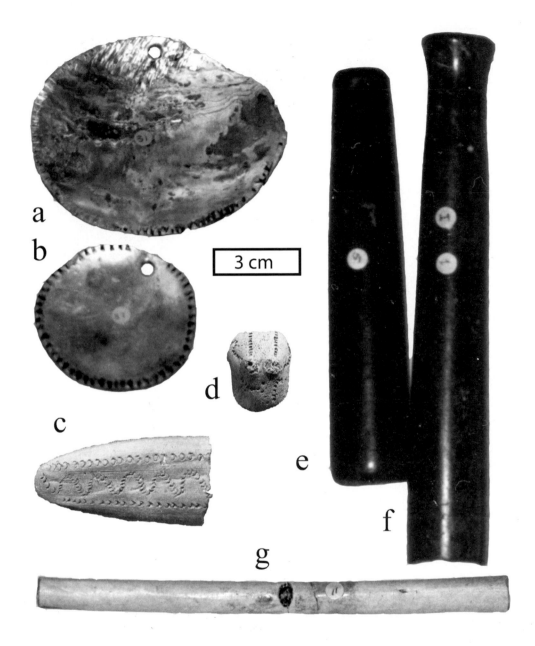

19 · Artifacts from archaeological sites in Marin County, collected from the 1930s to 1960s.
a. and b. Abalone shell pendants with hatch marks on the edges, found in Belvedere-Tiburon.
c. Baked clay decorated with zigzag lines and punctate marks, Sausalito. d. Baked clay figurine
of a female thorax, Novato Marin 365. e. and f. Soapstone pipes found in Belvedere-Tiburon.
g. Bone whistle found in Belvedere-Tiburon. Photos by John Niebauer (a., b., e., f., g.) and
Fraser Muirhead (c., d.).

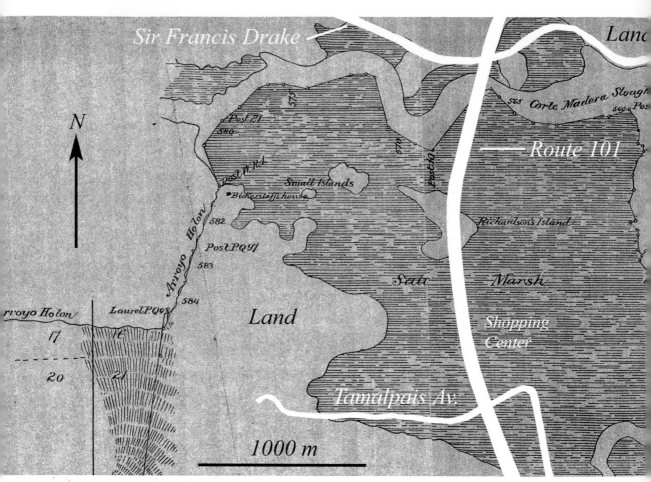

20 · Marsh and Corte Madera Creek, 1873, with an overlay of current Highway 101, Sir
Francis Drake Blvd., and Tamalpais Ave./San Clemente Dr. Survey by Leander Ransom.
Courtesy of Mary Alice Deffebach.

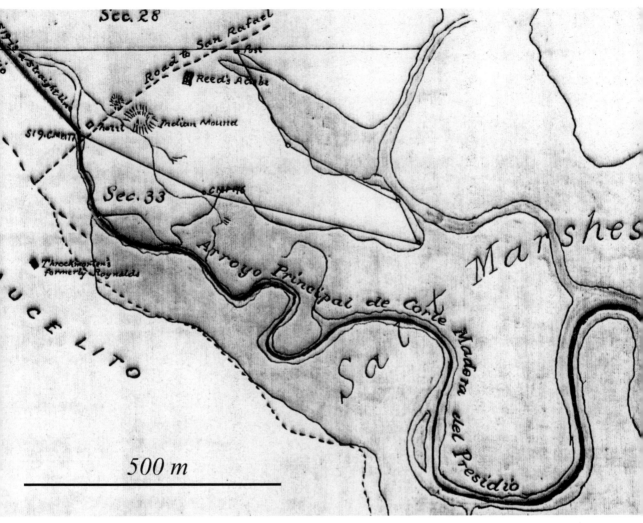

Sec. 28

Road to San Rafael

Reed's Adobe

Indian Mound

SEC.CORTE

Sec. 33

UCELITO

Arroyo Principal de Corte Madera del Presidio

Marshes

Sa

Throckmorton's
formerly Reynolds

500 m

21 · Marsh, creek, Indian mound, and Reed home in Mill Valley, 1841. Survey by G. F. Allardt. Courtesy of the Mill Valley Public Library, History Room.

22a *(opposite top)* · Drawing of what the *San Carlos,* the first European ship in San Francisco Bay, may have looked like in 1775. Courtesy of San Francisco Maritime National Historical Park.

22b *(opposite bottom)* · *Indian of California,* a portrait of a Huimen Indian at Mission Dolores, 1816. Artist Louis Choris. Work on paper 8 x 5 inches. From the Collection of the Oakland Museum, Museum Income Fund.

23 *(above)* · Soldier escorting a work party of mission Indians, with the San Francisco presidio in the background, 1816. Artist Louis Choris. Courtesy of The Bancroft Library, University of California, Berkeley.

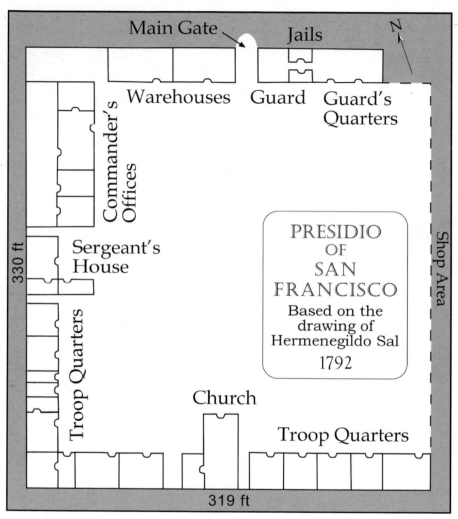

Main Gate

Jails

N

Warehouses   Guard   Guard's
                              Quarters

Commander's
Offices

Sergeant's
House

Shop Area

330 ft

PRESIDIO
OF
SAN
FRANCISCO
Based on the
drawing of
Hermenegildo Sal
1792

Troop Quarters

Church

Troop Quarters

319 ft

24 · San Francisco presidio in 1792. Redrawn by Jon Goerke and Rick Waterman.

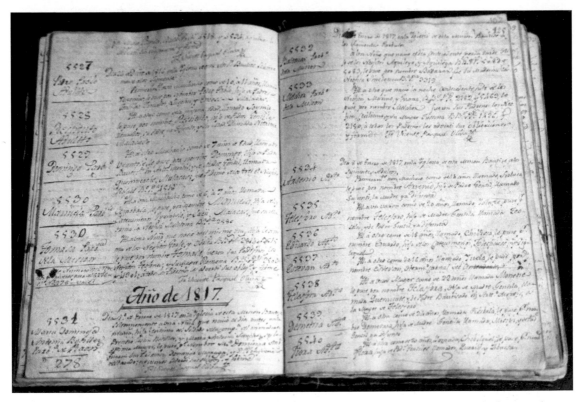

25 · San Francisco Mission (Dolores) baptismal record, 1816–1817, showing entry #5533, Melchior, child of Juana and Marino. Photo by Alonso Chattan. Courtesy of Jeffrey Burns, Chancery Archives, Archdiocese of San Francisco.

26a · San Francisco Mission baptismal record of Marino, adult #2182, March 7, 1801; "First a man of 20 years called Huicmuse, a Huimen, and I gave him the name Marino."

26b · Marriage record #1660. On August 28, 1816, Marino, widower, #2182, married Juana, single, #5463. Witnesses were neophytes Fausto, Calixto, and Teodorico # 2167, #2300, and #3310, respectively.

Photos on this page by Alonso Chattan.
Courtesy of Jeffrey Burns, Chancery Archives, Archdiocese of San Francisco.

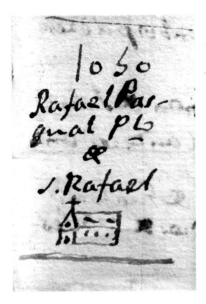

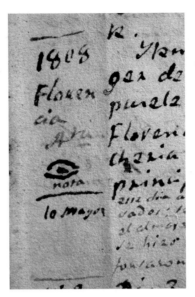

27a (left) · Drawing of the new San Rafael Mission church by Father Juan Amorós in the margin of the baptismal records, April 1824.

27b (right) · Father Amorós drew attention to his note of an attack on the mission by drawing an eye in the margin of baptism record #1808.

27c · Death record of Juana, #711.

27d · Death record of Marin, #783.

Photos on this page by Marvin Collins.
Courtesy of Jeffrey Burns, Chancery Archives, Archdiocese of San Francisco.

28a · Drawing of the San Rafael mission by Alphonse Sondag, based on the earliest sketch of the mission by M. G. Vallejo in 1878. The star window was not in Vallejo's sketch and is inaccurate. From the collection of the Marin History Museum.

28b · Plan of the San Rafael mission grounds, based on an 1854 survey by G. Black and the undated Hendry and Bowman Typescript at The Bancroft Library, University of California, Berkeley. Redrawn by Jon Goerke and Rick Waterman.

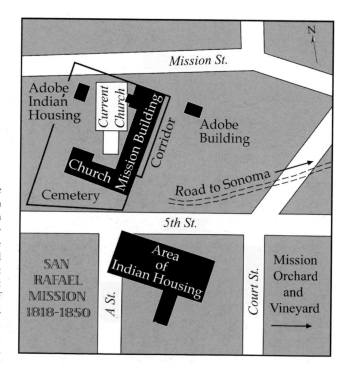

29a · Photo of Jose Calistro. Collection of the Anne T. Kent California Room, Marin County Free Library.

29b · Cabin on Halleck Creek in Nicasio that belonged to the Calistro family. Collection of the Anne T. Kent California Room, Marin County Free Library.

29c · Indian homes on the east shore of Tomales Bay at Reynolds, 1925. Courtesy of Virginia Jenson, from the collection of Dewey Livingston.

30 · Maria Copa's mother, Juana Bautista, was born May 6, 1829, and baptized the
following day as Juana Evangelista. She is shown here with her grandchildren Joseph
Monzaga, Julia Frease (daughter of Maria Copa), and Edward Monzaga. Photo
courtesy of Rita Elgin Carrillo.

31 · The Smith family at the Smith Brothers Fishery at Bodega Bay in the 1940s. Courtesy of Eugene Buvelot.

32a · Tribal elder
Eugene Buvelot with
his granddaughter at
a petroglyph rock,
Marin County, 2006.
Photo by Jon Goerke.

32b · Lanny Pinola,
Coast Miwok and
Pomo Indian, with
College of Marin
students at Kule
Loklo, Point Reyes
National Seashore, in
the 1990s. Photo by
Christina Noble.

7

MARINO JOINS AN EXPEDITION

At six o'clock on the evening of October 17, 1821, a group of Spanish soldiers and officers, along with a chaplain, an English-speaking interpreter, and at least two Indian guides—one of whom was Marino—marched to the San Francisco beach, where they spent the night at the water's edge. They would set out the next day on an exploratory trip that came to be known as the Columbia expedition.[1]

Their departure must have been a spectacle, full of color and contrasts. Captain Luis Argüello of the San Francisco presidio was in command. He and his officers typically wore large serapes over their uniforms and sported embroidered boots with large eight-pointed spurs, while the troops dressed in sleeveless deerskin jackets or coats and carried leather shields to protect them from Indian arrows. The priest would have been clad in a long gray tunic, belted with a double rope from which hung his rosary and wooden cross. Marino and the other Indian guide likely wore pants, befitting their status as bona fide participants in the expedition.[2] Supplies of ammunition and food, along with a cannon on wheels, completed this parade and were loaded on two large launches equipped with sails, which would carry the men and materiel across San Francisco Bay to the eastern shore of San Pablo Bay.

The travelers may have considered the upcoming journey to be a bit of a lark, but it had a serious purpose. Organized at the behest of Governor Solá, the expeditionary force was charged with looking for suspected English-speaking intruders and settlements in northern California. After the successful Lewis and Clark expedition to the Pacific Ocean via the Missouri and Columbia rivers in 1804 through 1806, it had become clear to the Spaniards that both the Americans and the British could move by land into California from the north, with or without support from the local native peoples. Solá, already leery of the Russian presence, wanted to nip this new threat in the bud. American ships were already plying the California coast, involved in clandestine trade,[3] and Solá may also have been concerned about the expansionist ideas of U.S. President James Monroe and about the fur traders associated with the Russian-American Company.[4]

Argüello had assembled the expedition and was well acquainted with many of those he selected to accompany him. He had chosen several of his fellow San Francisco presidio officers as the military leaders, Father Blas Ordaz from the San Francisco mission as the chaplain, an English-speaking interpreter from San Francisco, one Indian from the San Francisco mission, and Marino, formerly of the San Francisco mission. But Argüello had also drawn personnel from other California settlements, supporting his San Francisco troops with recruits from the San Jose and Santa Clara missions and with men and horses from as far away as Monterey.

As the two launches prepared to leave the San Francisco shore for the Carquinez Strait, Argüello dispatched some of his cavalrymen south with horses from the San Francisco presidio. They were to meet their counterparts from Santa Clara, Monterey, and San Jose and together proceed north up the eastern shore of San Pablo Bay to the Carquinez Strait, with plans to join Argüello and the rest of the expedition at the end of the following day.

The launches bearing Argüello's group departed in the morning, reaching the strait between San Rafael and San Pablo at five o'clock that afternoon, a trip that took at least six hours (indicating that the current, tides, and wind may have been less than propitious).[5] Off San Rafael, the launches had to wait another hour for high tide before continuing east to the San Pablo peninsula. The last leg of the day's journey ended around ten o'clock that evening, when the travelers beached their launches and spent the night on the eastern shore of San Pablo Bay.

The following day, after another trip of five and a half hours across the water to the southern shore of the Carquinez Strait, at the mouth of the Sacramento River, Argüello met the troops who were arriving from the south by land. By the next day, two additional launches had arrived from San Jose, one of them carrying an unusual ingredient for a successful expedition: ninety bags of ashes for making soap. The entire expeditionary force now consisted of sixty-three soldiers from the artillery, infantry, and cavalry; three military officers; the chaplain; the two Indian guides; the English speaker; and most likely other Indians who were acting as aides or servants. They also took along 235 animals, mostly horses and mules,[6] and the cannon, which had to be pulled over the rough terrain.

The next task was to transport the group on the launches across the Carquinez Strait to the opposite shore. Given his skills as a boatman, Marino was undoubtedly involved in determining when and where the launches would depart with their loads of men, horses, equipment, and cannon. Before crossing the strait, they met members of two tribal groups who were returning to their homelands on passes—the Ululato, a Patwin-speaking group originally from the area around Vacaville; and the Canicaymos, who were Wappos from Yountville. The Spaniards offered to ferry them across the river if the Indians would agree to remain with the troops for mass the next day, a Sunday.[7] (After the crossing, when the Ululato and Canicaymos travelers were sent on their way on foot, they were assured that they had nothing to fear if the expedition passed through their homelands, because the Spaniards were not pursuing them.)

The river crossing took two days to complete. Thus it was not until October 22, five days after Argüello had marched his troops to the beach at San Francisco, that the full expeditionary force finally started north in search of English-speaking intruders.

MEMBERS OF THE EXPEDITION

Captain Luis Argüello had grown up at the San Francisco presidio, as the son of the commandante. He had begun his military service there when he was only fifteen, in 1799. Moving up through the ranks, he was promoted to captain at age thirty-four, three years before the Columbia expedition set out.

Argüello was no newcomer to expeditions, having searched for runaways and explored uncharted territory in the north and the east in 1816, 1817, 1818, and possibly earlier. Popular with his soldiers for "his kindness, liberality, and affability," he was known as a "jovial companion [and] a bon vivant," fond of wine and raw brandy. (Seven years after the expedition, Argüello would lose his command, with Governor Echeandía commenting on his "loose" conduct and "excessive drinking.")[8]

The chaplain of the expedition, Father Blas Ordaz, was a relative newcomer to San Francisco. Argüello may have chosen this priest rather than Father Abella or Father Durán, who had accompanied him on previous expeditions, because of Ordaz's fun-loving personality. In any case, the captain and the priest became fast friends. In a letter Ordaz wrote to Argüello less than two months after the expedition, it was clear that these two had had a great time on the trip, perhaps drinking and womanizing. In his letter, Ordaz referred to Argüello as "Negrito" and "cabronzuela" (loosely translated as little bastard)—probably terms of endearment, since he also called God a "cabron" (bastard). Ordaz suggested that a visit of a month or two at San Luis Obispo, the priest's new post, would put Argüello in a good mood; and he asked Argüello to remind Chepita and other females he referred to as "Negras" (dark-skinned women) of the good times they had had.[9] (Apparently,

Ordaz fathered children, two of whom he baptized himself. His funeral in 1850 at Mission San Gabriel was arranged by a daughter and son-in-law.)[10]

Two of the military officers who helped to lead the expedition, Francisco de Haro and José Sánchez, had reputations as Indian fighters; Sánchez participated in at least twenty campaigns against Native Americans.[11] The English-speaking interpreter recruited for the expedition was John Gilroy, one of only eight English speakers in California in 1820. This Scottish sailor had left his ship in Monterey in 1814 when he fell ill with scurvy. He became the first non-Spanish, non-Mexican resident to settle permanently in California. (His rancho is known today as the town of Gilroy.)

Marino's Participation

Typically, Native American guides were nameless in the diaries of priests and the remembrances of soldiers. But Marino and Rafael were mentioned by name on the roster of participants for the Columbia expedition; Argüello listed them in his diary, which suggests that he considered them important to the success of the venture. By 1821, Marino had been in the mission system for twenty years and at San Rafael for nine years, and he knew Argüello from his days at Mission Dolores.

Argüello specifically identified Rafael as an interpreter for the expedition. As a member of the Suisun tribe, this twenty-five-year-old bachelor, known as Jobochea before his baptism, would have been an asset for his linguistic skills in communicating with other Patwin-speaking peoples along the proposed route north of the Carquinez Strait. Like so many Native Americans in the Bay Area, he was probably familiar with neighboring languages and, of course, must have been competent in Spanish.

Argüello did not describe Marino as an interpreter, although Marino may have served in this capacity, particularly on the return trip just north of San Rafael. Marino spoke Spanish and likely understood some of the Pomo languages spoken north of his homeland. Argüello may have believed that Rafael would be familiar with languages the expedition was to encounter to the north and east of the Carquinez Strait, while Marino would know the languages north of Colony Ross. Other Indians may have been acting as interpreters, too, for the diaries of Captain Argüello and Father Ordaz frequently mention "neophyte interpreters." In addition, Argüello picked up various Indian guides along the way to conduct the expeditionary force to neighboring villages.

It is more likely that Argüello chose Marino for his knowledge of the currents and tides in San Francisco Bay and his well-known competence as a boatman. The trip across the bay and the task of ferrying troops, animals, and equipment across the fast-moving Carquinez Strait at the mouth of the Sacramento River demanded good navigational skills. Referring to Marino as Marín, as the military usually did, Argüello's brother-in-law, Antonio Maria Osio, recalled that "Marín was accustomed to crossing in a tule craft whenever he wished or when he was sent with official or private communications from the Fathers."[12]

Argüello had previously experienced near-disasters on the bay as a result of fluctuations in current and tides: once, treacherous bay currents almost sank his barge as it was headed to pick up wood in the Marin area. In another incident, this same barge, loaded with wood, was swept out of the bay twenty-eight miles off shore to the Farallon Islands, where the crew had to spend the night.[13] According to earlier reports from European visitors, the Spaniards were not comfortable navigating the waters of San Francisco Bay. Langsdorff had considered it unusual for the soldiers and priests to rely on Indian transportation,[14] but it seems likely that the Spaniards continued to do just that.

Marino's experience as alcalde and mayordomo at San Rafael might have been another reason for his selection. Argüello may have hoped that Marino could help to enforce discipline among the other Indians involved in the expedition. According to two former soldiers who reminisced about their trip fifty years later, other Indian men were part of the expedition, with reports of at least one serious fight among them.[15]

Marino could also have had his own motivations for undertaking the trip: possibly a longstanding and special relationship with Argüello or a desire to seek adventure and freedom from the confines of the mission. During the journey, he undoubtedly earned a great measure of respect and appreciation for his talents.

THE TRIP

Many details of the trip can only be surmised—unfortunately, neither Argüello nor Ordaz sketched maps of their travel; and few, if any, of the names they gave to the rivers they crossed, the ridges they hiked, and the mountains they saw have persisted. There was even confusion about how widely the expedition ranged. José María Amador, Argüello's orderly, later recalled reaching the Columbia River, but Bancroft derided that idea, suggesting instead that they had never left California, and Milliken believes that the party reached no farther north than Chico. Milliken's interpretation of the route is based on the Indian names of the villages that Argüello and Ordaz reported in their diaries, and that route will be followed here.[16] (Appendix J, Map IV)

The expedition headed north along the Sacramento River through Patwin and Maidu tribal territory, eventually turned west at Stony Creek through Nomlaki villages, and then trekked south and west across the Coast Ranges by a tortuous route, passing through Lake Miwok, Wappo, and Pomo villages before reaching the Santa

Rosa plain, Olompali, and Mission San Rafael, and then returning to San Francisco. The diaries of Argüello and Ordaz and the accounts of soldiers written many years later provide not only information about the route but also some sense of the problems involved in managing such an unwieldy group, the difficulty of moving in unfamiliar territory, and the potential for conflicts with the Indian groups they encountered.[17]

After crossing the Carquinez Strait at the start of the land trip, the expeditionary force spent the next twenty-two days on the trail, often traveling seven to ten hours a day. "Officers and men were mounted, and their Indian interpreters followed on foot," Alvarado reported.[18] The expedition trekked through a number of territories whose inhabitants spoke languages unfamiliar even to the interpreters. They also passed large Indian rancherias that, according to Father Ordaz, contained as many as four hundred, nine hundred, and a thousand people. Amador described a large gathering at one rancheria where Argüello ordered all the Indians out of a large round house, some three hundred feet in diameter, and had the males, females, and children assemble in three separate lines. Amador insisted that the Spaniards counted a total of three thousand people, adding, "This will probably seem a falsehood, but it is nothing but the truth, without any exaggeration."[19] It is likely, however, that this was a ceremonial gathering involving many villages rather than the population of one large rancheria.

The troops often stopped near a rancheria to spend the night, no doubt for the same reasons that the Indians had settled there: accessible drinking water for people and animals, fields for grazing, protection from wind, and the potential runoff from winter rain-soaked slopes. These temporary camps must have posed a hardship for the local Indians, who at this time of year were usually busy collecting seeds and acorns. (At one village, most of the inhabitants were away gathering seeds.) The horses and mules brought by the Spaniards trampled, slept in, and disrupted the acorn-gathering areas as well as the fields of clover, brodeia, and other plants that the Indians would need the following spring.

Although many of the rancherias were friendly, providing guides and even giving gifts to the Spaniards, other Indian settlements resisted the incursion into their territory. Father Ordaz, who apparently had little to do besides holding mass on four Sundays, performed only two baptisms: a young Indian girl who was near death and a man who was dying from gunshot wounds inflicted by the Spaniards, who had fired on his village.

On October 23 the expedition traveled from what is today the Suisun City area, passing near Vacaville, and spent the night at Winters. On the following day they arrived at the village of Chila, whose inhabitants, Argüello believed, were seeing

Europeans for the first time. One older woman, however, had firsthand knowledge of the devastation the military could wreak: she had survived a Spanish attack on her Suisun village in 1810. She spoke to the interpreter Rafael and begged Argüello to treat the villagers where she now lived with kindness. Argüello wrote that he "succeeded in pacifying them and leaving them tranquil." The troop continued along Cache Creek and spent the night at Yolo.[20] They reached the Sacramento River at Knight's Landing on October 25 and the Indians at a village there offered the Spaniards gifts of baskets—and provided the first reports of foreigners in European dress with firearms.

The Spaniards first met resistance on October 26, when the villagers of Güillito (east of the town of Grimes) "threatened" the expedition in spite of Rafael's entreaties. Irritated by their "haughtiness" and "inflexibility,"[21] Argüello ordered the cannon fired to frighten them. The firing continued as the Indians fled across the Sacramento River, where they kept up their resistance into the night. The Güillitos suffered five deaths and some wounded, whereas the Spaniards lost only a horse that fell into the Sacramento River carrying a load of two thousand cartridges.

The next day, Rafael was able to talk to the villagers and find out what the expedition wanted to know. The Indians reported that there were two settlements of Europeans on the coast, which could be reached by traveling "three or four days, having previously to pass through the Sierra Nevada."[22] Although the identity of the mountain range as the "Sierra Nevada" seems uncertain, Argüello apparently continued north and northeast, following the Sacramento River, until October 30. Travelling through what is today Princeton and reaching Hamilton City they noticed twin mountain peaks in the distance that Gilroy believed indicated they were near the Columbia River. Instead, Milliken suggests that they were observing Mt. Lassen, sixty miles to the southeast, which appears as twin peaks from Hamilton City.

Shortly thereafter, on October 31, Argüello turned west and encountered another village (near the present Grindstone rancheria on Stony Creek). The Spaniards were met with a fusillade of arrows and responded with a volley of gunshots: "I determined to punish them for their haughtiness and obstinance, ordering the Infantry and Cavalry into battalion formation....I ordered them to fire." It was dark, and Argüello could not see how many Indians had been killed or wounded. But the "crowd fled with continuous howling that lasted about two hours afterwards from the woods along the river on the bank of which is found this village."[23] The next day, peace was secured, the Spaniards procured several guides, and the expedition continued on its way.

By the first of November, Argüello had deduced that the two European habitations being reported were probably the Russian settlements already known to the

Spaniards, but he wanted to continue the search to assure himself of that fact. He learned more when a group of Indians, whom an interpreter could only partially understand, reported that four men on horseback had been seen in the area and that a local resident had acquired a piece of blue cloth (of Russian origin) from other Indians on the coast.

The trek became especially hazardous between November 1 and November 9. "In the nine days' trip made on this ridge, there have died fifteen beasts, horses and mules, which have worn out completely in various precipices and descents in it, and it was therefore necessary to kill them," Argüello wrote in his diary.[24]

On November 6, while members of the expedition were following a local guide over steep, treacherous terrain in or near Lake Miwok territory, four mules carrying food fell into the stream below. Desperate for better information on trails, Argüello had picked local men who were generally competent as guides but were unaware of the hazards that foot trails through mountains and narrow gorges presented for horses and mules. The expedition continued to change local guides as the previous ones became less familiar with the terrain. Not all guides were willing participants; one of those who tried to slip away was punished, most likely with a beating. The following day, the expedition passed by Oleyomi, identified as a Lake Miwok village, and reached the spine of the Mayacama mountains and Mount St. Helena. At day's end, the travelers could see the ocean from a great height.[25]

On November 8, the expedition had another arduous day, crossing the Mayacama mountains and traversing the flank of Mount St. Helena. Argüello saw recent traces of horses that piqued his curiosity, suggesting the possibility of non-Russian European visitors. But after learning that two neophytes who had run away from the San Rafael mission had recently been in the area on horseback, he changed his mind. Despite the lack of a positive identification, Argüello felt that he had enough information to determine that the outsiders reported by the Indians were most likely Russians rather than Americans or Englishmen.

By November 9, the surviving horses and mules were growing weak from lack of pasture, and, according to one of the soldiers, the horse pulling the cannon had run away.[26] When he learned that the expedition had only three days of provisions left, Argüello decided to retreat and head south. Their troubles were not over yet, however: as the expeditionary force marched south toward San Rafael, "crowds of heathens" twice threatened their progress.[27]

North of Olompali, in the valley of Livantolomi (Libantiliyumi), the expedition found the bones of an Indian neophyte.[28] Marino may have been the translator who questioned the Pomo-speaking people and learned that these were the remains of Severo, a Coast Miwok of the Echajutti tribe, murdered two months earlier by

Indians from a rancheria beyond Livantolomi. Marino would have known this man well from their shared time at both the San Francisco and San Rafael missions. His wife, Severa, was from Juana's home territory of Olompali. The couple had been baptized in San Francisco and had later gone to the San Rafael mission, where their baby girl was baptized and died five months after the mission was established. Father Ordaz had Severo's bones collected for later burial. Three days later, Father Amorós buried the head, the spine, and a leg, all that was left of Severo, in the San Rafael mission cemetery.[29]

When the expeditionary force limped into San Rafael on November 12, Father Amorós greeted them and sang a special mass of thanksgiving for their safe return. A mere three hours after their arrival in San Rafael, two launches belonging to the San Jose mission arrived. Either someone had been sent ahead days earlier to San Rafael to pick up a tule boat and head for San Francisco and San Jose to arrange for the launches, or the launches had been tied up nearby since the crossing of the Carquinez Strait a month earlier. Over the next several days, other launches arrived and began transporting all the men and horses back to the various missions, a task that was finally completed five days after their arrival in San Rafael. Thus the Columbia expedition came to an end.[30]

RESULTS OF THE TRIP

Captain Argüello could report that he had learned of no English speakers north of the San Francisco mission; that he had visited more than thirty Indian villages, many of whose inhabitants had not seen Europeans before; and that some rancherias were friendly but others had to be subdued by firepower. His losses included the deaths of horses and mules as a result of the treacherous terrain in the mountains.

But what might Marino and Rafael have learned? They had a chance to observe firsthand the personal habits of the Spanish leaders: Argüello's drinking, and the camaraderie of the captain and the priest. They learned yet again how the military responded to a lack of deference from Indian communities. They saw the power of mounted military, the superiority of cartridge and cannon over bows and arrows, and the advantages of beasts of burden that could carry supplies for long journeys. They also observed villagers offering gifts of food baskets and precious feathered headbands, while Argüello, Ordaz, and Amador gave nothing in return.

It is clear that the expedition's safe return owed much to Indian help: the expertise provided by Rafael and Marino, the welcome offered by some of the villages, and the knowledge of local guides who led the force over trails to neighboring villages. Doubtless the trip reinforced Marino's and Rafael's feelings of self-worth, for their skills in translation and water transportation were critical. They became more familiar with the officers and soldiers, and perhaps more confident of holding their own in such company, especially as they gained greater fluency in Spanish. As members of the expedition, both Marino and Rafael received preferential treatment in contrast to the treatment of the local Indian guides. Perhaps the two men returned to San Rafael with a new sense of superiority, even a little cockiness, in regard to the mission fathers, whose lives were not as free as those of the soldiers with whom Marino and Rafael had just spent a month. It is not surprising, then, that a little over a year later Father Amorós complained about Marino's attitude in a letter to Argüello.

8

DEFIANCE:
MARINO, QUINTINO, AND POMPONIO

Just one year after the 1821 military expedition through northern California, Marino was in trouble with Father Amorós. Their relationship had soured to the point that on December 15, 1822, Amorós wrote to Luis Argüello requesting more soldiers from the presidio "to check the cattle and the fields, and perhaps our Marino will live with a little more subordination." Amorós did not describe Marino's insubordination in any detail, but his letter to Argüello suggested that "our" Marino was their common property and problem—a man they had discussed before and whose behavior was so well known to both of them that it did not need explaining. Argüello took the request seriously and sent two additional soldiers on January 24, 1823, to join Corporal Herrera, who was already stationed in San Rafael.[1] Apparently, even former alcaldes were not to be trusted.

His troubles with Amorós in December 1822 may have stemmed from Marino's perception of himself as a relatively free agent—a view apparently shared by others. Maria Copa described him as an "overseer for the priest....He used to go out in the fields and get wheat for pinole." But in addition to overseeing wheat fields, he clearly played many roles, among them alcalde, mayordomo, boatman, guide, and interpreter. The Californio Antonio María Osio, who noted that Marino was "accustomed to crossing [the bay] in a tule raft *whenever he wished* [emphasis mine] or when he was sent with official or private communications from the Fathers," portrayed an individual who had few restrictions, quite an extraordinary position for a neophyte.[2]

Even if Osio exaggerated, there is no denying the sense of freedom and power that a boatman such as Marino must have felt each time he pushed off from shore in his tule boat. As he set out across the open bay, watching the eddies around each dip of his paddle and the darkening of the water, he left the shore behind, feeling the current and the increasingly loud lap of the waves as he approached rougher water. The boatman was in control: he alone decided what route to take, how fast to go, and when to pull into a cove if the waves were too high or the current changed. Because Marino's maritime skills were needed and respected by the priests and the military, he became recognized for the very thing that may have given him a sense of power, pride, and a connection to his pre-mission roots. Ironically for his captors, this freedom also provided many opportunities for him to ignore the restrictions of his servitude.

In spite of Marino's "insubordination," he continued to act as a godparent at the San Rafael mission the following August and again in December 1823. The August baptismal entry is curious in that Father Amorós printed Marino's name in large black letters. Since the records contain only two other such entries, the notation must have represented a true emphasis, not simply the rapid flow of ink from a newly dipped quill pen.[3]

After December 1823, the San Rafael records fail to mention Marino for a year and a half. Where was he during this period? It is likely that he left the mission under mysterious circumstances and became the object of a search.

THE MILITARY PURSUES MARINO: VALLEJO'S STORY

According to General Vallejo, Marino and his lieutenant, another Coast Miwok named Quintino, were pursued and captured by soldiers from San Francisco in 1824 and were incarcerated for more than a year in the presidio jail.[4] The general included this tale in an 1849-1850 California Senate report from the legislative committee that named the state's counties (a committee that he headed), and it appeared again in Vallejo's five-volume history of California, published in 1875.

Hiding Out on the Islands

In Vallejo's narrative, Marino hid out on the "Marin Islands" near San Rafael, which were thereafter named "in honor of that chieftain, who, while maintaining his savage dignity, was a terrible and greatly feared enemy of the whites." An enduring story about how Marino reached these small islands in San Pablo Bay has captured imaginations over the years. According to an 1865 newspaper account, Marino used the islands as a hideout to elude the priests and the military and would frequently sally forth and cause trouble at the mission, returning safely to a cave on the island at night by wading from the mainland at low tide for most of the journey. Two maps, from 1841 and 1863, show a marsh extending from the Marin shore to the islands; even today, the water is very shallow here: at the mean low tide, the water is two feet deep between the mainland and the west island, and only a little deeper between the two islands.[5]

In 1895, an embellished newspaper version of this story described the wily Marino jumping into the bay when pursued, swimming away undetected by using a reed as a snorkel, and appearing "two weeks later safe in Mill Valley, everyone thinking he was dead."[6] Similar tales have been told many times in the past: the Greek historian Herodotus in the fifth century B.C. told of a Greek sailor who used a hollow reed to swim underwater so that he could cut the moorings of the ships in the Persian fleet; and Lanny Pinola, a Coast Miwok/Pomo ranger at Point Reyes National Seashore in the 1980s, described how Pomo children had survived a massacre by white marauders by hiding in the water and breathing through tule reeds until the attackers left.[7] The truth of Marino's snorkeling story cannot be proved—in fact, he could have reached the islands by wading at low tide, swimming, or using a tule boat at higher tide—but it certainly made a wonderful tale to tell around a Coast Miwok campfire on a cold winter night.

Archaeological evidence, however, confirms that Indians did use the island. On the west end of East Marin Island, four hearth-like areas on a bluff, excavated in 1992, indicate some occupation, although no cave was reported. The numerous retrieved artifacts included tools of obsidian and chert, bone awls, and four burned charmstones. The food remains at the site indicate that the diet of the seasonal residents included ducks, harbor seal pups, deer, voles, white seabass, sturgeon, mussels, oysters, and clams. A fugitive Marino would certainly have had ready access to sources of food, even on such a small island.[8] The absence of artifacts from the period of Spanish contact does not exclude the possibility that Marino was on the island once or many times.

The Capture of Marino and Quintino

The Spanish soldiers pursuing Marino were supported by an East Bay Indian chief named Marcelo and his followers in their tule boats (so Vallejo's story goes). Fearful that Marino's followers could surround them on the islands, they abandoned the chase and instead went a mile and a half south to what we know now as San Quentin Point, named after the Coast Miwok Quintino, who was captured in this action and taken to the San Francisco presidio.[9] Marino's luck ran out, Vallejo wrote, when the military returned with a larger force and finally cornered and captured him in an unspecified place in Coast Miwok territory. Marino then joined Quintino at the San Francisco presidio, where he stayed "for more than a year."[10]

Geographical records of the 1830s feature the names Marin and Quintín. Juan Reed's crudely drawn *diseño* from 1835 locates the "Islands of Marin" and a "Point of Quintín," as do Cadawalder and Ringgold's surveys of the bay from 1841 and 1849. The name "Marin Islands" also appears on Ringgold's surveys of the bay from 1841 and 1849. These designations clearly associate both Marino and Quintino with the earliest history of the area before Vallejo wrote about them, lending some credence to the story of their pursuit and capture.

Marino at the San Francisco Presidio

Soon after he was brought to the San Francisco presidio, Marino verbally challenged the mission priest. An excerpt from Alvarado's *History of California* illustrates Marino's confidence in himself, his facility with Spanish, and his irreverent attitude, all of which allowed him to poke fun at a priest. The Indians, Alvarado wrote,

> especially in the North, were not so witless as the priests thought them to be[;] they became very suspicious when such a rigorous attempt was made to force them to live according to the ideas of religion. I still recall that when Marin, the famous Licatint [Licatiut] warrior and companion of the Kintín [Quintino]…was a prisoner at the San Francisco presidio, he became very restive under the sedentary life forced upon him by his captors. One day when the priest of Dolores Mission was conversing with him in an effort to get him openly to accept community life for himself and his tribe, Marin angrily said to the padre, "Listen, man, I see you have horse that is saddle-horse, and you have horse you use for buggy. Now, if you hitch saddle horse to buggy, he kick and will not go, and if you put saddle on buggy horse, he won't go either. We Indians just like horses; we used to living in woods and hills and don't want live at mission. In hills we are free like stags and deer; at mission we are captives just like saddle and buggy horses."
>
> The friar recognized that Marin was not such a fool as he had imagined and, realizing that it was time wasted to try and persuade Marin that mission life, which was a type of slavery, was better than a life of freedom, abandoned that theme and tried to intimidate him with stories about hell and an eternal life of fire and torment. Marin, however, being an intelligent fellow and one who had learned many things in his dealings with the Cainamero Indians, addressed his interlocutor and told him with the greatest sang-froid that if the priest would not bother him while he was alive he would give him permission to make a Christian of his dead body. With this statement he dismissed his tormentor.[11]

Why Was Marino Pursued?

The reason for the soldiers' pursuit of Marino is not clear. Vallejo's explanation, that Marino had been harassing troops ever since his first escape from the presidio before 1817, is incorrect. As we know from the mission records, Marino was at Mission Dolores in 1816 and 1817 and at the San Rafael mission thereafter. Because Vallejo was stationed in Monterey and not in San Francisco or San Rafael at the time, his reporting likely contains errors.

A few letters and the mission records suggest various possibilities for why Marino was being chased. The simplest explanation is that he was defying the orders of Amorós at the San Rafael mission and was merely hiding out. A second possibility is that Marino either led or participated in an attack on the mission in 1824. A third explanation holds that he was collaborating with another Coast Miwok, Pomponio, a notorious runaway from San Francisco who played a cat-and-mouse game with the military for at least three years.

CLASHES WITH AMORÓS

Marino and Quintino may have taken advantage of the unrest at the San Rafael mission in 1823. That year was a particularly difficult time (see Chapter 6): Pomo and Wappo neophytes were refusing to return to the mission; Corporal Herrera, the soldier on whom Father Amorós had relied, had been jailed for committing an unspecified but horrible crime; and Father Altimira was attempting to close the San Rafael mission and had humiliated Amorós by taking both supplies and neophytes from San Rafael for his own use.

Given Herrera's jailing and the need to send soldiers out into the surrounding countryside to look for runaway neophytes, the San Rafael mission was probably left without sufficient troops to police the Indians who remained, some of whom may well have seized new opportunities to be "insubordinate." Marino and Quintino, both boatmen and thus usually freer than other neophytes, would have been sensitive to any efforts to curtail their personal freedom. If they had defied Amorós, and especially if they had convinced other members of their tribe to join them, they surely would have been pursued and jailed. It would have been particularly galling to Father Amorós that the former alcalde, Marino, chose to defy authority and disrupt the everyday working of the mission. Perhaps he would have agreed with the priest Gerónimo Boscana, who wrote about what he considered the devious character of the Indians, based on his experiences in southern California missions: "When they appear the most intelligent and entitled to the greatest confidence, they are the least to be trusted....All their operations are accompanied by stratagems and dissimulation, they easily gain our confidence, and at every pass we are deluded."[12]

The authorities must have perceived Marino and Quintino and their followers as a serious threat to the smooth running of the mission, considering the military force assembled to catch them, which was reinforced by Marcelo and his men. Other California missions had been attacked by mission Indians, and the military may have decided to quickly arrest and jail the ringleaders before they could attract any more dissidents.

AN ATTACK ON THE MISSION

Alternatively, it is possible that Marino and a group of like-minded Coast Miwok, including Quintino, had attacked the San Rafael mission in 1824 and were subsequently hiding out on the islands. Vallejo does not mention such a skirmish, but former governor Alvarado described an undated attack by Quintino in an 1874 letter to journalist G. W. Gift. Marino's role in the fight was unclear, however; Gift wrote that he was "probably among the attacking party."[13] (Chapter 9 provides more information on this attack.)

Kotzebue confirmed that the mission had been attacked and that buildings had been set afire before his October 1824 visit to San Rafael. Unfortunately, he did not say when the attack occurred, but he described the results: an uneasy mission, with Indians in shackles and two of the six soldiers on sentry duty at night on San Rafael Hill, "each of them beside a large fire; every two minutes they rang a bell which was hung between two pillars, and were regularly answered by the howling of the little wolf [coyote]."[14] It is difficult to assess whether the sentries' caution was typical or the result of a recent attack.

POMPONIO'S SAGA

Marino might have been imprisoned in 1824 because of an association with a fellow Coast Miwok named Pomponio, a runaway from Mission Dolores. Vallejo claimed that Marino's followers joined Pomponio after Marino was captured by the military. Alvarado connected Pomponio and Marino more directly, stating that Pomponio was under Marino's command.[15] The non-Indian Californios considered Pomponio an unsavory character. Vallejo noted that Pomponio had "quite a reputation as a murderer and thief";[16] priests and soldiers accused him of malevolence, murder, thievery, and rape. According to reports from the Californio J. E. Galindo, most of Pomponio's crimes were committed against other Indians—he reputedly set fire to an Indian woodcutter, "using the same wood the Indian had cut and collected earlier"[17]—although he was eventually executed for killing a Mexican soldier. Nevertheless, he was able to elude capture for at least three years by living on handouts from neophytes at the missions and various outstations (ranchos where livestock were tended and crops were grown). It is difficult to know how other Native Americans perceived him, however, since his reputation was recorded only by non-Indians.

Pomponio's biological father came from a respected family at the mission: his father's brother, Jacinto, a Huimen, was the major Coast Miwok interpreter and witness at weddings from 1800 to 1805, and he was both Marino's godparent and a witness at his first wedding (see Chapter 2). The priest entered Pomponio's tribal affiliation in the mission records as Guaulen, the tribe of his mother. His father, a member of the Huimen tribe, had entered the mission and married someone else three years earlier.[18]

When Pomponio's mother brought her son to the mission in 1803, he was only four years old.[19] At the time he was baptized, the youngster was surrounded by members of his extended family, soon to include a stepfather. But his good fortune was not to last. When Pomponio was seven, a series of illnesses killed his mother, his mothers' siblings, his maternal and paternal grandmothers, and his uncle Jacinto. When the boy was nine, his biological father died. By 1816, when he was seventeen, all his known kin were dead, including the spouses and children of his aunts and uncle.[20]

These tragic losses of his support network and role models must have affected the future course of Pomponio's life. Family bonds in the mission were a major force in neophytes' lives, not only helping them to sustain their belief system but also protecting them from threats such as sorcery. Pomponio may have retained some ties to the few survivors from his mother's Guaulen tribe, however, or to Huimen neophytes such as Marino from his uncle's village. When Marino left Mission Dolores for San Rafael in late 1817, Pomponio was a young adult of eighteen, giving them ample opportunity to have known each other in San Francisco.

By the time Pomponio was twenty-one, in March 1820, Father Juan Cabot at Mission Dolores was reporting to Governor Solá that the "evil" Pomponio and six other runaways from the San Francisco mission were causing damage and hiding out in rancherias on "the other side of the Puerto" (meaning in today's Marin County) and in "some [places] very far away."[21] This is the same month that Marino lost his titles of first alcalde and mayordomo in the San Rafael mission; conceivably, he could have been providing Pomponio and his companions with food, clothing, or shelter.

At about this time, Alvarado, then a young boy, traveled from Monterey to San Francisco on a horse behind cadet Don José Joaquín Estudillo. At the end of an exhausting twenty-hour trip, Alvarado recalled many years later, they were stopped by a sentinel and told of a dangerous incident involving one of Marino's men:

We have been invaded by one of the chiefs under Marin of Lompali [Olompali], named Pomponio, the bravest and most fearsome of the Cainameros....This story...made me tremble with fear; and exhausted as I was by my physical exertions I spent every moment thinking about the darkness of the night, the stormy noise of the icy winds that were blowing furiously from the harbor of San Francisco, which we were already nearing, and about how we had to pass through such a very dark place, just where Pomponio was known to be marauding.[22]

According to Alvarado, whose source was the corporal of the guard at San Rafael, Pomponio's "invasion" resulted from problems he had with "his people." At San Francisco, Pomponio had attacked a home in a rancheria at the mission and "seized the owner's wife and all his blankets and food supplies." The residents of the village had then asked to stay in the courtyard of the mission to be protected from Pomponio, whom they described as a "fierce and bold character...of great muscular strength."[23]

Did Pomponio Hide Out in Marin County?

The records contain no further references to Pomponio's whereabouts until three years later. During these three years, he might have been in the mountains south of San Francisco, where he hid out later; we have stories of his thefts from the San Jose and Santa Clara missions, which may have occurred at this time.[24] More likely, he was hiding out where he felt relatively safe: with other Coast Miwok neophytes he had known at Mission Dolores, especially those who were or had been runaways themselves. Coast Miwok territory would have been a good choice because only a few soldiers were stationed at San Rafael, and the mission had very few visitors. The foothills of Tamalpais and Mount Burdell or the hilly terrain of interior western Marin would have offered good hideouts. But Pomponio had grown up at Mission Dolores, not in Coast Miwok territory, so he would have needed help finding the safer locations and securing food and other supplies.

Marino could have had enough power to protect Pomponio. It may have been only a coincidence that Marino lost his privileged position as alcalde and mayordomo the same month that Pomponio was reported as a runaway, having fled to Marin County, where he might have needed help. But it is noteworthy that about three years later, in January 1823, with Pomponio still on the loose, extra soldiers arrived at San Rafael to keep an eye on Marino, perhaps because of suspicions about a clandestine association with Pomponio. Whatever the situation, Pomponio turned up three months later, in April 1823, south of San Francisco, needing food. He was with companions, but none of them were Coast Miwok.

Evading Capture South of San Francisco

One can pick up Pomponio's trail from April through July 1823 by examining correspondence among priests, the governor, and the commandante at the San Francisco presidio. Some of the letters, marked "secret," included their plans for surprising and capturing Pomponio south of San Francisco—and reflected their disappointment when these efforts failed.

In April, "the Indian robber" was at Rancho de San Pedro (today's town of Pacifica), an outstation south of San Francisco.[25] The following month, he was reported farther south, near the Santa Clara mission, trying to obtain food from sympathetic neophytes there. One neophyte told Father José Viader of Pomponio's presence, prompting Viader to send letters to Lt. Ignacio Martínez, commandante of the San Francisco presidio, detailing his secret plan to capture Pomponio. Viader requested that Martínez immediately send troops to surround Pomponio's hideout. Pomponio and a companion, Gonzalo, and four other southern California Indians, were hiding in thick brush, armed only with knives and bows and arrows. Another five southern California Indians were also in the band but were hiding in a different location in the mountains.[26]

Viader had a chance to capture Pomponio and Gonzalo when they went to the "barn" where food was dispersed, but he delayed, confident that by waiting he could catch all eleven with the help of the neophyte Filon, who would lure them into a trap. Although Viader promised Filon fine clothing and forgiveness for past transgressions in exchange for his cooperation, the plan backfired: Filon instead alerted Pomponio's band, allowing them to escape. The soldiers were left holding only Filon, whom they took to the San Francisco presidio jail.[27]

Raids on the San Francisco Mission and Presidio

In July 1823, Pomponio was back in the San Francisco area. Martínez explained in a letter to Argüello that the fugitive had abducted a young Indian woman and taken her to a temporary hiding place near Mission Dolores. While Pomponio and two companions went to a nearby ranchería to obtain food and supplies, the woman ran away and reported his whereabouts to the military. She led soldiers to the hideout, where they found horses and saddles, but no Pomponio. According to Martínez, Corporal José Reyes and his men then left the San Francisco presidio in pursuit. Aided again by the Indian woman, they were able to locate Pomponio's main hideout in the mountains south of San Francisco. There they found his meager supplies: two spears, one small machete made of a wheel rim, a hammer, and a chisel, all stored in two small huts.[28]

The fugitive, however, turned the tables on Reyes: while the search team was away from the presidio, Pomponio and a companion, Tadeo, surprised the young son of Corporal Reyes near the presidio, took all his clothes, and stole his horse and saddle. The boy later remarked that Pomponio "took him to the woods to kill him," but that Tadeo had intervened to save his life.[29]

Pomponio Survives a Series of Captures and Escapes
It is difficult to trace the next six months of Pomponio's life, especially since most of the available information is contained in conflicting recollections written years after the events. One of the authors, Vallejo, was the secretary at Pomponio's court-martial in February 1824, so we can use his account as a guide, even though his recollections were written fifty-one years later and his history of California contains some significant inconsistencies.

Apparently Pomponio was soon apprehended after stealing the horse and saddle and was jailed, for according to official documents, he was restrained while attempting to flee the San Francisco presidio jail in October 1823. On January 20, 1824, Argüello issued an order remanding the imprisoned Pomponio to the Monterey presidio, and six days later a shackled and handcuffed Pomponio was taken to Monterey for his trial and execution in February.[30] Beyond these bare facts, recorded in official letters, the details of what happened from August 1823 to February 1824 are not clear. The available sources often disagree, and some of the stories are clearly more imaginative and entertaining than edifying. Pomponio seems to have been captured two or more times during this period: in the Marin County area, near Soledad (southeast of Monterey), and possibly at Mission Dolores. We know some of the circumstances of these captures, but without any certain dates, it is difficult to establish a sequence of events.[31]

Guided by these official letters, however, we can postulate that Pomponio's story may have unfolded as follows. In late summer or fall of 1823, Pomponio was captured near Mission Dolores and taken to the presidio jail, from which he eventually escaped and fled to Marin County, only to be caught again in late December or early January 1824. Soldiers took him back to the presidio jail, where he reportedly spoke with a Russian guest. Later in January, he was sent to Monterey but escaped the presidio jail there. Recaptured near Soledad, he was returned to Monterey and executed in February. All this frantic activity, described in more detail in the following paragraphs, seems to have occurred in the space of five to six months.[32]

CAPTURED THROUGH TRICKERY According to Alvarado, who described Pomponio as preying on Indians and missions alike, an Indian who was in league with the military convinced Pomponio to join in a robbery near Mission Dolores. Alerted by this "friend," the soldiers promptly captured Pomponio and took him to the presidio.[33] On October 6, 1823, Pomponio was apprehended trying to dig his way out of the presidio jail.[34] Although this escape attempt was unsuccessful, he did manage to flee shortly afterward and remained free for about two months.

CAPTURE IN MARIN COUNTY Pomponio lost his freedom before January 20, 1824, when he was discovered by chance, along with two wives, in an isolated western Marin valley by Lt. Martínez and other soldiers. The captives were ferried back to San Francisco and placed in the presidio jail. In an 1828 summary of his military career, Martínez proudly described how he had captured Pomponio and an injured companion.[35] Osio, however, disagreed and derided Martínez for trying to take credit for what another soldier had done.[36]

Pomponio was caught in a secluded valley east of Hicks Mountain, on the east side of what is now the Point Reyes/Petaluma Road, perhaps in one of his earlier hideouts. The earliest written association of this cañada with Pomponio was in 1840;[37] it was still marked "Cañada Pomponio" on a 1916 U.S. Geological Survey map. Although the eroded banks of the stream in the canyon today lack the shrubs and trees of Pomponio's day, and barren hills show the effects of cattle grazing, one can still sense the isolation that he must have felt in this refuge.

The Coast Miwok village of Echatamal, on Halleck Creek in Rancho Nicasio, was less than four miles away from Cañada Pomponio as the crow flies. A trail connects the two through what would have been wild, uninhabited territory. The location of the canyon makes it unlikely that soldiers could have found Pomponio without the help of informants, but Vallejo wrote that Martínez, "falling upon him unexpectedly, took him prisoner."[38]

POMPONIO SPARES A RUSSIAN'S LIFE Returned to the presidio jail, Pomponio would have seen Marino (who Vallejo implied was imprisoned at the same time), and while there he apparently met Dmitry Zavalishin, a young Russian naval attaché. Zavalishin had arrived in San Francisco on December 12, 1823, when Pomponio was still at large. He was immediately warned by the troops to be on the lookout for the dangerous Pomponio. But this nineteen-year-old was headstrong, and he confidently set out on his adventures—traveling from San Francisco north to the Sonoma mission and San Pablo rancho, then east to Calaveras and south toward Santa Cruz—unaware that he was at times unwittingly near Pomponio's hideouts and that Pomponio had rejected opportunities to kill him.[39]

Zavalishin later learned about his narrow escapes when Pomponio asked to speak to him at the presidio where both were staying, one as a respected guest of the government and the other as a newly recaptured prisoner. Years later, when Zavalishin wrote of this meeting, he painted a sympathetic portrait of Pomponio, lauding him as a "Robin Hood figure" who was "courageous and resourceful," and supported by his fellow neophytes at the mission, who had previously protected him by not identifying him to the authorities.[40]

ESCAPE FROM MONTEREY—AND A FINAL RECAPTURE Governor Argüello probably acted quickly when he heard of Pomponio's forced return to the presidio. In any case, his order transferring Pomponio to the Monterey presidio was dated January 20, 1824. Six days later, Pomponio was put on a mule and taken to Monterey. Marino would have seen Pomponio's departure in shackles and handcuffs, escorted by six soldiers. Such a scene would have made a striking impression on Corporal Herrera and all the other prisoners, and they would have been reminded of it again the following month, when they heard of Pomponio's execution.

But Pomponio was not in Monterey long. Vallejo wrote that he escaped the Monterey jail by scaling the walls but was caught near Soledad, about thirty-five miles southeast of the presidio. Even though he was shackled for his return trip to Monterey, Pomponio outwitted his guard, Corporal Manuel Varela, by asking him for help in dismounting so that he could relieve himself. Then, according to Vallejo's account, Pomponio suddenly stabbed Varela to death. But he was unable to escape because Varela's companion managed to subdue him and put him back on the mule, as he testified at Pomponio's trial.[41] There are also other versions of this episode.[42]

The most preposterous tale, appearing in three different accounts, maintained that either Pomponio or his companion, Gonzalo, had been captured and had then cut off his own heel to escape from his shackles. Another account claimed that Pomponio subsequently survived for three years in the woods.[43] It is also interesting to note that these were non-Indians who were making Pomponio into a mythical figure.

Court-Martial and Execution
At his court-martial at the Monterey presidio, Pomponio was asked why he had murdered Varela. According to Vallejo, who was serving there as secretary, Pomponio replied that he believed the Spaniards were going to kill him anyway for the "killings imputed to me, and so I thought that killing one more would not make my plight any worse. One can only die once, and, as for me, it is all the same whether I die for something I did two years ago or for a killing committed a few days ago." Vallejo believed, however, that Pomponio would not have been executed for the additional killings because they involved mitigating circumstances.[44]

Pomponio was sentenced to death February 6, 1824. Before Pomponio's execution on the same date, he "confessed several times and was given Communion a few hours before being shot." As a deceased neophyte, Pomponio was buried in the chapel at the Monterey presidio, and his interment was duly written in the death records at the Carmel mission.[45]

MARINO AND POMPONIO

Did Marino and Pomponio lead separate, parallel lives joined only by circumstance and by the remembrances of two Californios, Vallejo and Alvarado, who wrote of a relationship that was tenuous at best? Or was there some organized resistance by a major chief, Marino, with the assistance of a subchief, Pomponio, and a lieutenant, Quintino? Even if Marino had been sympathetic to Pomponio, it is difficult to see how he could have played a central or sustained role in Pomponio's rebellion, since he was active at both the San Francisco and San Rafael missions from 1816 to December 1823. Nevertheless, Marino could have hidden Pomponio's presence from the priest or provided food to the fugitive, since he worked relatively freely within the system as alcalde and boatman. If Marino had been caught helping Pomponio—or had even given the appearance of doing so—he likely would have been punished, with the priest and military restricting his movements or even jailing him at the presidio. In apparent confirmation of this scenario, Vallejo implied that both men were indeed in the San Francisco presidio jail at the same time.

There are certainly similarities between Pomponio and Marino. They were both Coast Miwok from southern Marin who resided at Mission Dolores in the early 1800s. Both defied the mission system, spoke Spanish well, were runaways, and achieved reputations as troublemakers. Their self-confidence was striking, as was their ability to attract followers: Marino's from the core group of leaders at the San Rafael mission, and Pomponio's from a small band of non–Coast Miwok Indians.

But there are also some important differences in the experiences and backgrounds of these two men. Marino's formative years were spent in his native village in Huimen territory, not in the mission. He strongly identified with the Huimen people, and he could run to his homeland when escaping confinement. Later, he used familiar local islands as hideouts. Pomponio entered the mission system as a boy of four, probably too young to have identified very strongly with the native village of his mother in Guaulen territory. Lacking a native village, he was brought up in the rhythm of the mission—attending church regularly, performing required tasks in and around the mission, eating prepared meals, and adhering to the rules and regulations of the priest and the military.

Pomponio's known hideouts were in Marin and south of the San Francisco mission, in Ohlone territory. His known companions were not Coast Miwok: Tadeo was a young boy of fourteen from the East Bay, and Gonzalo and others were reportedly from the San Diego, San Gabriel, Carmel, and Soledad missions. Their only common language would have been Spanish. Such a following suggests that Pomponio might have been a charismatic figure who could attract others not only from different tribes but also from different language groups; without such a commanding personality, he would have been regarded with suspicion by these groups.

By camping south of San Francisco, however, Pomponio did have access to the outstations connected with the San Francisco, Santa Clara, and Santa Cruz missions. At these ranchos, he could approach the neophytes for food. He is portrayed as preying on other native peoples—"He killed at liberty, the assassination of his fellow savages being his particular delight," Bancroft wrote[46]—but we do not know how the other Indians perceived him. We also do not know whether they gave him aid freely or were coerced. He may have simply raided their supplies, without asking for help, since there were so few guards. Because he moved from one hideout to another in the mountains, it was impossible for him or his followers to store surplus food such as acorns or seeds. And, raised in the San Francisco mission, he may not have had his parents' skills for living off the land. In order to survive, then, Pomponio had to rely on food produced at the missions or their outliers. This meant that he would eventually be caught, and it is actually surprising how long he was able to evade capture.

Not all troublemakers came to Pomponio's end. Both the military and the priests could be surprisingly tolerant of defiant neophytes. The Spaniards frequently excused even the ringleaders who fomented revolt and were involved in crimes. Ironically, the alcaldes, chosen to keep order in the missions, were often the organizers of resistance; nevertheless, the latitude they were given is telling. Historian Steven Hackel notes that "incorporating Indian leaders...into their orbit was dangerous, but excluding them held greater risks still."[47]

For example, in 1828, the alcalde Estanislao, a Yokuts Indian at the San Jose mission who spoke and read Spanish, defied the mission priest, Father Durán, by not returning to the mission after receiving a pass. He notified the priest from his fortified village in the northern San Joaquin Valley that he and others were not returning and that they were not concerned about the firepower of a few young soldiers who were such poor marksmen.[48] Osio wrote that Estanislao defied Durán because "Estanislao could not tolerate anyone giving him orders."[49] Joined by Indians from other missions, including a group from Santa Cruz led by another alcalde, Cipriano, Estanislao's force included hundreds of neophytes and nonmission Indians. In 1828, after the Indians had won two battles, a group under Vallejo finally succeeded in putting down the uprising, with a loss of at least nine Spanish soldiers and an undetermined number of Indians.

Although Father Durán had demanded that Estanislao and Cipriano be returned "dead or alive" and threatened that they would be punished with the "good beatings that they deserve,"[50] Estanislao was welcomed back to the San Jose mission. Durán in fact hid Estanislao in his own rooms and then complained that Vallejo's actions had resulted in Indian deaths at Estanislao's rancheria. Estanislao received a pardon from the governor and died at the mission four years later.[51] Vallejo honored him by naming Stanislaus County after him.

An earlier example of leniency followed a revolt at the San Diego mission in 1775, during which Father Luís Jaume was shot with arrows and beaten to death. In the aftermath, Fathers Junipero Serra and Fermin Francisco Lasuén wanted to pardon the Indian leaders, reasoning that it was really the devil that had inspired the uprising.

Clearly, not all defiant Indians were treated equally. Compare these outcomes to the fate of Pomponio, who was not tolerated. Perhaps if Corporal Varela had been killed during a pitched battle, or if Pomponio had been perceived as having endured injustices at the hands of the mission, some compassion would have been shown toward him. But he was seen as dispensable, with nothing to offer the authorities and no special relationship with a priest or military officer who could argue in his behalf. In contrast, the reputations of Marino and Estanislao were so secure that Vallejo felt comfortable naming counties after them in 1850. Instead of being described as outlaws, they were perceived as worthy adversaries, respected by the military for their daring and prowess and for their willingness to stand up to Spanish and Mexican soldiers as equals.

9

MARINO'S WHEREABOUTS, 1825–1832

After Marino was released from jail, he returned at least briefly to San Rafael, where he served as a godparent in the summer of 1825. No doubt he was still near San Rafael in August, when his wife, Juana, was listed in the baptismal records as a godparent.[1] But his whereabouts from that time until after the death of Amorós in July 1832 largely remain a mystery. Although there is solid evidence that Marino was in the San Francisco and San Mateo areas at various times, most reports of his activities in these years are conjecture. It is hard to escape the impression, however, that he purposely avoided the San Rafael mission for almost eight years.

TWO STORIES OF CONFIDENT NEOPHYTES

Two intriguing stories from the mid-1820s may have involved Marino. In October and November of 1824, a Russian visitor, Otto von Kotzebue, needed an Indian guide for a trip from San Francisco to Colony Ross. Kotzebue's companion on the journey was Lt. José María Estudillo, who chose an Indian guide named Marco. In his journal, Kotzebue wrote that Marco had, "on account of his usefulness…been in many respects better treated than most of the Indians. He spoke Spanish with tolerable fluency, and when Estudillo endeavored to exercise his wit upon him, [Marco] often embarrassed him not a little by his repartees."[2]

This description of Marco bears a striking resemblance to accounts of Marino. Marco's facility in Spanish and his joking demeanor could have come only from someone who had frequent contact with soldiers, either on expeditions or at the presidio, someone who had confidence in his status and perceived himself to be an equal. Given that Kotzebue's writings contained numerous errors—for example, he referred to San Rafael as "San Gabriel"—it would not be unreasonable to speculate that he might have mistakenly written "Marco" instead of "Marino" and that his guide was actually Marino. It is also worth noting that Estudillo's son had participated in Argüello's 1821 expedition with Marino and therefore knew of Marino's skill as a boatman and guide and could have recommended him to his father.[3]

The second story was related by Antonio María Osio, Luis Argüello's brother-in-law. The incident he described took place near Olompali sometime before August 1826[4] and involved a boatman from San Rafael who talked back to Father Altimira—a boatman who again sounds suspiciously like a confident, brash Marino.

In this account, Father Altimira was approached by an angry Indian man who told him that a group of neophyte vaqueros from Mission Dolores had come to the North Bay on a barge looking for brides. Osio claimed that Father Esténega at Mission Dolores had approved their trip and had even provided gifts to entice the women. The irate man charged that his fiancée and other women had been forced to board the barge, which was already headed back to San Francisco.[5]

Father Altimira quickly arranged for a smaller, faster craft with a crew of Indian oarsmen, plus a corporal and four soldiers, to outrace the barge and bring back the women. When Altimira grew impatient with their progress, he kicked the boat and screamed at the oarsmen to speed up. According to Osio,

> the well experienced Indian chief ordered the crew to stop rowing so he could observe the currents. This, however, irritated the Father. It seemed to him to be a malicious delay and he hurled insults at the chief, who tolerated them in silence. The Indian who was at the front of the boat could not observe the force of the current, and it was necessary for him to stop rowing for a time. Fortunately he was confident of his skill, so he told the Father to shut his mouth because he did not know what he was saying.[6]

Because the boatman was able to read the currents correctly, they were able to intercept the barge and send it back to San Rafael Creek. But when the barge could not approach the landing spot closely enough, Altimira became angry and told the men to jump out and walk to shore, where each Indian "kidnapper" was punished with fifty lashes. They reboarded the barge, which eventually landed in Coast Miwok territory at Olompali, and the still wifeless men took off for the interior.

THE SAN RAFAEL MISSION SUSTAINS FURTHER ATTACKS

During these years, all was not as peaceful at Mission San Rafael as Father Amorós would have had the authorities believe. In January 1825, he had to request a "second soldier...primarily to chase a few elderly Christians who do a lot of damage to our cattle, horses and maize fields."[7] Several other attacks during Amorós's lifetime, including one mentioned by Kotzebue in 1824 (see Chapter 8), seem to have been more serious.

In later years, the grandson of Sonoma mission soldier Cayetano Juarez claimed that a group of marauding Indians had stormed the mission in 1829, bent on finding Father Amorós. Loyal neophytes surrounded the priest and escorted him to a marshy area where they could hide him in the tules. A speedy Indian runner from San Rafael alerted soldiers at Sonoma, who rescued Amorós and took him to Sausalito, where he was ferried in an "Indian balsa" (a tule boat) to San Francisco. Meanwhile, the attackers fled to an area north of Petaluma, where the soldiers confronted them. In two skirmishes, the Indians bested the soldiers and wounded Juarez.[8]

A second account concerned an assault on the mission by seventy-eight mission Indians on the afternoon of May 10, 1832. Amorós described this incident in the mission baptism records, calling attention to the entry by drawing an eye and writing "Nota" above it. (Figure 27b) Apparently, it was carried out by a non–Coast Miwok group who had come to retrieve the dying Indians of their tribe. They left the priest alone, and although shattering a window and breaking down a door, did not enter the warehouse or the soldier's house.[9] In the hope of preventing another assault, five soldiers were assigned to San Rafael from May through September, remaining there even after Amorós's death in July.

One hundred years later, Maria Copa related a story from her family's oral history that also describes an attack by a Pomo (non–Coast Miwok) group. In this rare historical description of an event from the Indian point of view, the Coast Miwok pursued the Pomo in an attempt to retrieve clothes stolen from the mission:

> Once they had a war when the priest was here. The Kainamako [Pomo from Healdsburg] went to San Rafael to fight. They took all the clothes the priest had and all the money and baskets—when everyone was away from the mission, working. They came and the priest was alone—not even a cook or the laundryman was there. He said to them, "Come in, come in; sit down, sit down." The leader said, "No come in. We want clothes. We want to fight." The priest said, "catcin, muchachos." He was telling them in Pomo to sit down. But he couldn't fight all alone. After the Pomo had left, he sent someone for the people [who resided at the mission]. They chased them and got some of the stuff back.[10]

Such accounts often mention the theft of clothes. José Fernández, a soldier stationed at San Francisco, reported that Indians fought "valiantly and cunningly, but they were not bloodthirsty. Their aim was to steal food and clothing, but not to kill the priests."[11] The disruption of Indian culture and society had made the traditional means of gathering food and producing clothes more difficult. Since warm clothing was provided at the mission, the Indians may have had little incentive to hunt for the rabbits, pelicans, and wood rats whose skins they had used to make clothing in the past. Traditional capes and blankets had become less essential to the Indians' ceremonial life and no longer conferred status and prestige on those who made or wore them. Mission-made blankets and shirts, in contrast, were given to neophytes at the mission, but they were not always readily available, especially to nonmission Indians.

A third tale of an Indian attack was dictated in 1883 by Nasario Galindo, an elderly former soldier. According to Galindo, the assault occurred in November 1833, the attackers were Cainameros, and loyal neophytes helped Amorós to escape. (In fact, Amorós had died more than a year earlier.)[12]

> One time the heathen Indians who were named in their tongue Cainameros... broke open the doors to the storehouses and stole everything that they could before returning to their rancheria. The padre, Juan Amoroso [sic], escaped with the help of some old Indians, Christians of the same mission, who led him out under cover of night, and, secreting him on a raft of tules, took him to San Francisco.[13]

Galindo reported that he and twenty-four other soldiers under the command of José Sánchez went to Sausalito from San Francisco, where horses were waiting for them. They surprised the Indians at their rancheria while they slept. "We came upon them at early dawn, before the sun rose...[and] recovered all the stolen goods, including blankets,...and captured four Christian Indians that had induced the others to do this crime. [At the presidio] they remained prisoners for about two years."[14]

Yet another account was penned by former governor Juan Bautista Alvarado in 1874, who described an attack led by Quintino and "probably Marin" without providing a date. According to Alvarado, the attackers belonged to the "Caynameros, a Marin County tribe." Allegedly, Corporal Rafael Garcia put both his family and Father Amorós on a reed boat or raft and "dispatched them with the tide to go elsewhere for safety. Strange to say this frail float and its precious cargo landed safely near the presidio."[15] But it strains credulity to believe that a priest and a soldier's family were left to drift with the tides and dangerous currents in the bay. Neither priest nor soldier could have controlled this craft in those treacherous waters; such a trip would have required the skills of an Indian boatman.[16]

Given the common elements in some of the stories, we can only speculate about whether they represent separate incidents or whether they all describe the same event, remembered differently in the telling and retelling over the years. Amorós's report of the 1832 attack was written soon after the episode, but many of the other descriptions are based on distant memories. Only Alvarado's account alleges that Marino participated in any of these attacks.

MARINO AND ARGÜELLO

Rather than leading attacks on the San Rafael mission, Marino was at Mission Dolores in 1826 and 1827 and was likely still in the San Francisco area with Juana in 1828. This would have put him in close proximity to Luis Argüello, who had left the governorship in Monterey in December 1825 to resume his former post as commandante of the San Francisco presidio. Marino's name appears in the San Francisco mission records as a godfather three months after Argüello's return.

Marino's fate may well have been linked with that of Argüello. According to his service record, Argüello participated in a number of expeditions both during and after his governorship between 1824 and 1828. Argüello may well have used Marino's expertise in reading currents and tides and his experience in transporting soldiers during some of the later journeys.

MARINO'S POSSIBLE EMPLOYMENT

In 1826, the government decided that a few responsible neophytes could be released from the mission system to live on their own, despite the objections of the priests, who did not want to lose the individuals they had come to rely on. Thus a number of Indians were released from San Francisco and other California missions, although none left San Rafael or San Francisco de Soláno (in Sonoma).

For many, however, living independently proved difficult. Some of the neophytes had spent all or most of their adult lives in the missions and found it hard to adjust to a new environment. Most who left went to new or unfamiliar towns and lacked guidance from local residents. A year later, many of those released had "gambled away their clothes, implements and even their land" and became destitute, forcing some to return to the missions.[17]

During this period, Captain William A. Richardson, a carpenter by training, was employing Indian boatmen on San Francisco Bay. Argüello would probably have looked favorably on Marino and others participating in these activities: while he was still governor, he had decried the way Indians were treated as slaves and "kept lazy when they could be trained to work as agriculturists or shipbuilders."[18] It is unclear whether Richardson's employees were newly released neophytes or individuals whom Father Esténega had excused from mission duties in order to help Richardson.

According to Vallejo, Marino turned to shipbuilding after he was released from jail.[19] It is possible that Argüello's belief in promoting gainful employment had opened an avenue for Marino both to participate in mission activities and to work on boats as a builder and a pilot. Unfortunately, this employment opportunity, with its relative freedom, ended after December 1829, when Richardson and his family left San Francisco for Mission San Gabriel in southern California. Richardson was absent from northern California for more than five years, building boats and sailing them to San Blas and the Sandwich Islands.

MARINO AT OUTLYING RANCHOS

Another clue to the whereabouts of Marino and Juana from 1826 to 1832 comes from a San Francisco baptismal record dated August 26, 1826, which indicated that both Marino and Juana were godparents to a dying Coast Miwok baby girl, south of San Francisco, near San Mateo.[20]

We do not know why Marino was in this area. He might have been carrying messages for Argüello or guiding and ferrying the commandante and guests between San Francisco and Argüello's rancho at Las Pulgas, near present-day Redwood City and Palo Alto. Alternatively, he might have been overseeing wheat production or cattle grazing at the outstation at San Mateo, jobs he had become familiar with when he was an alcalde at the San Rafael mission. From 1823 to 1825, San Mateo was an active outstation, with three hundred Indians; an 1835 inventory showed buildings, a chapel, and produce worth $2,753 on three leagues of land.[21] Neophytes were sometimes left in charge of these mission ranchos, running them without direct supervision. In 1824, Zavalishin described large storehouses of "grain, hides and wool" at a San Francisco mission outpost in San Pablo, noting that "two or three trustworthy Indian families usually lived beside the storehouses" and acted as guards. The Santa Eulalia rancho, associated with the Sonoma mission, had "a provisional house for the padres' visits, with a corral for horses,...[and a] neophyte alcalde was in charge of the rancho."[22]

In any case, Marino may have had some freedom of movement during this period. He and Juana may well have been "emancipated" in 1826 but continued to participate minimally in mission activities. Their names appear next in the mission records in April 1827, when they became godparents to a Coast Miwok child in San Francisco. Juana was a godparent in San Francisco again in 1828, a responsibility she shared with Teodorico, a longstanding Huimen friend who had remained at Mission Dolores.[23]

REVENGE AGAINST THE CAYMUS INDIANS

Another story about Marino in these "missing" years places him in Sonoma County, near present-day Yountville, around 1827 or 1828. Allegedly, he and Chief Sonoma massacred a band of Caymus Indians in that area. The source for this story was Jacob P. Leese, who acknowledged that he had heard these reports from others and had "no direct knowledge as to their truth." George Yount, the founder of Yountville, shared with his biographer in the 1850s a similar tale involving two unnamed chiefs.[24]

According to Leese and Yount, two Indian chiefs from the San Rafael area hid outside a Caymus settlement during the day. Then, at night, while the Caymus were gathered inside their sweathouse, the attackers threw firewood down the smoke hole. As the Caymus Indians fled the smoke-filled sweathouse, the two chiefs clubbed them to death, one by one. The sweathouse burned to the ground with all the remaining inhabitants inside.

Yount told his biographer that the "murderers were two Indian chiefs from San Rafael, monsters of evil and mischief," men that he "knew well."[25] Jacob Leese identified the chiefs as Marin and Sonoma and claimed that they were out to exact revenge on the Caymus after a previous conflict. Leese might have heard about this event from Yount and either supplied the names accurately or used the names of two of the more famous Indians in his story.[26]

The Indians' propensity for revenge had frequently been noted by priests, the military, and foreign visitors. A priest at the San Francisco mission said, "If one of their relatives is killed, even though some time passes, if they can, they take revenge,...aided by their relatives with the bow and arrow if the matter was serious enough." According to Captain Beechey, "The tribes are frequently at war with each other, often in consequence of trespasses upon their territory and property; and weak tribes are sometimes wholly annihilated or obliged to associate themselves with those of their conquerors; but such is the warmth of passion and desire of revenge that very little humanity is in general shown to those who fall into their power."[27] The Spanish, Mexican, and, later, American authorities frequently ignored such killings, particularly if other Indians were the only victims, with the rationale that the murders simply reflected Indian custom.

TWO DEATHS

The deaths of two powerful men, coupled with the absence of Captain Richardson from the Bay Area, undoubtedly influenced the next stage of Marino's life. In February 1828, Argüello was "suspended from his command"[28] by the governor for alcoholism. Behavior that had been tolerated for years was no longer ignored by his superiors. Even Argüello's troops, who admired him greatly, could not protect him from the wrath of Governor José María Echeandía. When Argüello died in San Francisco in 1830, Marino lost a valuable supporter, a powerful man who had provided him with work and a degree of protection.

In 1832, Father Amorós, head of the San Rafael mission, also died. Marino had stayed away from San Rafael during the last years of Amorós's tenure, possibly because the two no longer trusted each other or because Marino did not feel welcome there after his time in the presidio jail. It also seems that he may have enjoyed greater freedom in the San Francisco area. Nonetheless, whether he was motivated by the death of Argüello, the death of Amorós, or some other event, Marino soon made his way back to the San Rafael mission.

10

MARINO RETURNS
TO THE SAN RAFAEL MISSION

When Marino returned to the San Rafael mission in the 1830s, he found it greatly changed. After Father Amorós died in July 1832, the organization the padre had maintained began to break down. His successors, Jesús Mercado and José Lorenzo Quijas, proved intemperate and egotistical; and the military leader Mariano Guadalupe Vallejo took every opportunity to challenge their authority. Even more important, the Mexican government began to plan the dismantling of the mission system, a process known as secularization. For the Coast Miwok, it was a time of both hope and despair: the lands and property that they were promised and encouraged to claim were threatened by non-Indian settlers; and they did not know who could help them.

THE CLERGY AND THE MILITARY: A POWER STRUGGLE

After the death of Amorós, Father Tomás Esténega was sent from Mission Dolores to oversee the workings of the San Rafael mission; he remained in charge there for the next eight months. During that period he wrote the 1832 yearly report of the San Rafael mission, noting that there were only 300 Indians at San Rafael, a precipitous drop from Amorós's figure of 1,073 Indians in 1831. (Appendix D) Esténega claimed that Amorós's 1831 figures were incorrect, and that many Indians had fled the mission in 1831 and 1832 to live in the countryside or at the Russian Colony Ross. However, many Indians may have fled after Amorós's death, either fearing a change in regime, or to take advantage of a lull in ecclesiastical authority.[1]

Esténega was accompanied by Teodorico, the friend of Marino and Juana who had played an important role at Mission Dolores, assisting Esténega and serving as a witness at marriages. He was occasionally described in the mission records as a "sacristan," someone in charge of the sacred objects of the church. Teodorico's knowledge of the workings of the church and his familiarity with fellow Coast Miwok undoubtedly proved helpful to Esténega. Teodorico was a witness at two of the three weddings performed while Esténega was at San Rafael.

Father Esténega was eventually relieved by Father Jesús Mercado in the spring of 1833. Mercado, a Franciscan, belonged to the Zacatecan College, whose members were considered by the Californios to be coarser, more vulgar, and less sophisticated than their Franciscan predecessors from the San Fernando College in Mexico City. Yet Juan Bautista Alvarado, the former governor, described Mercado as an excellent fencer and dancer: the priest "knew how to tuck up his robes and dance exquisitely."[2] A former soldier recalled that Mercado "practiced all kinds of bad habits." Bancroft described Mercado both as a "quarrelsome and vicious padre who did much harm" and as a man of "fine presence [and] engaging manners," noting that he was "an intriguer, arbitrary in his acts and always ready to quarrel with anyone who would not accept his views…a hard drinker, a gambler and a libertine—the father of many half breed children at each of the missions where he served." The historian Father Maynard Geiger wrote that the padre who replaced Mercado at Mission Santa Clara, José María Suarez del Real, "took care of the woman and children of Mercado, and had some children of his own by her, some of whom went by the name of Real, others by the name of Mercado."[3]

Soon after Mercado's arrival at the San Rafael mission, he became embroiled in conflict with Vallejo, the commandante at San Francisco. The priest and the commandante initially clashed over the beating and physical abuse of mission neophytes, but, as subsequent months made clear, their conflict was much deeper. In fact, it went to the issue of who wielded the ultimate power, the cross or the sword—a problem that was magnified by the outsized egos of the two principals. Both in their mid-twenties, Mercado in a simple coarse robe with a rope belt around his waist, and Vallejo in his dashing military uniform, met with fists raised.

The Coast Miwok were merely pawns in this struggle. Both Mercado and Vallejo claimed to have the Indians' best interests at heart. But Vallejo seemed to be the more sincere, especially in contrast to Mercado's violent temperament and rash actions. Eventually, Vallejo would manage to best Mercado, aided both by the commandante's powerful family connections and by his sense of noblesse oblige.

Conflict over Whipping

Father Mercado began baptizing and burying at San Rafael in April 1833. Only a month later, a group of alcaldes led by Marino began complaining to Vallejo about this new priest's mayordomo, José Santos Molina. They wanted Vallejo to remove Molina from his job because the mayordomo was whipping and otherwise abusing neophytes without any "legal cause." Vallejo did not question the veracity of the alcaldes and wrote to the governor: "I believe what they said, because I observed it in another mission. I believe that if we don't remove Molina, they will kill him or they will go into the interior."[4]

Vallejo's indignation over the arbitrary administration of justice at the mission was clear in another document: "These poor Indians are being abused with the most dire results....The treatment would horrify the most feral man."[5] For a member of the military to be so incensed suggests that the actions allowed by the priests at the San Rafael and San Francisco de Soláno missions were indeed severe. Whipping was not an uncommon practice in the nineteenth century; U.S. explorers Meriwether Lewis and William Clark, for example, had disobedient soldiers whipped on their 1803-1806 expedition.[6] But in California, men of the cloth determined who should be whipped and why; the Indians, as virtual slaves at the missions, had no rights and no one to turn to for redress. At Mission Santa Cruz, the neophyte Asisara described the priest there, Father Ramón Olbés, as "fond of beating [neophytes] cruelly. He was never satisfied to prescribe less than fifty lashes, sometimes on the buttocks and very often on the belly. He even used to order 25 lashes given to little children eight or ten years old...on the buttocks or the belly as the whim struck him."[7]

By 1833, restrictions on whipping had already been ordered. A decree of 1813 had forbidden whipping "as a form of punishment for the Indians," although other forms of punishment were allowed. In 1822, prominent military, civil, and priestly authorities met and decided that "the lash being absolutely abolished, reliance must be placed on a stick applied to the clothed back, or to stocks, shackles etc., all 'gently' applied"; and in 1826, a decree from Governor Figueroa stated that Franciscans should not whip married or adult Indians and that children could not receive more than fifteen lashes a week.[8] Thus the priests who defied these orders by whipping adults were in fact acting illegally.

Vallejo's letter to his superior reveals the care with which he presented the Indian side of the story at San Rafael: for example, instead of writing that unnamed alcaldes or *neofitos* were complaining, he noted the name of each alcalde—Marino, Gerbacio, Joaquin, Pascual, and Jorge. Marino's name was listed first, indicating his importance in this matter. All of these men had personal ties to Marino and Juana, who had served as godparents or witnesses for the men's families.[9] In addition, although only Jorge and Marino were mentioned in the mission accounts as alcaldes, all of these individuals served as marriage witnesses under Mercado, which means that they were involved in church ceremonies and had firsthand knowledge of what was occurring at the mission.

Vallejo knew whom to contact to right a wrong, and so did Marino. Marino may have initially complained to Father Mercado, to no avail, and recognized that an appeal to the military authorities, who were frequently at odds with the priests, had a better chance of resolving the Indians' grievance. Alternatively, he may have bypassed the padre entirely and gone directly to Vallejo. But the alcaldes were not successful in their attempt to remove Molina at this point: five months later, he acted as godfather at the baptism of the son of Maria Copa's grandparents.[10]

In response to Vallejo's letter in May complaining about brutal treatment at San Rafael, Governor Figueroa answered four days later that he was writing to Mercado's superior, Garcia Diego (a Zacatecan), so that "he can find a remedy in order to avoid what you fear might happen."[11] Two of the priests responded to Governor Figueroa in a revealing manner. One, Father Francisco Garcia Diego of the Santa Clara mission, acknowledged that the alcaldes, "seeing the aversion I have for this type of punishment, say if I don't continue lashing, the mission will be lost....This punishment will be abolished at this mission because it shocks and torments my soul. I will follow laws, [as] a true Christian person."[12]

But Father José de Jesús María Gutierrez of the San Francisco de Soláno mission at Sonoma, and a member of the Zacatecan order, argued in great detail that whipping should be allowed and that the Indians should not be "indulged":

My being too indulgent with the neophytes seems to have brought upon the mission faults that we did not have before. The Indians miss mass, they miss the prayers to instruct themselves. They don't go to work,...flee from here to the fields for 15, 19 days or longer without letting me know. If we stop the lashings, what punishment would you use for these sinners?

Would it be enough punishment to give them a strong lecture? I know for a fact that they hate that, and it is useless; afterwards they mock the priest and go back to their bad ways. I am sure whoever made these charges against me did not inform you of these consequences. They must have told you however that I order lashings, this is true, but I do it rarely, and in moderation.

It is not the same to deal with uncivilized as with civilized men. The civilized men are directed by law, reason illuminates them, shame repels them and often they are stimulated by their honor. Not so Sir, not so with those who do not know law. Reason does not touch them nor honor nor shame. Nothing stops them but fear and precisely the fear of lashing because this is what they are used to since the establishment of the Mission....

You will see from what I have stated that my actions and sentiments are ruled by the feelings of pity towards these souls. I see them as small children and also as Mexicans as I am.

In conclusion: if you, after thinking over this matter, decide to absolutely abolish lashing as a form of paternal correction, I am ready to obey.[13]

Finally, in June 1833, whipping was curtailed at the missions, and the earlier decrees against it began to be enforced. Marino and his fellow alcaldes had achieved success by complaining to the one authority who could have halted these cruel practices, and the reverberations echoed from Sonoma to Santa Clara.[14]

Confrontation over Acisclo

Prior to the curtailment of whipping, in May 1833, Mercado's wrath was directed against a twenty-seven-year-old Coast Miwok named Acisclo,[15] resulting in a rash of letters exchanged between Vallejo and Mercado about Acisclo's whereabouts and his possible punishment. How he incurred the anger of Mercado is not clear. Acisclo was no renegade; he had participated in the mission community as a marriage witness under Father Amorós and Father Esténega. Mercado called Acisclo an adulterer, while Vallejo claimed that he had been charged with injuring another Indian, Redento.[16] But it seems evident that Acisclo's "crime" was of less importance than the issue of which power broker, Vallejo or Mercado, would have him under their control.

Apparently, the military guards at the mission were protecting Acisclo, even hiding him from Mercado, prompting the priest to write to Vallejo that he wanted to apprehend the "guilty Indian in order to do with him what I may deem convenient."[17] In another letter, an angry Mercado threatened Vallejo, warning him not to "overextend his military authority" at the mission and asserting that he, Mercado, was in charge and had the right "to expel anybody that would be morally harmful."[18] In this case, Vallejo backed down. He ordered the corporal at San Rafael to return Acisclo to the priest and asked him to try to get along with Mercado.[19]

We do not know Acisclo's fate at the hands of the mayordomo, but the mission records show that he was again participating in baptismal ceremonies a few years later under a different priest, Father Quijas.[20]

Hungry Soldiers

In August 1833, Ignacio Pacheco, one of five soldiers assigned to the San Rafael mission, requested some meat from the priest to feed the soldiers, because the "soldiers didn't have anything to eat." According to Pacheco, Mercado replied that he "did not have any meat to feed the wolves." Persisting in his request, Pacheco returned the next day. When he was rebuffed again, he ordered a soldier to take a lamb from the mission flock and kill it. The priest railed against the soldiers and denounced Pacheco and Vallejo as public thieves. Turning on Pacheco in a most unpriestly fashion, Mercado let him know that he too had "gunpowder and bullets" at his disposal and that "the lamb would kick in the stomach" of not only Pacheco but also Vallejo and the soldier who had killed the animal.[21]

Mercado's anger was really directed at Vallejo, whom he suspected of privately ordering Pacheco to "take by force anything he wanted." Moreover, Mercado was now able to accuse Vallejo of stealing the Indians' property (the lamb) instead of protecting it. He described the neophytes as "these unfortunate people who work so hard to care for" the mission larder, warning that he would hold Vallejo responsible for any regrettable outcome.[22] Vallejo then did an about-face and requested that Pacheco avoid disagreements and "take no supplies without politely asking the missionary first."[23]

Mercado Deems Colony Ross a Threat

Threats to Mercado's authority also came from outside the area. For the Coast Miwok, life at the Russian settlement of Colony Ross continued to be an increasingly attractive alternative to the more structured and punitive existence at the mission. Both Amorós (in 1828 and 1830) and Esténega (in 1832) noted in their annual reports that San Rafael neophytes were living at Colony Ross; Esténega wrote that "considerable numbers" of Indians were there.[24] The Russians seemed to appreciate the Indians in ways that Father Mercado was apparently incapable of understanding. In the 1870s, Vallejo reminisced about a trip he had taken to Colony Ross in the spring of 1833, noting that he had been surprised to see "hundreds" of Indians there, freely coming and going, "bringing hides of wild animals which they traded for tobacco, kerchiefs and liquor."[25] Among the various groups, the Bodega Miwok, known to the Russians as the Olementke, were the most closely involved with the Russians.

Both the Russian governor, Baron F. von Wrangell, and manager, P. Kostromitonov, wrote about the Olementke and the Pomo in positive terms. Wrangell described the Indians as individuals who were "soft-hearted and not vengeful by nature," who could "easily learn diverse arts and crafts," who were "nimble and daring horsemen" and "accomplished in speaking the Spanish language." In their lighter moments, he added, they "love dance, song and gambling."[26] Kostromitonov pointed out the Indians' intelligence, noting that they "catch on quickly." Both observers reported that the Indian women seemed stronger than the men; Kostromitonov commented that the women "did the hard work."[27]

Father Mercado complained to the Mexican governor that male and female neophytes at the San Rafael mission were fleeing north, leaving their mission-sanctioned spouses behind and finding new mates at Colony Ross. In addition, other Indians in the Tomales area were selling mission cattle and horses to the Russians, clearly without permission. Mercado warned the governor of "dire consequences" if the Russians' activities were not stopped; he argued that while the Russians were pretending to be fishing, they really had their eyes on acquiring both land and Indians.[28]

Apparently Mercado hoped that by accusing the Russians of nefarious activities, he could convince the governor to send troops to Colony Ross and rid the mission of this nuisance forever. But this was 1833, and the governor was involved with other matters—not the least of which was the imminent dismantling of the missions.

Mercado's Attack on Toribio's Band

In April 1833, Vallejo was in the Bodega area and learned that Toribio, a Coast Miwok neophyte and the capitán of the Licatiut, was warning other Coast Miwok there to be wary of Mexican soldiers. Toribio claimed that although the soldiers were feigning friendship, they were really coming to "violently imprison [the Indians] and take them back to the missions at San Rafael and...Sonoma, [where] they would be forcibly converted to Christianity."[29]

Gaulinela, described as "chief" of the rancheria at Bodega Bay, told Vallejo that both neophytes from San Rafael and nonmission Indians had joined forces, some two hundred strong, to prevent soldiers from entering their lands—an unusual example of cooperation between mission and nonmission Indians. If the group was indeed that large, it probably included more than one Coast Miwok tribe, perhaps the Licatiut, the Yoletamal of the Bodega area,[30] the Petalumas, and even southern Pomos, since Toribio spoke Pomo and had been a godparent to Pomo neophytes.

Vallejo warned his troop of twenty men to behave with "consideration" toward this defensive force. He then tried to persuade the Indians that Toribio's assessment was incorrect. Vallejo was, however, willing to admit that the Indians had been "ill treated" by Mexican troops, and he criticized the missionaries in particular for "their detestable policies" of "forcing Christianity and taking [Indians] from their homes."[31]

Having thus been reassured by Vallejo (who in turn had been reassured by Governor Figueroa), Toribio then encouraged a group of Indians from Pulia to come to the mission some months later, telling them that they would be safe and welcome there. There was no reason for the Pulia to doubt him: as capitán of the Licatiut, he was respected by his own people; and he had been familiar with mission procedures at San Rafael since 1820, serving as an interpreter, a sacristan, and a witness at weddings. Toribio had also become part of the power structure at the mission, a position that was solidified when Juana served as godmother to both his wife and his mother. At some point, Toribio had met Governor Figueroa at the mission and was referred to by Vallejo "as a very important name in this area."[32]

No one could have foreseen that Mercado would cause any difficulties, much less a string of troubles. But when Toribio and an advance party of fourteen non-mission Indians from Pulia arrived at the mission on November 16 and requested an audience with Mercado, the priest, for some reason, refused to see them until the following day. The next morning, Mercado learned that some items belonging to the mission had been stolen, and he immediately leaped to the conclusion that the guests were responsible for the theft. He had them rounded up and sent to jail at the San Francisco presidio. Then, fearing that the rest of the newly arriving party from Pulia might storm the mission, Mercado sent his mayordomo, José Molina, with a troop of armed neophytes to attack them, killing twenty-one, wounding others, and imprisoning the remaining twenty Indians.[33] Understandably, both groups of Pulia believed that Toribio had betrayed them.

When he heard of this deadly confrontation, Governor Figueroa sent Vallejo to the presidio. Vallejo freed the fifteen prisoners and took them to his house in San Francisco. When he left San Francisco for San Rafael, he took not only the former prisoners but fifteen "well armed men," probably to protect Toribio and possibly himself from angry neophytes at the San Rafael mission. Meanwhile, "the captains" of those Pulia who had survived Molina's assault ordered the hands and feet of Toribio's mother and nephew tied to a stake in retaliation for his supposed betrayal.[34] When Vallejo arrived at San Rafael, he did his best to convince the capitáns that the fault lay with Father Mercado and not with Toribio. Nonetheless, Toribio and his son, Anselmo, chose to stay in the mission until the Indians from Pulia had been assured that he had not set them up for an ambush.

The next afternoon, angry alcaldes spoke again with Vallejo about ousting Molina, who had led the attack. Apparently, they received no satisfaction. By nine that evening, the alcaldes and a "mob" of angry neophytes brandishing lances "confronted" Vallejo and demanded Molina's dismissal. The commandante was able to calm the crowd, and he spoke to the Indians again the next day before leaving for

Sonoma. There, at the San Francisco de Solάno mission, he found that the story was well known, although it had not generated such great tension. Vallejo reported to the governor that the returning Pulia "were in Santa Rosa trying to convince the nearby rancherias that neither you, nor I, nor Toribio were at fault for the imprisonment or deaths that Mercado had caused."[35] Vallejo did not mention having Molina removed from his post; nevertheless, Molina was not heard from again. The Coast Miwok may have found their own way to solve the problem.

Father Mercado's last baptism at San Rafael occurred December 6, 1833, just before he responded to a summons from his superior demanding that he report to Mission Santa Clara to explain this disastrous incident. But he was exonerated at a hearing that included Father José Lorenzo Quijas. Ironically, it was Quijas who replaced Mercado at San Rafael, performing his first baptism there on January 3, 1834, and remaining there until 1843.[36]

Quijas Arrives at San Rafael

The departure of the hotheaded Mercado provided some relief to the neophytes at the mission, but the appointment of another Zacatecan, Father Quijas, did not rescue the reputation of the priests assigned to San Rafael. José Fernández, the former soldier, complained that both Mercado and Quijas set bad examples for the Indians, being interested solely in "spending a good life." Alvarado described their motto as "Amuse yourself today, tomorrow will be another day."[37] Similar complaints about both Mercado and Quijas continued into the 1840s. According to Vallejo, Governor Micheltorena condemned the two priests with these words:

> The Spanish missionaries slept on a floor with an adobe brick for a pillow and a cowhide for a mattress, while today Fathers...Quijas, Mercado...and others have luxurious beds adorned with curtains and provided with good mattresses....In the old days only as a special favor were the missionaries allowed to put on underdrawers when they traveled on horseback, while at the present time priests are to be seen at any time mounted upon good horses, elegantly dressed and, instead of sandals, a symbol of humility, they wear grenadiers' boots which they lace with silken cords.[38]

When Fernández compared the two priests, however, he recalled that although Quijas "forgot his Christian duties when he was drunk," he was "not as bad as Mercado [and] had some good qualities when he was sober."[39]

Father Quijas was assigned to officiate at both of the North Bay missions—San Rafael and San Francisco de Solάno—but in June 1835 he settled permanently at San Rafael, vowing that he would not return to San Francisco de Solάno until Antonio

Ortega, the insulting mayordomo appointed by Vallejo, had been removed from his post.[40] By that time, Quijas had lost much of the power the missionaries had once enjoyed; as a result of the Mexican government's decision to secularize the missions, his authority had become comparable to that of a parish priest.

Ortega and Vallejo's brother Salvador, "a rough, hard-drinking, unprincipled fellow,"[41] both seemed to go out of their way to humiliate and insult Father Quijas, and it is unlikely that this would have continued if Vallejo had not condoned it. The priest accused Ortega of ordering praying neophytes to leave the church and go to work and of teaching a recent convert to say a Spanish swear word after "Gracias a Dios." Quijas also complained of the "barefaced manner [Ortega] has given to the infamous vice of lust. He spares neither young girls nor married women or widows, neither heathen nor Christian, as is affirmed by the majority of inhabitants of San Soláno."[42]

Quijas was accused, perhaps unfairly, of neglecting his duties as a priest at San Francisco de Soláno in 1835. The charges included failing to celebrate mass and not baptizing or burying members of his flock. It is difficult to support the charges from information in the mission records, however; Quijas was required to officiate in both Sonoma and San Rafael, and he could not have been in both places at once.[43]

Father Quijas did have a problem with alcohol, and the issue began to surface in 1836. Bancroft noted, "All testify to his drunkenness, and his fondness for dancing and debauchery," but the historian tempered his remarks by adding that Quijas was a "large, fine looking man,…kindhearted and popular when sober" and who had no "enemies."[44]

THE PROMISE OF SECULARIZATION

In 1833, the Mexican government decided that it would no longer be responsible for managing and maintaining the far-flung mission system. Instead, the missions would be "secularized." The government wanted to open California for colonization, and it was also interested in ending the system of fiefdoms in which the missionary priests had ultimate authority and the neophytes had few if any rights. Instead, the government decreed, each mission would become a local church, part of a *pueblo,* a town or civil municipality that was not subject to priestly authority. The priests would no longer control the vast mission estates with their herds of cattle, sheep, and horses; and a portion of the mission lands, the stock, and the mission assets would be distributed to the neophytes.

Many military personnel also anticipated receiving grants of mission land for their years of service. For years, the military had strongly resented the priests for their wealth at a time when there was little or no money to pay soldiers; with secularization, they expected their grievances to be redressed in the form of land grants.

Moreover, the troops and their commanders were also looking forward to escaping the control of the priests, each of whom, according to Vallejo, exercised "beneath his cowl the civil, ecclesiastical and military authority, [since] the troops...were subject to his orders." Vallejo gave voice to the resentments of both soldiers and Indians in his history of California, commenting that the padres "possessed the keys to the public conscience and to the treasure chests which held the public wealth," and that "the missions acquired great wealth, but the unhappy neophytes got little benefit of it."[45]

On the heels of the 1833 law requiring secularization came a decree supporting colonization, with promises of mission land, livestock, and tools for potential Mexican settlers as well as money for transportation from the rest of Mexico to California. But among the old Californios, feelings against this plan ran high. They suspected two agents of the settlers, José María Híjar and J. M. Padrés, of deliberately plotting to seize the California government as well as taking all the mission lands for themselves.[46] Bancroft could not find proof of these allegations, however, and it is certainly possible that the old-time Californios criticized the colonization plans because they themselves wanted to control the dispersing of land and mission resources.

Plans for the Indians

Governor Figueroa's *reglamento* (rules and regulations) of 1834 spelled out the new duties and restrictions under secularization: an inventory of each mission's goods and assets would be conducted; mission lands would be surveyed; boundaries of each pueblo would be established. A parcel of mission land at least 100 but not exceeding 400 square *varas* (roughly, a minimum of 1.8 acres to a maximum of 28.8 acres)[47] would be distributed to each neophyte "head of family and to all over 20 years old" (presumably restricted to males), along with half the mission livestock and no more than half the tools and seed. The women's dormitories were to be "abolished at once, [and] the girls and boys are to be given to their parents, to whom their parental duties are to be explained." Although selected neophytes were to be emancipated, they did not attain complete freedom from mission control: "those emancipated" were "obliged" to work when "necessary for the cultivation of the vineyards, gardens and fields," and they had to "render to the padre the necessary personal service." The nineteenth-century historian Theodore Hittell interpreted this as "a sort of qualified tutelage," now coming under secular rather than priestly control.[48] This granting of greater freedom was not a new idea; when the missions were founded, it had been argued that the Indians could live on their own after they were "civilized." Overall, the initial period of secularization, with its promise of land and property for Indians, seemed to be an exciting and hopeful time for the Native American community.

Secularization at San Rafael and Sonoma

In October 1834, Ignacio Martínez, the secular administrator assigned to San Rafael, took "alcalde Marino" with him to survey the lands of the San Rafael mission, as required by the recent government decrees. Marino would have been particularly helpful in confirming the location of Anamas, the Huimen village said to be his birthplace, which marked the southern boundary of the mission lands. Other Coast Miwok participating in the survey were Jacome, the alcalde from Olompali; Camilo, the ranch foreman, *"el caporal,"* from Olompali; and Tiberio, the vaquero from Bolinas. Gregorio Briones, a former soldier stationed at San Francisco, accompanied this group in his new role as the mayordomo.[49]

At San Rafael, secularization seemed to proceed flawlessly, with the inventory completed in September 1834, the boundaries of the pueblo of San Rafael determined by Ignacio Martínez and Marino the following month, and stock given to the Indians in December. The animals were distributed to 343 Indian men (heads of households and those older than twenty), who received 1,291 sheep and 439 horses from the mission stock.[50] Strangely, the distribution of the available 2,000 head of cattle is not mentioned.[51] The cattle may have been held back in order to pay off the mission debts of $3,448, before half of the herd was given to the Indians. But less noble motives—such as making loans or sales to friends who were settling nearby, or setting aside personal gifts for the administrator or for Vallejo in Sonoma—may also have been in play.

In comparison to San Rafael, the San Francisco de Soláno mission at Sonoma had a greater Indian population: 996 Indians were associated with the mission in 1832. The livestock holdings available to be distributed were also greater: in 1833, they included 4,849 cattle, 1,148 horses, and 7,114 sheep.[52] The steps toward secularization were completed in 1836, when the Indians were given some property and were released to return to their rancherias.

Because of conflicts with other Indians on the periphery of the Christian Indian settlements, however, the property was returned to Vallejo for "safe keeping," although it is not clear how voluntary this transfer might have been. Bancroft, impressed with Vallejo's skill at handling colonists, Indian problems on the frontier, the Indian chief Solano, and the militia stationed at Sonoma, nevertheless commented that this meticulous keeper of records had little to say and provided few papers concerning what happened to the property of the Indians: "Vallejo had many difficulties to contend with...and the credit due him is not impaired by the fact that the development of his own wealth was a leading incentive."[53]

The Coast Miwok Receive Land at Nicasio

In 1835, a group of neophytes petitioned the governor for a part of the former San Rafael mission land known as Nicasio. The petition was signed by Teodorico, Sebastian, Juan Evangelista, Luis Gonzaga, and Luis Antolin—all of whom, except Teodorico, may have come from that area originally and may have been living and working there as stockmen.[54] Teodorico had neither family nor marriage ties to this part of the Coast Miwok lands; he was likely chosen to head the list of petitioners because of his political sophistication, his ability to read and write Spanish,[55] his many years of dealing with the authorities, and his respected reputation among the clergy. In later years, Sebastian referred to himself as Sebastiano and claimed to be the capitán of Nicasio. María Copa remembered him from Echatamal and described him as having been a cook at the mission.[56]

Sebastian and Juan Evangelista carried the petition to Monterey, where Governor Figueroa gave the two men the necessary papers for the land. They took the papers back to Vallejo, who then gave them to Teodorico. Figueroa's notification to Vallejo read: "You will notify the referenced neophytes that the government...grants the... rancho Nicasio to the claimants....You must be careful...that nobody interrupts or obstructs the peaceful possession of these lands."[57] On the bottom of the page, Vallejo wrote that he had carried out these instructions.

The administrator of San Rafael, Ignacio Martínez, and his father-in-law, Captain William Richardson, determined that the boundaries of the Nicasio land were twenty leagues, enclosing approximately eighty thousand acres. Even this large block of land was but a pathetic substitute for what the Indians had had before the priests and soldiers arrived to set up the mission at San Rafael eighteen years earlier.

Guequistabal, a Tamal Indian who was baptized as Nicasio at Mission Dolores in 1802, is no doubt the namesake of this piece of land.[58] The San Rafael mission records mention him as an alcalde. His mother lived with him away from the mission, which suggests that he was taking care of livestock, perhaps near the town that now bears his name.

Other prominent alcaldes, including Marino, did not petition for land. We do not know how many Coast Miwok returned to their tribal rancherias without attempting to apply for an official grant from the governor. More and more neophytes began to leave the missions; the Indian population at San Rafael fell from 365 in 1838 to approximately 195 in 1839.[59] Many former neophytes probably resumed a nomadic lifestyle, with seasonal stays at favorite bayside locations adjacent to major streams and periodic visits to the mission. Others remained at the mission, and still others, who settled at nearby locations such as San Pedro Point, were frequent visitors.

The settler Charles Lauff listed specific locations, most of them in or near San

Rafael, where Indians were living in 1836 after they left the missions. Although Lauff's locations may be accurate, he was not in California during much of the 1830s, and he cited unrealistic population figures for each location. He claimed that five hundred Indians were "camping in the lower part of San Rafael at Bay View and Taylor Street. Another five hundred were located in the Coleman Addition," near today's Dominican University in San Rafael, and "another tribe lived in the willows on the lot bound by Tamalpais Avenue, Mission Street, Grand Avenue and Fourth Street. A few hundred were located at San Quentin Point and at McNear's Point" in eastern San Rafael. The rest, he asserted, settled in Miller Valley (Miller Creek) and Nicasio Valley.[60]

Broken Promises

What seemed, on paper, to be a reasonable plan for California's missions—a secular political structure containing a parish church, an inventory of goods at the mission, a survey of mission lands, determination of pueblo boundaries, the payment of debts, and the distribution of livestock to the neophytes—quickly spun out of control as the avarice of those who were supposed to help the Indians deprived them of their rights and property. Administrators and priests at various missions around California ordered the slaughter of cattle, with the proceeds from hides and tallow going to the well-placed individuals who sold them and not to the Indians. This also meant that fewer animals were available to the neophytes, despite the governor's order. Animals were "loaned" to friends and relatives, but administrators were reluctant to hold accountable the men who did so, and cattle and horses were never returned to the mission for distribution to the rightful owners, the Indians. In later years, Vallejo tried to explain why property disappeared from the missions: "No one was ever able to account for what became of the great wealth which the reverend mission fathers had turned over to be distributed among the Indians." He turned on his childhood companion Juan Bautista Alvarado, the former governor, blaming him in part for choosing and tolerating unethical administrators: "It was in his power to remove them and he did not."[61]

The first warnings of trouble in San Rafael and Sonoma arose in October 1835, when Vallejo wrote to the governor that he was ready to take back the property (in this case, the tools and animals) that he had distributed to the Indians; he argued that they had "limited ability to enjoy liberty and property."[62] He did not act until 1837, however, when he collected the property, according to Bancroft, with the "promise of redistribution when circumstances should be more favorable."[63] Thus, while Marino was still alive, there were clear indications that the Coast Miwok would have to fight or maneuver politically to retrieve the material goods and land that had been promised them.[64]

Vallejo admitted:

I cannot hide the fact that the Indians did not receive at our hands the treatment they deserved, for their property was, to a certain extent, wasted and devoted to uses very different from those to which it should have been applied. In defense of the authorities, however...; after I had made a trial at San Rafael and San Francisco Soláno ex-missions where in a few short days after having received land and herds, the Indians had been stripped of all the property which had been distributed among them, it was not considered prudent to put them in possession of the property...for there was plenty of reason to believe they would make bad use of everything turned over to them.[65]

Vallejo put the onus on Alvarado, noting that the governor had ordered that "distribution of property be suspended, and...[that] neophytes should resume their communal residence" at the missions, although exceptions were made for industrious Indians.[66] How many Coast Miwok, if any, from Nicasio were affected by this order is not known; it was directed primarily at those who were living in larger towns such as Santa Barbara.

Essentially blaming the priests for the Indians' lack of willpower, given that the individuals raised at the mission "had no will of their own," Vallejo wrote that the Indians "gave themselves over blindly to the vice of drunkenness and stripped themselves of their property for much less than its value." Philip Edwards, an American visitor in 1837, claimed that the Indians at San Rafael "were so extravagant that it is thought they will soon have...[no possessions] unless taken from them [and preserved for them,] as has been done at other missions."[67]

Neither Vallejo nor Edwards was an impartial observer, however. The person who would have benefited most from taking the Indians' livestock was Vallejo himself, who probably wanted the cattle and sheep for his own rancho. Edwards had come to northern California specifically to help purchase cattle for the Willamette Cattle Company of Oregon, and he had a lot at stake in promoting the sale of cattle formerly held by the missions. His group was eventually successful in persuading Vallejo and Alvarado to sell them seven hundred head of cattle for three dollars a head. It is most unlikely that the profits from the sale were ever passed on to the Indians.

The success of secularization depended on radically changing the culture of California. In spite of good intentions, however, it allowed those with larceny in their hearts to become rich on the spoils of the missions while stealing from the Indians. Writing in the 1880s, Bancroft judged that "failure was a foregone conclusion" and "inevitable."[68]

In 1836, Vallejo was named commandante general for the northern area, and from then on, he was referred to as General Vallejo, although the highest official rank he ever held was that of colonel. His first major confrontation with Indians on the northern frontier occurred in June 1834. While on a fourteen-day trip to Sonoma to establish a pueblo there on the orders of Governor Figueroa, he encountered both hostile and friendly Indians.

Vallejo and his men were traveling by boat, while horses were sent overland from San Rafael to meet him. Off Novato Point, in Omiomi territory (a Coast Miwok group), his two schooners with eighty cavalrymen aboard ran aground in mud. Observing his predicament, Indians came as close as they could on shore and shot arrows at the ships. Failing to inflict any damage from that range, they waded out into the water and either became mired in the mud or tried to swim to the ships. When Vallejo's crewmen fired on them, they dropped their bows and arrows, ducking under the water at times to escape detection. Approximately fifteen Indians died in this encounter.[69]

On this same trip, Vallejo described meeting several Indian groups, including the northern Coast Miwok of the Licatiut and Sonoma tribes, as well as the Pomo and Patwin tribes, all of whom received him cordially. His gifts of blankets, tobacco, and glass beads to the chiefs helped to ensure their acceptance of his presence. Vallejo claimed that at one point almost eleven thousand Indians gathered near Sonoma to welcome him, including three thousand warriors under two Indian chiefs. This may have been the first contact between Vallejo and Solano, a Patwin chief, baptized at San Francisco,[70] who urged the assembled throng to join him in supporting Vallejo so that together they could conquer the Satiyomis, a Wappo tribe. Vallejo came to greatly admire Solano, and they relied on each other for support.

This large pan-Indian group was joined by two hundred Coast Miwok neo-phytes, accompanied by five soldiers who arrived with horses for Vallejo from San Rafael,[70] and five hundred Licatiut, led by the soldier Rafael Garcia. Vallejo's esti-mate of the number of Licatiut is puzzling, however; of those who had been bap-tized at northern California missions, only twenty Licatiut males older than twelve survived in 1834, including the spouses of Licatiut women. Vallejo may well have used the term "Licatiut" to identify all Coast Miwok except those at San Rafael. Although estimates place the total Coast Miwok population at about five thousand at the time of contact with Europeans,[71] by 1834 the majority of those who had entered the mission had died of diseases, which they had spread to their nonmission friends and family when they ran away or returned to their homes. Moreover, no archaeological evidence supports as high a population figure as Vallejo suggests.

Vallejo may have exaggerated the numbers of the large pan-Indian group who joined under his leadership, in order to draw attention to his courage in being surrounded by such a large number of "untamed" Indians. He compared his successful reception by the local population with the negative experience of the two priests at the San Francisco de Soláno mission, who "very seldom left their church, since they were extremely fearful about going out into the surrounding country…because of their fear that the Indians would attack them."[72]

Marino was active in the San Rafael mission community at the time of Vallejo's trip; the mission records show that he was a godparent at a baptism on June 21. It is highly probable that Marino either accompanied Garcia and the "Licatiuts" or was with the group who brought the horses from the mission. When Vallejo named the northern county after Marino in 1850, he identified him as "the great chief" of the Licatiuts and other tribes, but Vallejo also said that Toribio was the captain of the Licatiuts. If Marino had been with a Licatiut group on this trip, it may have reinforced Vallejo's idea that Marino belonged to and led the Licatiuts.

Chief Solano

Vallejo supported his new friend Chief Solano by joining him in an attack on the Yolos west of Sacramento in 1835. Charles Brown, an American from New York, accompanied them and later described an expedition led by General Vallejo in 1835,[73] which included Vallejo's brother Salvador. This trip lasted three rain-filled weeks as they traveled two hundred miles north of Sonoma. The expedition is significant because it illustrates cooperation between a major military figure and a powerful Indian chief against an unnamed Indian enemy—as well as Vallejo's tolerance of Solano's vicious treatment of his innocent victims.

The eighty-two-man expedition included Californios, Mexicans, twenty-two foreigners, Chief Solano, and two hundred Indian auxiliaries. Brown justified the attack as retribution for the plundering of livestock. In this case, and others that followed it, however, it is never clear that vengeance was directed at the rancheria responsible for the alleged crime. Here, the expeditionary forces attacked an Indian rancheria in the middle of an unidentified valley; although the attack lasted only an hour and a half, the Indians lost between two and three hundred people after having "fought desperately." Brown observed Solano killing a pregnant woman with a child: he "first lanced the child on her back and then kneed the woman, ripping the belly open and pulling the fetus out." Enraged, the American was prevented from killing Solano by Vallejo, who told him that Solano "was his best friend."[74] Ironically, Solano had an opportunity later in this same raid to save Brown's life.

The expedition returned with sixty to sixty-five captured "bucks" as well as women and children. The prisoners were divided among different rancho owners, and the young women were placed in the women's dormitory at the Sonoma mission. Brown's reward for participating was sixty-five beaver pelts that had been found at the rancheria. This was the first documented example in northern California of what would become a pattern in white/Indian interactions: raiding Indian settlements, capturing male laborers for the rancho owners, murdering others, stealing valuable goods, forcibly removing women to the mission, and selling children into servitude.

Vallejo did not approve of all of Solano's actions. When he later heard that Solano had kidnapped and sold thirty Indian children, he had the Indian chief jailed. The children were found and returned. Vallejo blamed the incident on his enemies, who, he alleged, had served alcohol to Indian chiefs.[75]

Attacks by the Californios

The arrogance of some Californios toward the Indians was evident in yet another kidnapping. This crime was committed by a nineteen-year-old rancher, Victor Castro, and his brother, Antonio, who went to the Santa Rosa area in 1836, confiscated property (probably cattle, sheep, horses, or plows) from the Indians there, and bought children from some of the chiefs, intending to force them to work on the Castro rancho at San Pablo in the East Bay. Vallejo responded swiftly to Indian complaints: he had the Castro brothers arrested in San Rafael and made sure that the children were returned to their families. In spite of their brief detentions, however, Antonio Castro continued to prey on the Indians (see Chapter 12), and Victor Castro remained politically prominent enough to be given a land grant to Mare Island four years later.[76]

INDIAN LEADERS DURING THE LAST DAYS OF THE MISSION

At the San Rafael mission, the leaders of the Coast Miwok—the capitáns of rancherias, the alcaldes, the surveyors, the signers of petitions to redress wrongs—all continued to participate in the sacraments of the church, getting married, having children, acting as marriage witnesses, and serving as godparents. Some were returning to the mission for these events; others had never left. Whether all of those at the mission willingly chose to reside there is not clear, however. Two of those who signed the petition to remove Molina—Jorge and Pasqual—had their children baptized in

1837; and after Jorge was widowed, he remarried at the mission. Teodorico, one of the petitioners for land at Nicasio, had his child baptized in 1835.[77]

Marino played an active role in the last years at San Rafael as a godparent and a marriage witness.[78] From 1833 to 1836, his name was usually listed first among witnesses at weddings. In the mission records, Father Mercado and Father Quijas seemed to use the names Marino and Marin interchangeably. There is little doubt that both names refer to the same person, because they are both associated with Juana. In the last entry, when he was listed as a godparent in August 1836, Marino was identified as "Marin grande,"[79] perhaps to distinguish him from a younger Marino, his namesake and godson. In 1832, this younger Marino, then eighteen years old, was referred to as a page, or an assistant to the priest.

Teodorico also appears in the records as a witness both at the San Francisco de Soláno mission in 1834 and at San Rafael beginning in late 1835. A third witness often associated with the names of both Marino and Teodorico, and a newer member of the Coast Miwok leadership, was Elzeario, Maria Copa's grandfather. His name is spelled various ways in the mission record;[80] the anthropologist Isabel Kelly heard it as "El Siario." Although Elzeario lived a hundred years before Copa shared her family's oral history with Kelly, she nevertheless recounted numerous facts about him that have been verified in the mission records, a reminder of how important and enduring oral history can be, especially in the absence of a written record. For example, Amorós described Elzeario in the 1829 mission records as a musician and a carpenter;[81] Maria Copa, not aware of the content of the records, told Kelly that her maternal grandfather, El Siario, had played the violin for mass. Copa also provided intimate details about her grandfather that were not included in the dull mission accounts: he washed and ironed the priest's clothes, for example; and he once ran away from the mission, returning because "every time he tried to take a drink of water he heard something hissing. It frightened him so that he went back to the mission."[82]

In the years after 1832, Marino, Teodorico, and Elzeario were leaders in a number of spheres: political, religious, and social. As such, they were highly visible within the Indian community and took advantage of the positions of leadership that were still available to neophytes. Nereo, also part of the Indian power structure in earlier years at San Rafael, acted as an assistant to the team that surveyed Juan Reed's land in November 1835. And just as Marino became Marin, Nereo became Neri in the records.[83]

Another contemporary of Marino was Camilo, a witness only twice during the last years of the mission, but a man whose name is better known to posterity than Marino's because he received a grant from the governor for the land of Olompali and became a friend of both Vallejo and the Patwin chief Solano.[84] Olompali was a common eating and resting stopover for travelers on their way from San Rafael north to Colony Ross or to the Sonoma mission.

Camilo was not identified with Olompali until 1831, at the time of his second marriage. Born in 1803, he was some twenty years younger than Marino but knew him well; Camilo's baptism, at age sixteen, occurred in January 1819, at a time when Marino was active in mission affairs. Camilo's parents came from villages on the lower Petaluma River associated with Olompali.[85] When Marino returned to the San Rafael mission in the 1830s, Jacome was the alcalde at Olompali, and Camilo was working there; all three surveyed the mission land together.

Shortly after the widowed Camilo married his second wife, a southern Pomo woman named Candida, she was kidnapped by the Cainameros, a southern Pomo group, and died with them in March of 1835. Four months later Camilo married Cayetana.[86] This was an important marriage for both of them; Camilo's status was likely assured because his new wife was the widow of the previous Olompali alcalde, and his wife's half-brothers were the well-known Teodorico and the deceased alcalde José María. Their father's Indian name was Quilajuque, and his stature was significant enough that Teodorico was known as Teodorico Quilajuque and Father Quijas entered Cayetana's name as Cayetana Quilajuque in her marriage record.[87]

By 1839, Camilo was clearly the headman at Olompali.[88] This was not a hereditary post, and neither he nor his father was mentioned in any mission records as a capitán, chief, or alcalde. Camilo and his wives Candida and Cayetana seldom participated in mission activities as godparents, perhaps because they were rarely at San Rafael, residing instead at Olompali, where Camilo was busy looking after the mission herd (see Chapter 12).

Teodorico and Elzeario must have been living near the mission, however, because they continued to act as witnesses at weddings until the last marriage at the mission, which took place in February 1839. For some reason, Marino was no longer participating in mission affairs after 1836; he may have been sick or living farther away, but apparently he was at or near the mission at the time of his death.

11

THE OWL BRINGS BAD NEWS:
DEATHS AT SAN RAFAEL

In many Indian cultures, the owl presages death. The Miwok of the Tuolumne River foothills, for example, believed that when the great horned owl hooted, it meant "that someone is dying. [The owl] is himself the Ghosts of dead people." If Maria Copa's grandmother saw an owl, she talked to it, saying, "Don't follow me; don't follow me....Take your bad news somewhere else." For Copa herself, owls were not the only harbingers of disaster: if two blackbirds ("smaller than crows") were observed flying and calling together, they were "bringing bad news. Maybe somebody was going to die."[1]

In the mission death records, the priests noted the name of the deceased and that person's closest kin, but these accounts did not record the names of those who participated in mourning ceremonies and did not describe the acts of mourning that would have preceded and followed the final disposition of the body in the mission cemetery. If a priest arrived in time, a dying person received the sacraments, which included penance (confession), extreme unction (anointing the body with oil), and, less frequently, the Eucharist (communion). Those neophytes who died away from the mission were noted in the death records only if someone told the priest about the death.

Old-timers at San Rafael, many of whom had come from the San Francisco or San Jose mission, were well aware of the signs of numerous diseases, and they recognized the symptoms that preceded death. But they did not avoid their sick relatives; instead, observers were impressed with the concern and support that native Californians gave to their kin. In 1826, Frederick William Beechey noted "the very great care taken of all who are affected with any disease....When any of their relations are indisposed, the greatest attention is paid to their wants, and it was remarked by Padre Arroyo [at Mission San Juan Bautista] that filial affection is stronger in these tribes than in any civilized nation on the globe with which he was acquainted."[2]

Traditions such as cutting hair, not speaking the name of the dead, crying, and wailing were usually part of commemorating the deceased. The first notice a priest might have had that one of the neophytes had passed away was the sound of keening (public wailing) in the mission village. A Pomo woman described her childhood experience of an old man's death: "A person died and my mother was crying. And I was scared. I sure hate to see my mother cry. That was my mother's relation...that old man who died.... Never heard her cry before. And my aunt started to cry too, and all the women crying. Women cry, but hardly men cry. They have the tears but not so loud."[3]

There were dangers associated with the dead, including the suspicion that the deceased person might have been harmed by the stealthy actions of others who were still alive nearby. According to Copa, even if you were not mourning, it was important to keep quiet to show your respect, so that one of the mourners would not come and poison you.[4]

The priest's involvement with the deceased probably ended with the last toss of soil over the body and the entry in the death records, but the Indian survivors continued to concern themselves with the whereabouts of the spirit of the dead. Such spirits could return and scare them by reappearing unexpectedly. Tom Smith told of a frightening nighttime experience when a deceased woman, his brother-in-law's sister, "came down through the ceiling. She had a fine dress, with abalone shells attached so that they make a noise when she walked"; the ghost ordered Smith to tell her brother not to remarry. Copa told of ghosts who asked for food and clothing; when they requested food, it was gathered the next day and burned for the ghost.[5] A narrative collected by C. Hart Merriam and attributed to the Coast Miwok of Nicasio and Tomales speaks of the movement of this spirit:

> When a person dies his Wal'-le or Ghost goes to Hel'wah, the West, crossing the great ocean to Oo-ta-yo'-me, the Village of the Dead. In making this long journey it follows hinnan mooka, the path of the Wind. Sometimes Ghosts come back and dance in the roundhouse; sometimes people hear them dancing inside but never see them.[6]

Although Father Amorós rarely mentioned the cause of death in the mission records, the priests who followed him did record such information when it was known. The most commonly reported cause of death among the neophytes was syphilis, followed by chest infections (including cough, tuberculosis, and pneumonia) and old age. Other deaths at the San Rafael mission were described as the result of fever, craziness, stomachache, wounds, pustules, being attacked by a bear, or being "kicked by a horse."[7]

THE DEATH OF JUANA

Marino's wife, Juana, was forty-three years old when she died in September 1836,[8] but the changes that occurred during her lifetime were so dramatic that it might have seemed as if she had lived for a hundred years. Born in 1792, probably in or near Olompali, she grew up in a village untouched by the mission system, where she practiced the ways of her parents and grandparents. She was fully acculturated as a Coast Miwok woman when, at age twenty-four, she joined others from her village in resettling at Mission Dolores. While in San Francisco, she married Marino and gave birth to a baby boy, who died five days later, perhaps from a European disease. She then accompanied Marino to the asistencia at San Rafael, where she played an even more prominent role than her husband as a godparent.

Juana was with Marino for most of their married life; the evidence suggests that she moved with him frequently, since her name is not found in the mission records for any year in which Marino's name is missing. They were also together in San Francisco and San Mateo after 1825. Every mention of Juana in the mission accounts includes the phrase "wife of Marino" or, later, "wife of Marin." Her last years were spent with him at the San Rafael mission. During her lifetime, she was doubtless exposed to all the diseases and illnesses that were endemic to the mission, yet she survived, perhaps because as a married woman she spent so little time in the women's dormitory, which was a breeding place for European diseases.

We do not know what caused her death. She may have been ill for a while, because her last role as a godmother was at a baptism in June 1834, more than two years before she died.

Maria Copa remembered Juana as "Juanita" and claimed that she ran off once with Marino's brother but returned. This event, part of the oral history of Copa's family, illustrates that even headmen or chiefs were not without marital problems, but that they could expect others to help out if necessary:

> Marino had a wife called Juanita. She was a great big fat woman with no children. He had no other wife. Once Marino's brother was playing with his brother's wife and she went off with him. They [Marino's brother and Juanita] had been with other people getting dry chamise to burn in the sweathouse. They went to the hills and used to meet there. But this time they ran away.[9]

Copa's words in Isabel Kelly's original field notes indicate that Marino was very much in charge: "Marino ordered the people to get them. He brought them home. He had man [his brother] punished. After that everything was quiet. They went together again. It's okay if you don't run away."[10]

Copa's oral history helps to put a human face on at least one Indian woman. In the mission records, it was rare for a priest to mention a woman other than to note her duties at the mission. Unfortunately, then, it is impossible to tell what kind of role Juana may have played in the community other than as a godmother.

After September 1836, Marino's name does not appear in the mission records. He was a wedding witness six days after Juana died, but that is the last time his name was listed as a participant in mission affairs. We cannot determine whether he left the mission or whether he simply lost his motivation for fulfilling mission duties. But it seems safe to speculate that Juana's death dealt him a psychological blow.

THE EPIDEMIC OF 1838

In the spring of 1838, a devastating smallpox epidemic hit the Indians of central California. Spreading from Colony Ross, it took its toll, according to Sherburne F. Cook, particularly in valleys north and east of today's Marin County. He estimated a thousand dead in the Sonoma and Russian River valleys, and a thousand more in the Clear Lake area and on the western side of the Sacramento Valley, areas occupied by northern Coast Miwok, Lake Miwok, Pomo, Wappo, and Wintun tribes.[11]

Oddly, however, the San Rafael mission records list only forty-five deaths during that year.[12] Of these, thirty died of smallpox, all at the peak of the epidemic in May and June; the rest succumbed to syphilis, old age, pneumonia, tuberculosis, skin disease, indigestion, chest infection, or fever.[13] But Father Quijas's entries are almost certainly incomplete. For example, there are no deaths recorded among the Indians at Nicasio, and other deaths may have gone unreported when people were too sick to summon the priest. In addition, Quijas was apparently at San Francisco de Soláno in Sonoma during July and August and thus did not record deaths at San Rafael for those months. Horrifying contemporary accounts describe rancherias in the Sacramento Valley decimated by the smallpox epidemic; had this been the case at rancherias in Marin and southern Sonoma, there would have been no one left to report to the priest.

The only other account of deaths from smallpox in the San Rafael area is found in the reminiscences of Charles Lauff, reported in *The Independent of San Rafael* in 1916, when he was ninety-four years old. Lauff was not in the area during the epidemic, however, and his numbers are most likely inflated. He told of "over 1200

Indians dying at San Rafael alone" and claimed that priests had to "dig trenches" for five hundred dead at the foot of B Street, three hundred at the Nicasio rancheria, and two hundred in the Miller Creek area. But this masterful storyteller also said that he had been in Sausalito "at the time when I heard that the Indians had contracted smallpox"—although he did not arrive in the Bay Area until 1844. Further, the priest he names as being involved in the burials, Father Amorós (which he spelled Amoroso), had died in 1832, six years before the epidemic. Most compelling, none of the mission records suggests that the Indian population was ever as high as his figures imply, even at its peak in the 1820s.[14]

THE DEATH OF MARINO

Marino survived the smallpox epidemic as he had survived many other diseases over the years. His last days came two and a half years after Juana's death, in March 1839. We do not know whether anyone in the Indian community heard the mournful hooting of the great horned owl or saw two blackbirds flying and calling together, but at this time of year, birds such as the orange-crowned and Wilson's warblers were returning from the south and beginning to usher in spring with their distinctive songs that presaged sun and warmth. The hillside above the mission would have been green and covered with colorful wildflowers for the first time after months of rain, and the hillside springs would have been flowing as they still do today. If it was a warm and calm March, the butterflies, perhaps the appropriately named mourning cloak, would have been out as well.

Marino died of an ulcer or abscess (apostema). Father Quijas was near enough in Marino's last hour to give him the sacraments, typically penance and extreme unction. When Quijas was in a hurry, he usually noted the administration of these sacraments in a form of shorthand in the record books as "P and E." In Marino's case, however, he wrote out the complete phrases and included a note that a third sacrament, the Eucharist, had been performed—the only occasion on which Quijas so honored and recognized a Native American.[15] We know, then, that Marino was physically able to receive communion before his death, and he might even have requested it; he had actively participated in church activities after returning to San Rafael in 1832 and may have considered receiving the sacrament his due. According to Alvarado, when Marino was a prisoner at the presidio years earlier, he had told a priest that "if the priest would not bother him while he was alive he would give him permission to make a Christian of this dead body."[16]

We do not know who mourned Marino's death or whether his godchildren or Juana's relatives were nearby, but once they heard of his death, they must have come to mourn him in the old ways. Smith related that when a hoipu died, "they danced six days as a goodbye to him";[17] such a ceremony, if allowed by Quijas, would have been a deserved tribute to Marino's leadership. Given his status, his reputation, and his accomplishments, the mourning and crying among those still living in the Indian settlement at the mission would have been loudly demonstrative and widespread, even if some had experienced friction with him during his lifetime. Six years earlier, Marino had taken the lead in stopping the brutal whipping of Indians and in ridding the mission of Father Mercado's hated mayordomo. In his last years, at age fifty-eight, no longer the brash young man who had defied the military and been imprisoned for his defiance, he had discovered ways to help his fellow Coast Miwok by working within the system. Respected at the time of his death as an elder, Marino must have been admired for his courage and conviction.

During nighttime storytelling, youngsters, parents, and grandparents may have gathered to hear stories of Marino: his life in Anamas before he went to Mission Dolores, his adventures and mishaps on the bay in his tule boat, his experience on the Columbia expedition, and his escape to the islands off of San Rafael. We do not know whether he was an orator in the hoipu tradition, but there is evidence that he was a spokesperson and a storyteller—witness both his place as the first man in the group who complained to Vallejo about Molina and his irreverent treatment of the priest at the San Francisco presidio, with his comparison of buggy horses and saddle horses (see Chapter 8).

Marino's grave was dug by fellow neophytes, and he was laid to rest in the mission cemetery adjacent to Amorós's 1824 church, along with Juana, José María, and other neophytes; thus the church continued to cast its shadow on Marino in death as in life. In 1885, the marked graves of Amorós and American settlers were moved to Mount Olivet Cemetery; the unmarked graves, those of the Indians, were left where they were.[18]

This intelligent and multifaceted man had both defied and acquiesced to the demands of the mission system and the military. This complexity does not make him less Indian or less noble, but it certainly helped to ensure his survival, as he adapted to the inevitable power of the cross and the sword. Why did the priests accept Marino back into the mission community in 1816 and 1833? Perhaps it was priestly compassion, but more likely it was the clergy's need of his gifts: leadership ability, intelligence, navigational and maritime skills, knowledge of Spanish, and the respect he received from other Indians and the military. It was also to the priests' advantage to have the known troublemakers visible at all times and working within the system rather than hidden and fomenting trouble from the outside.

By the same token, why did the Indians agree to return? Leaders no doubt had certain privileges; in Marino's case, he could ply the waters of the bay with some independence. His activities, even as a godparent and marriage witness, provided visual evidence that he was a leader in the community. Moreover, by being at the mission, he was able to maintain his ties with tribal members and participate in their shared religious and ceremonial traditions. His presence at the mission thus became an act of spiritual and cultural survival.

12

THE LAST DAYS OF MEXICAN CALIFORNIA

The Coast Miwok could turn to only a few authorities for advice and support after secularization: Father Quijas, General Vallejo, and the secular administrators who were assigned to San Rafael. Quijas was not dependable because he also officiated at the Sonoma church and thus was away for weeks at a time; in addition, he was not always sober. The new administrators were more reliable but could not act independently of Vallejo, who kept a sharp eye on events at San Rafael, although his residence was in Sonoma. When Vallejo was named commandante general for northern California, San Rafael came under his official jurisdiction.

When the United States later took over California, Vallejo was clearly the most politically astute Californio and a force to be reckoned with. Although he was imprisoned for more than six weeks by a small American force in 1846, he carefully sized up the political situation and became one of the earliest advocates for aligning California with the United States rather than with France or England. This turned out to be a propitious move, which boosted his personal fortunes and prestige. It was as a Mexican citizen prior to the American takeover, however, that Vallejo was at his most imperious, openly disagreeing with the governor, appropriating what he wanted, befriending the Indians with one hand and taking away with the other, jailing those who disagreed with him, and even decreeing a death sentence for one Indian without evidence or a trial.[1] At that time, he was indisputably the most powerful man in northern California.

HARTNELL AND ALVARADO CHALLENGE VALLEJO

In 1839 and 1840, it became evident that Vallejo could be as prickly as Father Mercado had been when his authority was questioned. Mercado was long gone, but

Vallejo was about to have his authority questioned by two men he had known since childhood: Governor Juan Bautista Alvarado, Vallejo's nephew and boyhood companion, who had been raised in the home of Vallejo's parents;[2] and W. E. P. Hartnell, the former teacher of both Vallejo and Alvarado. Vallejo had worked for Hartnell in Monterey as a clerk and bookkeeper when he was fifteen.

In 1839, Governor Alvarado, concerned about his lack of control over the former missions and about the general mismanagement of mission property, decided to send Hartnell to examine the status of all mission Indians, to inspect the lands and property (stock, supplies, vines) in mission holdings, and to remind local civil administrators of the limits of their power. His *reglamento* of 1839, which tried to protect the cattle herds for the Indians and prevent the administrators from using mission cattle for their own ends, decreed that the administrators "shall not...slaughter any cattle beyond what is necessary for the maintenance of the Indians" and that salaries "must not be paid in livestock." Hartnell was to "regulate the weekly and annual slaughter of cattle in such a manner that the livestock may not decrease."[3]

Hartnell first visited San Rafael in September 1839. Despite the ink blots and torn pages that mar his diary and conceal some of the figures he recorded for San Rafael, it is clear that he accounted for 438 horses; the numbers for cattle and sheep are missing. In addition, his inventory found twenty-six yoke of oxen, three mules, cow and deer hides, an ample supply of wheat, and lesser amounts of beans and peas—in short, it was a well-provisioned community.[4]

Since Hartnell arrived in San Rafael only six months after Marino's death, the conditions at the mission must have been similar to those Marino had experienced during his last years. According to his diary, Hartnell spoke to at least 190 Indians, former neophytes. They gave him an earful of bitter complaints about their lack of freedom and their lack of success in retrieving their property and land. They also pointed out that the clothing they had been promised had not been forthcoming, and they expressed their outrage at the kidnapping of two young boys.[5]

Their freedom indeed remained limited. Governor Figueroa's 1834 reglamento listing the duties of the neophytes at the mission was apparently still in force. Vallejo, for example, gave Talio, the capitán of Tomales, a pass in January 1838 that allowed Talio and his followers to stop at San Rafael only on the condition that some Indians had to return to the mission every eight days to perform unspecified duties at the church.[6] Hartnell's instructions from Alvarado included an admonishment to the administrators to "treat the Indians kindly, inflict but moderate punishments and see that they attend faithfully to their religious duties."[7]

Indian Land Disappears

At San Rafael, some Coast Miwok also complained that "there was not much land left."[8] The men with whom Hartnell spoke were particularly concerned about areas of mission lands that they needed for their planting, mentioning specifically the cañadas (valleys) of San Anselmo, San Geronimo, and Las Gallinas; the arroyo de San Jose (Ignacio Valley); and Point San Pedro. These were all areas on which non-Indian squatters were grazing their stock, believing that they would soon receive land grants from the governor. This period of transition from church to civil control of mission property was still fluid; the Coast Miwok were not only correct in their fears of losing their land, but wise to complain to Hartnell, since neither the governor, nor Vallejo, nor the priest, nor the administrator of the mission seemed to be able to stop the encroaching settlers.

By the time Hartnell conducted his inspection at San Rafael, much of the non-Nicasio land had in fact been effectively granted to others. (Appendix J, Map V) Unbeknownst to the Coast Miwok, Domingo Sais had already been to Monterey to ask the governor for the San Anselmo land; he eventually received title to the 6,600-acre rancho named Cañada de Herrera.[9] As for the cañada of San Geronimo, Rafael Cacho, a friend of Vallejo, freely ran cattle and horses there from at least 1839, receiving a grant for the land in 1844. East of the Nicasio property was the area known as San Jose (today's Pacheco and Ignacio valleys), occupied by another former soldier from San Rafael, Ignacio Pacheco, and granted to him in 1840.

South of Cañada de Herrera, the rest of San Anselmo went to Vallejo's brother-in-law Juan B. R. Cooper, who received a grant for Punta de Quintín in 1843, land that consisted of the San Quentin peninsula, plus a portion of San Anselmo and the areas that became Ross, Kentfield, and Greenbrae. The first settlement was established there in 1840.[10] No squatters had yet claimed Point San Pedro, another piece of land requested by the Indians, but Timothy Murphy, the administrator at San Rafael, had his eye on it and received a grant in 1844 entitling him to San Pedro and the contiguous ranchos of Las Gallinas and Santa Margarita. Thus squatters and non-Indian landowners became bona fide grantees and surrounded the Nicasio Indians.

While Hartnell was examining the mission and Murphy's accounts, he had an opportunity to meet Camilo, apparently now the headman at Olompali, whom he described as "the best Indian in San Rafael" and "very hardworking."[11] Camilo was upset about non-Indians encroaching on Olompali, which he considered his own land. He complained that the sons of Juan Miranda, a soldier from the San Francisco presidio, were building a corral on this property. Although he pleaded through

Hartnell for title to the land, Camilo waited until 1843 before applying for and receiving the 8,878 acres at Olompali from Governor Manuel Micheltorena.

Hartnell Returns in May 1840

Hartnell's second visit to San Rafael, in May 1840, did not go smoothly. He was there to enforce Alvarado's new reglamento, which attempted to reduce mission expenses, to tie the Indians more firmly to the priest and the parish church by requiring them to perform unspecified duties, and to give the priest a hand in disbursing goods to the Indians. This reglamento replaced the civil administrator with an official chosen by Alvarado, who was to "make the Indians work for the community [that is, the former mission] and chastise them moderately for faults,...to enforce morality and attendance on religious duties,...to see that the padres lack nothing needed for their personal subsistence, [and]...to attend to the proper distribution of goods among the Indians, the padres approving the lists."[12]

But Vallejo claimed that he had written to the governor to argue that San Rafael was "already a pueblo and not a mission...and that the Indians should not be disturbed in the peaceful possession of their ranchos and property."[13] Vallejo disagreed not only with Alvarado's order but also with Hartnell's authority to carry it out.

The greatest conflict seemed to be between Alvarado and Vallejo, with each man believing that the other was treading on his turf. Hartnell, caught in the middle, spoke to the Indians, explaining that the governor was not aware of Vallejo's promises to them. But the Indians were not passive in this exchange: they forcefully complained to Hartnell about the governor's orders, telling him that they did not want to remain at the mission, that they had been "deceived too many times," that their land had been taken from them, and that they wanted their freedom and the return of their goods. When asked whom they would obey, Vallejo or the governor, the Coast Miwok were concerned not to offend either man; Hartnell described the Indians as between "the sword and the wall." He decided to leave things as they were, lest his actions cause an "uprising."[14]

Hartnell may have believed that his duties were finished when he left San Rafael with his report and headed back to San Francisco. To his surprise, however, Vallejo had his former teacher arrested upon his arrival in San Francisco. According to Hartnell, he was literally pushed into a boat that carried him back to San Rafael. Vallejo felt that he was within his rights: he was the commandante general of northern California, and he had previously given orders that no one was allowed to go to San Rafael without his permission—a prohibition that included even a representative of the governor. Hartnell was freed the next day after an interview with Vallejo, in which he acquiesced to the general's demands. The two agreed that the neophytes would be freed and that, after paying off the debts of the mission and setting aside a fund for the priest and church, the Indians should also have their possessions *(bienes).*[15]

Vallejo's position was that all the rules and regulations of the reglamento had already been carried out and the mission closed, making Hartnell's presence in San Rafael unnecessary. His touchiness at the idea of Hartnell checking up on him may have simply been irritation at the questioning of his authority, but perhaps he also did not want to be questioned about the whereabouts of the livestock or the vines from the mission vineyard.

It took Vallejo five months, but eventually he kept his promise to the Coast Miwok by ordering Murphy to return three cows and a horse to each Indian (probably each adult male).[16] This allotment no doubt paled in comparison to the Indians' rightful portion of the vast herd of mission cattle and horses that had been available in 1834 before Vallejo took possession of much of the stock for "safe keeping" and before Murphy helped himself to part of the herd in the 1840s. In his annual report for 1840, Quijas reported that on October 26 Vallejo had dismissed all the Indians from the mission, "allowing them to go wherever they wanted, therefore the mission is left with only my servants....The rest have gone to various ranches, some to the *gentilidad* [non-Christian Indians]...and others [to a location that is undecipherable]."[17]

Although the Coast Miwok welcomed even this meager recompense of stolen property, their major concern was the land that had provided their tribal identity and linked them with their ancestors. The governor's latest reglamento did not address the issue of land, however, and vast tracts of land were fast going to Vallejo's relatives and friends. His mother-in-law eventually received a generous 8,800 acres, but this was a small amount compared to Vallejo's own 66,000 acres at Petaluma and Sonoma or the total of 100,000 acres that went to his five brothers-in-law in separate grants.

VALLEJO IMPRISONS QUIJAS AND MURPHY

Hartnell was not the only one to be jailed at San Rafael in 1840. Vallejo again flaunted his authority when he jailed both Father Quijas and Timothy Murphy, the San Rafael administrator, for going to Fort Ross to obtain liquor. When Vallejo sent five soldiers to pick up the two men, they tried to bribe the soldiers so that they would not be taken to Sonoma.[18] It is not clear whether Vallejo objected to the alcohol itself, to acquiring it from the Russian enemy, or to these men leaving their posts. Apparently, the relationship between Vallejo and Quijas had been a little testy for some time, and on one occasion, Quijas had publicly pointed his finger at

Vallejo during mass at the Sonoma mission because the general would not permit the collection of tithes. After Vallejo ordered the priest to his office, however, Quijas rescinded his objection.[19]

According to an irritated Vallejo, the priests were living an easy life after secularization, enjoying gifts of fresh fruit from the Indians and cash from the parishioners for performing baptisms, marriages, and burials. He commented that the priests "always managed to get together enough money to secure for themselves good clothing and excellent food." Singling out Quijas for particular scorn, Vallejo noted that "Padre Quijas, who administered one of the poorest communities of the entire Territory, earned enough to take a weekly trip to Ross or Bodega to purchase an assortment of foreign liquors, which were openly consumed within the sacred precincts of his badly administered parish."[20] Yet Quijas, in his 1840 annual report, complained that for the celebration of mass he had not been given "even half a penny....I had to pay for everything."[21]

A year later, in 1841, the American H. A. Peirce experienced firsthand an out-of-control Father Quijas when both were guests at John Reed's adobe home in Mill Valley. Arriving in the company of the homeowner, Peirce saw a "person dressed in the coarse, grey habit of a Dominican priest. He was very drunk and embraced each of us in the affectionate manner of Spanish people." Reed found his wife hiding in the woods, where she had fled to "avoid the insults and beastly conduct that the priest had exhibited to her, just prior to our arrival." Reed attempted to quiet Quijas, who was raving like a "madman," accusing the family of not showing him respect. The priest then suddenly lunged at his host with a penknife, hitting Reed's thumb. At that point, struck with remorse, Quijas asked Reed to punish him by stabbing him in the heart with the same knife. Somehow Reed managed to calm the priest down sufficiently to allow dinner to be served, but Quijas, a native of Ecuador, proceeded to rail against the Spanish people, the governments of Mexico and California, and the secularization of the missions.[22]

THE STATE OF THE MISSIONS

While the church affairs at San Rafael seemed to be in disarray, there was a concomitant breakdown in the physical structures at the mission. After secularization, little effort was made to maintain the buildings, and in a very short time they had begun to deteriorate. Col. Philip L. Edwards, visiting in 1837, described the mission as "poor and decaying. The buildings, though spacious, are very rude and inconvenient." In 1840 and again in 1841, Quijas wrote that the church itself was in need of repair, that it was in danger of falling down, and that he had removed items from the church because objects were being stolen.[23] In 1841, H. A. Peirce, looking for food and a place to spend the night, turned to San Rafael in spite of a warning from John Reed that "San Rafael was famous for its fleas." Peirce did not mention the fleas, but he chose not to spend the night there because he found the accommodations "disappointing and disgusting," noting that the mission buildings were both "dilapidated and forbidding."[24]

The physical and social collapse of the missions was not confined to San Rafael. At the San Jose mission, Hartnell appointed José María Amador as administrator, probably in 1840, but Governor Alvarado soon dismissed Amador, who had objected to turning over $1,300 "belonging to the community to defray the expenses of a grand ball which the Governor had given at Monterey." Before his dismissal, Amador inventoried the mission's livestock holdings, which were extensive: sixteen thousand head of cattle, thirty thousand sheep, and five to six hundred mares. Later, Amador described how it had all been removed in just two years, accusing Joaquin Castro and José Estrada of carrying off the mission's possessions to San Pablo [Castro's rancho], including "even the shelves of the storehouse. Of the livestock nothing remained....Mission stills and earthenware jars in which fat were rendered out may be found this very day [1877] at San Pablo."[25] At the Soledad mission, even Governor Alvarado helped himself to cattle and roof tiles from the mission for use at his home, giving what was left over to a friend.

At San Rafael, Vallejo and Murphy, the very people responsible for protecting the mission property for the Indians, were depleting the mission of its goods and supplies. An official French visitor, Eugene Duflot du Mofras, reported that in 1841 Vallejo had removed "two thousand feet of vines" and "confiscated livestock" from the San Rafael mission for his rancho at Petaluma.[26] The use of the word "confiscated" indicates that he appreciated the import of Vallejo's action. In the same year, the visitor Sir George Simpson stayed with Murphy and later described Murphy's cattle as the "spoils of the church."[27]

COAST MIWOK SETTLEMENTS

In spite of the deterioration of the San Rafael mission buildings, Indians were still living nearby in adobe houses on the east side of the mission as well as near the area that is known today as Courthouse Square. For example, Lauff claimed to have observed nearly a hundred Indians attending mass at the mission church sometime in the late 1840s.[28]

Leading families continued to participate in church ceremonies, but we do not know whether they were living nearby or traveled some distance to bring their babies for baptism. Teodorico and Micaelina, Elzeario and Escolastica, Camilo and Cayetana, and Pasqual and Isabel all had babies baptized at the parish church and acted as godparents during the 1840s. Maria Copa's grandparents, Elzeario and Escolastica, had four of their children, including Copa's mother, baptized at the parish church between 1840 and 1858.[29]

Although baptisms appear to have been meticulously recorded in the 1840s and beyond, the death records are a different matter. For a time, Father Quijas, who remained at San Rafael and Sonoma until 1843, when he was transferred to San Jose, was as precise as ever, even including causes of death. But deaths were no longer recorded after May 1841, and recordkeeping was not resumed until the years from 1850 to 1854, when only a few notes were made. Unfortunately, the marriage records are completely missing, perhaps destroyed when the Americans billeted at the mission for a few days in 1846 and burned valuable papers.

Workers at Richardson's Rancho

In addition to the Indians who lived at or near the mission after secularization, there were scattered small settlements in areas that became Marin and southern Sonoma counties, as well as larger enclaves in Nicasio, Marshall, Bodega, Bodega Bay, and around Petaluma. One post-mission Indian settlement was at Captain William Richardson's rancho, which encompassed Sausalito and much of Mill Valley, the result of an 1838 land grant.

In 1837, Richardson had employed twenty Indians from Sonoma while building his house in San Francisco. When he moved to Sausalito in 1841, he continued this practice. Settling first in "old Sausalito," near Whaler's Cove, he next moved to a large adobe on what became Pine Street, between Bonita and Caledonia, near a large Indian mound. Whether his Indian workers lived there, where generations had preceded them, or at another location nearby is unknown.

In Sausalito, Richardson employed at least eight Indian boatmen, who piloted ships through the Golden Gate. Each incoming ship reportedly sounded a two-gun salute as it approached the headlands.[30] One of these workers, the Indian Monico, stood six feet tall and was described by Richardson's son, Stephen, as "an able seaman, the peer of the best who ever manned a ship. He knew the name and use of every appurtenance of a sizeable ship, a brigantine for instance. He possessed the primitive instinct that forecasts storms and recognizes a meaning in the portents of the weather invisible to cultured man." In 1841, Monico and Richardson helped to rescue José Yves Limantour, whose ship went aground on the spit later named after him on the Point Reyes peninsula.[31]

Monico was famous for his explanation of how the San Francisco Bay formed. According to his native oral tradition, water had not flowed to the sea through the

Golden Gate in the past. Instead, a mountain range towered there, and the river waters emptied into the ocean at Monterey via the Santa Clara Valley. But, as a result of a catastrophic event, an opening occurred where the Golden Gate is today, and the bay began to empty there instead of at Monterey.[32]

Richardson's children praised the helpfulness and ability of the Indians with whom they had contact. His daughter said that the women "did excellent work with the needle, all the bed clothing being done by hand, all the sheets and pillow slips [and]...table linen. [They] took good care of children, and were fine cooks and very trustworthy."[33] Richardson's son believed that the Indians had been misjudged. He wrote that his father, who died in 1856,

> maintained an Indian refuge at Sausalito for as long as he lived. The remnant so protected was large enough to have formed the nucleus for a rehabilitated race. But one strange factor concerning these people marked their future— doubtless a shock due to inhuman persecution—they cease to breed, a tragic instance of race suicide—of a race whose wrongs were so great that the inherent wish to perpetuate the species perished.[34]

Camilo's Olompali

Although an unknown number of Coast Miwok may have continued living at Olompali, the impression conveyed in his original land grant in 1843 is that Olompali was specifically Camilo's home, not the home of a band of Olompali-associated Indians: the grant from Governor Micheltorena states that it was for "his own benefit and that of his family." A traveler in the early 1840s observed that an Indian chief north of San Rafael, no doubt at Olompali, was "assisted by some of this tribe," indicating that some vaqueros or cooks probably helped with duties at the rancho, which included tending livestock and seeing to the needs of guests such as Vallejo and the Patwin Indian chief Solano, who, according to Maria Copa's mother and grandmother, came to visit Olompali with his forty wives.[35]

Camilo continued to be respected by non-Indians, who called him a chief. One American said: "I knew this chief, who was a fine, intelligent and shrewd man....He owned 600 cattle, numerous horses and sheep, and was quite a noted breeder. He was punctual in meeting his obligations, and owing to this and to his affability and intelligence, was highly esteemed by us all."[36] A visitor in the early 1840s, G. M. W. Sandels, and an early settler, W. H. Davis, also referred to Camilo as a chief. During the U.S. Land Commission trials in the 1850s, however, the Californios referred to him as Camilo, José Camilo, or Citizen Camilo, but not as a captain or chief.[37]

The Petaluma Adobe

East of Petaluma, the Petaluma adobe housed some six hundred Indians who worked for Vallejo, sixty of them Coast Miwok,[38] including members of Maria Copa's family. Her paternal grandfather was a Mexican soldier who had been a captain under Vallejo and had married a Solano Indian woman. When he deserted with the Indian soldiers under his command, he was cornered, and the military offered him a choice: surrender or death. Copa said that when he chose death, he and his troops were killed and their bodies were "piled...like wood and burned."[39]

Copa also told of Calistra, her great-aunt on her father's side, who worked for Vallejo's wife. Calistra was punished severely after Vallejo learned that she had provided a file that allowed her husband, accused of murder, to file through his shackles and escape from custody: "They got the poor old woman, and tied her to a cannon wheel and whipped her. Her back was all cut up." When she was young, Copa's mother had piqued Vallejo's interest, but she successfully avoided him. "The old people always said, 'Why does this old fellow always look for [young] girls? He might do something to them.' Twice he came, looking for my mother, but he did not find her." Others lied to Vallejo to conceal the young girl from him.[40]

MARAUDERS AND RAIDERS

The late 1830s ushered in many years of depredations against Native Americans, first carried out by soldiers and Californios, sometimes with Indian accomplices, and later continued by American settlers even before California became a state. These bands of marauders—composed of settlers, owners of large ranches, soldiers transferred from the San Francisco presidio to Sonoma, former military men, sons of soldiers who had served at the presidio, members of the militia formed after secularization, and Indians of often unknown tribal affiliation—terrorized peaceful Indian settlements, launching raids to seize cattle and horses and to ransack the rancherias, taking captives for forced labor on ranches, and murdering as they went.

Before secularization, both runaway neophytes and nonmission Indians had sometimes raided ranches for cattle and horses, which had irritated the rancho owners. But now some of these bands of marauders used purported cattle and horse rustling as an excuse for ransacking Indian rancherias and inflicting brutality on Indian communities. The American Charles Brown, who had accompanied the two Vallejo brothers on a raid in 1835 (see Chapter 10), wrote that he continued to go on small raids as late as 1848. Their alleged purpose was to pursue Indians "who had stolen and run off stock, which happened very often....On such occasions a few Indians were killed."[41]

In the East Bay, Indians stole a hundred "head of stock" in 1837 from José María Amador's rancho in San Ramon. Retaliation by Amador and his men was delayed but deadly. The Californios initially retrieved sixty head of stock, but lost the animals to "200 Indians" who attacked in the early hours of the morning. When the Indians were caught almost a month later, they were taken prisoner, forcibly baptized, and then shot in the back. Not all Californios accepted this cruelty, however: one of General Vallejo's brothers, José de Jesús Vallejo, complained about Amador's actions.[42]

In 1839, the non-Indian alcalde/administrator at San Jose told a posse sent out to recapture stock stolen by Indians "to exterminate all male thieves from 10 years up and to capture all women and children." Even the Mexican governor, Pio Pico, permitted the killing of Indians for stock rustling. In one case in 1845, he not only offered a group led by two Americans a reward of five hundred head of cattle and half the spoils, but he also agreed that "resisting" Indians should be killed and that captured women and children should be put in the hands of the government.[43]

In the North Bay, according to most accounts by the settlers and the military, the Indians were pursued for capture rather than murder, because the rancho owners needed men to work as laborers. The goal may have been different, but the outcome was the same: murder, rape, and enslavement.[44]

Revere's Raid

Joseph Warren Revere, a San Geronimo rancho owner and the grandson of Boston's Paul Revere, described one raid on an Indian rancheria, which took place sometime between 1846 and 1849, as something of a lark. He reported that the Indians who participated in the raid were men "who enter into the spirit of these *razzias* with great zest, and take keen delight in entrapping their wild relatives." The raiding party consisted of five rancho owners, including Rafael Garcia, accompanied by five to ten Indian vaqueros from each rancho, led by Garcia's mayordomo. The rancho owners used their annoyance over alleged horse rustling by local Indians as an excuse for the raid, but their aim was to capture Indians, to "keep them as hostages, and to use them, meanwhile, as laborers."[45]

The raiders rode north for two days, arriving first at an Indian village where a friend of one of the rancho owners lived. The intruders sought to trade various goods for hostages, but the Indians there were not interested in giving up the freedom of people from their own village, even when enticed with "many-colored beads, great needles, awls, mirrors and knives."[46]

As the raiders scouted around for another rancheria to attack, they foolishly left behind their fifty horses, guarded by only three men. Indians from a different rancheria spotted the horses and drove them to their village, where the raiders eventually discovered them. Now with a good excuse for a battle, the raiding party attacked the rancheria, capturing numerous Indians and retrieving all but one horse (which had been eaten by the kidnappers).

In keeping with the tone of his account, which almost seems to portray schoolboys on an outing, Revere never mentioned any dead or wounded Indians, even after describing the sabers, lances, and firepower inflicted on the villagers. The spoils of the battle were the captured Indian men and women, who, Revere rationalized, had been "legitimately acquired according to the notions prevalent at that time in California" and who submitted "resignedly and even joyfully to their fate."[47] The hostages claimed by Revere were assigned to manufacture adobe bricks on his rancho. Eventually, they were dismissed, with shirts and blankets; two of the young men elected to stay at his rancho.

Attack by Castro and Garcia

One raid in the summer of 1845 was so outrageous and sordid that it resulted in charges being brought before a judge at Sonoma. The twelve marauders were led by Antonio Castro, who had previously been in trouble with the authorities for purchasing Indian children (whom he was forced to return); and Rafael Garcia, who was a former soldier from the San Rafael mission, a recipient of a land grant in Bolinas, and a participant in the Revere raid.[48]

When the raiders returned, they divided the captured Indian families among themselves, but not before a "fistfight, because Antonio Castro did not want to distribute the groups of Indians they had caught." One young Indian woman went to Luis Leecs; one family was assigned to the Bodega rancho of Victor Prudon, Vallejo's secretary; twelve or thirteen Indian families went to Garcia's rancho; and the remaining 150 prepared to leave for Antonio Castro's rancho in Contra Costa.[49] But before this last group set out, the non-Indian alcalde at Sonoma, Cayetano Juarez, apprehended Antonio Castro with his captives and ordered him to report to the judge at Sonoma.

The court testimony described the brutal assaults on the Indians that had occurred between July 29 and August 3, 1845. The first witness, José María Treviño, explained that Antonio Castro had promised him a change of clothes if he could direct Rafael Garcia to certain Indian villages. Garcia ordered an attack on the first quiet rancheria and took Indian captives by force. At a second rancheria, frustrated at finding only the two capitáns, Garcia tied up one of them and beat him with the butt of his rifle, while Castro struck the other capitán with a spade. After tying their captives' heads together and threatening them, Garcia and Castro let them go on the condition that they return with their villagers. The Indian leaders of course disappeared. Outside another village, Mariano Castro killed an Indian who was trying to defend a woman who was being kidnapped. Another Castro brother, Siberiano, killed an old man and wounded another in a different village.

The marauders then headed toward the home of caretaker William Benitz at Fort Ross. (This settlement had by now been vacated by the Russians because the decimation of both otters and fur seals had made it unprofitable.) Benitz was not at home that day, but seven of the raiders gang-raped at least two women there. The rapists were Rafael Garcia, Antonio Castro, Manuel Sais, Nazario Sais, Sebero Alviso, Mariano Elizaldi, and an unnamed Indian vaquero, whom Antonio Castro tried to exclude from the rape by saying, "Get out of here, you are an Indian, and are not to 'take' with the gente de razon." The marauders also ransacked Benitz's house and took his belongings. Benitz complained to Timothy Murphy that the raiding party had broken into his house, "abused the Indians which I kept in charge, and have nearly killed the chief. They have stolen a number of things from me and plundered the Indian village. The Saises [a large family, recipients of land grants in the San Anselmo area] have threatened to shoot me, I am afraid to leave this place to come and see you."[50]

There was no record of formal sentencing after the trial, so we do not know whether these men were exonerated or punished. A few months later, however, during the fall of 1845, Rafael Garcia was doing his Christian duty at the church in San Rafael, serving as a godparent to five children and one young woman, all Indians who were probably part of his spoils in the raid.

Raid at Clear Lake

Another disastrous raid occurred the same month in 1845, in Lake Miwok territory at Clear Lake. Salvador Vallejo, one of General Vallejo's brothers, left Sonoma with a troop of soldiers and Indians, looking for laborers. On an island in Clear Lake, Indian men were killed as they tried to swim away, while others were forced into the sweathouse at their rancheria and then burned.[51] Sandels reported seeing the raiders return to Sonoma, led by the "blood thirsty" Salvador Vallejo:

> These barbarous incursions into the Indian territory are often made from mere wantonness, or result from the Indians being cheated out of their lands or the reward of their labor. As consequence, they retaliated by stealing cattle; never, as far as I could learn, by committing murder. Advantage is taken of these misunderstandings by the Californians, who, joining with the military forces, scour the country, committing every cruelty that can be imagined.

Whenever a ranch requires laborers, you hear of some Indian outrage, followed by the taking of prisoners by the Californians.[52]

THE U.S. FLAG RAISED IN THE BAY AREA

In June 1846, José Castro, the new military chief of California, ordered another dispersal of San Rafael mission property to the former neophytes, although he reserved "a few horses" for the defense of the country[53] and approximately two hundred for himself. The Indians never saw these horses again. At the same time, a short but intense period of unrest commenced, as American settlers seized horses meant for the Mexican militia, formed themselves into a loose group, and, in what came to be known as the Bear Flag revolt, arrested Vallejo and those with him at Sonoma, including Salvador Vallejo, Victor Prudon, and Jacob Leese. The prisoners were sent to Sutter's Fort, where they were held for more than six weeks. This reversal of fortune for the powerful Vallejo family happened with astonishing rapidity and was a blow to Vallejo's plans of rapprochement with the Americans.

Other misfortunes for the Californios followed in quick succession. American Bear Flaggers led by Lt. Henry L. Ford rousted a group of Californio militiamen who had reconnoitered at Olompali. Then Lt. John C. Fremont, believing incorrectly that the Californio militia had fled to the San Rafael mission, stormed that empty establishment and garrisoned his troops there. (During this brief occupation, the military destroyed many of the priceless historical documents stored at the mission.) Fremont ordered Stephen Richardson to deliver horses to these Americans at San Rafael the next day, where Richardson witnessed the senseless slayings of three Californios.[54] In short order, Commodore J. D. Sloat of the U.S. Navy arrived in California from Mexico and ordered the American flag to be raised at Monterey. By the middle of July, it was flying over Sausalito, Bodega, San Rafael, and San Francisco.

The following spring, in a disturbing portent of things to come, U.S. General S. W. Kearny asked Timothy Murphy to send an inventory of San Rafael's "horses, mares and cattle and other public property" to the assistant quartermaster at San Francisco,[55] making it obvious that potential Indian property was now "public property." Under the new administration, it began to appear that whatever had been left for the Coast Miwok at San Rafael was going to be appropriated by the Americans.

The Mexican period of California came to a close in January 1847, although the United States did not finally win its war with Mexico until 1848. Two years later, in 1850, California was accepted into the Union as a state. The Coast Miwok at Olompali and Nicasio soon realized that the once all-powerful Californios had lost to another group of white men speaking a different language. The church, the military, and the rancho owners were replaced by a new group of outsiders who could question and even decide the ownership of large tracts of land that had been granted to the Indians and Californios under the Mexican government. The puzzling changes of land ownership during these last years of Mexican California and the first years of the state of California are exemplified in the convoluted way the Coast Miwok lost their land at Nicasio.

13

THE COAST MIWOK
LOSE THEIR NICASIO LAND

Between 1835 and 1855, the group of Coast Miwok Indians at Nicasio lost and regained their twenty leagues of land many times over. This group, led by Teodorico, Sebastian, Juan Evangelista, and others had received the original grant for Nicasio from Governor José Figueroa in 1835 (see Chapter 10). But they soon lost control to a series of Californios, among them General Vallejo, Governor Alvarado, and Secretary of State Casarín (Manuel) Jimeno, who either separately or together manipulated the configuration of the Nicasio land to their liking, shrinking or expanding its size at their whim. These powerful men alternated between supporting the legitimate Indian grant for Nicasio and acting as if it had never existed. This betrayal by civil and military leaders who had gone out of their way to blame the priests for the problems faced by the Indians caused the Coast Miwok to suffer one of their most crushing losses: their land. Throughout all the maneuvering and confrontations that occurred, no one of influence was acting solely on the Indians' behalf.

THE COAST MIWOK APPEAL TO GOVERNOR ALVARADO

In August 1839, just five months after Marino's death, the Indians at Nicasio became concerned that they might lose their land. Squatters were settling all around them, and a succession of Mexican governors had granted large tracts of land to various individuals: to a retired military officer in Point Reyes, to Rafael Garcia in Bolinas, and to the Mexican colonist Fernando Feliz in Novato. (See Chapter 10 and Appendix J, Map V) Despite all its promises, secularization was proving to be a quagmire for the Indians. The governor's reglamentos had attempted to limit their freedom, and Vallejo had withheld or retaken the livestock and tools to which they were entitled. Now the Coast Miwok were demoralized by the new threat of losing the land that they had only recently secured for themselves and their descendants. How could their claim to the land be at risk, particularly when it had been verified by the highest authority, the Mexican governor, in 1835?

Fortified by the belief that Mexican law was on their side, the Coast Miwok wrote to the new governor, Juan Bautista Alvarado, on August 1, 1839, requesting assurances that the Nicasio land was theirs.[1] Their letter to Alvarado stated that "certain persons[2] say that we are going to be dispossessed....We pray your excellency to take into consideration that we are poor and have large families, so that you may be pleased to help and protect us." It continued by reminding Alvarado that his predecessor, Governor Figueroa, had "granted us the land at Nicasio" and that these lands "were reserved for us." Alvarado's response to their letter on August 18 acknowledged that the Indians were "in actual possession of the land therein mentioned and granted by my predecessor [Figueroa]" and assured the petitioners that they could rely on the protection of the government. It suggested that, if need be, they could apply to the military commander of the northern area, Vallejo, for help "until a plan can be prepared for said lands."[3] A copy of Figueroa's order to Vallejo was attached.

The worrisome phrase "until a plan can be prepared" hints that Alvarado might have already been preparing a loophole in order to avoid giving all the land to the Indians. Asking the Coast Miwok to turn to Vallejo for help would have been reasonable if they had trusted Vallejo, but they most likely did not. After all, he had decided in 1837 that the Indians' possessions could be confiscated for "safe keeping" and redistributed only "when circumstances [were] more favorable." So instead of feeling mollified by the governor's response, the Coast Miwok, led by Teodorico, "stormed into San Rafael and threatened to lay siege to the pueblo," according to Jack Mason.[4] Small wonder that the Indians were in no mood to compromise a month later when W. E. P. Hartnell, by order of Governor Alvarado, came to San Rafael to inspect the progress at the mission (see Chapter 12).

VALLEJO STEPS IN

In October 1841, Vallejo seemingly overstepped his authority and gave the Indians at Nicasio a square league of land called Tinicasia, within their original grant, at the southern end of Nicasio Valley. This strange move might suggest that Vallejo knew or suspected that the larger grant was not viable and was trying to secure at a minimum the land where the Indians had built their homes. It was also an example of Vallejo asserting his control in northern California, since the legal power to grant land was nominally in the hands of the governor.[5]

Two years later, in November 1843, under a new administration, the status of the large Nicasio rancho came into question when two non-Indians, Pablo de la Guerra and Vallejo's brother-in-law Juan Cooper, applied to Governor Micheltorena for sixteen of the twenty leagues of Nicasio. Secretary of State Jimeno wrote to Father Quijas in November, asking him about the status of the land. Rather than reminding Jimeno that it had been granted to the Indians, Quijas responded a month later that "Nicasio is the only [mission] land left and is used for stock."[6] The priest's failure to support the Indians at a time when it could have made a difference was a blow.

Then, acting quickly, on December 27 Vallejo sent a request to Governor Micheltorena asking that the Nicasio land be given to the Indians. Juan Evangelista and Sebastian, two of the five original Coast Miwok claimants to Nicasio, personally delivered Vallejo's letter to Monterey, where the governor resided.

But the commandante general's seemingly generous gesture on behalf of the Indians was in reality a stab in the back. Instead of requesting the original twenty leagues of land for the Indians, Vallejo asked for only eight leagues—and he did not refer to the original Figueroa grant to substantiate his case. It is likely that Juan Evangelista and Sebastian were unaware of the contents of this letter.

Vallejo's letter explained that the Indians

> applied to me yesterday, demanding of me that the departmental government should grant to them the tract of land [known as] Nicasio whereon they at present have their property which is not less than 800 head of cattle and as many horses....Their object is to establish there a pueblo that all the Indians who were formally in San Rafael live reunited. There is a large number of families which do not number less than 500 persons,...the greater proportion of them are industrious and very laboreous [sic]....[I want to] remind you that Nicasio is not vacant and that no one has more right to a grant of it than its natural owners, particularly when they have occupied and are very laborious....I believe it will be convenient to grant them 8 leagues for their pueblo and stock raising, or more if you deem it proper, because the land known as Nicasio is very extensive....It is six or seven years that I promised to give them ownership of it, but the government then looked with disconfidence [sic] upon everything that was done in the frontier.[7]

Vallejo was trying with a single stroke to satisfy two incompatible constituencies. On the one hand, he could present himself as a friend of the Indians by requesting eight of the twenty leagues for them; on the other hand, he could please his relatives, friends, and other Californios by trying to free up the twelve remaining leagues for them. This latter group included one of Vallejo's brothers, another brother-in-law, and Vallejo's secretary, who had submitted their own petition for land, which had been denied.[8]

But the land was not available. As early as February, the governor had issued "a decree in favor of" the application of de la Guerra and Cooper. Then, in August, ten leagues had been formally granted to de la Guerra and six to Cooper, "leaving the overplus to the benefit of the natives of San Rafael."[9]

The convoluted chain of events did not end here, however. On October 14, 1844, without approval from the governor, Vallejo tried to gain the upper hand by once more giving the Nicasio lands to the Indians.[10] This time, he based his authority on the original 1835 order of Governor Figueroa, which his previous letter had ignored, and he did not mention any dimensions of the rancho. He must have known that the land had already been granted to de la Guerra and Cooper, but he seemed to be testing the waters, hoping that his military authority as well as his physical presence would outweigh any decisions made in Monterey. What he hoped to gain by this maneuver did not become clear until the next day.

ALVARADO BUYS THE NICASIO LAND

In a surprising move the following day, October 15, 1844, Alvarado "bought" twenty square leagues of the Nicasio land from the original five Coast Miwok applicants of 1835, with a promise to pay them one thousand dollars, much less than the land was worth. And who would be responsible for the payment? Mariano Vallejo, who only the day before had granted the Nicasio land to the Indians. Although the terms of the purchase allowed the Indians to retain both grazing and cultivation rights on the land and offered them payment "in a manner that they will prefer," Alvarado also insisted that they pass their title to Nicasio to him and pay any legal expenses that he might incur in defending his title against the claims of all others.[11] We do not know what arguments were used to convince the Coast Miwok to part with their land; William Richardson's son Stephen hinted that they had been plied with alcohol.[12] We can only assume that this deal, which flagrantly disregarded their rights, was presented as their only chance to remain on their land. Furthermore, there is no evidence that the Coast Miwok received either money or goods from this disreputable deal.

Alvarado of course knew that Governor Micheltorena had already deeded sixteen leagues of the Nicasio grant to non-Indians, but this was his end run. He also surely knew that lawsuits would follow, but, according to the terms of the deal, the Coast Miwok, the victims of this maneuver, would be forced to pay his legal expenses.

We do not know when Alvarado and Vallejo decided to join forces, in what was probably a marriage of convenience for both of them. The papers describing this sale of Nicasio were witnessed by one of Vallejo's brothers-in-law, the alcalde Jacob Leese, and signed by the five original Indian claimants and the same three individuals whose application had been denied earlier: one of Vallejo's brothers, another brother-in-law, and Vallejo's secretary, implicating all of them in the land grab.[13]

On October 19, Alvarado's sale documents were sent to Governor Micheltorena, who passed them on to Secretary of State Jimeno for clarification. In November, Jimeno reminded the governor that he (the governor) had already granted a total of sixteen leagues to de la Guerra (Jimeno's brother-in-law) and to Cooper, leaving the remaining four leagues "to the benefit of the Indians of San Rafael." Jimeno suggested that Alvarado could buy Nicasio from the "legitimate owners." Fairly bristling with irritation, he referred to Vallejo's "impudence" and labeled as fraudulent Vallejo's claim that the land had been granted to the Indians: "The vending Indians do not present, nor have they at any time had, sufficient instrument of title to enable them to sell their land....There never was a grant of any kind, but only a mere offer of [Vallejo's] own."[14] But if Jimeno was correct, why had Alvarado reassured the Indians in 1839 that Nicasio had been granted to them by Governor Figueroa?[15]

Meanwhile, Alvarado acted as if he owned the land, grazing his cattle on the Nicasio rancho and hiring one of the Castro brothers to tend them. Later, when de la Guerra, the other putative owner, came to survey the land, Castro chased him away. Castro promptly appealed to Timothy Murphy, the legal authority at San Rafael, who supported Castro and told de la Guerra that the land belonged to Alvarado. Nevertheless, by 1850, de la Guerra had begun trying to sell off his portion of the land.[16]

U.S. LAND COMMISSION INVESTIGATES LAND CLAIMS

The conflicting land claims were eventually settled during the 1850s by an American commission that saw land as part of the spoils of war. The treaty concluding the war between the United States and Mexico specified that the land grants made by the Mexican government should be respected, but this principle was ignored in practice. As the nineteenth-century Missouri Senator Thomas Hart Benson described it, the Act to Ascertain and Settle Land Claims in California, which created the U.S. Land Commission, became in effect the "Act to Despoil Owners of Land Under Mexican Grants."[17]

Many Mexican ranch owners opted to sell their land rather than participate in lengthy and expensive court procedures that they might eventually lose. This was the route taken by Camilo, whose Mexican land grant was, ironically, one of the few accepted by the U.S. Land Commission. Camilo sold the bulk of his property in 1852 to the Marin County assessor, James Black, keeping only 1,480 acres, one-sixth of his original holdings.

During the Land Commission meetings, the Coast Miwok had a slight hope of recovering some of their land—perhaps the tiny parcel of Tinicasia, which had been granted by Vallejo, or at least permission to graze stock and cultivate the soil at Nicasio under the "sale" agreement the five Coast Miwok leaders had made with Alvarado. The best evidence supporting Coast Miwok rights at Nicasio would have been the original 1835 grant from Figueroa.

Decision on Tinicasia

Regarding the one league of Tinicasia, Timothy Murphy filed a brief on the Indians' behalf in 1852. Murphy argued that Vallejo had granted the land in 1841 to sixty Indians who lived there, "until certain persons without valid title…tried to dispossess them of their land and drive away their cattle." But the Land Commission judged the case to be "without merit" and rejected the claim, finding "no proof of any of the statements…in the…petition."[18]

Decision on Nicasio

The second hearing on Nicasio land dealt with Alvarado's claim to all twenty leagues of Nicasio. Although the land had supposedly been "sold" to Alvarado, this was an extremely important case for the Indians. If the commission upheld Alvarado's claim, the Coast Miwok would be allowed to continue cultivation and grazing of stock on what was, in reality, their own land.

Unfortunately, the U.S. Land Commission could not address the more important issue of whether the land should revert back to the Coast Miwok. Rather, it was charged only with establishing whether Alvarado had a right to it. The rumor that the Indians had been plied with alcohol before the sale to Alvarado was not part of the commission's investigative responsibility. In any case, no Coast Miwok had the clout or the money to pursue that avenue for their lost land. The only person who could have helped them was Vallejo, but his power had been greatly diminished since the American takeover, even though he served as a senator in the first California state legislature.

Key to Alvarado's case was the paperwork that could have verified Figueroa's 1835 grant to the Indians. Numerous Californios testified in support of Alvarado's claim to all twenty leagues of Nicasio—testimony that was in effect verifying that the land had belonged to the Coast Miwok. But in spite of the additional documents he produced, Alvarado lacked the actual 1835 grant.

Vallejo claimed that he could not find the grant among his papers, asserting that essential documents had been lost and destroyed during the Bear Flag revolt.[19] He produced only a partial copy of what he described as a decree or order from Figueroa that had accompanied the lost official grant, instructing him to give possession of the land to the Indians. This document posed a serious problem for the claim investigator. At the time, all copying was done by hand, and the copyist occasionally misspelled names and words, added quotation marks, and omitted words and phrases deemed unimportant. Vallejo's copy of the order lacked both its heading and Figueroa's signature, yet he insisted that it was a "true copy" of the original that he had received from the governor.

Everything hinged on how the commission chose to interpret Vallejo's copied order, which read like a grant in its own right:

> Having informed the government of the petition of Teodorico Quilaquequi, Sebastian, Juan Evangelista, Luis Gonzaga, Luis Antolin and other christianized Indians of the ex-mission of San Rafael and also of the reports furnished by you relative to their claims which they make to the lands appertaining to the ranch of "Nicasio" which they themselves have selected to live upon with their families.
>
> You will notify the said christianized Indians that the government, in consequence of the preferences they are entitled to and of their right to have lands for colonization does grant to them in full ownership of the said land above mentioned called Nicasio.
>
> You will take due care that good order be maintained among the said Indians and their families and that none disturb them in the peaceful engagement and possession of the said lands.
>
> and in compliance they were notified
>
> Sonoma, May 1, 1835 (signed) MGV.[20]

When Sebastian was called to testify, he recalled having received the actual grant from Governor Figueroa in 1835, when he and Juan Evangelista went to Monterey. On returning, they gave the document to Vallejo, who then gave it to Teodorico. Sebastian testified that at Teodorico's death, his daughter had burned his papers "to show her affection and respect for her father, as that was the custom among us." The commission decided to discount Sebastian's testimony, however, ruling that he was "incompetent on account of being Indian."[21] But non-Indians had also supplied depositions relating to the events of 1835, all supporting Indian occupation and legitimacy.[22]

All of this testimony was to no avail. The commission rejected Alvarado's claim to the Nicasio land. The commission members did not accept the copy of the order submitted by Vallejo from Figueroa as a substitute for a bona fide grant, nor did they find the witnesses, all Californios and one Coast Miwok, convincing.

The commission's decision was in part influenced by the laws governing mission lands that were in force during these years. Although many priests had believed that the vast lands surrounding the established missions on which wheat and livestock were raised would return to the Indians after secularization, the Spanish government had never formally granted these lands either to the padres or to the missions. Only land that lay within one league surrounding each mission was considered mission property and thus available for distribution to the Indians. The forests, the vast grasslands, and the potential farmland between the missions became part of the public domain and hence available for the establishment of private ranchos.[23] The U.S. Land Commission used this restricted concept of mission lands as a legal, though hardly moral, basis for future land grant rulings.

Three people deserve the most blame for the loss of Nicasio: Alvarado, Vallejo, and Jimeno. Despite the frequent condemnations of the priests issued by Vallejo and Alvarado on behalf of the Indians, the general and the governor were clearly the major power brokers during the last days of Mexican California, whereas the priests had relatively little to do with the loss of Indian lands such as Nicasio.

Alvarado had assured the Indians in 1839 that the land was theirs, granted to them by Governor Figueroa, but subsequently he ignored this truth. In fact, he may have had a plan to dispose of Nicasio otherwise as early as 1839. The most charitable interpretation of Alvarado's purchase of Nicasio is that he snatched this land out of the hands of de la Guerra and Cooper in order to preserve it for the Coast Miwok, and made the best deal possible by promising that the Indians could graze their livestock on his land. But such an idea cannot be found in either his or Vallejo's writings.

As for Vallejo, his role in promising support to the Coast Miwok at Nicasio is disturbing, particularly after he failed to cite Governor Figueroa's grant when he deeded Tinicasia in 1841 and then, in a turn, four years later acknowledged Figueroa's grant but requested only eight of the twenty leagues for the Indians. Perhaps he thought that this maneuver would at least safeguard eight leagues for the Coast Miwok, in the face of an inevitable land grab by his relatives and friends. But it is difficult to attribute such kindly motives to him when one considers that his name was involved in Alvarado's "purchase" of the land from the Indians. The two competitors, Alvarado and Vallejo, had apparently joined hands by 1845 in a scheme to obtain the Nicasio land.

The role of Secretary of State Jimeno in these transactions is most suspicious. As secretary of state under two governors, Alvarado and Micheltorena, he was privy to essential documents and was involved in approving or disproving applications. He awarded the rancho adjacent to Nicasio to Domingo Sais in 1839, and he facilitated the grants to de la Guerra and Cooper. The die was cast in 1845, when he denied to Governor Micheltorena that there had ever been a grant to the Indians. Jimeno apparently either purposefully ignored, lost, or destroyed the paperwork from Governor Figueroa's transaction.

We cannot know the hidden motives of the principals, nor can we completely trace the web of changing and conflicting loyalties. We do know that before California became a state, Vallejo was the only person who could have protected the Indians; he was the only man with enough personal influence and enough determination to bend or ignore custom and law to protect their land. But Vallejo's goals were essentially incompatible: he wanted land for the Indians, but he also wanted the spoils for himself, his relatives, and his friends. Without his full support, either open or covert, the Indians were unable to withstand the onslaught of settlers. Vallejo professed his overwhelming desire to help the Indians—his self-righteousness and indignation are evident in his writings—but apparently he was even more determined to help himself and his heirs. Nicasio and other lands were lost because of competition among Vallejo's contemporaries, ineptitude, poor bookkeeping, a sense of manifest destiny on the part of grantees, and, most of all, greed.

14

AGAINST ALL ODDS

In the early days of California statehood, the Coast Miwok and other Native American peoples were increasingly overwhelmed by the juggernaut of American settlers, gold rush miners, and land grabbers. Hordes of people poured into the state, establishing ranches, farms, homes, and businesses on what had once been Coast Miwok land. Many of the new residents were oblivious to the pain and despair suffered by the people they had displaced; others saw the injustices forced on the Indians as a small price to pay for realizing America's manifest destiny, rationalizing that the triumph of an "advanced" culture over the "savages" was inevitable and right. Thus California's native peoples, most of whom now lived in scattered settlements, faced continued assaults, the loss of their land and property, and the shattering of their cultures. Each census in the last half of the nineteenth century showed a decrease in the number of Indians residing in Marin County, which did not bode well for the survival of the Coast Miwok.

INDIAN NAMES BECOME PART OF THE LANDSCAPE

Ironically, it was at this time that the names of several Indian leaders became a permanent part of the new state. In 1850, the newly formed state legislature chose General Mariano Vallejo to head a committee to name California's counties. His selections ensured that the names of at least a few notable Indians would be spoken every day in the state, long after their life histories had been forgotten.

Just eleven years after Marino's death, Vallejo honored him by giving the name Marin County to the region north of San Francisco. Vallejo had a number of possible choices, among them San Rafael, Camilo, Amorós, Reed, Richardson, or Tamalpais (for the mountain that is the most obvious local geographic feature). But, considering two of Vallejo's choices for other counties, Solano and Stanislaus (for Estanislao), he seemed determined to honor Native Americans. It is interesting that these three Indian leaders shared some of Vallejo's own characteristics: confidence, courage, intelligence, defiance, obstinance, and a pragmatism that allowed them to survive.

Vallejo named Marin County when his own recollections were fresh and when Marino's reputation was still familiar to the priests, military, and civilians. Vallejo accompanied his recommendation for using the name of "the great chief" with vivid descriptions of Marino's two confrontations with the military, his escape from the San Francisco presidio jail after his first capture, and his hideout on the Marin islands.[1]

Other Coast Miwok place names still dot the landscape of Marin and Sonoma counties: Bolinas (from Baulenes, derived from Guaulenes), Cotati, Olema, Olompali, Petaluma, Sonoma, and Tomales. Mount Tamalpais is traversed by the Ho koo e koo trail; Maria Copa noted, "We [Nicasio people] call ourselves hukuiko."[2] The name of the mountain itself, spelled in a variety of ways in historical documents, comes from two Coast Miwok words, "tamal" and "pais." "Tamal" has been translated variously as "coast," "bay," "west," and "bay country"; all authorities agree that "pais" means mountain.[3]

In contrast, the Indian names of most of the neophytes have been forgotten, no doubt because the Spaniards had difficulty pronouncing them. Instead, the Coast Miwok are remembered by the Spanish names given to them at baptism. Most likely, towns such as Ignacio, Nicasio, Novato, and Solano were named after Indians, not Spanish luminaries or saints, as some might think.[4] Americans in California unwittingly changed Punta de Quintín (Quintín Point), named after the battle between Quintino and the military, to Point San Quentin, thus elevating Marino's companion to sainthood. Vallejo was amused by this and recounted that he had also heard of "Santa Sonoma," "San Monterey," and, ironically, "San Diablo."[5] Just north of San Pablo Bay, Indian peoples are remembered in the native names of Carquinez, Napa, Suisun, and Tolay.[6] We can appreciate how enduring these names are: Tamalpais and Ho koo e koo have been in use for thousands of years—conceivably, for more than five thousand years—while the names of Marino and Quintino date back to their baptisms, just over two hundred years ago.

INDIAN LIFE AFTER STATEHOOD

The lawlessness experienced in Mexican California in its closing years did not cease once California became part of the United States in 1850. Among the waves of settlers and miners arriving in the state were violent men who had little compunction about lynching Indians, offering bounties for Indian heads and scalps, massacring entire rancherias, raping girls and women, or kidnapping and selling children. Most of these atrocities occurred in the far northern counties and were often followed by retaliation from the Indians. In 1851, the governor of California, John McDougall, spoke of a "war of extermination" against the native population, which "must be expected" until they are "extinct."[7]

Involuntary servitude continued to exist in California as Indians were abducted and enslaved, in spite of California's status as a free (nonslave) state. During the Mexican administration, raids by the Californios had supported a peonage system in which captured Indians performed manual labor on large ranchos in return for food and clothing. But historian Sherburne F. Cook believed that, under the Americans, "the boundary was at last crossed from technical peonage to actual slavery."[8] Children and women were sold throughout California, even in Sacramento and San Francisco. Of the Indian children baptized in Contra Costa County between 1850 and 1853, most had white "sponsors" but no known parents,[9] suggesting that they had been kidnapped or that their parents had been killed. A case investigated by the Marin County coroner in 1863 revealed that Charlie, a twelve-year-old Indian boy, had died after being "kicked in the breast and stomach" by Peter, his employer, for complaining that he was too sick to work. Peter had obtained the boy when he was six years old from Indians in Mendocino, perhaps in a kidnapping. The jury's verdict at the inquest was that the boy had died of "causes unknown to us."[10]

With California statehood, the Coast Miwok suddenly found themselves deprived of citizenship rights within their homeland, and their word was no longer trusted or accepted in any court of law. In 1854, the California Supreme Court upheld a state law that ruled nonwhites incompetent to testify against whites, with Chief Justice Hugh J. Murphy warning that allowing nonwhites to testify "would admit them to all the equal rights of citizenship, and we might soon see them at the polls, in the jury box, upon the bench, and in our legislative halls…an actual and present danger."[11]

The second half of the nineteenth century proved to be a difficult time for California's Indian population in other ways, too. Many of the skills that had been essential to tribal life or the economy of the mission were useless in the post-mission world: creative work with stone, feathers, or shells was no longer culturally valued or economically useful, for example; and the ability to make adobe bricks, learned at the mission, became obsolete as wooden houses replaced adobe structures. After the secularization of the missions, most of the able-bodied Coast Miwok men worked as laborers on ranches or as fishermen, while women served as washerwomen and housekeepers. In Sonoma County, Indian men in the Bodega

Bay area were fishermen and did seasonal work such as harvesting Red Bodega potatoes, hops, and fruit.

Beginning in the 1850s, the U.S. government began to create tribal reservations for many groups of Native Americans in the West, forcing tribes to relocate to parcels of land assigned by the government. The reservation system was in part a response to the continuing conflicts between settlers and Indians, and some saw it as an attempt to protect the Indians from those who would take advantage of them. Some government officials reasoned that by gathering the Indians in a few locations, the government could more easily supply them with goods for farming and eventually with schools and health services. But it was also clear that the reservations provided a way to remove Indians from their former tribal lands, which could then be opened up to settlers. In addition, settlers moved to the borders of reservation lands and frequently managed to intercept and take supplies destined for the Indians. The reservation system also separated Indians from their cultural roots by moving them to land that had never been associated with their ancestors and often forcing them to live side by side with traditional enemies.

It is not clear whether Coast Miwok from the Bodega area were forced by the military to go to the Round Valley reservation in Mendocino County in 1857 or whether they fled there to avoid vigilantes.[12] But the Smith family remembered the 147-mile walk from Bodega Bay into central Pomo territory as the "long march" or the "death march." Grant Smith recalled hearing about his grandmother's experiences: "They herded them like cattle, like animals. Old people couldn't make it, couldn't keep up and died on the road. [When I was a boy,] they talked about it; they would talk about what happened on the road and they would cry, go all to pieces. It was misery, it was hardship. It was death."[13] Kathleen Smith's great-grandfathers, Jim Antone, a Pomo, and Bill Smith (Tom Smith's half-brother), a Coast Miwok, were "forcibly removed from their homelands and made the death march, forced by militia to Round Valley Reservation; they were some of the very few who later returned." Bill Smith's wife did not survive the experience.[14]

In the 1870s, some Americans, who thought that they had the Indians' best interests at heart, argued that the tribes would have a better chance of surviving if their children could be assimilated into the dominant culture by being sent to boarding schools, where they would be taught American culture and American norms of behavior. Little thought was given to the devastating psychological effects this might have on the children, who were separated physically and culturally from their parents and were not allowed to live with the members of their tribe or even to speak their native languages. In some cases, the students were not able to return home easily during school vacation, since they were required to work as domestics for non-Indian families "with only token remuneration."[15] There were also reservation day schools, local Indian schools, and public schools that included Indians; all of these schools allowed children to return home each day to live with their parents. Indian children were not required to attend school until 1891.

Well into the twentieth century, Indian children were still being sent to Indian boarding schools. Kathleen Smith recalled that in 1918 her father, Stephen Smith Jr., was not "allowed to go to the public school, but schoolmaster Watson at Kidd Creek took on the role of mentor" and arranged for him to go to the boarding school at Carlisle in Pennsylvania. Although young Stephen went voluntarily, Eugene Buvelot's grandmother reportedly said that at the turn of the century they "would hide the young children for fear they would be taken."[16] Buvelot's father had to have written permission from the Sonoma County Board of Education to attend a public high school in 1926.

Before 1880, Marin County paid small sums to aid elderly Indians through the county's Hospital and Infirmary Fund. But in that year, the civic authorities established what became a self-sustaining farm, including housing and a hospital, in Lucas Valley, a site that became known as the Poor Farm. Although their intention was to house indigent Indians at this site, there were never many Indian residents. (Juan Garcia, son of the mission soldier Rafael Garcia, spent his last days there.) There were Indian patients at the hospital, however, and four Indians were buried on the grounds in the 1930s and 1940s. The Poor Farm remained open until 1963.[17] Another institution, St. Vincent's Orphanage, opened in the 1850s, originally as a school. By 1884, it housed 554 orphaned boys, mostly of Irish descent. In 1882, an Indian family from Novato placed two of their six children there as "half orphans," a common practice for children whose parents could not support them and who remained at the school for various lengths of time. These two Indian children, ages ten and eight, stayed at St. Vincent's for one and two years, respectively, until their parents were able to take them home again.[18]

Coast Miwok Figures

CAMILO In the latter half of the nineteenth century, various Coast Miwok individuals continued to be well known in the Bay Area, whether for their prominence or their notoriety. One such individual was Camilo, still at Olompali. The land grant he had received for Olompali in 1834 was the only such grant issued to an Indian by the Mexican government.

After California became a state, Camilo lost his privileged position as the friend of General Vallejo, who no longer wielded substantial power in northern California. While the U.S. Land Commission was deciding which land grants were legal,

Camilo sold most of his land to James Black, the Marin County assessor. (The where-abouts of the gold Camilo received from this land deal has never been determined.) Camilo seems to have remained at Olompali, hosting travelers between San Rafael and Sonoma and retaining enough cattle and wheat to prosper. After his third wife, Cayetana, died in 1850, he married his fourth wife, the young Susanna, in 1852.

In 1931, when Maria Copa shared her tribal history with Isabel Kelly, she told of Camilo's last days, stories that she had likely heard from her mother and grandmother. She spoke of her grandfather, Camilo, who "spent all his money for whiskey;…those old timers were crazy for whiskey." Elzeario, she said, "drank heavily" and "fought a lot," including two fights with her grandfather.[19]

Camilo died violently in July 1856.[20] Apparently he was murdered, but there is no agreement on what happened, nor is there any extant record of a coroner's inquest. Camilo may have been buried at Olompali before an inquest could take place. Stories abound about Camilo's death, including one that a jealous brother shot him in Camilo's own corral, and another that an Indian shot him with a bow and arrow because Camilo had romanced and married his woman.[21]

According to Copa, however, Camilo died as a result of a drunken fight. "An Indian fought with him. They were always fighting with him," she recalled.[22] "It was a fight—not after money." Camilo had been outside by a small creek. When he returned, he said, "'Somebody killed me; I'm dying.' He fell in door and fell down. He pulled out arrow—point stayed in.…Sheriff came—caught man—They never found the money." Copa did not explain who the bowman was, but she described him as the "last Indian to use bow and arrow."[23] Yet another account cites a "family oral history," which claims that "Camilo awakened one night to check on a sheep tethered outside his adobe and was murdered by a hidden assassin."[24] This "hidden assassin" or the "last Indian to kill with a bow and arrow" may have been Eliseo (also known as Elisco), an Indian who was indicted for murder in Marin County in August 1856, although this conjecture cannot be verified.[25]

Copa's grandmother told her that Camilo had "lots of money" and that he was "too high toned with his cigar." Other Coast Miwok may have been envious of his wealth and possessions, perhaps leery, even suspicious, of his friendship with Vallejo.[26] After Camilo's death, his family moved to Mendocino County, and the property was sold in 1860. The remains of Camilo's adobe house can still be seen at Olompali State Park.

JOSE CALISTRO Only one Indian had sufficient funds to buy Coast Miwok land during these years. In 1872, Jose Calistro purchased a small but significant parcel of the Nicasio land, an area that included Echatamal on Halleck Creek, where a few Coast Miwok, including Maria Copa's family, were still living. We know little of Calistro's background, and we don't know the source of the funds with which he purchased the land. Although Maria Copa, age seven at the time of his death, referred to him as a "half-breed,"[27] his marriage record gives the names of his Indian mother and father. Church records also detail the birth of four of his children, baptized in San Rafael, as well as the names of the mothers of these children and his marriage to Rafaela (Maria Copa's aunt and the daughter of Elzeario and Escolastica) at St. Vincent's in Petaluma in July 1875.[28]

Calistro had only three years to enjoy being a landowner before he died in 1875, leaving his young widow, Rafaela, with the responsibility of looking after the Coast Miwok who were living on his land. (During his lifetime, county officials had selected Calistro, and later Rafaela, to be responsible for dispensing funds for the care of the old and infirm who lived on his property at Nicasio.) The previous April, he had written a last will and testament leaving his property to his "wife" Rafaela and his children, although he and Rafaela were not yet married. Perhaps the marriage in July, only one month before he died, was to guarantee that Rafaela would legally inherit her share of Calistro's property at his death.

SEBASTIAN In the late 1800s, one of the few Coast Miwok known outside the Indian community was Sebastian, one of the five original claimants to Nicasio in 1835. At the U.S. Land Commission hearings in 1855, he introduced himself as "Sebastiano, chief of the Nicasio Indians," and he was commemorated this way when he died in 1880. His obituary in the county newspaper, titled "Death of a Chief," described Sebastian as having been the chief of more than three hundred people in the Nicasio Valley in his earlier years, with vast herds of horses and cattle and clothing that was "handsome and very costly."[29]

At the time of his death at age ninety, Sebastian was blind. Copa remembered bringing him blackberries at Echatamal. He followed the old ways, she recalled, angering her by throwing some of the berries to the supernatural being *si'ika,* who "have to eat before I do." Making a "ss" sound, Sebastian threw some of the blackberries "outside, some in fire, and some in water."[30]

SALVADOR In 1879, the notorious criminal Salvador confessed to committing six murders during the 1860s and 1870s.[31] Salvador was well known in the Indian community because of his illustrious relatives. Through his mother, Escolastica, he was a first cousin (once removed) of Marino and an uncle of Maria Copa. He was also said to have been a grandson of the infamous Pomponio (see Chapter 8). In 1879, a local newspaper published an article by someone who claimed to have encountered the young Salvador years earlier, as both were riding by Pomponé Canyon in Novato. The writer had derided the young Indian for throwing an offering into this canyon for Pomponé (Pomponio). Bristling and looking "as vindictive as a young wildcat," the young boy said that he was Pomponé's grandson.[32] Little else is known of Salvador's background, except the date of his birth, 1842, based on his prison records at San Quentin.[33] His relationships with his half-siblings, children of Escolastica and Elzeario, were mixed: although he killed one, threatened to kill another, and was a fellow fugitive with a third, his family nevertheless came to visit him before he went to the scaffold.

When Salvador confessed to multiple murders in 1879, he spoke of three killings that had taken place in the 1860s: the murders of his half-brother Cruz at Nicasio, a man named José at Paper Mill Creek, and another man known as Whiskey Bill at Bodega. He argued self-defense in Whiskey Bill's death and was acquitted. Salvador was also accused of killing T. J. McKeon at Tomales Bay in 1867 and was pursued by the sheriff for this crime. During the chase, one Indian was killed, and Salvador and his half-brother Agaton were wounded. (Agaton died in jail.) Salvador was sentenced to San Quentin prison for seven years. Years later, however, authorities came to believe Salvador when he denied killing McKeon.[34]

At San Quentin, Salvador became convict #3626. He was described as a stocky Indian, age twenty-five, five feet nine inches tall, with "round nice features" and a "sallow complexion and black hair and eyes." Further identifying features included both "cupping marks" and a tattoo of a "cross on his right arm in India ink," scars "between his eyebrows, right cheek and left wrist [and a] large black spot on the center of his back."[35] Salvador was released after serving five years and ten months of his sentence. Soon afterward, he killed an unidentified Indian near Hopland in Mendocino County and then murdered a "Chinaman" by "kicking him to death" in 1878.[36] At some point, his half-sister Rafaela, widow of Jose Calistro, "swore out a warrant at Nicasio for Salvador's arrest for threats to kill her."[37]

In 1879, Salvador was accused of killing Paul Rieger at Tocaloma. After eluding the sheriff for a month and traveling as far as San Jose, Salvador was finally caught, but not before he had thoroughly confused a Sonoma sheriff, who went twice to the suspected hideaway and left empty-handed each time after being told by Salvador himself, "Salvador gone. Not here." Salvador was wearing Rieger's pants at the time of his arrest, which helped to convict him. He was sentenced to death.[38]

Sheriff Tunstead had a high fence built around the courthouse area where the scaffold was erected and sent out five hundred invitations to witness the hanging. The day before his execution, members of Salvador's family visited him at San Quentin: his mother, Escolastica; his half-brother Jose Antone, "a good Indian" (as reported in the newspaper); and his half-sister Rafaela. According to one account, "he embraced them all, standing the wailings of his mother without flinching. His mother then uttered a weird, wild prayer in the Indian dialect, and laid her hands upon the head of her son who had sunk down upon his knees."[39] The next day, Salvador was hanged, accompanied to the scaffold by two sheriffs and two priests. He thanked Sheriff Tunstead "for the kind treatment he received" while in jail and then "behaved with a firmness quite remarkable."[40]

THE SMITH FAMILY In 1844, before hostilities between the Californios and Americans surfaced, an American sea captain named Stephen Smith received a large land grant from the Mexican government, encompassing 35,787 acres in Bodega. His first living quarters at Bodega, where he also housed the three pianos he had brought with him, were in buildings that had been abandoned by the Russians. Smith established one of the earliest steam-powered sawmills in California and became an admired figure in the community. In 1846, he "was appointed the civil magistrate for the region." Although his sawmill was temporarily put out of business during the Bear Flag revolt, when the Americans took his horses and his Indian laborers fled, he was able to return to this lucrative endeavor in 1847 and 1848. Before his death in 1855, he had built a two-story home, a tannery, a bowling alley, and a hotel.[41]

Smith married the Coast Miwok woman Tsupu, who was also known as Maria Cheka. Their child William (Bill) Smith became an important figure in the Coast Miwok community, with numerous descendants who are leaders in the tribe today. Another child born to Tsupu/Maria Cheka was Bill's half-brother Tom, who took the last name Smith although his father was not Captain Smith. His interviews with Isabel Kelly in the early 1930s, when he was in his nineties, are some of the most valuable records of the words, narratives, religious ceremonies, historical events, and songs of his tribe.[42] His descendants are equally respected in the Coast Miwok community today.

Tom Smith became a singer and healer; as early as 1875, he was one of the better-known Indian dream dancers and was soon famous in northern California for his spiritual power. A new spiritual emphasis on ritual dreaming had swept parts of northern California after the Ghost Dance was introduced from Nevada in the 1870s. Followers of the Ghost Dance believed that dancing could bring back their dead ancestors and cause all white people to die. New cults based on these beliefs grew from the desperation that Indians in the western United States felt in these years, after the theft of their land and numerous massacres by whites. In north central California, these ideas took on many forms. One variation held that the imminent end of the world could be averted by believers dancing in an Earth Lodge.

Nine such lodges were built in Pomo territory and were visited by Pomo, Coast Miwok, and Wappo Indians. Because some of these dances suggested that the world would end for all who did not dance, and for whites in particular, non-Indians typically did not see the dances.

Another cult that evolved from the Earth Lodge movement, was the Dreamer, or Bole-Maru, religion.[43] It featured healing by a dream leader, whose dreams inspired the creation of songs and the designs of cloth costumes. A dance house pole representing the center of the world was erected, and in some rancherias dancers performed a ball dance. Tom Smith's daughter, Carrie Smith, was also a dreamer. In the round house at Middletown, her version of the ball dance included twelve cloth-covered balls decorated with red crosses, which were thrown by six men and six women standing opposite each other. Adherents of this cult were urged to avoid "drinking, quarreling, stealing and disbelief."[44]

The practice and interpretations of these dances at the turn of the century varied among individual dreamers within a rancheria as well as among rancherias. Tom Smith was one of the leaders in this tradition, becoming a well-known dream dancer. He told Isabel Kelly that he had "learned this dance from the dancers at Bodega. My father paid them."[45] Although he was famous for his dreaming, he insisted to Kelly that he never danced to bring back the dead.

His dreams did, however, determine the design of women's costumes for his four-day dances, including dresses patterned with crosses and headdresses consisting of a circlet of crow feathers. The men dressed in trousers decorated with crosses and wore yellowhammer (flicker) feather headbands. A Pomo Indian told Cora Du Bois, one of Kelly's colleagues, that when Smith became a dreamer, "stripes grew all over his face and body. They looked like paint but they wouldn't wipe off. After a while they went away by themselves. Many came to his dance and saw him that way. He didn't put them there himself. His dance lasted four days."[46]

The Californios

Under the Americans, life did not go well for another group of old-time residents: the Californios. Many of those who had been granted land by the Mexican government found that the U.S. Land Commission would not honor their claims. Even Vallejo's claim to the eighty thousand acres of Rancho Soscol, granted to him by Governor Micheltorena in 1843, was lost in 1862 in a U.S. Supreme Court decision.[47] Others had been living for years on land they assumed to be their own, but arriving American settlers considered it available for the taking and began to build on it.

In the 1850s, these individuals of Spanish and Mexican heritage were puzzled and outraged at their change in status. One of their defenders, the state senator

Pablo de la Guerra, complained bitterly to the California legislature in 1856 about the Californios losing their land to American settlers in a country where they no longer "understand the language of their native soil. They are strangers in their native land....They have been refused the privilege of drawing water from their own wells. They have been refused the privilege of cutting their own firewood....They have been abased and insulted....[They have been] in possession of large tracts of soil which, in many instances, have been in the possession of the same family for over half a century."[48] It is an ironic twist of history that the speaker seemed not to appreciate that the Americans were doing to the Spaniards and Mexicans what the Spaniards and Mexicans had done to the Indians.[49] Even more ironic is that when de la Guerra himself was granted Nicasio in 1845, he had in effect taken the land away from its legitimate owners, the Coast Miwok.

The Coast Miwok "Disappear"

Public ignorance, lack of interest, and perhaps shame at what had happened to the Indians in California all contributed to a public perception that the native peoples, including the Coast Miwok, were disappearing in the American West and that nothing could be done to prevent it. Many whites, believing in racial superiority, considered Indians to be impediments to the progress of the white race. The deaths of fifteen to twenty Indians at Nicasio of "chicken pox or measles" in 1878[50] fit the pattern of Indians succumbing to diseases that the supposedly "stronger" white race could easily withstand. The disappearance of Native Americans was interpreted as a natural and inevitable process.

Population figures seemed to bear this out, as disease, murder, and the effects of alcohol decimated the Indians. After 1850, the officially recorded population of California Indians dropped precipitously, reinforcing the belief that the tribes were disappearing. The accuracy of the U.S. Census records was questionable when it came to counting Native Americans, however. Some Indians lived in isolated areas and were not counted; others were simply ignored by census takers. And, increasingly, people had begun to keep information about their heritage to themselves to avoid prejudice, discrimination, and violence.

George Yount, from his vantage point at Yountville, northeast of Sonoma, told his biographer that in the Napa Valley "the natives had been hunted by the murderous white man....The same intruders have usurped their land, scattered and exterminated their game and fish, corrupted the habits, as well as infected the persons of their females, which has rendered them feeble, torpid and indolent." The remnants of five different tribes, he asserted, who had once been "noble, proud and athletic nations [now]...sit broken-hearted and disconsolate by the sides of the streams and under the ancient wide spreading oaks,…most of them mere bundles of corruption and [suffering from] the most loathsome of all diseases [syphilis], offensive even to themselves—Their ardor and vivacity is gone;…unpitied and unlamented they die." "The tribes," he wrote, "are wasting away like the dew of a summer's morning."[51] Yount's metaphor was repeated by J. P. Munro-Fraser in his 1880 *History of Marin County, California:* the Indians of Nicasio, he wrote, were said to have "vanished before the silent forces of civilization, like the dew from off the grass beneath the ardent rays of a mid-summer sun."[52]

Horace Bell, in 1881, asked how it was possible that the Indians, who had covered "mountain and valley, forest and plain," were gone, only thirty years after the gold rush. "Thirty years seems too short a period of time to annihilate a great population extending more than a thousand miles of country." Nonetheless, in his view, there was cause for despair: "They are gone! all gone! It is sad to contemplate; they were so docile and harmless in disposition….But what is the use of useless lamentation? The Indians are all gone and that is the end of it, and we can only hope that they have all gone to happy hunting grounds."[53]

History Distorted: Marino's Parentage

As the Indians began to fade from public consciousness, their tribal history and the histories of their ancestors were sometimes revised in startling ways. A series of articles by Alex S. Taylor in the *Daily Alta* in the 1860s, for example, included a discussion of Marino. Taylor had an avid interest in early California and was an important collector of mission and military letters, which are still extant. His interpretations and recital of events are sometimes faulty, however. Taylor arrived in California after Marino's death, so he was not speaking from firsthand knowledge when he claimed that Marino and some other chiefs had lighter skins and a more "intelligent appearance" than the local Indians because they were descendants of a Spaniard from a shipwrecked galleon. This claim was repeated in the 1880s by the historian H. H. Bancroft, who, while praising Marino's bravery and intelligence, wrote that "it has been suspected that the chief Marin was not a full-bred Indian." Bancroft asserted, much as Taylor had done, that Marino's lineage and that of other Indian chiefs included men from a Spanish galleon shipwrecked in 1750. At least Bancroft was willing to admit that "of this we have no proof."[54]

The diaries of the earliest explorers of California and the writings and drawings of early visitors to the San Francisco mission all indicate that the skin color of the Indians was not uniform. Both the priest Francisco Palou, who visited near San Carlos and in San Bruno on the San Francisco peninsula in the 1770s, and Juan Crespi, who hiked on the east side of San Francisco and San Pablo Bay, noted in their journals that some of the Indians they encountered were light-skinned and bearded.[55] Yet the legend of a map drawn in the 1770s and credited to Juan Crespí included the words *"Gentiles…hallaran rubio blancos,"* translated as the "heathen had ruddy complexions."[56]

While there was variation in the Indians' skin color, suggesting a mixed heritage from other groups, possibly European, Bancroft's assertions that Indian chiefs had European ancestors cannot be confirmed. His assumptions that such a lineage made them qualified to be leaders were examples of nineteenth-century racism and ethnocentrism, which held that European appearance connoted intelligence.[57] This was not the view of Father Vicente Santa María or Captain Juan Manuel de Ayala of the ship *San Carlos* (see Chapter 3), who voiced their admiration for the intelligence of the Coast Miwok and Ohlone individuals they met in 1775, with no mention of any similarities to European males.

THE COAST MIWOK IN THE TWENTIETH CENTURY

The Indians, of course, had not disappeared from California. In the 1920s, Indian communities were still found in locations where they had existed for centuries—for example, at Bodega and Bodega Bay as well as on both the east and west shores of Tomales Bay. Bill Smith (the son of Captain Stephen Smith and Tsupu) bought property at Bodega Bay after returning from the Round Valley reservation. He and his many children flourished in their commercial fishing business, purveying the fresh catch to restaurants in Sonoma, Marin, and San Francisco counties. When Bill Smith died in 1936, all but one of his eleven children were still alive, as were twenty-nine grandchildren and eleven great-grandchildren. (Figure 31) As a child in the 1950s, Eugene Buvelot, the great-grandson of Bill Smith, was able to join a three-generation extended family at Bodega Bay during weekends and summers, where he slept in the warehouse of the Smith Brothers firm.[58] But most Coast Miwok families did not have such a thriving community of relatives to help in successfully managing a large business. Buvelot suggested that if Bill Smith's father had not been white, he would have had trouble buying property and building up his fishing business after his return from Round Valley.[59]

In the early 1900s, there were settlements at Laird's Landing as well as in coves north and south of there and at Pelican Point on the west side of Tomales Bay. Elizabeth Campigli Harlan's mother, who lived at Laird's Landing, went to Marshall on the east side of the bay to give birth to her daughter in 1925, in order to be closer to medical help. Elizabeth had to row across the bay to Marshall to buy groceries, leaving "early in the morning to avoid the wind."[60]

Coast Miwok families also lived on the east side of Tomales Bay, just above the tide line at Reynolds (see Figure 29c), where Marshall Boat Works and Tony's Seafood are today, and at Fisherman's, now known as Marconi Cove. Indians living in these communities were engaged in clamming, selling their catch to passengers of the Northern Pacific Coast Railroad. They also caught herring and worked in processing the fish at the Booth plant at Hamlet, north of Marshall.[61]

Thirty-three people from nine families lived at Fisherman's in 1920.[62] A survey of landless Indians taken from 1919 to 1920 found that only one woman at Fisherman's, age ninety, was a full-blooded Indian. In fact, most of the individuals at Fisherman's were less than one-half Indian. (In a system similar to that used for African Americans, individuals whose ancestry was at least one-eighth Indian were tallied as Indian rather than white.) The surveyors wrote that all of the individuals who were interested in joining a rancheria at Sebastopol or Stewart's Point, in Sonoma County, should have "Indian rights," which included "additional aid" for the "old people who are needy."[63] Not all northern California Indians were living in scattered settlements, however. Coast Miwok and Pomo people were residing in Santa Rosa, Healdsburg, and Sebastopol, as well as in larger urban areas such as San Rafael, Novato, and Petaluma.

Graton Rancheria

In 1920, the federal government decided to purchase land for "landless Indians" and chose the Coast Miwok and Pomo from Marshall, Bodega, Tomales, and Sebastopol to be the recipients. The Indian agent L. A. Dorrington reported to his superior, however, that "there is no necessity for the purchase of land by this band. They are quite happy and continue in their present status and there is no objection to their continued residence at their present site. The children are welcome and attend the Marshall public school."[64] He may have been speaking of the families at Fisherman's.

Nevertheless, the U.S. government purchased land through the Bureau of Indian Affairs. Instead of prime property on the coast or even in Marin County, the site the government chose was inland at Graton in Sonoma County, a small 15.45-acre piece of property that had little to offer in terms of arable land, water, or building sites. If the "landless" Indians had had any political clout, they would have refused it. They received neither an irrigation system nor the funds and supplies to build homes, although these had been promised. Despite the steepness of the land and the limited water supply, some of the Coast Miwok and southern Pomo used it seasonally, living on tent platforms while they picked hops or fruit on local farms.

Behind the Scenes

In the late 1800s, Native Americans themselves had begun to hide or downplay their Indian identity and history, and this continued into the twentieth century. For many, it was an attempt to protect themselves from bigotry and hostility, from the disrespect and discrimination they faced in white society. Others simply expressed a desire for privacy and a wish to avoid exposing themselves to the insensitivity of others. Eugene Buvelot's aunt, for example, always denied that she was Indian and said that someone must have mistakenly identified her. Patricia Cummings, a Miwok genealogist, did not learn of her Indian heritage until the 1970s because her grandmother had kept it a secret; and Jeanne Billy found that her grandmother had cautioned her children not to speak the Coast Miwok language: "They did not want to appear different from the community where they lived."[65]

Outside public view, however, many Native Americans had continued their ceremonial life over the years. Originally, Indian customs were hidden in order to protect those who were practicing old religious and ceremonial ways that were not understood by the white culture. Dances, particularly those associated with dreaming and curing, were still performed in rural rancherias and on reservations, and the belief in and ritual use of dreaming continued to be a part of the Indian belief system.

According to one of Bill Smith's daughters, Rosalie Smith Cody, her uncle Tom Smith would sometimes wake up in the "middle of the night and he'd start singing. I wish we had a tape recording of his songs. They were beautiful, and he had a good voice." She had been taught not to "interfere" when her uncle was singing. One morning after he had been singing, she asked him how he was, and he answered: "'Bad....Somebody is sick up there [at Stewart's Point]. Very sick.' Sure enough, he'd [later] get word that...somebody in his family had died."[66]

Rosalie Smith Cody also spoke of a "bear in human skin" that could put poison in the well water. Her father chased such a human bear once and shot at it but did not kill it. Once, however, when it was outside the Smith home and the dogs were upset, "Uncle Tom" came down from upstairs, and "this is what he done. I'll never forget it. We had a fireplace. So he brought his tobacco...bag....And he...threw that in the fire, and he was mumbling some magic words...and making motions like he was praying. And do you know that that thing went away."[67]

Tom Smith suddenly stopped dancing in the early 1920s. He explained to Du Bois: "My brother was poisoned and I quit that dance. I burned all the things."[68]

Oral Tradition and Mission Records

The oral tradition of the Indians allowed them to preserve links to their history and ancestry. Sometimes the details became vague and incorrect, but in some cases, the strands of memory proved quite accurate. Maria Copa, for example, recounted astonishing details of mission and pre-mission life from well before her birth, probably based on stories told by her grandmother. She told Isabel Kelly about her great-grandparents, about an attack on the mission by the Pomo, and about Marino. Concerning her famous ancestor, she stated: "I heard the reason they called this country Marin was because of a man named Marino. He was my grandmother's first cousin, and overseer for the priest at San Rafael mission."[69]

Because Copa knew the Spanish names given to her great-grandparents when they entered the mission, it is possible to locate them in the mission records today and to learn their origins. Her grandmother's parents, Otilio and Otilia, came from Olompali, were born in 1780 and 1785, and were baptized at the San Jose mission. The parents of her grandfather, Ysidro and Ysidra, were Coast Miwok from the Alaguali area, born in 1771 and 1777, and baptized at San Francisco. Her grandfather was Elzeario, and she recalled that he often drank with Camilo. When her grandmother was baptized in 1812, she was given the name Escolastica, which was mentioned in her first children's baptismal records. During the 1840s and 1850s, her name was written by a different priest as Colastica and Scolastica. By the 1880 census, the name had evolved to Mary Colasti, and Copa remembered it in 1932 as Maria Nicolasa.[70] (Appendix H)

At the end of the nineteenth century, only two of the Indians mentioned in the census records, ages eighty-two and seventy-two, could have known Marino personally, yet Copa and probably others were familiar with Marino and other relatives as part of their oral tradition in 1932. By the end of the twentieth century, however, Marino had been forgotten by most Indians and non-Indians alike.

Citizenship

With the advent of the First World War, Indians volunteered for service in the U.S. military and fought abroad, even though they were still not recognized as U.S. citizens. One of Eugene Buvelot's great-uncles was gassed in France and suffered from the aftereffects. This participation in the war may have been the impetus for the U.S. Congress to finally grant citizenship to Indians in 1924, thus conferring the civil rights that had been denied to the Native Americans of California since 1850.

Termination

In the 1950s, the U.S. government decided to end federal ties to Indian communities and "terminate" its relationship with the rancherias in California. These settlements could choose to maintain their status in a sort of trust relationship, akin to being wards of the government, or to be terminated, receiving ownership of their own lands but giving up whatever health, education, and other services they had periodically received from the government. Although Professor Edward Castillo of Sonoma State University, a southern California tribal member, described termination as a "plan for cultural and tribal suicide," the government offered inducements to encourage settlements to opt for termination: "upgrading of squalid housing, paving roads, building bridges, constructing water projects and even providing college scholarships in return for a vote to terminate."[71] The Kashaya Pomo reservation voted not to terminate, but Graton Rancheria was one of the twenty-three California rancherias and reservations that were terminated between 1958 and 1970.

The results were predictable. Most individuals, lacking sufficient funds, could not afford the taxes on their property, and they lost their holdings and their last cultural tie to the land of their ancestors. The promised roads and sewer lines were never put in. Although Graton had not been traditional land for the Coast Miwok, it was nevertheless the only land that had been granted to them by the government. At this rancheria, only one family, that of Gloria Truvido Ross Armstrong, was able to retain its property, which consisted of just one acre. Economic conditions in the Indian communities also deteriorated, with the loss of federal benefits and services. Termination was partially reversed in 1983, twenty-five years later, but the Coast Miwok were not recognized, nor was their land restored.

"WE ARE STILL HERE"

The Coast Miwok have survived. In a small museum in Bolinas, the title of a 1993 Indian tribal exhibit announced: "We Are Still Here." Old and contemporary photographs taken at graduations, family picnics, and other gatherings formed a major part of the show and, accompanied by family histories, provided clear evidence that the Coast Miwok people are indeed "still here." Although most of these survivors had moved to Pomo territory in Sonoma County's Santa Rosa, where many had intermarried with the Pomo and non-Indians, some people of Coast Miwok descent were still living on traditional Miwok land, for example, in Corte Madera, San Rafael, Novato, Petaluma, and the area of Tomales Bay, Bodega, and Bodega Bay.

A year before the museum exhibit opened, some 150 Coast Miwok survivors had come together in an emergency meeting at the home of Rita Carrillo. They were assembling to oppose a proposal by the Cloverdale Pomo to build a marina, homes, a golf course, and a casino at Marshall, on the coast of Marin County, which was clearly former territory of the Coast Miwok.

In spite of their common heritage, many of the guests at Carrillo's home had not spoken with one another for more than fifty years, a consequence of what Greg Sarris referred to as an "angered history" between families. But they soon found their own close relatives in shared family photographs, realized their "connectedness, and saw it as a sign from the ancestors."[72]

They agreed to form a group called the Federated Coast Miwok and to seek federal recognition. Pursuing this goal meant that they would have to be more public about their tribal identity and would have to garner support from non–Indians. If they were successful in gaining federal recognition, they would be in a better position to prevent other Indian groups from encroaching on their territory and would also be able to receive health care, education, and housing benefits.

The newly elected chairman, Greg Sarris, traced his family history to Tom Smith, a Coast Miwok,[73] and Eugene Buvelot, treasurer of the new tribal organization, was a descendant of Bill Smith, Tom Smith's half-brother. Rita Carrillo, vice chairwoman, shared an ancestor with Marino through her grandmother, Maria Copa. But this was not an exclusively Coast Miwok tribe, because Coast Miwok and southern Pomo people had intermarried over the years. For example, Tom Smith's mother was Coast Miwok, but his father was Pomo.[74] At least three of Tom Smith's wives were Pomo, and Eugene Buvelot's great-grandfather Bill Smith had married a Pomo woman, Rosalie Charles (1852–1922). Others also had ancestors from both Coast Miwok and Pomo groups, and they would now have to align themselves with one tribe or the other.

Federal Recognition

The Coast Miwok group requested federal recognition of the Graton Rancheria site and eventually changed their name accordingly from the Federated Coast Miwok to the more inclusive Federated Indians of Graton Rancheria. This linked them to the one remaining acre at the site that belonged to Gloria Truvido Ross Armstrong, whose daughter, Lorelle Ross, is currently vice chairwoman of the tribe.

Greg Sarris led the fight for recognition. Congresswoman Lynn Woolsey, who represented the area, introduced a bill for recognition. After its passage in the House of Representatives in June 2000, it went to the Senate, where it was shepherded through the process by Senator Barbara Boxer.

At this point, the tribe decided to be inclusive rather than exclusive and opened up membership to anyone who could trace his or her ancestry to a designee of Graton Rancheria from 1922, when it was established, for "the homeless Indians of Tomales Bay, Bodega Bay, Sebastopol, and vicinities thereof."[75]

Greg Sarris, tribal chairman since 1993, is a charismatic figure. He is a problem solver and a fence mender, but he can also talk tough when necessary. For example, when he was visibly concerned about what he perceived as greediness, he spoke to the tribal members in the tradition of the hoipus of old, exhorting them to make the right choices between greed and kindness: "Greed has divided tribes and families….Can we work in harmony for the greater good, will we be ethical, or will we be greedy and fight with each other? Who do we want to be? [If we turn to] kindness rather than greed, then we'll have a future which is boundless, a future for our grandchildren and great-grandchildren."[76]

Sarris gave his first speech when he was a student at Santa Rosa Junior College; his adopted mother was there to hear him and was the first person to tell him of his gift for speaking. Later he would attend Stanford and become a professor of English, first at the University of California at Los Angeles and then at Sonoma State University.

Sarris says that his leadership model is the famous Pomo basketmaker and doctor Essie Parrish. Such healing doctors of the Bole-Maru religion continued to play an important role into the 1960s. Parrish's son Otis, a Kashaya Pomo, remembered how he used to cry as his mother left him at home when she took one of her many trips to heal someone.[77] In a photograph taken in 1963, Essie Parrish is wearing her Bole-Maru dress with stars on it and a "big head" headdress of many feathers. A documentary film produced by U.C. Berkeley in the 1960s shows her performing a healing ceremony.[78] In addition to this work, she was also a manager in an apple-canning factory and raised fourteen children. According to Sarris, for her there was "no such word as 'can't.' She was a great orator. Her English may not have been grammatically correct, but she was charismatic,…eloquent,…and had the ability to lead without jealousy. People respected her for her fair, cautious, strong sense of ethics and morals, her sense of psychology, and her great doctoring."[79]

Sarris is an accomplished storyteller. One of his stories is about the power struggle between two elders, Tom Smith and a powerful Kashaya Pomo doctor named Big Jose, each trying to "out feat" the other. Tom Smith played the winning card, however, when, as Sarris explained it, "he caused the 1906 earthquake, [thus] winning…the contest once and for all."[80]

Sarris once wrote about the possible burial sites of Tom Smith. He described the broader aspects of sacredness and place and mentioned locations that would have been sacred to Smith's memory:

Certainly the knoll overlooking the mouth of the Russian River, where our last traditional round house stood, would be such a place. And we can't forget…the spot near the town of Bodega where he demonstrated his authority to Big Jose.…Or the field just east of Healdsburg where he raised a dying man to his feet? Or the rancheria in Middletown where one hot summer night he carried the fog with him from the coast?

[If one drew lines on a map connecting all these locations, there would be] so many places and connecting lines that the map would look like a tightly woven, intricately designed Miwok basket. The patterns would circle around, endless, beautiful, so that the map would, in the end, designate the area in its entirety as sacred.[81]

Meeting at Kule Loklo

Members of the newly recognized tribe and their guests gathered in the round house at Kule Loklo in Point Reyes National Seashore on February 17, 2001, to celebrate their renewed sovereignty. It was a wet, overcast day, with water dripping from the huge eucalyptus trees near the re-created Indian village. Smoke from the fire inside the round house was visible, and the village was quiet.

The round house, some 55 feet in diameter, is a simple, serene, and contemplative space. It is supported by four inner poles and twelve outer poles; a center pole does not meet the roof. The fire pit is aligned with the center pole, while at the far side an eighteen-inch drum is placed over another pit. Two rows of benches almost encircle the structure; the outer bench sits against a low wall of rough-hewn rocks many feet thick. On that day of celebration, folding chairs had been added.

Individuals are expected to turn counterclockwise just before entering the round house, a disorienting movement that helps to prepare them for passing into a sacred place. On that February afternoon, some two hundred people had passed through the door and crowded into this space. Gathered together were members of the tribe, their families, dignitaries, park personnel, and longtime park volunteers, along with volunteers from the Miwok Archaeological Preserve of Marin (MAPOM), an organization that helped to build the Indian village Kule Loklo and offers classes in native skills.[82] Some of those attending were seated on the folding chairs or benches, but many were standing, squeezed between tables filled with food in a crowd so dense that wet, steaming bodies were pressed together even in the twenty-foot entrance hall. Rain fell though the smoke hole and onto the fire, causing smoke to permeate the building. Everyone's eyes were wet, both from the smoke and from the emotion of the event. The light of the fire illuminated the faces of those in attendance, all united in happiness and relief that they had finally achieved federal status for the tribe.

Greg Sarris stood up and the crowd fell silent. All that could be heard was the dripping of water as it ran down the seams of the roof and the sizzling of raindrops that fell onto the fire. A few people shuffled their feet as those standing tried to find a way to see the speaker. Sarris's first words were "Thank you." People who were there remember how they felt, and some can recall who was sitting beside them. But the emotion was so intense that no one, including Sarris himself, can repeat his exact words, other than his eloquent remembrance of the ancestors. It was a sacred moment in a sacred place. Later, Sarris would write:

> If we want to identify and mark a place as sacred,…we must also see that place as only the beginning, the knot a basketmaker ties to start her basket, from which a sacred world rolls out and coils around us in every direction.…It is place that can remind us of what the Coast Miwok people always believed: The sacred is everywhere, in everything, and in us. In the old roundhouse above the Russian River, Grandpa Tom often spoke of this all-encompassing notion of sacredness and place. Gesturing with his hand to the earth and the heavens, he admonished us: "Remember."[83]

APPENDIX A

CAST OF CHARACTERS

ALVARADO, JUAN BAUTISTA. Governor of California, 1836–1842; boyhood companion of Mariano G. Vallejo; wrote a history of California, 1876.

ABELLA, JOSÉ RAMÓN. Priest at Mission Dolores, 1799–1818.

ALTIMIRA, JOSÉ. Priest originally at Mission Dolores, 1823; founded Mission San Francisco de Soláno at Sonoma, 1823.

AMORÓS, JUAN. Priest at Mission San Rafael, 1819–1832.

ARGÜELLO, JOSÉ DARIO. Commandante at San Francisco presidio, 1791–1806; father of Luis Argüello.

ARGÜELLO, LUIS. Commandante at San Francisco presidio, 1806; made captain in 1818; led 1821 expedition (accompanied by Marino and Blas Ordaz); governor of California, 1822–1825; returned to San Francisco from Monterey, 1825.

ARGÜELLO, SANTIAGO. Brother of Luis Argüello; second lieutenant of San Francisco presidio company, 1817–1827.

BEECHEY, FREDERICK WILLIAM. Captain of British ship in California, 1826–1827.

BILLY, JEANNE. Coast Miwok descendant.

BUVELOT, EUGENE. Coast Miwok descendant of Bill Smith.

CALISTRO, JOSE. Name also spelled Calisto; Coast Miwok; purchased land at Nicasio, 1872.

CALISTRO, RAFAELA. Coast Miwok; aunt of Maria Copa; half-sister of Salvador; married to Jose Calistro.

CAMILO (HUEÑUX UNUTIA). Name spelled by Americans as Ynitia; parents from Puscuy (in the Chocoay tribal area of Coast Miwok); received Mexican land grant of Olompali, 1843; married to Cayetana.

CASTRO BROTHERS, ANTONIO, JOAQUIN, AND VICTOR. Pillaged Indian villages and mission for their rancho in San Pablo.

CAYETANA (GUALULU QUILAJUQUE). Huimen tribe of Coast Miwok; half-sister of Teodorico and José María; married to Jacome and, after his death, to Camilo.

CHORIS, LOUIS ANDREVITCH. Artist; visited San Francisco with Kotzebue, 1816.

COPA, MARIA. Coast Miwok interviewed by Isabel Kelly, 1931–1932.

CUMMINGS, PATRICIA. Coast Miwok descendant; genealogist.

DURAN, NARCISO. Priest at Mission San Jose, 1806–1833.

ELZEARIO (SACNEPA). Alaguali tribe of Coast Miwok; grandfather of Maria Copa; married to Escolastica.

ESCOLASTICA (TOLLEPALE). Olompali tribe of Coast Miwok; grandmother of Maria Copa; married to Elzeario.

ESTANISLAO. Lakisamne tribe of Yokuts; alcalde at and 1828 runaway from San Jose mission; captured, 1829.

ESTÉNEGA, TOMÁS ELEUTERIO. Priest at Mission Dolores, 1821–1833; priest at Mission San Rafael, 1832–1833.

ESTUDILLO, JOSÉ JOAQUIN. In San Francisco presidio company, 1816–1823; accompanied Luis Argüello on expedition of 1821; son of José María.

ESTUDILLO, JOSÉ MARÍA. Accompanied Kotzebue and Marco to Ross, 1824.

FIGUEROA, JOSÉ. Governor of California, 1833–1835; granted Nicasio to Coast Miwok, 1835.

GALINDO, JOSÉ EUSEBIO. Soldier in San Francisco presidio company, 1828–1829; wrote "Apuntes para la historia de California," 1877.

GALINDO, NASARIO. Corporal and sergeant of San Francisco presidio company, 1832–1843.

GARCIA, JUAN. Son of Rafael Garcia; described his father's life at Mission San Rafael.

GARCIA, RAFAEL. Corporal in San Francisco presidio company, 1823–1834; frequently assigned to Mission San Rafael, 1825–1834.

GERONIMO (JUMLE). Coast Miwok; alcalde at San Rafael, 1819; killed by non-mission Indians in Pomo area, 1824.

GIL Y TOBOADA, LUIS. Priest at Mission San Rafael, 1817–1819.

GOYCOCHEA, FELIPE DE. Commandante of Santa Barbara presidio, 1747–1814; led soldiers through Marin County to Bodega, 1793.

HARLAN, ELIZABETH CAMPIGLI. Coast Miwok descendant.

HARTNELL, WILLIAM E. P. British citizen; sent by Governor Alvarado to inspect missions, 1839–1840.

HERRERA, JOSE. Corporal (promoted to sergeant second class) of San Francisco presidio company, 1811; stationed at San Rafael, 1818–1823; jailed for atrocities to Indians, 1823–1824.

JACINTO. Huimen tribe of Coast Miwok; from village of Anamas; interpreter, witness, and godparent at San Francisco mission, 1800–1805; witness at Marino and Juana's wedding, 1816; uncle of Pomponio.

JACOME (COIS). From Puscuy area of the Chocoay tribe of Coast Miwok; alcalde of Olompali, 1828; witness at the mission; married to Cayetana.

JIMENO, CASARÍN MANUEL. Secretary of State under Governors Alvarado and Micheltorena, 1839–1845.

JOSÉ MARÍA (LULUECUEC). Huimen tribe of Coast Miwok; alcalde at Mission San Rafael; half brother of Teodorico and Cayetana.

JUANA (SOTOATIJEIUM). Olompali tribe of Coast Miwok; married to Marino.

JUSTINO (CHALI[E]CHI). Guaulen tribe of Coast Miwok; godfather, witness, interpreter, sacristan, and nurse at Mission San Rafael, 1818–1821, 1824–1825; brother of Nereo.

IÓLLO. Coast Miwok chief of Bodega Bay, 1810; subject of watercolor by Tikhánov.

KELLY, ISABEL. Interviewed Tom Smith and Maria Copa in 1831 and 1832 while a graduate student at the University of California, Berkeley.

KHLEBNIKOV, KIRIL. Agent for Russian American company; visited Fort Ross, 1818–1832; wrote about Coast Miwok of Bodega Bay.

KOTZEBUE, OTTO VON. Visited San Francisco, 1815–1816; visited San Francisco and San Rafael, 1824.

LANGSDORFF, GEORGE H. VON. German naturalist; visited San Francisco, 1806.

LAUFF, CHARLES. Arrived in Marin County, 1845; wrote of life in early Marin County.

LEESE, JACOB. Mariano G. Vallejo's brother-in-law.

MARCO. Coast Miwok Indian guide with Kotzebue, 1824.

MARINO/MARIN (HUICMUSE). Huimen tribe of Coast Miwok; married to Juana; namesake of Marin County, as chosen by Mariano G. Vallejo.

MARTINA (CHONCHONMAEN). Olompali tribe of Coast Miwok; mother of Juana; married to Nemenciano Telemele.

MARTINEZ, IGNACIO. Commander of San Francisco presidio company, 1822–1827; wrote that he captured Pomponio.

MERCADO, JESÚS. Priest at Mission San Rafael, 1833; in conflict with Mariano G. Vallejo.

MICHELTORENA, MANUEL. Governor of California, 1842–1845.

MOLINA, JOSÉ SANTOS. Assistant to Mercado; accused of injustices toward Indians at Mission San Rafael.

MURPHY, TIMOTHY. Administrator at Mission San Rafael after secularization, 1837–1842.

NEREO (GUENUNGUBOC). Olema tribe of Coast Miwok; alcalde, witness, interpreter, godparent, and nurse at Mission San Rafael, 1819–1833; brother of Justino.

ORDAZ, BLAS. Priest at Mission Dolores at the time he accompanied Luis Argüello on his 1821 expedition.

OSIO, ANTONIO MARÍA. Brother-in-law of Luis Argüello; wrote an early history of California.

PACIFICO (HUYUM). Guaulen tribe of Coast Miwok; captain; son of Telemele (Nemenciano); accompanied Payeras on trip north, 1819; witness and godparent.

PAYERAS, MARIANO. Priest at and president of numerous missions, 1815–1822; visited Mission San Rafael, 1818, 1819, 1820, and 1822.

POMPONIO (LUPUGEYUN). Guaulen tribe of Coast Miwok; runaway from Mission Dolores, 1820; executed for killing soldier Manuel Varela, 1824.

QUIJAS, JOSE LORENZO. Priest at San Rafael and Sonoma (San Francisco de Soláno) missions, 1834–1843.

QUINTINO/QUINTÍN (TIGUACSE). Aguasto tribe of Coast Miwok; neophyte at Mission Dolores; Mariano G. Vallejo wrote of battle of Quintín and Marín against the Mexican military, 1824.

RAFAEL (JOBOCHOLA/JOBOCHEA). Suisun tribe of Patwin language family at Mission Dolores; interpreter on Luis Argüello's 1821 expedition.

REED, JUAN. Mill Valley settler; received land grant of Rancho Corte Madera del Presidio in Tiburon and Mill Valley, 1834.

SALVADOR. Coast Miwok; executed for murder, 1879.

SANCHEZ, JOSE ANTONIO. Soldier in San Francisco presidio company, 1791–1832; campaigned against Indians.

SARRIS, GREG. Chairman of the Federated Indians of Graton Rancheria, 1993 to present; professor at Sonoma State University; author of several books, including *Keeping Slug Woman Alive, Mabel McKay, Grand Avenue, Waternelon Nights,* and *The Sound of Rattles and Clappers.*

SMITH, BILL. Coast Miwok from Bodega Bay; half-brother of Tom Smith; son of Tsupu and Captain Stephen Smith.

SMITH, KATHLEEN. Coast Miwok; descendant of Bill Smith; artist.

SMITH, TOM. Coast Miwok from Bodega Bay; interviewed by Isabel Kelly, 1931–1932; son of Tsupu (Coast Miwok) and a Pomo father.

SOLANO (SINA). Suisun tribe of Patwin language family; baptized Francisco Solano at Mission Dolores, 1810; friend of Mariano G. Vallejo.

TAYLOR, ALEX S. Writer; collector of mission letters, 1860s.

TEODORICO (TAUALSSUTUPUTTI QUILAJUQUE). Huimen tribe of Coast Miwok; neophyte at Missions Dolores, San Rafael, and Sonoma; witness at Marino and Juana's wedding; half-brother of Cayetana and José María; claimant of Nicasio; married to Micaelina.

THALMAN, SYLVIA. Co-edited Isabel Kelly's manuscript; one of the founders of the Miwok Archaeological Preserve of Marin (MAPOM); genealogist of the

Federated Indians of Graton Rancheria.

TIKHÁNOV, MIKHAIL. Russian artist in Bodega region, 1818.

TORIBIO (PIXPIXUECAS). Licatiut tribe of Coast Miwok; captain of Licatiut, interpreter, witness, godparent, alcalde, 1820–1826.

TSUPU. Also known as Maria Cheka; associated with Petaluma, Tomales, and Bodega tribes of Coast Miwok; mother of Bill and Tom Smith.

VALLEJO, MARIANO G. Named county of Marin after Marino, 1850; wrote *Documentos para la historia de California (History of California)*, 1875; secretary to Governor Alvarado in Monterey, 1820s; in military at Monterey and San Francisco presidios; commander at San Francisco presidio, 1831–1834; founder of Sonoma mission, 1835; commandante general of northern California, 1836; known as General Vallejo.

VALLEJO, SALVADOR. Brother of Mariano G. Vallejo; captain of militia at Sonoma, 1836, campaigned against Indians.

ZAVALISHIN, DMITRY I. Russian naval officer; visited San Francisco, 1823–1824.

APPENDIX B

TIMELINE FOR MARINO

1781   Born in tribal lands

1801   Baptized March 7 at Mission Dolores
        Married Marina March 7 at Mission Dolores

1802   Marina died in July at Mission Dolores
        Witness at weddings in April and December at Mission Dolores
        Married Doda in September at Mission Dolores

1804   Witness at wedding in August at Mission Dolores

1806   Witness at weddings in August at Mission Dolores

1811   Witness at weddings and a godparent in March at Mission Dolores
        Doda died in August at Mission Dolores

1816   Baptized a six-year-old girl in "el monte" in July
        Married Juana in August at Mission Dolores
        Godparent in August at Mission Dolores

1817   Juana's child Melchior baptized in January and died five days later at Mission
        Dolores
        Became (in December) the first Indian to act as a godfather at Mission San
        Rafael

1818   Godparent in May, June, and October at Misson San Rafael

1819   Named "alcalde mayor" in July at Mission San Rafael
        Godparent in October at Mission San Rafael
        Named "primero alcalde and mayor" in October and December at Mission San
        Rafael

1820   Godparent in February at Mission San Rafael
        Named "mayordomo" in February at Mission San Rafael

1821   On expedition with Argüello and Ordaz from October to November

1822   Godfather in February (brought dying child to San Rafael for baptism) and April at Mission San Rafael
Written up for insubordination in a letter from Amorós to Argüello in December

1823   Godfather in August and December at Mission San Rafael

1825   Godfather in June at Mission San Rafael

1826   Godfather in August in San Mateo outstation, recorded at Mission Dolores

1827   Godfather in April at Mission Dolores

1833   Met with Vallejo in May to complain of mayordomo at Mission San Rafael
Godfather in July at Mission San Rafael
Witness at wedding in August at Mission San Rafael

1834   Witness at weddings in April, May, and June at Mission San Rafael
Godfather in May and June at Mission San Rafael
Surveyed San Rafael mission lands with Martinez in October

1835   Witness at weddings in May, October, and November at Mission San Rafael

1836   Witness at weddings in June and August at Mission San Rafael
Godfather in August at Mission San Rafael
Juana died in September at Mission San Rafael
Witness at wedding in September at Mission San Rafael

1839   Died March 15 at Mission San Rafael

1850   Vallejo named county after Marino

APPENDIX C

THE COAST MIWOK LANGUAGE:
CATHOLIC PRAYERS AND WAR SONGS

CATHOLIC PRAYERS

A Catholic Prayer from Mission San Rafael, August 15, 1825

Canipu oy opa muye usguisu suaigi itti Ma Sma illingela masca sa uni omchus (72 anos; itti imguelac Dios ope muye inico, opeia inti masca omu incapo: ope catovitam menea numa culesco: ope itti maxca isac unu J.C. eay Dios isactais: itti sucugi tupeca lileto cucui floyaco uni Angelisco:ope ittica unpattu chague mayen ope enpecadona lileto: itti macono jaus itti opunvelac macono unu:ope macono guelac itti muye usguisu. Amen

—Pinart, A. L. Prayer from "Catechism and Prayer in the San Rafael Dialect."

The Lord's Prayer as Said at Mission San Rafael

Apí maco sa liléto manénas mi aues oniá mácano michauka oiopa mitauka chakenit opu negato chakenit opu liléto tumako muye quenunje naya macono sucuji sulia macóno masojte chake mat opu ma suli mayaco maco yangia ume onut ulemi macono mu in capo. neteni Jesus

—Duflot du Mofras, *Travels on the Pacific Coast*, 203.

WAR SONG OF THE BODEGA MIWOK

At the beginning of a battle, or in making ready for war, the warriors sing:

Temoi hoibu	Leaders, let us
Onigi tschinami	Go out to war!
Temai ilawak	Let us go and capture
Temai o tomai	A pretty girl!

Upon approaching the enemy settlement, they sing:

Indi mi schujugu	When do we cross the mountain?
Pari o londo	Who do we see first?

Upon beginning to shoot, they sing:

Buteki landa	Sharp are our missiles;
Junawschi landa	Keep putting forth yours.

To give his warriors courage, the toyon sings:

Otilek – otilek lilem	Forward, forward,
Lile oje lippe	Now to the battle,
Lile oje ili lippi	Stouthearted, follow me!
Nawu elendu	Fear nothing, enemy arrows
Indi kotscht ma iwid elendu.	Do you no harm.

—Transcribed by P. Kostromitonov in 1839, translated by
Fred Stross in Wrangell [1839] 1974, 11.

APPENDIX D

SAN RAFAEL MISSION CENSUS, 1815–1845

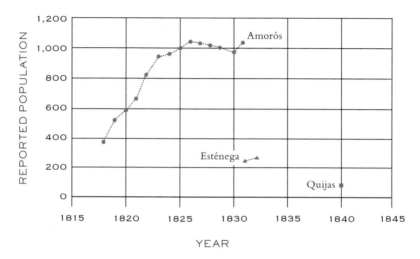

From annual reports of Amorós, Esténega, and Quijas. On file at Santa Barbara Mission Archives Library.

APPENDIX E

INDIAN BAPTISMS, MARRIAGES, AND DEATHS
AT MISSION SAN RAFAEL, DECEMBER 1817 TO 1839

YEAR	BAPTISMS	MARRIAGES	DEATHS
1817–1818	212	50	61
1819	147	44	34
1820	117	28	28
1821	156	51	45
1822	199	71	55
1823	118	30	43
1824	228	55	65
1825	158	33	70
1826	137	39	63
1827	45	17	38
1828	83	29	61
1829	17	11	35
1830	23	15	29
1831	157	66	29
1832	15	9	37
1833	14	9	39
1834	10	2	8
1835	13	12	23
1836	12	7	28
1837	10	10	15
1838	12	1	45
1839	19	4	28

The figures are based on the annual and biannual reports submitted by the priests and are on file at the Santa Barbara Mission Archives Library. When the reports were missing (1833–1839) the data in the mission registers were used. The annual reports and the mission registers did not always agree; deaths were underreported in the annual reports, particularly in the years 1818, 1819, 1821, and 1826, by five to twelve people, the result of omitting those who died at baptism or who were tallied only at Mission Dolores, even though they died at San Rafael.

APPENDIX F

CONFESSIONS AND COMMUNIONS
AT MISSION SAN RAFAEL, 1824–1830

YEAR	NUMBER OF ADULTS	CONFESSIONS (%)	COMMUNIONS (%)
1824	763	26.6	1.8
1825	803	24.9	1.7
1826	823	24.9	1.5
1827	822	27	1.8
1828	815	28.2	1.6
1829	806	27.9	1.7
1830	777	2.6	2.6

From annual reports of Amorós. On file at Santa Barbara Mission Archives Library.

APPENDIX G

POPULATION, LIVESTOCK, AND PRODUCE
IN FOUR CALIFORNIA MISSIONS, 1828

		SAN RAFAEL	SONOMA	SAN FRANCISCO	SAN JOSE
INDIANS AT THE MISSION		1,027	705	936	1,767
LARGE ANIMALS	CATTLE	873	1,400	4,332	15,000
	HORSES	393	525	900	1,000
	MULES	2	6	17	40
SMALL ANIMALS	SHEEP	2,957	4,000	4,093	15,000
	PIGS	15	60	0	30
WEIGHT OF PRODUCE (FANEGAS)	WHEAT	333	514	505	1,700
	CORN	5	25	80	400
	BEANS	34	2	10	70
	BARLEY	274	208	230	30
	CHICKPEAS	12	21	32	37

Data from José María Guzmán, "Breve Noticia," 1926, *California Historical Society Quarterly,* vol. 5, no. 3, 216-217.

APPENDIX H

FAMILY TREE OF MARIA COPA

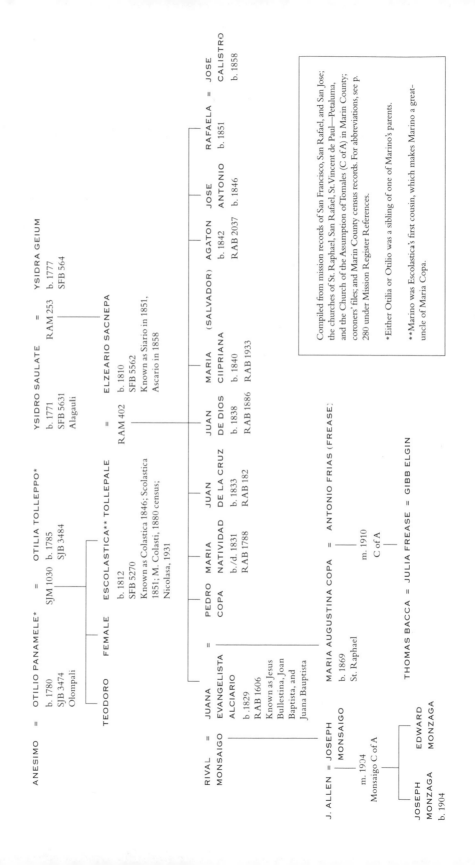

Compiled from mission records of San Francisco, San Rafael, and San Jose; the churches of St. Raphael, San Rafael, St. Vincent de Paul—Petaluma, and the Church of the Assumption of Tomales (C of A) in Marin County; coroners' files; and Marin County census records. For abbreviations, see p. 280 under Mission Register References.

*Either Otilia or Otilio was a sibling of one of Marino's parents.

**Marino was Escolastica's first cousin, which makes Marino a great-uncle of Maria Copa.

APPENDIX I

MARIN COUNTY CENSUS RECORDS OF INDIANS, 1850–1900

TOWNSHIPS	1852	1860	1870	1880	1900
San Antonio		5	0	1	0
Tomales		10	11	1	0
Novato		18	17	8	0
Bolinas		1	16	5	0
Sausalito		3	5	7	1
Point Reyes		0	18	34	0
Nicasio		0	33	39	0
San Rafael		72	10	0	1
San Quentin		0	16	0	4
TOTAL	218	109	126	95	6

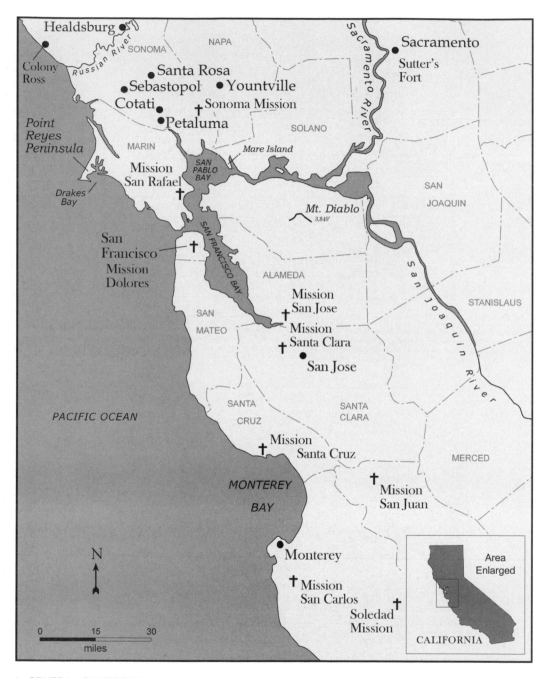

Healdsburg
Colony Ross
SONOMA
NAPA
Russian River
Santa Rosa
Sebastopol
Yountville
Cotati
Sonoma Mission
Petaluma
SOLANO
Sacramento River
Sacramento
Sutter's Fort
Point Reyes Peninsula
MARIN
Mare Island
SAN PABLO BAY
Drakes Bay
Mission San Rafael
SAN FRANCISCO BAY
Mt. Diablo
3,849'
SAN JOAQUIN
San Francisco Mission Dolores
ALAMEDA
Mission San Jose
SAN MATEO
Mission Santa Clara
San Jose
San Joaquin River
STANISLAUS
PACIFIC OCEAN
SANTA CRUZ
SANTA CLARA
MERCED
Mission Santa Cruz
MONTEREY BAY
Mission San Juan
N
Monterey
Mission San Carlos
Soledad Mission
Area Enlarged
CALIFORNIA
0   15   30
miles

I · CENTRAL CALIFORNIA

216

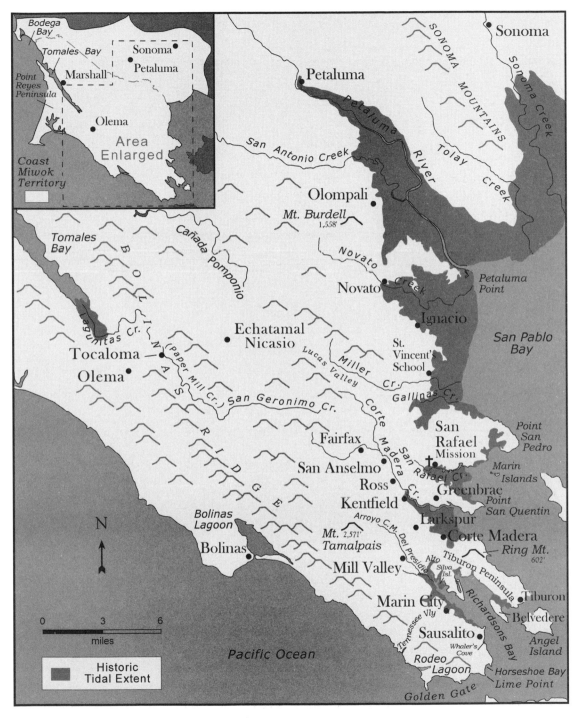

II · COAST MIWOK TERRITORY *(Information on historic tidal extent from http://www.sfei.org/ecoatlas/Habitat/maps/SFBay/*
pastDist.html)

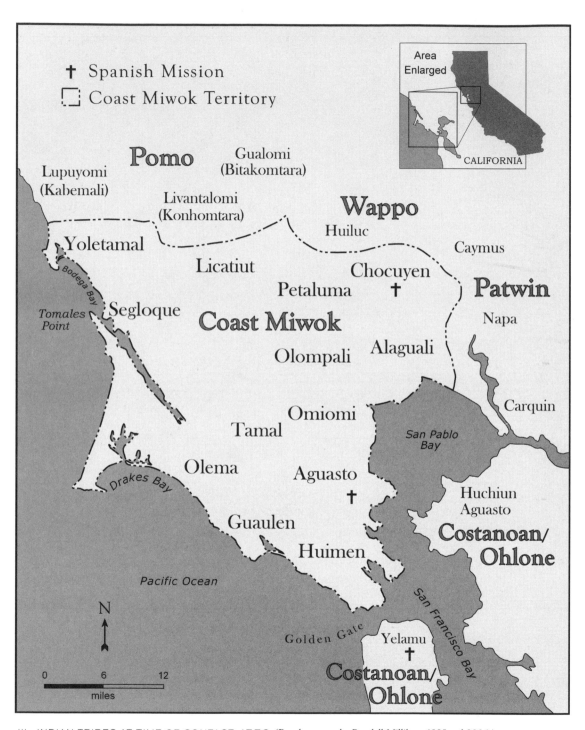

Spanish Mission
Coast Miwok Territory

Area
Enlarged

CALIFORNIA

Pomo

Gualomi
(Bitakomtara)

Lupuyomi
(Kabemali)

Livantalomi
(Konhomtara)

Wappo

Huiluc

Caymus

Yoletamal

Licatiut

Chocuyen

Patwin

Bodega Bay

Petaluma

Napa

Tomales
Point

Segloque

Coast Miwok

Alaguali

Olompali

Carquin

Omiomi

San Pablo
Bay

Tamal

Olema

Aguasto

Huchiun
Aguasto

Drakes Bay

Guaulen

Costanoan/
Ohlone

Huimen

Pacific Ocean

N

San Francisco Bay

0   6   12
miles

Golden Gate

Yelamu

Costanoan/
Ohlone

III · INDIAN TRIBES AT TIME OF CONTACT, 1776 *(Based on maps by Randall Milliken, 1995 and 2006.)*

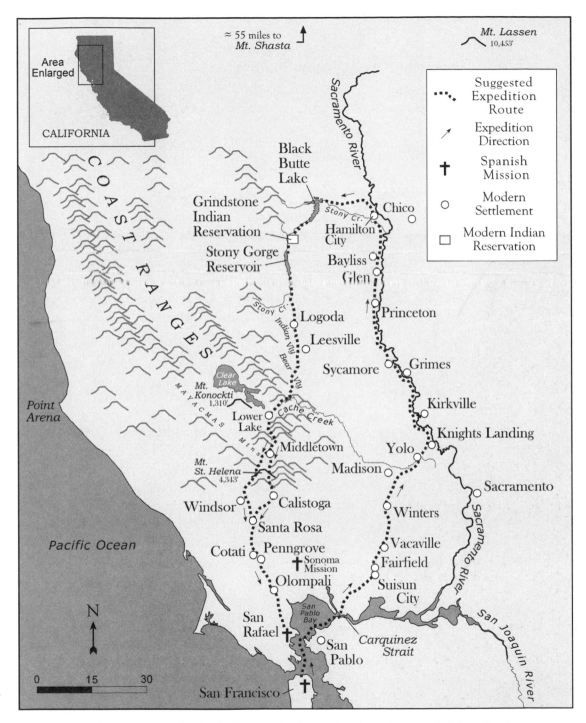

Map labels:

Area Enlarged

CALIFORNIA

≈ 55 miles to *Mt. Shasta*

Mt. Lassen 10,453'

Suggested Expedition Route

Expedition Direction

Spanish Mission

Modern Settlement

Modern Indian Reservation

Sacramento River

COAST RANGES

Black Butte Lake

Stony Cr.

Chico

Grindstone Indian Reservation

Hamilton City

Stony Gorge Reservoir

Bayliss

Glen

Stony Cr.

Princeton

Bear Vlly

Stony Indian Vlly

Logoda

Leesville

Sycamore

Grimes

Clear Lake

Mt. Konockti 1,310'

Kirkville

M A Y A C M A S

Cache Creek

Lower Lake

Knights Landing

Point Arena

Middletown

Yolo

Mt. St. Helena 4,343'

Madison

Mts.

Sacramento

Windsor

Calistoga

Winters

Santa Rosa

Pacific Ocean

Cotati

Penngrove

Vacaville

Sonoma Mission

Olompali

Fairfield

Suisun City

N

San Pablo Bay

San Rafael

San Pablo

Carquinez Strait

Sacramento River

San Joaquin River

0   15   30

San Francisco

IV · EXPEDITION OF 1821 *(Based on Randall Milliken undated manuscript and author's extensive field observations.)*

219

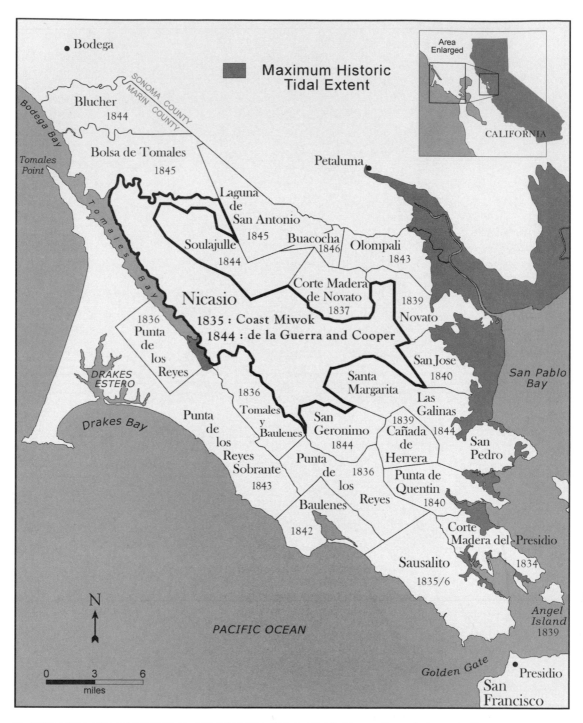

Bodega

Maximum Historic
Tidal Extent

Area
Enlarged

CALIFORNIA

Bodega Bay

Blucher
1844

SONOMA COUNTY
MARIN COUNTY

Tomales
Point

Bolsa de Tomales
1845

Petaluma

Laguna
de
San Antonio
1845

Tomales Bay

Soulajulle
1844

Buacocha
1846

Olompali
1843

Nicasio

Corte Madera
de Novato
1837

1839
Novato

1835 : Coast Miwok
1844 : de la Guerra and Cooper

1836
Punta
de
los
Reyes

San Jose
1840

San Pablo
Bay

DRAKES
ESTERO

Santa
Margarita

Las
Galinas

1836

Drakes Bay

Punta
de
los
Reyes
Sobrante
1843

Tomales
y
Baulenes

San
Geronimo
1844

1839
Cañada
de
Herrera

1844

San
Pedro

Punta
de
los
Reyes

1836

Punta de
Quentin
1840

Baulenes

1842

Corte
Madera del Presidio

1834

N

Sausalito
1835/6

Angel
Island
1839

PACIFIC OCEAN

0   3   6
miles

Golden Gate

Presidio

San
Francisco

V · MEXICAN LAND GRANTS IN MARIN COUNTY, 1834–1846 *(Sonoma County land grants in Coast
Miwok territory were granted between 1840 and 1846.)*

NOTES

CHAPTER ONE

1. Muir 1938.

2. Wilma Follett, personal communication.

3. Copa quoted in Kelly 2003, 491, 485; Smith quoted in Kelly 2003, 485. Copa's observation is quite close to the familiar sailing adage "Red sky at night, sailors' delight; red sky at morning, sailors take warning."

4. Wood and Heck described the earthquakes that occurred between 1769 and 1940 in *U.S. Coast and Geodetic Survey* 1941; Smith quoted in Kelly 2003, 492.

5. Merriam 1993, 228. Portions of these redwood forests are preserved in Muir Woods and Samuel P. Taylor State Park. Remnants of towering redwood groves can also be seen at the entrance of Baltimore Canyon in Larkspur and at the head of Homestead Valley adjacent to Mill Valley.

6. Kelly 2003, 193.

7. Kelly 2003, 394-395; Merriam [1910] 1993.

8. Kelly 2003, 91, 177, 178, 185, 160, 500, 496.

9. Beechey 1941, 64; Kelly 2003, 37-54, 42.

10. Anderson 1993, 162, 167.

11. Richardson 1918, 40, 151; Davis 1967, 31.

12. Slaymaker 1977, 158; Smith quoted in Kelly 2003, 194.

13. Peacock, 8; Fages quoted in Stanger and Brown 1969, 22.

14. Beechey 1941, 65; Duhaut-Cilly 1929, 239.

15. Kelly 2003, 29; Kelly 1931-1932, Notebook 10, 24.

16. Lauff 1916, 6; Richardson 1918, 151.

17. The Nisenan tribe east of Sacramento used forty rabbit skins, according to Wilson and Towne 1978, 391; Tom Smith recalled using only fourteen jackrabbits for a blanket (Kelly 2003, 160), but this number seems too low.

18. Stanger and Brown 1969, 54; Smith quoted in Kelly 2003, 139; Beechey 1941, 66; Choris 1932, 367.

19. Ogden 1941, 58-59; Richardson 1918, 152.

20. Kelly 2003, 194.

21. Kelly 2003, 194.

22. Kelly 2003, 195.

23. Kelly 2003, 195, 412-413; Geiger and Meighan 1976, 160.

24. Shuford 1993, 430 (in Koford 1953, *National Audubon Society Research Report 4*).

25. Kelly 2003, 409.

26. Kelly 2003, 121, 494; Hudson and Bates 1984.

27. Golovnin 1979, 152; Richardson 1918, 156.

28. Kelly 2003, 493; Merriam 1993, 213.

29. By the 1930s, the fifty-five thousand acres of wetlands in the North Bay had been reduced to ten thousand acres. Earlier, the waters of San Pablo Bay had reached Sears Point and Black Point, today on Highway 37 in southern Sonoma County.

30. Richardson 1918, 156; Geiger and Meighan 1976, 84.

31. Kelly 2003, 130-131.

32. Richardson 1918, 157.

33. Heizer and Elsasser 1980, 210.

CHAPTER TWO

1. Tom Smith reported that a large rancheria might have had ten houses, although the smaller villages more commonly had five to six houses, supporting thirty to forty inhabitants (Kelly 2003, 62, 67).

2. SFB 2182; The term "Coast Miwok" is a linguistic classification, but it commonly refers to a tribe. The separate tribes within this language group were first described by Kroeber as "tribelets," but this term is no longer in favor.

3. Milliken 1998. The Aguasto are also identified as Habasto and Abasto in the San Francisco mission records. Milliken has suggested that the Tamal Indians also be included in this branch of the Coast Miwok (personal communication, 2004).

4. Recollections of long-time neighbors at the Alto site in Mill Valley, collected in the 1970s by Katy Jo Sebastian and the author. In 1909, a local newspaper touted the "good soil" that could be found in Mill Valley shellmounds (*Mill Valley Independent,* April 23, 1909).

5. Archaeologists today work cooperatively with Indian observers to ensure that all excavations on Indian sites are done respectfully and professionally and that Indian people are increasingly involved in decision making, in what has been described by Kent G. Lightfoot as "indigenous archaeology" (Lightfoot 2005a, 39). Research includes such topics as cultural change through time, the organization of villages, use of natural resources, kinship and migration patterns, diet, and the general health of the community.

6. Nelson 1909. Field notes for Mrn (Marin) 10. Archaeological sites in California are usually identified by three-letter abbreviations for each county. "Mrn" represents Marin County.

7. Author interviewed the informant, who wished to remain anonymous, in 1994.

8. Land Case 183 N.D., p. 3, Corte Madera del Presidio, United States District Court, Bancroft Library, University of California, Berkeley. The surveying team included Fernando Felix, Francisco Haro, and Nereo (spelled "Neri" in the documents).

9. Testimony, October 28, 1875. "Before the U.S. Surveyor-General of California..., Rancho Corte Madera del Presidio: Testimony and Proceedings," 1876.

10. Both a mound in Sausalito (at the Marin Movie Theater on Caledonia Street) and one in Belvedere were larger: 650 feet by 350 feet by 20 feet high, and 500 feet by 270 feet by 22 feet high, respectively.

11. Henry Fontine, personal communication, 1988.

12. Schoolboys Don McGeein and his brother rode their bicycles around Mill Valley and collected artifacts from other sites as well. Eventually trained at the University of California at Berkeley, Don McGeein practiced archaeology during vacations into his eighties, working with professional archaeologists. Personal communication with Don and Doug McGeein, 1988.

13. Thomas Bickerstaff (born 1892), oral history, 1970, Mill Valley Public Library.

14. As observed by the author; Nick Davoren found a piece eight inches long (see Pahl 2004).

15. In the 1980s, Tom Origer of Sonoma State University dated a few of the obsidian stone tools from the McGeein collection using the obsidian hydration dating method, which revealed that the site was occupied at least in the late sixteenth century.

From 2003 through 2005, three different projects had an impact on the already disturbed mound. Archaeologists and a Coast Miwok observer, Frank Ross, worked together to ensure that all projects were in compliance with the laws of California (the California Environmental Quality Act, CEQA) and the federal government (the Native American Graves Protection and Repatriation Act, NAGPRA).

16. Allardt map, 1841.

17. James Bennyhof, personal communication, 1982.

18. A salvage dig in the 1970s under the supervision of the author included students from the College of Marin, volunteers from the Miwok Archaeological Preserve of Marin (MAPOM), and an Indian observer.

19. See also Moratto, Riley, and Wilson 1974; Riley 1979.

20. See also Pahl 2004.

21. See also Goerke and Davidson 1975; Bill Roop, personal communication.

22. Merriam 1907, 356. Merriam listed the pronunciation of this name as Le'-wan-nel-lo wah'.

23. This village, located where the Marin Movie Theater now stands, was excavated by Nelson. His 1910 notes mention that at least nine skeletons and approximately eighty artifacts were found at the site (Nelson 1910). The artifacts are listed in the Hearst Museum catalog and include obsidian blades, ear plugs, abalone pendants, and bone awls.

24. Beads at these two sites were studied by James Bennyhof. See the manuscript of W. J. Wallace, 1940 and 1943-1944; and the notes of Jack Smith, 1957 (both in the late Bennyhoff's personal collection). Neighbors collected the beads.

25. Ray Weeks, personal communication, 1994.

26. Obsidian hydration dates on a few obsidian tools found at this site indicate that it was occupied at least by 200 A.D. and as recently as the sixteenth century (Tom Origer, personal communication).

27. Interviews with elderly residents and former residents of Tiburon and Belvedere, conducted by the author during the 1990s.

28. Ray Weeks, personal communication, 1994.

29. T. F. King 1970; T. F. King 1974.

30. These designs are described as the "pecked curvilinear nucleated" (PCN) style of petroglyph (T. Miller 1977).

CHAPTER THREE

1. Isabel Kelly notes that there was no round house at the Nicasio rancheria and that people gathered in the sweathouse; this may have been typical in smaller rancherias (Kelly 2003, 463).

2. See also Margolin 1993, 7.

3. Kelly wrote that while she was interviewing Tom Smith, "he spent his evenings singing [in order to] remember things to tell [her] the following day" (Kelly 2003, xvi).

4. In 1850, the boy's father, former U.S. Army officer William Mayfield, who was working as a stockman, left his motherless son, Thomas Jefferson Mayfield, in the hands of the Choinumne tribe in the San Joaquin Valley. What must have appealed to the senior Mayfield was the loving, supportive, and stable lifestyle of the Choinumne, an environment that he could not provide his child given the frequent moves and economic instability of a stockman's life. See also Mayfield 1978.

5. Mayfield 1993, 69-70.

6. Margolin 1993, 139.

7. Kelly 2003, 421. California tribes usually told these stories at night; the Pomo in particular believed the narrator would become a hunchback if the story were related during the day. Nevertheless, Smith told Kelly that it was "all right to tell stories in the daytime"; and the Achumawi in northern California purposefully told narratives during the day in colder months, "all lying down in the earth lodge...on cold winter days...[and] huddled together for warmth" (Olmstead and Stewart 1978, 234).

8. Margolin 1993, 140.

9. Kelly 2003, 421, 434.

10. Merriam [1910] 1993, 18.

11. Merriam [1910] 1993, 204-205.

12. Kelly 2003, 421-423, 434-436.

13. Kelly 2003, 444-445.

14. Hinton 1994, 45-47.

15. Kelly 2003, xvi; Otis Parrish lecture, November 2002. The current chapter relies extensively on interviews with Tom Smith and Maria Copa that were conducted by Isabel Kelly from 1931 to 1932. Published in 1991 by the Miwok Archaeological Preserve of Marin, these interviews contain a wealth of detailed information on Coast Miwok culture. Most of the quotations from Smith and Copa included in this chapter come from this 2003 publication; others come from Kelly's field notes, as indicated. Quotations from Smith and Copa were edited minimally, for clarity, in the 2003 book. Overall, Smith and Copa had similar remembrances; differing recollections can usually be traced to their differences in age (Smith was ninety-four, Copa sixty-three), gender, or place of origin (Smith came from Bodega, Copa from Nicasio).

16. Kelly 2003, 499, 497.

17. Kelly 1978, 421; Bean and Theodoratus 1978, 295.

18. Kelly 2003, 504-506.

19. Kelly 2003, 509, 382, 175. The comment about the scratching stick is quoted from Kroeber 1970, 254.

20. Kelly 2003, 496.

21. Geiger and Meighan 1976, 68-69.

22. Kelly 2003, 327, 332. The Miwok were divided into two groups known as moieties, one designated as land, and the other water. Based on patrilineal exogamy, married couples belonged to different moieties, and their children belonged to the moiety of the father.

23. Kelly 2003, 495-496; Kroeber 1970, 46, 497.

24. Kelly 2003, 401, 408, 450, 432.

25. Kelly 2003, 397; Kelly 1978, 422-423. Bev Ortiz describes the dances as "visible prayers" (Bay Miwok Conference, October 2003).

26. Kelly 2003, 423.

27. See Kelly 2003 for the details of more than twenty dances.

28. Kelly 1978, 422; Kelly 2003, 100.

29. Kelly 2003, 297.

30. Kelly 2003, 409-411. The hoipu kulele was not the same person as the primary female leader, the maien.

31. Effigies were used in bird and bear dances. The effigies were representative of one of the moieties, and members of the opposite moiety shot at the effigy.

32. Kelly 2003, 253-256, 153.

33. Kelly 2003, 369, 359.

34. Margolin 1993, 108; Kelly 2003, 360.

35. Kelly 1931-1932, Notebook 9, 8; Kelly 2003, 360, 361.

36. Greg Sarris, personal communication, 2000; Munro-Fraser 1880, 46. Another version of this tale can be found in Bingham 1906.

37. Merriam [1910] 1993.

38. Loeb 1926, 226; Geiger and Meighan 1976, 92. The sun of the winter solstice rises just feet away from two different archaeological sites in Coast Miwok territory.

39. Kelly 2003, 490, 489, 491.

40. Jeff Fentriss, personal communication, 2000; Hedges 1985.

41. Elsasser and Rhode 1996, 1.

42. "Tolay Lake Regional Park: Cultural and Natural History," www.sonoma-county. org/parks/pk_tolay_history.htm, County of Sonoma Regional Parks Department.

43. Sarris 2003.

44. Kelly 1978, 419; Kelly 2003, 347; Kelly 2003, 350.

45. Kelly 2003, 343-347.

46. Kelly 2003, 346, 351.

47. Bean 1978, 678.

48. Kelly 2003, 454, 407.

49. Kelly 2003, 118.

50. Tom Smith describes the children's chores in Kelly 2003, 207, 131, 502.

51. The feathered belts seen by Hudson and Bates at the Kunstkamera in St. Petersburg, Russia, had "shell disc beads (white) that were incorporated into the fabric as it was woven" (Hudson and Bates 1984, 186).

52. Kelly 2003, 206, 207.

53. Visitors from Europe admired the skills of these central California Indian artisans and collected baskets, headdresses, belts, capes, and other objects. Some of these items are exhibited prominently in European museums. Strangely, the Spaniards and the Mexicans did not collect or even seem to admire the work of the Indians; it was as if they did not recognize the Indians' craftsmanship. Museo de América in Madrid contains only nineteen objects from California, all from the Chumash people of the Santa Barbara area, collected in 1791, whereas museums in Paris, London, Helsinki, Frankfurt, Berlin, Offenbach, Munich, and particularly St. Petersburg (which houses more than one hundred pieces), have fine collections of these rare and priceless pieces of art, the majority of which are not on public display, except at Offenbach. The German collections are stored in controlled environments and are in very good condition, save for the loss of some feathers. The much larger and most spectacular St. Petersburg collection has not fared as well.

54. Beechey [1831] 1941, 62; Kotzebue 1830, 116.

55. Ralph Shanks, basketry expert, personal communication, 2005.

56. Kelly 2003, 118.

57. C. King 1978, 61; Kelly 2003, 198.

58. The most common headdress, observed by Sir Francis Drake in 1579, was a type of hairnet, sometimes decorated with beads, that was worn by men. This type of hair covering was one of the gifts offered to the first Spanish arrivals, as described by Father Santa María two hundred years after Drake (Francis Fletcher cited in Heizer 1947, 287).

59. Langsdorff quoted in Paddison 1999, 113; Craig Bates, MAPOM lecture, March 1998.

60. Heizer 1947, 283.

61. Craig Bates, personal communication, 1998; Hudson and Bates 1984, 156.

62. Kelly 2003, 169; Zavalishin 1973, 382-383; Hudson and Bates 1984, 187b.

63. Craig Bates, MAPOM lecture, March 1998.

64. Langsdorff quoted in Paddison 1999, 111; Bates, personal communication.

65. Margolin 1993, 65.

66. Stross 1974, 11, 5.

67. Kelly 2003, 360; McCorkle 1978, 697; Kroeber 1970, 235; Otis Parrish at the Native Voices Conference, Dominican University, San Rafael, California, July 2004. There was, however, a serious conflict involving deaths and scalping in northeastern Pomo territory sometime between 1830 and 1840. The dispute concerned the ownership of a salt deposit and payments for it (Kroeber 1970, 236).

CHAPTER FOUR

1. Galvin 1971, 3; Treutlein 1968, 64; Stanger and Brown 1969, 30, 41, 31. Stanger and Brown reported that the ship was 7½ feet long.

2. Ayala in Galvin 1971, 91.

3. The Ohlone people are also known as Costanoans, an anglicized version of the Spanish name for coast people.

4. Fages also visited the Pittsburg area in the east before turning back through Amador Valley to Pleasanton and over Mission Pass to Monterey.

5. Santa María in Galvin 1971, 19.

6. Ibid. The decorated rod was a mark of authority, observed by Drake in 1579 (Heizer 1947, 287).

7. Santa María in Galvin 1971, 21. José de Jésus Vallejo also commented on this speechmaking: "Indian orators used to make their speeches while walking back and forth very quickly in the nude" (1875 s3:13). The minerals for body paint were available on the Tiburon peninsula.

8. Santa María in Galvin 1971, 25.

9. The string of shells looked like a rosary to the priest, but Randall Milliken (1995) has suggested that it was a central Californian invitation string, the knots representing how many days remained before a festival or gathering. In his 1930s interview, Tom Smith, an elderly Coast Miwok, described unmarked invitation sticks, rather than strings, with the number of sticks sent to another village representing the number of days until a dance (Kelly 2003, 227).

10. Santa María in Galvin 1971, 29, 31.

11. Stanger and Brown 1969, 31; Santa María in Galvin 1971, 31.

12. Santa María in Galvin 1971, 43.

13. Ibid., 45.

14. Ibid., 61, 63. Captain Ayala in Galvin 1971, 84, 91.

15. Santa María in Galvin 1971, 61.

16. Ibid., 63; Ayala in Galvin 1971, 91.

17. Ibid., 65-66.

18. One Alabado that has survived and was sung in the missions is similar to a chant; as transcribed, it is in the Phrygian mode, with no sharps or flats. It is possible that Santa María sang words similar to these: "Lift your heart in joy and exalt Him / In the blessed Sacrament all Holy / Where He the Lord, His glory veiling / Comforts souls true and lowly" (from Father da Silva's transcription of the Alabado that Fernando sang for him; Juan Pedro Gaffney, Instituto Pro Musica de California, personal communication, 1980s).

19. Santa María in Galvin 1971, 63.

20. Ibid., 69.

21. Hinton 1994, 13.

22. Santa María in Galvin 1971, 69.

23. A round house. The best examples of these structures today can be seen at Kule Loklo at Point Reyes National Seashore or at Indian Grinding Rock State Park.

24. Santa María in Galvin 1971, 73.

25. Stanger and Brown 1969, 162.

26. Canizares in Galvin 1971, 96. George Vancouver in 1792 described them as 10 feet in length and 3 or 4 feet wide, "made up of rolls the length of the canoe, the thickest in the middle, and regularly tapering to a point at each end" (Paddison 1999, 70).

27. Ayala in Galvin 1971, 91.

CHAPTER FIVE

1. Milliken 1995, 62.

2. Ibid., 64.

3. Ibid., 63-65.

4. Palou quoted in Milliken 1996, 12.

5. J. Vallejo, 1875, 22. The missions also experienced food shortages, however. At such times, they allowed the Indians to fish and gather traditional greens and seeds.

6. Beechey 1941, 16.

7. Beebe and Senkewicz in Osio 1996, 66, 28.

8. Milliken 1995, 270-271, tables 8 and 9. These figures do not include the numbers of East Bay Ohlone who were also at Mission Dolores.

9. Most of the sixteen Guaulen and thirty-seven Aguasto were baptized in 1800 (ibid., 271).

10. Hendry and Bowman, 1062.

11. Captain Frederick William Beechey, an Englishman, ridiculed the artwork displayed in northern mission churches for the visual representations of hell ("disgusting") and heaven ("ludicrous"), "the former exhibiting in the most disgusting manner all the torments the imagination can fancy, for the purpose of striking terror into the simple Indians" (Beechey 1941, 14). At the mission in Carmel, the painting "Glory of Heaven" can still be seen; its companion piece, "Horrors of Hell," is now lost. Both were ordered from Mexico City in 1771.

12. Language diversity increased when Patwin speakers from north of the Carquinez Strait on the Sacramento River began coming to the mission in 1809 (Milliken 1995, 272). By 1815, 39 percent of the neophytes spoke Coast Miwok, 21 percent spoke Patwin, 20 percent Ohlone, and 10 percent Bay Miwok (Milliken 1998, table 3).

13. SFB 0769; SFB 2292. Jacinto, Marino's godfather, was the most frequently mentioned godfather and witness at weddings from 1800 until 1805. Jacinto died in 1806.

14. The greatest number of baptisms, 290, were among the Omiomi tribe of the Novato area. Other Coast Miwok baptisms as of December 1817 included 177 Tamal from the Nicasio area; 175 Costa from the coast, including Point Reyes; 148 Aguasto from the greater San Rafael area; 191 from Olema, north of Bolinas Bay; 116 Guaulen from Bolinas; 65 from Olompali; and 53 from Petaluma. Smaller numbers came from other Coast Miwok villages: 54 Chocoay, 47 Geluasibe, and 26 Puscuy, all tribes from the sloughs of the Petaluma River; 50 Alaguali from the north side of San Pablo Bay; 43 Chucuyen from the Sonoma Creek valley; and 13 Echajute from the mouth of Tomales Bay. The number of Huimen baptisms

may be inflated, since the priest may have labeled some Native Americans as Huimen simply because they came from the Marin peninsula. See SFB records transcribed by Milliken (1998, 20, table 1).

15. Milliken 1995, 266, table 5. In 1801, the mission total increased to eight hundred.

16. This village was located just south of today's Sixteenth Street, on the east side of Dolores Street. Excavations of this site in 1999 yielded few tools associated with traditional rancherias, such as chipped stone tools of chert or mortars and pestles for grinding acorn meal. Instead, archaeologists found cattle remains and seeds of domestic plants, suggesting that the residents were consuming rations provided by the priests (Nancy Valenti and Richard Ambro, personal communication, 2000). According to Ambro, there were other villages nearby, at present-day Fourteenth and Mission Streets, at Seventh and Mission Streets, and at the "willows" south of Eighteenth Street, between Valencia and Mission Streets, but tribal associations with these locations are unknown.

17. Vancouver quoted in Paddison 1999, 81.

18. Vancouver quoted in Milliken 1995, 90.

19. Vancouver quoted in Paddison 1999, 70; Choris 1932, 95.

20. Vancouver quoted in Paddison 1999, 79-80.

21. Choris in Mahr 1932, 95; Kotzebue 1830, 95.

22. La Pérouse 1989, 70; Kotzebue 1830, 79; Bancroft 1888, 231; Beechey 1941, 18.

23. Weber 1979, 44; Beechey 1941, 15.

24. Amador 1877.

25. Osio 1996, 33. Osio was a brother-in-law of Luis Argüello.

26. Chamisso in Mahr 1932, 83.

27. Beechey 1941, 18.

28. See also Milliken 1995, 299-303.

29. Osio 1996, 67.

30. Letter from Abella to Solá, January 1817, Taylor Collection #695.

31. Bancroft 1886, vol. 4, 759.

32. See also Beechey 1941, 28; Zavalishin 1973, 411, n. 4.

33. Beechey 1941, 16; Shishmarev quoted in Shur and Gibson 1973, 44; J. E. Galindo 1877, unpaginated.

34. Kotzebue 1830, 97-98. According to Bancroft, Kotzebue picked up his ideas from the Spanish officer José María Estudillo, who was "a bitter foe of the padres" (Bancroft 1886, vol. 2, 524).

35. Vancouver quoted in Weber 1979, 28; Botta [1828] 1952, 4.

36. Schabelski 1993, 8.

37. Margolin 1989, introduction to La Pérouse 1989, 15.

38. California Indian Conference, San Francisco State University, February 27-28, 1998.

39. The walipo "used to get the shoulder bone of a dead person—one who was murdered, hence not cremated. Held this bone on the windward side of a rancheria and killed

the people. There was poison in that bone; left the bone there in the night, he is going to finish that rancheria. When they see that person they are afraid. If there is a spring nearby, they are afraid he might poison the water" (Kelly 2003, 380).

40. Margolin does not see real similarity between Spanish and Indian religion (1993, 58).

41. Milliken 1995, 93-94.

42. Geiger and Meighan 1976, 127-128.

43. The alcaldes sometimes set their own timetable by not returning with a work party of Indian laborers until they wished. "Not infrequently the alcalde and the men spend their time in play and remain away for another day despite the fact that their task is an urgent one," wrote Father Abella and Juan Sainz de Lucio in an 1813-1815 questionnaire about Indian customs (Geiger and Meighan 1976, 128).

44. Milliken 1995, 131.

45. Beechey 1941, 15.

46. The records are somewhat confusing because the book of marriages cites the baptism number of Doda as SFB #1603, which was actually the recorded baptism number of her younger sister Dora, who would have been only nine years old at the time of the marriage. The death records show that Doda (#1602) died in 1811, and Dora (#1603) died in 1817; neither death record mentions a marriage.

47. SFM 1304.

48. For the marriage record, see SFM 1660; for the baptismal records, see SFB 5463, 5462, 5231.

49. Bancroft 1888, 227-228.

50. Milliken 1995; Milliken, personal communication, 2005.

51. Geiger and Meighan 1976.

52. Geiger and Meighan 1976, 88; De Roquefeuil and Langsdorff quoted in Weber 1979, 53, 43. Sources on the inadequacy of the diet include Jackson and Castillo 1995, chap. 3; and Cook 1976, 55.

53. Choris in Mahr 1932, 359-360.

54. Geiger and Meighan 1976, 152; Langsdorff quoted in Paddison 1999, 111.

55. Khlebnikov 1829, 333.

56. Golovnin 1979, 168; Beechey 1941, 29.

57. Botta [1828] 1952, 8-9.

58. Kelly 2003, 218-223.

59. Choris in Mahr 1932, 363.

60. Geiger and Meighan 1976, 137.

61. Weber 1979, 51.

62. Choris 1932, 97.

63. Beechey 1941, 26-27.

64. In the early 1990s, the Santa Barbara mission bookstore offered not a single book about the culture of the Chumash, one of the most successful of all California tribes. In 2001, the Carmel mission bookstore contained only one book about the Ohlone Indians,

and this was written for schoolchildren; the bookstore also did not offer the important diary of La Pérouse, who visited the Carmel mission in 1786, perhaps because he described the neophytes as "slaves."

65. Milliken 1995, 300–301.

66. Ibid., 303, 299; Cook 1976, table 5.

67. Fernández 1874, 50.

68. C-A 17.

69. Alvarado 1876, vol. 1, 171.

70. Osio 1996, 67.

71. Kotzebue quoted in Mahr 1932, 63.

72. Chamisso in Mahr 1932, 83 n.11; Choris in Mahr 1932, 95.

73. For example, 21 Indians ran away from Mission Dolores in 1793, and 280 fled in 1795. Subsequent records show between 150 and 200 runaways in 1796, 13 in 1805, 62 in 1807, 6 in 1816. In 1819, "all ran away temporarily" (Cook 1976, 60).

74. Kotzebue in Mahr 1932, 63. In 1817, Father Abella asked some captured runaways why they had fled; he reported being told "that it occurs to them as it occurs to all sons of Adam. That naturally we want our freedom." Some indicated that they were also seeking single women (letter from Abella to Governor Solá, January 29, 1817, Archivo del Arzobispada de San Francisco, C-C 1, 2, and 3, 125–126).

75. La Pérouse 1989, 82.

76. California Indian Conference, San Francisco State University, February 27–28, 1998.

77. Milliken 1995, 11.

78. Langsdorff quoted in Milliken 1995, 197; Beechey 1941, 16.

79. A drawing based on M. G. Vallejo's recollections shows the jail in 1820 as one room. Zavalishin 1973, 376.

80. Bancroft 1886, vol. 2, 598; Hittell 1885, 1897, vol. 2, 794; Huggins 1945, 166.

81. Vallejo was referred to as "General" after being appointed commandante general of northern California, even though he never actually rose above the rank of colonel.

82. J. Vallejo 1850, 530; M. G. Vallejo 1875, vol. 1, 106–110; Bancroft 1886, vol. 5, 759.

83. M. G. Vallejo 1850, 530.

84. M. G. Vallejo 1875, vol. 1, 110.

85. Lists of Indians held in the presidio jail were not kept, despite the governor's request in April 1816 for the names of all Indian prisoners, who were to be released only on his order (C-A 55, Tomo 8, 63). Entire years of soldiers' records at the San Francisco presidio are missing, and the 1816 records are blurred and difficult to read. From extant letters, it is obvious that not all expeditions were recorded.

86. Letter from Luis Argüello to Solá, May 1816, Taylor Collection #480. This capture may have been the result of an expedition led by Lt. Santiago Argüello to Sonoma and Bodega in October 1816 (C-A 56, Tomo 10, 17, 82, 91).

87. Luis Argüello, October 20, 1815, C-A 21, 78; C-A 17, Tomo 46, 37, October 1815 (or 1816); letter from Argüello to Solá, May 1816, Taylor Collection #480; Argüello report to Solá, February 29, 1815, C-A 21.

88. The Petaluma people were slow to join the San Francisco and San Jose missions. In 1815, only four Petaluma people were baptized at either mission. In 1816, forty were baptized at San Francisco and twenty-eight at San Jose.

89. SFB 5364.

90. C-A 13, Tomo 20, 102.

91. SFM 1741.

92. Milliken 1995, 92.

93. SFB 5533; SFD 4263.

94. Geiger and Meighan 1976, 99-100.

95. Jon Goerke, M.D., personal communication, 1998; Cook 1976, 190.

96. Milliken 1995, 193.

97. Cook 1976, 23, 24.

98. Ibid., 27.

99. Geiger 1969, 230; Asisara 1877, 55.

100. Langsdorff quoted in Milliken 1995, 173; Merck Manual, http://www.merck.com/mmpe/sec14/ch194i.htm.

101. Ibid; letter from Abella to Governor Solá, July 31, 1817, Archivo del Arzobispado, C-C 1, 2, and 3, 146.

102. Letter from Abella to Governor Solá, January 29, 1817, Archivo del Arzobispado, C-C 1, 2, and 3, 125-126.

103. These figures are based on Milliken's unpublished transcription of San Francisco mission records.

104. SFB 4859.

CHAPTER SIX

1. Letter from Abella to Solá, January 1816, Taylor Collection #698. Abella referred to the soldiers as "low grade soldiers recruited in Mexico from the scum of society."

2. Lightfoot 2005b, 120-121.

3. In the early twentieth century, an elderly Juan Garcia, son of the Spanish soldier Rafael Garcia, reported that his father had told him about the many Indians who had camped at McNear's on the San Pedro peninsula in eastern San Rafael to greet the new arrivals to the mission site, describing a crowd that swelled from five hundred to five thousand in a few hours. If this account is true, it suggests a prearranged ceremonial gathering. A crowd of such size seems unlikely, however, because so many central and southern Coast Miwok had already died at Mission Dolores and Mission San Jose. Neither mission records nor archaeological evidence supports such a large number of native Californians in this area at this time. There is also some doubt as to whether Rafael Garcia was actually present. Other statements made by Juan Garcia about his father's experiences are similarly not supported in the mission records and may be exaggerated, if not fabricated. Juan Garcia's recollections were given to the San Rafael newspaper *The Independent* at an unknown date and were not published until August 1917.

4. Milliken 1998, 31. Bancroft put the figure at "about 230," but he was not certain (Bancroft 1886, vol. 2, 330). Sixty-one of these individuals (21 percent) came from the San Jose mission (State of the San Rafael Mission, 1818, Taylor Collection #2365).

5. Milliken 1998, 31. Thirty survivors from the Aguasto tribe, who had originally come from the San Rafael area, were still alive at Mission Dolores, but a majority did not return to San Rafael (ibid.). Indians from Olompali who made the trip to San Rafael included Marino's mother-in-law, Martina, and Telemele (baptized as Nemenciano), capitán of Olompali in 1816 and father of one of Martina's children. He arrived with his wife Nemenciana.

6. RAB 1-26; letter from Sarría to Payeras, January 5, 1818, Archivo del Arzobispada, vol. 3, pt. 2, 21. The prescribed procedure for founding a mission included the raising of the cross by priests and a religious superior in an *enramada* (a three-sided enclosure) that contained the altar and from which bells were hung (Mackey and Sooy 1932, 13).

7. Geiger 1969, 104; letter from Gil to Argüello, April 1818, Taylor Collection #835. But Gil was not alone. Abella may have remained at San Rafael: he was there baptizing five children on January 15, 1818, returning to officiate again on September 8 and between September 19 and 23. Sarría also returned in October, participating in sacraments.

8. Santa Barbara Mission Archives (SBMA) 1181.

9. The Spanish navigator Bodega y Quadra was in Tomales Bay in 1775. Both he and his pilot, Francisco Antonio Maurelle, wrote of their friendly contacts with the Indians at Tomales (C. R. Edwards 1979, 12). In 1790, the English captain James Colnett landed at Bodega Bay to repair his ship after a storm. The Indians alerted the Spaniards, who eventually sent Juan Bautista Matute to establish a settlement there in 1793 to protect the area from other foreign incursions. (He found the area unsuitable, however.)

The English were also at Bodega Bay in 1793. Botanist Archibald Menzies and a naval lieutenant named Puget found evidence of previous Spanish contacts—the Indians were speaking "a mixture of Spanish and their own provincial dialect," even calling them "*amico*"—but no Spaniards. As usual, the Indians were hospitable, offering food and showing no fear of the visitors even when they saw their guns (Wagner 1931, 14).

10. See C. R. Edwards 1979.

11. Wagner 1931, 345.

12. SFB 3794, 4414, 4415.

13. The date of spying on the Russians was not given (M. G. Vallejo, no date, 2). Ogden described the Native Alaskan otter hunters (1941, 57-59).

14. Nanaguani may have been the village identified variously as Awániwí (Barrett 1908, 309), Ah wan´ me (Merriam 1907, 356), and Awani-wi (Kroeber 1970, 274) and described as being at San Rafael, although this identification is uncertain, since other archaeological sites in San Rafael are also possibilities. Because construction at Courthouse Square in the 1970s did not include an Environmental Impact Report, the known neophyte housing from the mission period was not investigated, nor was there a search for evidence of an earlier village in the same area. Settlements have been identified northeast of the mission at today's Dominican University (Mrn 254) and west of the mission on D Street; Charles

Lauff reported that others existed closer to the mission in the 1830s, but Lauff's veracity is doubtful. Artifacts were found before 1908 in the vicinity of Lootens Place and Fifth Street by Farrington Jones (Richard Torney, personal communication, 1998).

15. Kelly 2003, 13.

16. The inventory of artifacts from a village in the Pacheco Valley suggests that it was a trading center benefiting from its location on this well-traveled trade route (Goerke et al. 1983, 16).

17. Bancroft 1886, vol. 2, 330.

18. Gil, State of the San Rafael Mission, 1818, Taylor Collection #2365; Amorós, State of the San Rafael Mission, 1820, Taylor Collection #2366. The church bell was 16 inches high and 20 inches at the base (L. Little 1989-1990, 14).

19. Vasilyev is quoted in Shur and Gibson 1973, 42. Father Amorós's sketch appears in RAB 1050. The church's interior is described in Garcia 1917, 3.

20. Richardson quoted in Hendry and Bowman, 55.

21. Register of Brands 1828, 3-5. See Chapter 2 for discussion of the possible location of Anamas in Mill Valley. The name Corte Madera is Spanish for "cut wood." If the western boundary of the mission lands included Bodega Bay, the northern boundary, the "San Antonio Valley," must have been located in what is known today as Chileno Valley. It is clear from the 1834 map that the geography was far from accurate.

22. Gil, State of the San Rafael Mission, 1818, Taylor Collection #2365; Amorós, State of the San Rafael Mission, 1820, Taylor Collection #2366; Amorós, State of the San Rafael Mission, 1823, SBMA.

23. RAB 300, 303.

24. RAB 444.

25. RAB 339, 300; letter from Amorós to Solá, September 25, 1819, SBMA 1779.

26. RAB 332-335, 338-339, 450, 452-455, 467-468. Later, there were others in 1826 and 1832; see also RAB 1351-1352, 1815.

27. Amorós, State of the San Rafael Mission, 1820, Taylor Collection #2366.

28. RAB 380, 385, 325, 615.

29. Amorós, State of the San Rafael Mission, 1826.

30. Amorós's 1820 yearly report states that the twenty-eight baptized adults were "dead or infirm in their rancherias" (State of the San Rafael Mission, 1820, Taylor Collection #2366).

31. In his annual report for 1818, for example, Father Gil reported sixty-one deaths without recording the names of the deceased; thirty-two of these individuals had originally been baptized at San Francisco and four at San Jose (Gil, State of the Asistencia, Residencia, Rancho…of San Rafael from December 14, 1817, to December 18, year 1818, Taylor Collection #2365).

32. RAB 237, 238, 240.

33. At least five single adult men were listed in the death records as never having married (RAD 311, 476, 539, 708, 784).

34. RAB 902; RAD 463; RAB 1329.

35. Kotzebue 1830, 62; L. Little 1989-1990, 14-16. The bell described by Kotzebue can be seen today at the site of the old mission.

36. Garcia 1917, 21; Kelly 2003, 319, 324.

37. Garcia 1917, 3; State of the San Rafael Mission, 1818-1823.

38. State of the San Rafael Mission, 1824-1828, SBMA. For a full discussion of San Carlos, see Hackel 2005, 157-176.

39. Hackel 2005, 172.

40. In 1829, 225 neophytes (22 percent) at the San Rafael mission confessed. But in 1830, the number of confessions dropped to 20 (0.02 percent) (State of the San Rafael Mission, 1829-1830, SBMA). We have no record of serious problems at the mission that year; such a low figure may indicate that Amorós was ill during the Easter period.

41. Letter from Amorós to Argüello, 1822, Taylor Collection #1374; letter from Narciso Durán to Juan Amorós, 1822, Taylor Collection #1406; Faulkner 1928; Vallejo, *Documentos* 1769-1850, 17.

42. When Auguste Duhaut-Cilly traveled from San Francisco to Sonoma to purchase deer tallow in 1827, he and his group bypassed San Rafael because "the mission is very poor and has nothing for barter" (Duhaut-Cilly 1929, 239).

43. In 1820, the mission stock included 500 head of cattle and oxen, 2,000 sheep, 11 horses, 20 old mares, 70 brood mares, and 3 stallions (State of the San Rafael Mission, 1820, Taylor Collection #2366). By 1823, the numbers of both cattle and sheep had doubled, and the mission claimed 200 horses and 30 pigs. Although Father Guzman reported lower totals for all animals except horses in 1828 (873 cattle, 2,957 sheep, 15 pigs, and 383 horses) (Guzman 1926, Breve Noticia of 1828), these numbers increased during the 1830s. In 1832, the mission cared for a total of 5,508 animals (Bancroft 1886, vol. 3, 716n18).

44. Letter from Vicente Francisco de Sarría to missionaries, January 12, 1818, SBMA 1534. Amador described the vaqueros' mode of dress at the San Jose mission (Amador 1877, 117-118).

45. Zavalishin 1973, 411n5, 383.

46. Letter from Father Durán to Amorós, 1822, Taylor Collection #1406; Bancroft 1886, vol. 2, 597; SBMA 3267; Guzmán 1926, 216-217. The San Rafael mission exceeded its closest mission neighbors only in the number of bushels of barley and beans (see Guzman in Appendix G).

47. Pinney 1989, 238; Bowman 1943, 20; Bancroft 1888, 371-372.

48. RAB 346, 331.

49. Although the Native Americans had no written record of how old they were, societies with an oral rather than a written history typically reconstruct age by connecting memorable events, allowing most individuals to have a general idea of their age. The priests must have guessed at the ages of some: Father Gil listed Luis Gonsaga's age as one hundred and described him as near death at the time of his baptism, although Father Amorós recorded Gonsaga's death at age ninety more than two years later (RAB 177; RAD 56).

50. During the early days at San Rafael, the most frequent godmothers for women were Toribia and Melitona, Coast Miwok from Mission Dolores who had originally come from

the Omiomi (Novato) and Guaulen (Bolinas) tribes, respectively. Melitona knew Marino from Mission Dolores, where they had been godparents together in 1816 (SFB 5411).

51. RAB 634; RAD 131.

52. RAB 327, 111.

53. Letter from Amorós, 1809, Taylor Collection #334; Tac 2001, 334.

54. Heizer 1947, 287; Galvin 1971, 21-22.

55. Alvarado 1876, 70-71.

56. RAB 228, 327, 367, 372.

57. A tragedy occurred during Marino's time as alcalde. Six men on a voyage in a *cayuco* (a dugout canoe) presumably drowned as they returned to San Rafael, and their bodies were never found (RAD 48, SFD 4717). Marino had a special relationship with at least one of them: he had been a witness at Pio and Pia's wedding in Mission Dolores, and he and Pio may have been boatmen together in San Francisco.

58. RAB 437, 438.

59. Milliken, personal communication, 1996.

60. RAD 334B.

61. SFB 3506, 3502.

62. RAD 250.

63. RAB 792; RAM 249.

64. Both Justino and Nereo were baptized at San Francisco (SFB 2493, 2667).

65. Justino and Nereo were witnesses at Pacifico's wedding to Juana Nepomuceno (RAM 337), and both Pacifico and Justino had been witnesses at the first wedding of Pacifico's wife.

66. SFB 4859. The baptisms of three of Quilajuque's children are recorded in SFB 3502 (José María), SFB 3310 (Teodorico), and SFB 4173 (Cayetana).

67. SFB 5231. Telemele married his first wife at San Jose, where they were baptized as Nemenciano and Nemenciana. The couple transferred to the San Rafael mission at its founding. Telemele married Martina three months after his wife died.

68. RAB 217.

69. Kelly 2003, xvii.

70. Letter from Abella to Solá, June 1, 1817, Taylor Collection #711.

71. Ibid.; letter from Abella to Solá, January 29, 1817, Taylor Collection #698.

72. RAB 232. The word Amorós wrote in the mission records was *cocindera,* which may be a colloquialism for *cocinera.*

73. Letter from Amorós to Argüello, January 3, 1825, Taylor Collection #1746.

74. M. G. Vallejo 1875, vol. 1, 4.

75. Kelly 1931-1932, Notebook 10, 27. Another Coast Miwok informant, Tom Smith, reported more favorably on relationships between his people at Bodega Bay and those from the Healdsburg area who came to coastal Marin to fish and clam: "Never fight in the old days; good friend all the time" (Kelly 2003, 354). As for those from Fort Ross: "We were good friends…although some of the old people were enemies" (ibid., 355).

76. Letter from Abella to Solá, June 1, 1817, Taylor Collection #711.

77. SFD 4392, 4393. This assignment for Sergeant Sánchez is not reflected in the presidio records for June 1817, which show Sánchez assigned to the pueblo San Jose (Vallejo, *Documentos* 1769-1850, 16, 1).

78. Letter from Father Gil to Luis Argüello, April 26, 1818, Taylor Collection #835; Lihuantuleyomi was one of the many variant spellings of Livantolomi.

79. Diary of Altimira, June 26, 1823, quoted in Smilie 1975, 6.

80. Kelly 2003, 354.

81. RAB 772.

82. Letter from Amorós to Argüello, February 1, 1823, Taylor Collection #1540. In the presidio records, Herrera's first name is listed as Josef. His rank is a puzzle. In 1811, he was promoted to sergeant because of "bravery" in fighting the Indians (Bancroft 1886, vol. 3, 782). Osio, however, described him as a corporal (Osio 1996, 105). The San Francisco presidio monthly records list him with other corporals but include the words "corporal rank sergeant" (Vallejo, *Documentos* 1769-1850, 19, 1).

83. Letter from Amorós to Payeras, March 8, 1823, Taylor Collection #1433.

84. Ibid.; letter from Amorós to Argüello, April 10, 1823, Taylor Collection #1541; RAB 855, 854.

85. C-A 56, Tomo 11, 16. Santiago Argüello had departed on an expedition to the north on October 23 with twenty-five men (C-A 56, Tomo 11, 17).

86. Letter from Amorós to Argüello, November 18, 1823, Taylor Collection #1542.

87. Farris 1990, 5; Golovnin 1979, 167.

88. Letter from Amorós to Argüello, November 18, 1823, Taylor Collection #1542.

89. Tarakanoff 1953, 34, 5; RAB 1343. According to Kent Lightfoot (2005b, 152), the Russians were not interested in proselytizing, concerned that it could disrupt their trade relations with the Spanish.

90. Shelikhov to K. T. Khlebnikov, quoted in Shur and Gibson 1973, 47.

91. RAB 262. Amorós, who recorded the baptism, apparently heard Tadeo's Indian name as Gualinlela, which differed from Valinela in the initial sound ("Gua" instead of "Va").

92. Farris 1994, 4. This information was given to Father Payeras in 1822 by Vicente and Rufino, two neophytes from the San Rafael mission, when he visited Fort Ross (and Bodega). The daughter of Ióllo, who may have been Xisemaen, was baptized as Alexandra (RAB 217) at San Rafael in January 1819. Amorós identified her as the daughter of the capitán at Bodega. Alexandra apparently remained in the mission system, with both her marriage (1819) and death (1824) recorded by the priest.

93. Khlebnikov 1829, 77-78; Schabelski quoted in Farris 1993, 9.

94. Kotzebue 1830, 126.

95. Taylor Collection #1541.

96. Letters from Amorós to Argüello, May 17, 1823, Taylor Collection #1447; June 26, 1823, Taylor Collection #1453.

97. Bancroft 1886, vol. 2, 502n37, 497-500.

98. Milliken 1998, 32.

99. Letter from Altimira to Argüello, October 18, 1823, Taylor Collection #1478.

100. Tchitchinoff 1956, 11; letter from Altimira to Argüello, September 18, 1823, Taylor Collection #1478.

101. Bancroft 1886, vol. 3, 94. See also M. G. Vallejo 1875 and Alvarado 1876. According to Geiger, Altimira was unwilling to vow allegiance to Mexico and fled after hearing that Mexico intended to expel all Spaniards (Geiger 1969, 9).

CHAPTER SEVEN

1. This chapter is based on the diaries of Captain Luis Argüello and the priest Blas Ordaz. Their diaries are so similar that the translator of Argüello's diary believed that Argüello had based his diary on the writing of Ordaz. In referring to one of the barges used to transport horses for the expedition, Argüello claimed that it belonged to the Sonoma mission, which was not established until 1823, indicating that he must have written his version after that date.

2. Descriptions of the clothing worn by members of the expeditionary force are conjectural, but they are based on accounts by the participants (Amador 1877, 13; Fernández 1874, 20) and the observations of contemporaneous foreign visitors, including Langsdorff (who described the serapes worn by Argüello and other officers as bedspreads and the spurs as "unusually large"; Langsdorff 1927, 37-38), Beechey, Kotzebue, Choris, Zavalishin, and Mackey and Sooy.

3. Bancroft 1886, vol. 2, 268.

4. In later years, Governor Alvarado wrote that it was a Russian officer who had spread the rumor that English-speaking settlers were nearby. According to Alvarado, the officer had reported this story to a Spanish priest, hoping that it would reach the ears of the Spanish governor, who would then act to rid California of Russia's unwelcome competitor (Alvarado 1876, vol. 1, 156).

5. According to Argüello's diary, the group set out across the bay at 8:00 A.M.; Ordaz describes an 11:00 A.M. departure.

6. Argüello 1992, 13.

7. Ordaz 1958, 232; Bancroft 1886, vol. 2, 445.

8. Bancroft 1886, vol. 3, 13; Langsdorff 1927, 37-38; Bancroft 1886, vol. 3, 12n22.

9. Letter from Ordaz to Argüello, January 7, 1822, Taylor Collection #1364. Luis Argüello was described as being of "ruddy complexion" (Bancroft 1886, vol. 3, 13), and his father was said to have been very dark-skinned. It is not clear whether Ordaz's use of the words "Negrito" and "Negra" referred to dark-skinned Mexicans and Spaniards such as Argüello or to the Indians.

10. Father Ordaz's reputation as a man of loose morals was the subject of numerous letters exchanged by the priestly authorities. For arguments and counterarguments concerning Ordaz's immorality, see Bancroft 1886, vol. 4, 759, and Geiger 1969, 174. Ordaz's letter also mentions a Father Luis, who "says that if he had gone with you [on

the northern expedition] he would have had a grand time. He sends regards and affection" (Taylor Collection #1364). This is probably Father Gil, with whom Argüello was reportedly "especially close" (Brown 1975, 7), another priest whose morals were questioned (Geiger 1969, 105; Bancroft 1886, vol. 3, 691n8).

11. Beebe and Senkewicz 1996, 336.

12. Osio [1851] 1996, 33. Osio's information most likely came from his later acquaintance with Luis Argüello; Osio did not settle in Alta California until 1825 and does not mention Argüello's 1821 expedition. Writing in 1850, Osio also referred to Marino as Marin, the name with which Marino was associated more frequently, but not exclusively, by 1833.

13. Osio, 33-34.

14. Paddison 1999, 123.

15. Fernández 1874, 21; Bojorques 1874; Boronda 1878.

16. Amador 1877, 12; Bancroft 1886, vol. 2, 446; Milliken, unpublished manuscript in possession of the author. The present day locations from Suisun City to Mount St. Helena are based on Milliken's research.

17. The manuscripts of Amador 1877, Bojorques 1874, Boronda 1878, and Fernández 1874.

18. Alvarado 1876, vol. 1, 157; Bojorques 1874; Boronda 1878; and Fernández 1874.

19. Amador 1877, 11.

20. Ordaz 1958, 233; Argüello 1992, 23.

21. Argüello 1992, 24.

22. Ibid., 26.

23. Ibid., 30.

24. Ibid., 39-40.

25. Ordaz 1958, 239; Callaghan 1978, 265; Argüello 1992, 37.

26. Bojorques, 1874. Amador recalled fifty-six years later that the cannon was "transported on a mule along with its gun carriage" (Amador 1877, 10).

27. Argüello 1992, 40-41.

28. Ordaz 1958, 240.

29. RAD 121.

30. Although the entire trek lasted only a month, from October 17 to November 17, the memories of some of the participants grew fuzzy over the years. Interviewed more than fifty years later, soldier Juan Bojorques claimed that the trip had taken two months, while José Fernández indicated that the expeditionary force had traveled for one year (Bojorques 1874, 3; Fernández 1874, 20-22). Governor Alvarado, who was only eight years old at the time of the expedition, reported in his *History of California* that the group had been out for eighteen months (Alvarado 1876).

CHAPTER EIGHT

1. Letter from Amorós to Argüello, December 15, 1822, Taylor Collection #1391; letter from Amorós to Argüello, January 24, 1823, Taylor Collection #1539. Amorós's December

15 letter was the only time the priest mentioned an Indian by name in his correspondence. After Marino's death, Jacob Leese (Vallejo's American-born brother-in-law) reported that he had heard that Marin quarreled frequently with the priests (*Daily Alta,* March 30, 1865).

The records of presidio assignments for January 1823 indicate that Corporal Herrera was stationed at San Rafael from January 1822 through March 1823 but do not include the names of the two additional soldiers. Because assignments and expeditions were not always reflected in the presidio records, it is often difficult to trace the whereabouts of the military. Herrera first arrived at San Rafael in July 1818, but the records for the period from December 1818 through December 1821 are missing.

2. Kelly 2003, 9; Osio 1996, 33. Osio referred to Marino as Marín. In October 1822, Marino may have had another opportunity to help Argüello and absent himself from the mission: Argüello and Payeras were traveling from San Francisco through Olompali on their way to Bodega Bay and Ross, and it took two days to transport horses across the bay for their trip (Bancroft 1886, vol. 2, 463-464n31).

3. RAB 877.

4. M. G. Vallejo 1875, vol. 1, 108.

5. Ibid., 110; Leese, in *Daily Alta,* March 30, 1865. The 1841 survey was done by Cadwalader Ringgold and Lt. Charles Wilkes at the behest of the U.S. Congress (Ashcroft). Today, the tide in this area varies from the extreme low of -1.6 feet to 7.1 feet. The overall water level has risen about 24 centimeters since the 1820s (Permanent Service for Mean Sea Level, Proudman Oceanographic Laboratory, Bidston Observatory, United Kingdom, 1998).

6. *San Francisco Call Bulletin,* September 7, 1895.

7. Lanny Pinola, personal communication, 2002.

8. Mrn (Marin) 661, indicating that the site is the 661st recorded site in Marin County. The archaeologist believed that this site was occupied only seasonally and was a "specialized camp rather than habitation site" (Luby 1994, 115) from at least A.D. 210 to A.D. 1510.

9. M. G. Vallejo 1875, vol. 1, 108. Quintino, a Coast Miwok of the Aguasto tribe and eight years younger than Marino, had been known as Tiguacse before he was baptized at the San Francisco mission (SFB 2038) in 1800 at age eleven. It was logical for him to be found in the Aguasto tribal territory, which included the San Quentin peninsula. In his later years he worked as a boatman for Vallejo, who described him as a "very good sailor" and noted that the priests often used him in this capacity. Vallejo hired Quintino on the recommendation of two Indian chiefs, Marcelo and Solano (M. G. Vallejo 1875, vol. 1, 108).

10. M. G. Vallejo 1875, vol. 1, 109-110.

11. Alvarado 1876, vol. 1, 75-76. Alvarado may have included this account in his *History* because it provided him with an avenue to attack the mission priests; he particularly loathed the power, wealth, and hypocrisy of many of the priests he had known.

The reference to a buggy horse may be anachronistic, but in 1820 Father Mariano Payeras complained to his superior in Mexico about the priests at some missions who rode in carriages and coaches drawn by one or more horses, rather than riding a "little horse or a mule"

(Farris and Jones 2005, 95). The Russian Khlebnikov brought a carriage and parts to the mission at Santa Cruz in 1824 (ibid., 97.) A Russian visitor had earlier derided the large, awkward wheels he saw on wagons pulled by oxen, suggesting that the conveyances lacked spoke wheels. If Marino made a comment about horses, he may have referred to a different comparison, perhaps comparing a horse that was accustomed to being saddled to one that was not.

12. Boscana 1947, 63. Boscana was speaking particularly about the neophytes' lack of faith.

13. It is not clear whether the report of Marino's involvement came from Alvarado or whether it should be attributed to George W. Gift, the author of the *San Rafael Herald* article in which Alvarado's letter appears (Gift 1875, 8). I have not been able to locate Alvarado's original letter, and thus Gift's article is the only available source. Gift was a "newspaper man" in San Rafael and Napa sometime after 1861; his article contains numerous errors.

14. Kotzebue 1830, 114. The San Francisco presidio account books registered only one soldier assigned to San Rafael in September and October 1824, and two in November 1824.

15. Alvarado 1982, 33. Alvarado believed that Pomponio was one of the defiant chiefs led by Marino.

16. M. G. Vallejo 1875, vol. 1, 109-110.

17. J. E. Galindo 1877, 65-66. Galindo also claimed that Pomponio refused to take a wounded companion, Baltasar, to the Santa Cruz mission for last rites and shot him instead.

18. Pomponio's mother was named Antonina (SFB 2581); his biological father was Francisco (SFB 2100).

19. SFB 2546.

20. SFD 1611, 1953, 2057, 2082, 2100, 2197, 2387, 2535, 3466, 3477, 3923.

21. Letter from Juan Cabot to Governor Solá, March 21, 1820, Taylor Collection #1142.

22. Alvarado 1982, 33-35. The reference to the Cainameros is puzzling. Milliken (personal communication, 2005) believes that they were a Pomo group who lived north of the Coast Miwok. Alexander S. Taylor (1865) also related Marin to the Cainameros. Perhaps in the 1860s, when these stories were told, this tribe had a reputation for being ferocious, and thus both Marin and Pomponio were said to be associated with it.

23. Alvarado 1982, 34.

24. Alvarado 1982, 37.

25. Martínez in C-A 32, Tomo 10, 82.

26. Letter from Viader to Argüello, May 31, 1823, Taylor Collection #1510; letter from Viader to Argüello, June 1823, Taylor Collection #1670. Confident that he would be successful in capturing Pomponio, Viader requested help from Father Durán at Mission San Jose and from the town of San Jose, suggesting that they take a circuitous route so as not to alert Pomponio (letter from Viader to Don Ignacio Martínez, May 31, 1823, Taylor Collection #1510).

27. Letter from Viader to Argüello, June 7, 1823, Taylor Collection #1512; letter from Viader to Argüello, June 23, 1823, Taylor Collection #1573.

28. Letter from Martínez to Argüello, July 31, 1823, C-A 56, Tomo 10, 94-97.

29. C-A 56, Tomo 10, 94-97; Bancroft 1888, 683; J. E. Galindo 1877, 65. The Mission Dolores baptismal records list an Indian from the East Bay named Tadeo (SFB 4144). If this is the same individual mentioned as Pomponio's companion, he would have been fourteen years old and a Huchiun/Aguasto rather than a Coast Miwok.

30. C-A 56, Tomo 10, 88; C-A 56, Tomo 14, 3.

31. M. G. Vallejo 1875, vol. 1, 110. Vallejo wrote that Pomponio was captured twice.

32. This sequence of events does not follow the one described by Alan Brown 1975, but Brown did not have access to the translation of Zavalishin's experiences in California (personal communication, 2004.)

33. Alvarado does not provide a date for this capture, and it appears in no other accounts (Alvarado 1982, 38).

34. C-A 56, Tomo 10, 88.

35. C-A 56, Tomo 11, 66-67; C-A 19, Tomo 66, 92-93; Vallejo, *Documentos* 1769-1889, 141. The wounded companion was likely from another mission: in the death records at San Rafael and San Francisco, no one is identified as an associate of Pomponio or as having been injured in a battle with him. M. G. Vallejo (1875, vol. 1, 110) claimed that Pomponio was caught with two wives, but this cannot be verified in the mission records.

36. "So that the record of his combat experience would not be entirely blank, [Martínez] inserted into the record that he had apprehended a fugitive Indian named Pomponio, even though old Corporal Herrera had actually done this" (Osio 1996, 105). Perhaps Martínez believed that he could get away with stretching the truth because the disgraced Herrera was no longer around to defend himself, and because Martínez's own superior officer had been suspended from his command ten months earlier. Vallejo wrote that the other soldier was José Sánchez.

Martínez did not include the month he captured Pompino. If Osio was correct and Herrera had indeed apprehended Pomponio, the capture must have occurred before November 1823, prior to Herrera's imprisonment at the San Francisco presidio for a serious crime. But if Osio was wrong, the incident could have occurred as late as January, confirming Vallejo's account that Marino was caught in 1824 just before Pomponio's capture.

37. Cañada Pomponio (written as "Cañada de Poniponi" in the land grant) was the southern boundary of John Martin's 1840 land grant, Corte Madera de Novato (Land Case 134 N.D., p. 15, Corte Madera Novato, United States District Court, Bancroft Library, University of California, Berkeley).

38. M. G. Vallejo 1875, vol. 1, 110. Vallejo wrote that Pomponio was first captured in Marin County and sent to the presidio jail in San Francisco along with his two wives. According to this account, he was captured a second time in the area of the Soledad mission and sent to the presidio jail in Monterey, from which he escaped by climbing over the walls (ibid., 110).

The only expedition listed in the San Francisco presidio records for this period commenced in July 1823; it was led by Luis Arguëllo, not Ignacio Martínez. This seventeen-man force may have been responding to Amorós's request to bring the Pomo back to the San Rafael mission.

39. Zavalishin's description of his meeting with Pomponio is compatible with Vallejo's account of Pomponio being free for two months before finally being sent to Monterey.

According to Zavalishin, Pomponio had spared his life because of the Russian's good reputation for supporting the Indians in their conflicts with the authorities. But this story seems to have been merely a vehicle for lauding the Russians, and Zavalishin in particular; he quotes Pomponio as saying, "You alone have always been affectionate and kind to the poor Indians: why you are fairly well known everywhere, including the missions and rancherias....We know that you came to take this land from the accursed Spaniards and to free the poor Indians!" (Zavalishin 1973, 377). Such a statement seems difficult to reconcile with the reality that Zavalishin had been in California only about six weeks before Pomponio was sent to Monterey.

40. Zavalishin 1973, 376, 383. Zavalishin wrote that the location where Pomponio spared his life was in Calaveras, which seems highly unlikely, because it would have been too dangerous for Pomponio to be in alien territory.

41. M. G. Vallejo 1875, vol. 1, 111.

42. A different version of Varela's death appeared in an 1869 newspaper, which claimed that both Pomponio and a companion named Gonzalo were caught at a fandango. This account stated that, as they were being taken back to the presidio, Pomponio held Varela while Gonzalo murdered him (*Santa Clara News,* November 13, 1869). The two Indians then reportedly escaped after beating off their shackles. According to Bancroft, Pomponio later stabbed and killed Gonzalo after "a horse fell on [Gonzalo] and broke his leg" (Bancroft 1888, 683), and refused to take the wounded man to the San Carlo mission for last rites (Torre 1877, 46½.)

43. Duhaut-Cilly 1929, 215; Torre 1877, 46½; Bancroft 1888, 682.

44. C-A 15, Tomo 11, 7; M. G. Vallejo 1875, vol. 1, 111.

45. C-A 17, Tomo 52, 7; CAD (Mission San Carlos death records) 2478 (cited in Brown 1975, 16). After Pomponio's death, fanciful stories about his life began to appear. In May 1879, a newspaper article about Pomponio said that he was remembered for having "robbed and murdered settlers...dislodged by...the rancheros of Marin, and [was]...captured south of Yerba Buena. The authorities burned him alive" (San Francisco *Argonaut,* May 31, 1879). The author, identified as "Angle," included another tale about meeting a young Indian boy who claimed to be Pomponio's grandson (see Chapter 14).

46. Bancroft 1888, 682.

47. Hackel 2005, 262.

48. Sandos 1998, 212-213; Jackson and Castillo 1995, 79.

49. Osio 1996, 89.

50. Letter from Father Durán to Ignacio Martínez, commandante of presidio, November

8, 1828, Taylor Collection #2037.

51. On Durán's complaint about Vallejo, see Beebe and Senkewicz in Osio 1996, 94. On the pardon of Estanislao, see Sandos 1998, 212.

CHAPTER NINE

1. RAB 1264, 1312.

2. Kotzebue 1830, 107-108. The San Francisco, San Rafael, San Jose, and San Carlos mission records contain no mention of a neophyte named Marco, although an Indian named Marcos from Petaluma was baptized at San Francisco and resided at the San Rafael mission. Marcos's baptism is recorded in SFB 5217. He had been a witness at San Rafael in 1820; his brother was a page, assisting the priest in 1831.

3. If Marino was the man who accompanied Kotzebue, however, it means that he had been freed from the presidio jail by October 1824 rather than serving a term of "more than a year" as Vallejo later wrote (M. G. Vallejo 1875, 110).

4. The incident Osio described may have occurred during the summer of 1825, when Altimira was away from Sonoma, visiting as far south as Mission Buenaventura, or in 1826, after the burning of the Sonoma mission buildings when Altimira fled to San Rafael (Smilie 1975, 23-24).

5. Osio 1996, 122-123; Bancroft, who repeated a version of this story, citing Osio as his source, does not name the priest at San Rafael (Bancroft 1886, vol. 2, 596n20).

6. Osio 1996, 122-123.

7. Letter from Amorós to Argüello, January 3, 1825, Taylor Collection #1746.

8. Donnelly 1967. According to Bancroft, Juarez was a soldier of the San Francisco company from 1828 to 1831 and a corporal from 1832 until 1835. Juarez's reminiscences do not mention such an experience (Juarez 1875). The grandson's story placed the attack in February, but the records show an increase in soldiers, from two to five, only in October of that year, perhaps indicating that a disturbance had occurred the previous month

9. RAB 1808, 1809.

10. Kelly 2003, 358.

11. Fernández 1874, 12.

12. Galindo's account is quite specific, citing the date of the attack as Sunday, November 23, 1833. During Amorós's time at San Rafael, however, that date fell on a Sunday only in 1823 and 1828.

13. N. Galindo 1883, 104-105. Amorós's escape in a tule boat is similar to the account by Alvarado, but in Galindo's version, it was the Indians who took Amorós to San Francisco.

14. Ibid.

15. Alvarado quoted in Gift 1875, 8; Milliken has identified the Cainameros as a southern Pomo tribe (personal communication, 2004).

16. Garcia may not have been the soldier involved; his son, Juan Garcia, never mentioned such a dramatic incident in his published story about his father. The elder Garcia

was assigned to the San Rafael mission from July 1825 through January 1829. After the 1832 attack, Garcia was one of the five soldiers assigned to guard the mission.

17. Beechey 1941, 73.

18. Letter from Luis Argüello to the Minister of State, May 25, 1825, Luis Argüello Papers, Bancroft Library [CA 309].

19. M. G. Vallejo 1875, vol. 1, 110.

20. SFB 6493. The child was the daughter of two Coast Miwok, Nestor and Maxima. Priests from San Francisco visited the chapel at San Mateo for mass and baptisms (Stanger 1994, 249), but we do not know how large the chapel or outstations were in 1826.

21. Stanger 1944, 254; Bancroft 1886, vol. 3, 714n16.

22. Zavalishin 1973, 381-382; Bancroft 1886, vol. 2, 505.

23. SFB 6500; SFB 6511.

24. *Daily Alta,* March 30, 1865; Camp 1923, 58-59.

25. Camp 1923, 59.

26. Yount was baptized at the San Rafael mission in April 1835, which means that he could have known Marino and other capitáns who were participating in mission affairs that spring. There is, however, no record that Sonoma was also at the San Rafael mission. In fact, the evidence of Sonoma's existence is sparse. A man named Sonoma was still remembered in the early twentieth century as a hoipu, or a headman; his Indian name was reportedly "hōīpūs-tōlōpo'kse," which S. A. Barrett translated as "from hoipus, captain and tolopo, to respond" (Barrett 1908, 313). Stephen Powers in 1877 wrote that Sonoma Valley "was named from one of their celebrated chiefs" (1976, 195). The derivation of the name seems to be native: the Coast Miwok peoples from the Sonoma area who entered Mission Dolores called themselves the Chocuyens, Sonomas, and Chocoime (Milliken 1995, 240). An Indian known as Sonoma, a Chocuyen from the Sonoma area, was baptized at Mission Dolores and died in 1815 at age sixty (SFB 5047, SFD 3753).

27. Geiger and Meighan 1976, 115; Beechey [1831] 1941, 64.

28. Bancroft 1886, vol. 3, 12n22.

CHAPTER TEN

1. It is difficult to know if Amorós's 1831 figures were an exaggeration. It may be that Esténega did not want to appear responsible for the dramatic drop in the mission population after he arrived. On the other hand, the two men may have been counting population differently, with Amorós's figures based on the number of people who would attend an occasional mass, particularly at Easter, and Esténega's assessment on just those who were living on or near the mission grounds.

2. Alvarado 1876, vol. 3, unpaginated.

3. Fernández 1874, 46; Bancroft 1886, vol. 4, 738, 682n20; Geiger 1969, 262. Although the Californios decried the morals of the Zacatecan priests Mercado and Quijas, there were other Franciscans at San Rafael, including Father Gil (described in Chapter 6), who also behaved badly. Agustin Fernandez de San Vicente, a cleric who visited San Rafael in 1822,

was described as a bon vivant, debtor, and gambler, with an "unclerical fondness for wine and women" (Bancroft 1886, vol. 2, 469). Two governors complained of his conduct: Solá found him a "scoundrel" (ibid.), and Alvarado wrote of his immorality.

Asisara, a neophyte at Santa Cruz, reported that another Franciscan, Father Ramón Olbés, claimed that he could ascertain why a female neophyte was sterile if he could observe her having sex with her husband. When the husband refused to participate, the priest demanded to see his penis. Olbés then had the husband tied up. When the priest tried to examine the woman's genitalia, a struggle ensued; she tried to bite his arm, he screamed, and when the interpreter and alcalde rushed into the room, Olbés had her bound and whipped with fifty lashes. According to Asisara, "all the women who were sterile became alarmed" by this incident (Asisara 1877, 53). It is hard to escape the conclusion that at some of the missions, the Indians must have recognized that a key reason for locking women in the dormitories at night was to protect them from the priests.

4. Vallejo to Commandante General, May 5, 1833, Vallejo, *Documentos* 1769–1850, 40. This looks like a draft. The copy of this letter (Vallejo, *Documentos* 1769–1850, 124bb) spells Marino's name "Mariano," but the original is spelled "Marino."

5. May 5, 1833, SBMA 3414. It is not clear to whom Vallejo intended to send this letter.

6. Ambrose 1996, 148.

7. Asisara 1877, 51.

8. Bancroft 1886, vol. 2, 461–462n28; Hackel 2005, 376.

9. Gerbacio's name was missing from the San Rafael mission record books for much of the time that Marino was away; it is possible that they were together during that period.

10. RAB 1828. Given that Maria Copa's grandmother and Marino were related, it is puzzling that Molina rather than Marino or another Coast Miwok was the godfather at this baptism. Was Molina the only person in the church that day? Had his behavior changed? Did Mercado order his participation? Had the parents (Elzeario and Escolastica) been absent from the mission during these disagreements and were thus unaware of Molina's reputation?

11. Letter from Figueroa to Vallejo, May 13, 1833, Vallejo, *Documentos* 1769–1850, 143.

12. Letter from Francisco Garcia Diego to Governor Figueroa, June 30, 1833, SBMA 3434.

13. Letter from José de Jesús María Gutierrez to Governor Figueroa, June 16, 1833, SBMA 1216.

14. It is curious that at some of the missions today, histories either deny that priests had Indian neophytes whipped during the mission period or attempt to whitewash the issue. A retired priest at St. Raphael Parish, the church at the site of the San Rafael mission, told the author in the 1990s that Indians had never been beaten at the missions.

15. Acisclo was either a Tamal/Omiomi born in 1806 (SFB 3482) who was married at San Rafael in August 1831 (RAM 523A), or he was an individual born in 1806 (RAB 58) whose father was from Petaluma.

16. Letter from Mercado to Vallejo, May 17, 1833, Vallejo, *Documentos* 1769–1850, 149,

167 b–f, 141a–c.

17. Letter from Mercado to Vallejo, May 9, 1833, Vallejo, *Documentos* 1769–1850, 140.

18. Letter from Mercado to Vallejo, May 17, 1833, Vallejo, *Documentos* 1769–1850, 149, 167 b–f.

19. Letter from Vallejo to Corporal, May 9, 1833, Vallejo, *Documentos* 1769–1850, 141d.

20. RAB 1869, 1895.

21. Letter from Pacheco to Vallejo, August 22, 1833, Vallejo, *Documentos* 1769–1850, 167a. Soldiers believed that they were living in poverty while the priests had both money and supplies. Beechey mentioned that when he was in San Francisco in 1826, he had arranged to pay the military for "medicines [and] provisions" rather than paying the priest. This had upset the cleric, who felt deprived of the profits that he considered his due (Beechey 1941, 5).

22. Letter from Mercado to Vallejo, August 22, 1833, Vallejo, *Documentos* 1769–1850, 168aa.

23. Bancroft 1886, vol. 3, 323n40.

24. State of the San Rafael Mission, 1828, 1830, 1832, SBMA.

25. M. G. Vallejo 1875, vol. 2, 168. Russian commentary typically lauded their relations with the Indians in comparison with how the Indians were treated at the missions. But when the Russians needed more Indian laborers, they could act aggressively too. In 1833, a Russian search for Indian workers resulted in "75 people, including women and children…brought to Ross against their will with their hands tied, from a distance of 43 miles inland" (Cuneo, unpaginated). Kent Lightfoot believes the Russians were "the lesser of two evils" (Lightfoot 2005b, 155). For an excellent discussion of the Russian colony see Lightfoot 2005, and for a comparison of advantages and disadvantages for the Indians at Colony Ross and the missions, see particularly pages 152–153 and 155–158.

26. Wrangell 1839, 5, 6.

27. Kostromitonov 1974, 7, 8.

28. Letter from Mercado to Figueroa, November 25, 1833, SBMA 3463.

29. C-A 53, Tomo 2, 97–111. Although Vallejo described Marin as chief of the Licatiut, the mission records listed Toribio as capitán of the Licatiut (RAB 386, RAM 107) in 1820. At the time of this incident, Toribio was thirty-nine years old.

30. Slaymaker (1977) applied the name of one village, Yoletama, to a group of villages in the Bodega Bay area.

31. C-A 53, Tomo 2, 97–111.

32. Letter from Vallejo to Figueroa; Vallejo, *Documentos* 1769–1850, 255B; RAB 387, 388.

33. Bancroft 1886, vol. 3, 323. Geiger (1969, 159) incorrectly attributed this act to Father Rafael de Jesús Moreno, another Zacatecan priest.

34. Letter and report from Vallejo to Governor Figueroa, January 12, 1834, Vallejo, *Documentos* 1769–1850, 255, B–C. At this time, Father Quijas had replaced Mercado.

35. Ibid., D–F.

36. RAB 1830, 1831.

37. Fernández 1874, 46; Alvarado 1876, vol. 3, unpaginated.

38. M. G. Vallejo 1875, vol. 4, 68.

39. Fernández 1874, 46. A tribute to Quijas can be seen today in San Rafael, inscribed on a metal plate on the sidewalk at Fourth Street and Cijos (named after Quijas), which is, appropriately, across the street from a bar. It refers to Quijas as a "black sheep" and "a good man when sober."

40. Ortega was removed from his post in 1837.

41. Bancroft 1886, vol. 5, 759.

42. Letter from Quijas to Father Francisco Garcia Diego, August 2, 1835, cited in Smilie 1975.

43. Letter from Quijas to President Rafael Moreno, SBMA 3538. In one case, an eighty-year-old woman in San Rafael died in January 1835 "without sacraments because the priest was out of town" (RAD 697A). In another case, Quijas was in San Francisco (RAD 687B); and in 1836 a man died "without sacraments because the priest was in Soláno" (RAD 690B). Quijas had an explanation for why three other San Rafael neophytes died without sacraments: he had not been notified of their illnesses.

44. Bancroft 1886, vol. 4, 681n18.

45. M. G. Vallejo 1875, vol. 2, 108, 109, 286.

46. See Osio [1851] 1996, 125-131; Bancroft 1886, vol. 3, 262.

47. This equivalence is based on information provided by Rose Marie Beebe and Robert M. Senkewicz, translators of Osio's history of Alta California, who note that a vara was approximately 2.8 feet (Osio 1996, 347).

48. Bancroft 1886, vol. 3, 342n4, 344n4, 343n4; Hittell 1885, 1897, vol. 2, 189.

49. C-A 51, Tomo 10, 11. When Jacome was baptized at San Francisco in 1816 (SFB 5429), his home was recorded as Puscuy, an area that Milliken locates "along the sloughs" of the Petaluma River, with "extensive family ties to Olompali" (Milliken 1995, 240). Tiberio, a Guaulen from the Bolinas area, was also baptized originally in San Francisco (SFB 3102).

50. Bancroft 1886, vol. 3, 348, 716n18.

51. Mission livestock in 1832 included an estimated 2,120 to 2,442 head of cattle, 372 horses and mules, and 3,000 sheep. The total number of animals was 5,508 (ibid., 716n18).

52. See Appendix G.

53. Bancroft 1886, vol. 3, 723.

54. Except for Luis Antolin from Tamal, all of the other petitioners had the same baptismal name as other neophytes, so we cannot determine precisely which tribal area they came from. For each petitioner (except Teodorico), however, the mission records include an individual of the same name and appropriate age from western Marin.

55. Land Case 404 N.D., p. 68, Nicasio or ex-Mission San Rafael, United States District Court, the Bancroft Library, University of California, Berkeley.

56. Kelly 2003, 320.

57. Vallejo, *Documentos* 1769–1850, 29, May 1, 1835.

58. Baptized as Nicasio at Mission Dolores in 1802 (SFB 2434), Guequistabal first married a Coast Miwok woman from Olemoloque; after her death, he married another Coast Miwok woman, this time from Omiomi (SFM 1174, 1382). The name of his second wife was spelled Ubnceslaa in the San Francisco records and Wenceslaa at San Rafael; she was still alive when Nicasio died in 1841.

59. Lauff's unreliable manuscript claims that there were two thousand Indians around the San Rafael mission in 1835, but it is unlikely that he was actually in California at the time (Lauff 1916, 68).

60. Ibid. 70. Juan Garcia also mentioned that Indians lived on the site of the McNear home near McNear's Point, as well as at the foot of what is today B Street in San Rafael as well as the San Anselmo area known as the "Carrigan tract" (Garcia 1917, 3).

61. M. G. Vallejo 1875, vol. 4, 13, 18.

62. Letter from Vallejo to Figueroa, October 12, 1835, SBMA 1276.

63. Bancroft 1886, vol. 3, 718.

64. In the face of this travesty, the irony and inappropriateness of the phrase "Indian giver" are striking. Today, the *American Heritage Dictionary* defines an "Indian giver" as "one who gives something to another and [then] takes or demands the gift back." Originally, the term referred to the American Indian practice of giving a gift and expecting one in return; if the second gift was not of equal value, the original gift was returned.

65. M. G. Vallejo 1875, vol. 4, 18.

66. Ibid., vol. 3, 291. Alvarado's decree ordering neophytes to return to the missions affected nine-tenths of those Indians who had previously been granted their freedom.

67. Ibid., vol. 3, 29; P. E. Edwards 1890, April 6, 1837.

68. Bancroft 1886, vol. 4, 44, 48.

69. M. G. Vallejo 1875, vol. 3, 10.

70. Vallejo said they were from the "Aguanui" tribe, probably a variant of the name of the San Rafael area, Nanaguani.

71. Milliken, personal communication, 2004.

72. M. G. Vallejo 1875, vol. 3, 18.

73. There is some doubt that Brown remembered the correct year.

74. Brown 1975, 12.

75. M. G. Vallejo 1875, vol. 3, 271–273.

76. Bancroft 1886, vol. 2, 755. Francisco Castro, father to the two brothers, had received a grant for San Pablo.

77. RAB 1874, 1878; RAM 546; RAB 1853.

78. RAB 1838, 1839; RAM 517, 520B, 522B, 523B, 524B, 525B, 526B, 530B, 534B, 539B, 541B.

79. RAB 1862.

80. The variant spellings are many, including Elisario, Elseario, Eliserio, Elciario and Eseario.

81. RAM 452.

82. Kelly 2003, 26.

83. Land Case 183 N.D., p. 48, Corte Madera del Presidio, United States District Court, the Bancroft Library, University of California, Berkeley. Nereo's name appeared as a member of the leadership group at the mission and was often associated with that of Marino, who was the godparent for Nereo's son. Nereo had many roles at the mission: alcalde, interpreter of the Coast Miwok and Pomo languages, godparent on many occasions, marriage witness, and "caporal of the Tehases." His wife was also a frequent godparent.

84. Somewhat inexplicably, the spelling of Camilo's Indian name changed over the years. At the time of his baptism, his Indian name was Hueñux, and his father's name was Vnutia. At his first marriage, Camilo was unitia (RAM 241) and his father was Vnitia. At Camilo's second marriage, the priest wrote Camilo unutia (RAM 509A), and at his third wedding, his name was spelled Benú (RAM 527B), possibly a short version of Vnutia, his father's name. (In Spanish, the letters *b* and *v* are interchangeable.) The first use of Ynitia to refer to Camilo was in his land grant for Olompali in the 1840s.

85. Camilo's parents were baptized Aurelio and Aurelia. Aurelio came from Canuinpuxcui, and Aurelia from Puscuy (see note 49 in this chapter). Camilo's mother died from burns in 1824 (RAD 242), and his father passed away six years later (RAD 587).

86. Other than noting her death, the priest did not explain Candida's death further (RAD 670B). There is no death record for Jacome; he was last mentioned in the mission records in 1833. The wedding of Camilo and Cayetana was duly recorded in 1835 (RAM 527).

87. Teodorico was also referred to as Teodorico Quilajuque.

88. Hartnell, September 17-18, 1839-1840.

CHAPTER ELEVEN

1. Merriam 1993, 212; Kelly 2003, 494, 403.

2. Beechey [1831], 65.

3. Margolin 1993, 81.

4. Kelly 2003, 403.

5. Kelly 2003, 451.

6. Merriam 1993, 217.

7. Amorós, State of the San Rafael mission, 1827; RAD 202.

8. RAD 711.

9. Kelly 2003, 338. Unfortunately, this mention of Marino's brother is the only existing reference to Marino's family of origin, except for Maria Copa's statement that he was her grandmother's cousin. We have no way to identify Marino's brother or even his parents.

10. Kelly 1931-1932, field notes, vol. 10, 16. At Mission San Diego, the priest Luís Jayme learned from the Indians that "if a man plays with any woman who is not his wife, he is scolded and punished by his captains" (quoted in Hackel 2005, 184).

11. Cook 1976, 214. Cook reported the year of the epidemic as 1837. He dismissed Governor Alvarado's figures (two hundred thousand to three hundred thousand deaths), which he considered inflated, and gave more credence to Vallejo's more modest estimate of

"hundreds" of deaths in his district (ibid., 213-214).

12. RAD 734-779.

13. One of those who did not die of smallpox was the long-lived Ysidro, Maria Copa's great-grandfather, who died of "old age" (RAD 776).

14. Lauff 1916, 71. The elderly Lauff's misrepresentations were perhaps no worse than the exaggerations and errors reported by younger observers throughout the mission period. And it is worth noting that Lauff's statistics did not hurt anyone or deprive the Indians of land or possessions. But untangling his claims does present obstacles in the attempt to set the historical record straight. At least he was consistent in his variability, changing both his birth date and his arrival dates in California (see also Munro-Fraser 1880) continually over the years.

15. RAD 783. Amorós administered this third sacrament, also known as Viatico, only ten times in fourteen years, notably to the alcalde José María (RAD 334B); to Justino (RAD 398), who had served as a witness, an interpreter, and a nurse; and to Toribia (RAD 538), the wife of Tiberio (SFB 3102), a vaquero.

16. Alvarado 1876, vol. 1, 76.

17. Kelly 2003, 403.

18. *San Francisco Monitor*, June 3, 1885. The original cemetery was in the area of Fifth Street, near the bookstore, office, and rectory of today's Saint Raphael Church.

CHAPTER TWELVE

1. Seven months after Marino died, Vallejo personally ordered one of his men, Lt. Lázaro Piña, to kill on sight a Coast Miwok neophyte from the San Rafael mission. Vallejo's order attempted to resolve what he saw as a serious miscarriage of justice from years past. A soldier from the San Francisco presidio, Francisco Rubio, had been accused of killing two children at Mission Dolores in 1828 and was executed by a firing squad in 1831; Vallejo and others at the presidio, however, doubted that Rubio was the murderer, and eight years later, Vallejo became convinced that the real killer was the Coast Miwok Román.

Román would have been thirty-eight at the time; he was single and had been baptized in 1819 on the same day as his parents, when he was eighteen years old (RAB 286). He may have been the same Román from San Rafael who was tried in 1831 on a charge of receiving stolen clothing from a soldier, Felipe Gomez of the San Francisco presidio.

Dispensing with judge and jury, and with no known evidence for Román's guilt, Vallejo decided that Román should be shot four times (Osio 1996, 105-106). Soon thereafter, Father Quijas recorded Román's death in the San Rafael mission death records, expressing no judgment but noting that he had been shot by Piña "while in a ravine, [and] died without confession because no one said anything until Piña himself came to inform me" (RAD 803). Quijas wrote that Román had been *arcabuceadado,* or harquebused. (A harquebus was a small-caliber long gun.)

2. Vallejo's older sister came home to live with her parents after the death of her husband and brought her young son, Juan Bautista Alvarado, with her. Vallejo was only a year older than this nephew.

3. Bancroft 1886, vol. 4, 56n23.

4. Hartnell 1839-1840, September 18, 1839.

5. The Indians complained that they had not received any clothes for two years; the flocks at San Rafael had not produced sufficient wool for clothing for the Indians. Hartnell was able to report, however, that Murphy, the administrator, was requesting sheep from San Jose to replenish the flocks at San Rafael (Hartnell 1839-1840, September 23, 1839; Vallejo, *Documentos* 1769-1850, 291). The Indians also "demanded" that Hartnell ensure the return of two boys, Pedro and Papa, who had been taken to Monterey by a man named Robbins—most likely Captain Thomas M. Robbins, an American employed by Alvarado and Vallejo as captain of the government schooner *California* (Bancroft 1886, vol. 5, 697). According to the mission records, five young boys named Pedro, between the ages of six and eight, still survived in 1839; two of them (RAB 1716, 1822) were motherless. There is no record of a boy baptized as Papa at San Rafael.

6. Vallejo, *Documentos* 1769-1850, 23. Ink blots make the wording of the pass difficult to read, but the impression is that Talio (RAB 1343) left Sonoma armed with his pass, which allowed him to stop at San Rafael to pick up supplies but also required him to send some of his followers back to San Rafael every eight days for duties at the church. This translation differs from Bancroft's.

7. Bancroft 1886, vol. 4, 56n23.

8. Hartnell 1839-1840, September 18, 1839. Bancroft considered the 190 Indians described by Hartnell to be those living in the "community," the word used to designate those who lived at or near the mission, with another 150 "scattered" (Bancroft 1886, vol. 3, 717). This suggests that the Indians Hartnell spoke with at San Rafael were not the Coast Miwok from Nicasio, who just a month earlier had been reassured by Governor Alvarado that Nicasio was their land.

9. The name of this land grant may have come from a name associated with the parcel of land, referring to Corporal José Herrera, who was stationed at the San Rafael mission for many years during the time of Father Amorós. Osio gave Herrera credit for capturing Pomponio, but he is also remembered for committing a serious crime, for which he was jailed and dismissed from the San Francisco company in 1824 (see Chapter 6). Another interpretation of the name, as "valley of the blacksmith" (Mason 1971, 47), seems less likely; the Spanish word for "blacksmith" is *herrero* rather than *herrera*.

10. In 1840, Cooper engaged Timothy Murphy, the San Rafael administrator, to "make improvements and carry on a farm in the cañada." Murphy in turn had Rufino (a Coast Miwok) and others build a "large stick house there near a creek on a road from Corte Madera to San Rafael." Rufino and his family lived there while working for Cooper, planting "corn, beans, potatoes, barley, wheat and pumpkin" (Beales 1978, 3-5). Rufino eventually left and joined other Coast Miwok at Nicasio, and Cooper received this 8,895-acre parcel from former governor Alvarado, who used it to pay off a debt (Mason 1971, 57). Cooper himself spent little time on this extensive rancho, apparently preferring to reside in Monterey and San Francisco while accumulating property elsewhere.

11. Hartnell 1839-1840, September 16 and 17, 1839. Camilo was seriously ill at the time of Hartnell's visit and wrote a will, making Murphy his executor.

12. Bancroft 1886, vol. 4, 59n28.

13. M. G. Vallejo 1875, vol. 1, 151.

14. C-A 51, Tomo 11, 12-17.

15. Ibid.

16. Order from M. G. Vallejo to T. Murphy, October 23, 1840, Vallejo, *Documentos 1769-1850*, 291.

17. Quijas, State of the San Rafael Mission, Informe annual, 1840, SBMA.

18. Simpson [1850] 1930, 57. Quijas and Murphy may have traveled to Fort Ross to obtain alcohol that was not available at San Rafael, such as vodka (either imported or locally prepared from grain) or sherry prepared from the white Palomino grape.

19. Alvarado 1876, vol. 3, unpaginated.

20. M. G. Vallejo 1875, vol. 2, 198.

21. State of the San Rafael Mission, 1840, SBMA.

22. Peirce, undated, 80-83.

23. State of the Mission, Informe annual, 1840, 1841, SBMA.

24. P. L. Edwards 1890, April 6, 1837; Peirce undated, Memoranda, 24; Peirce undated, Rough Sketch, 80.

25. Amador 1877, 6-7. Bancroft claimed that small items at the missions were sold for cash that was used in gambling (Bancroft 1886, vol. 4, 51).

26. Wilbur 1937, 237. Apparently, Vallejo did not take all the grapevines that had been tended by the neophytes at the mission; in 1845, 210 plant stocks were still extant (Bowman, May 1943, 11). Within the next five years, Charles Lauff, visiting San Rafael on a Saturday afternoon, reported that "to my surprise a dozen Indians passed down the street to spend the afternoon in working in the mission orchard, which then comprised 100 acres of grapes, pear, apple, olive trees and grain" (Lauff 1916, 64).

Vallejo's appropriation of the mission's vines is ironic, given the poor reputation of the wine produced from these grapes; it was described as "lacking in bouquet and flavor,... rough and acid" (*Los Angeles Herald,* October 28, 1887, 1); and a wine industry official in the 1880s claimed that "he never used Mission brandy without suffering afterwards from a dull headache with almost a suicidal tendency" (Wetmore 1884, 9).

Two reds and two whites were produced from the black grapes. The unfortified white was used in the church and described by Father Durán as "rather unpleasant, because it has no sweetness." Of the two reds, the priest mentioned that one was sweet and the other dry and "good for the table" (Teiser and Harroun 1983, 7).

27. Simpson 1930, 56.

28. Lauff 1916, 64.

29. RAB 1920, 1931, 1933, 1947, 1949, 1991, 2013, 2037. Baptism numbers were not used after 1848. The spelling of some of these names changed over the years when recorded by different priests (see Chapter 14).

30. R. R. Miller 1995, 102.

31. Stephen Richardson is quoted in Wilkins 1918, 25. R. Miller 1995 (102) describes the rescue of Limantour. Monico was baptized originally at San Jose (Milliken, personal communication, 2004).

32. See also Davis 1967, 40.

33. Mariana Richardson Torres quoted in the *Oakland Tribune,* March 4, 1928.

34. Richardson 1918, 33-34.

35. The grant was included in the papers of the U.S. Land Commission, ND, Case 10, 54; Sandels 1880, 6; Kelly 2003, 320.

36. Davis 1967, 103.

37. Sandels 1880, 6; Davis 1967, 103; U.S. Land Commission ND, Case 10, 2-105. At a time when most (but not all) Coast Miwok had Indian godparents for their children, it may be significant that prominent Californios Gregorio Briones and María Antonio Martinez served as godparents for Maxima Antonio, the daughter of Camilo and Cayetana, in 1841 (RAB 1947). María Antonio Martínez was the wife of Captain Richardson and the daughter of Ignacio Martinez. By the time Camilo and Cayetana's second daughter, María Antonia, was born in 1845 (RAB 2013), having Californio godparents—in this case, Captain Richardson and his wife—was the norm.

38. Milliken, personal communication, 2004.

39. Kelly 2003, 75.

40. Kelly 1931-1932, vol. 10, 50; Kelly 2003, 75.

41. Brown 1975, 15.

42. Amador 1877, 14-20, 21.

43. Bancroft 1886, vol. 4, 75n66, 543n60.

44. Such raids may help to explain the presence of more than forty unbaptized Indians at the Bojorques rancho near Petaluma in March 1843. Rather than representing a small pocket of Coast Miwok who had resisted mission surveillance, they may have been victims of a raid. Reportedly, these Indians left the Bojorques rancho later for Napa County (perhaps their area of origin), returning to the rancho yearly for seasonal work.

45. Revere 1872, 171, 170.

46. Ibid., 173.

47. Ibid., 178.

48. During the court trial, Rafael Garcia testified that Antonio Castro had led the raid and was the commandante of the group. This assignment of leadership is puzzling, if true, because Garcia himself had been a soldier at the San Francisco presidio and would have been the logical choice to lead a paramilitary band. We have no record that Antonio Castro had been in the military.

49. C-A 39, Tomo 5, 389; *"una indita que le marido a Don Luis Leecs"* (ibid., 388).

50. C-A 39, Tomo 5, 391, 393-394.

51. Bojorques 1874, 24-37.

52. Sandels 1880, 7-8.

53. Bancroft 1886, vol. 5, 669n3.

54. Mason 1971, 171.

55. Taylor 1850, 286.

CHAPTER THIRTEEN

1. Someone else may have helped the Indians compose their letter; it is unlikely that even the gifted Teodorico would have had the drafter's linguistic skills in Spanish. Timothy Murphy spoke Spanish with some flair, but, according to Bancroft, Murphy's Spanish was "peculiar...and vulgar" (Bancroft 1886, vol. 4, 750). Quijas or Vallejo might have provided such aid.

2. Vallejo used the expression "certain persons" in his history of California when he disapproved of someone's opinion but did not want to identify the individual. In this case, the phrase may have referred to the secretary of state or even to Alvarado himself.

3. Land Case 404 N.D., pp. 17-18, Nicasio of ex-Mission of San Rafael, United States District Court, the Bancroft Library, University of California, Berkeley. It is possible that Secretary of State Jimeno actually wrote the response to the Indians on Alvarado's behalf, because Alvarado was sick much of the time between July and September 1839. Bancroft described him as "nervous and ill from the effects of too much aguardiente [brandy]" (Bancroft 1886, vol. 3, 596). During this time, Jimeno was in effect acting governor. Alvarado was so busy in August, when the letter was received, that he could not attend his own wedding and was married in absentia, although he was well enough for the wedding festivities early in September.

4. Mason 1971, 71. I have been unable to ascertain the source of Mason's information.

5. Later, Vallejo would claim that the previous governor, Figueroa, had given him the power to grant land. In his deposition in the land case, Vallejo stated: "I had the power to grant mission lands...from said governor. Those instructions [to grant lands] were a matter of public notoriety and I suppose they are in the Archives of the Governor taken by the Bear Flag Party in 1846. I have not seen them since" (Land Case 404 N.D., p. 63, Nicasio or ex-Mission of San Rafael, United States District Court, the Bancroft Library, University of California, Berkeley).

6. Dietz 1976, 27.

7. Land Case 404 N.D., pp. 44-46, Nicasio or ex-Mission of San Rafael, United States District Court, the Bancroft Library, University of California, Berkeley. Notice that Vallejo wrote, "I promised to give them ownership of it" rather than "Governor Figueroa promised to give them ownership of it." The "disconfidence" Vallejo mentions no doubt refers to the earlier arguments between himself and Governor Alvarado, in which both claimed ultimate authority in northern California (land case 45).

8. Land Case 404 N.D., pp. 34-36, Nicasio or ex-Mission of San Rafael, United States District Court, the Bancroft Library, University of California, Berkeley. Vallejo's secretary, Victor Prudon, recipient of a land grant in Bodega, must have known about the history of the disputed land. He was privy to the arguments between Alvarado and Vallejo and had been Alvarado's secretary during his governorship before coming to work for Vallejo.

Where did his loyalties lie? Did Prudon apply for the land in order to help Vallejo, in the hope that an application under Prudon's name might be received more favorably than under Vallejo's? When Prudon testified at the U.S. Land Commission, he said that he did not know whether the "grant was made before or after our petition was presented" (Land Case 404 N.D., p. 59, Nicasio or ex-Mission of San Rafael, United States District Court, the Bancroft Library, University of California, Berkeley).

9. Land Case 404 N.D., pp. 34-36, Nicasio of ex-Mission of San Rafael, United States District Court, the Bancroft Library, University of California, Berkeley.

10. Land Case 404 N.D., pp. 41-44, Nicasio of ex-Mission of San Rafael, United States District Court, the Bancroft Library, University of California, Berkeley.

11. Land Case 404 N.D., pp. 20-23, Nicasio of ex-Mission of San Rafael, United States District Court, the Bancroft Library, University of California, Berkeley. The terms specified that "the sum of one thousand dollars ($1000) is hereby acknowledged an order on Mariano G. Vallejo."

12. Mason 1971, 71.

13. Land Case 404 N.D., pp. 22-23, Nicasio of ex-Mission of San Rafael, United States District Court, the Bancroft Library, University of California, Berkeley.

14. Land Case 404 N.D., pp. 34-37, Nicasio of ex-Mission of San Rafael, United States District Court, the Bancroft Library, University of California, Berkeley. Jimenez said that Alvarado's transaction was illegal because the price was too low and because no arrangements had been made for the date of the payments.

15. Jimeno and Vallejo had long-running difficulties with each other, and Jimeno may have been trying to embarrass Vallejo by saying that the Indians had never held title. Nothing more was ever heard of the land that Jimeno claimed had been left for the Indians.

16. Land Case 404 N.D., p. 69, Nicasio of ex-Mission of San Rafael, United States District Court, the Bancroft Library, University of California, Berkeley; Dietz 1976, 33.

17. Hittell 1885, vol. 3, 693.

18. Land Case 210 N.D., p. 5, Tinicasia, United States District Court, the Bancroft Library, University of California, Berkeley.

19. Vallejo claimed that he had kept the original decree because it was an archive of the "frontier," but that when he looked for it, he could not find it. Witnesses at the hearing testified that Teodorico had had the original, so it is not clear how Vallejo could have had it.

20. Translation in Exhibit A, Land Case 404 N.D., pp. 16-17, Nicasio of ex-Mission of San Rafael, United States District Court, the Bancroft Library, University of California, Berkeley; also found in Vallejo, *Documentos* 1769-1850, 29 (an original copy, and a copy of a copy). Apparently, Figueroa's order was dated March 13, 1835, and it was signed by Vallejo on May 1, 1835.

21. Land Case 404 N.D., pp. 67-68, Nicasio of ex-Mission of San Rafael, United States District Court, the Bancroft Library, University of California, Berkeley.

22. Ranch owner William Richardson testified that he had seen an order that Ignacio Martinez (his father-in-law and the administrator at San Rafael) had received from the

governor, "directing him to place these Indians in possession of the land named Nicasio." Richardson, Martinez, and several Indians who had done the original survey had sent a "rough plan" (presumably the diseño) to the governor (U.S. Land Commission 1855, ND 404, 60). Victor Castro also reported that he had seen the title to Nicasio while Teodorico was still alive and recognized the seal and signature of Figueroa, although he had not read the body of the grant (ibid., 69). Rafael Garcia's statement mentioned that the Indians had been living at Nicasio up to that day (presumably 1855, the year of the hearing) without any authority ever preventing them from freely exercising their just rights (ibid., 17-18). Victor Prudon's deposition referred to the sale of the land by the Indians to Alvarado and "the right of the Indians to graze cattle and cultivate the lands they had yearly cultivated" (ibid., 23).

23. Bowman 1947, 29-30.

CHAPTER FOURTEEN

1. M. G. Vallejo 1850, 530.

2. Kelly 2003, 87. Tom Smith said that hukúiko was "the name for Tomales and Bodega people," whereas Maria Copa told Kelly that the Nicasio people "call the Tomales and Bodega people tamalko (coast people)" (Kelly 2003, 1).

3. The various translations of "tamal" are found in Kelly 2003, 1; Barrett 1908, 307; Kroeber 1970, 897; Callaghan 1970, 70; and Merriam 1907, 355, respectively. Tamalpais was pronounced "tamal pa-yee" by the grandmother of a Coast Miwok descendant (Eugene Buvelot, interview with the author, March 2004).

Spanish and European visitors had other names for this peak, such as Table Hill (Beechey 1827 map [Stanger and Brown 1969, 62-63] and Duflot de Mofras 1843 map [Map 12 1850d, Bancroft Library) and Palmas, shown in the 1835 survey of Reed's land grant (Francisco de Haro, U.S. Land Commission 1853, ND 183, 45). The word "Tamalpais" appeared on the 1845 Bolinas (Baulenes) map for lands granted to Gregorio Briones.

4. It is unlikely that the towns of San Geronimo and San Anselmo commemorate the two Coast Miwok alcaldes Geronimo and Anselmo. References to both San Geronimo and San Anselmo were in common usage during the Mexican period, and the Californios would not have added "San" (for "Saint") in front of an Indian's Spanish name.

5. M. G. Vallejo 1875, vol. 1, 109. Today, there is even a San Marin.

6. Until the 1930s, the name of the Guilucs, mentioned so often in the San Rafael mission records, was associated with the Los Guilicos Warm Springs, located in Glen Ellen, north of Sonoma; in 1938, however, the name was changed to Morton Springs.

7. California Legislature 1851, Senate and Assembly: 1.

8. Cook 1976, 311.

9. Arrigoni 2003, 25-27.

10. Marin County Coroner's Files #61, 1863.

11. State of California Supreme Court 1854, vol. 3, 404-405.

12. See Edward Castillo, cited in Elliott 1995, 3.

13. Elliott 1995, 2.

14. Kathleen Smith, interview with the author, May 19, 2004; Eugene Buvelot, interview with the author, March 12, 2004.

15. Castillo (1978, 116) cites as his source the book *Battlefield and Classroom: Four Decades with the American Indian, 1867-1904*, by Richard Henry Pratt.

16. Kathleen Smith, interview with the author, May 19, 2004; Eugene Buvelot, interview with the author, March 12, 2004.

17. Hurley 1995, unpaginated.

18. Records of St. Vincent's Orphanage.

19. Kelly 2003, 151, 316; Kelly 1931-1932, Notebook 9, 20b.

20. The date is based on the notice signed by Joseph A. Knox, "executor of Camilo Ynitia deceased' in the *Petaluma Weekly Journal,* August 9, 1856 (Glass 2002, 2). No deaths were recorded at the San Rafael church between January 1854 and the 1870s.

21. Mason 1971, 125-126; Stephen J. Richardson in Wilkins 1918, 31.

22. Kelly 2003, 316.

23. Ibid.

24. Carlson and Parkman 1986, 247.

25. Eliseo's victim is not named in the few records that still exist. If he had murdered a white man, the individual would probably have been identified, so it is more likely that the victim was an Indian. Eliseo was sentenced to two years for manslaughter and was incarcerated at San Quentin beginning in November 1856. At the prison, he was described as a thirty-year-old man with a dark complexion and black eyes and hair. He had a blue tattoo on his forearm, described as two scars of blue ink, as well as scars "on his forehead and between his shoulders" (San Quentin Records #1043). An Indian named Eliseo, born in 1817 and the son of a man from a village near the lower Petaluma River, not far from Olompali, was baptized at the San Rafael mission (RAB 728); but he would have been thirty-nine years old in 1856.

26. Kelly 2003, 316. Greg Sarris, the tribal chairman in 2004, stated that Camilo was not liked by other Coast Miwok (personal communication, 2002).

27. Kelly 2003, 63.

28. In his marriage record, his surname is spelled Calisto, his father is listed as Teodorico Calisto, and his mother as Maria Michaelina. All are said to be Indians. (St. Vincent's, Petaluma, marriage records, 1875.) It is possible that he was the son of Teodorico Quilajuque, the well-known land claimant at Nicasio (and witness at Marino's wedding), whose wife was Michaelina, and whose child, Jose, was baptized at the San Rafael church in 1840. Based on the Nicasio census of 1870, Jose Calistro was born in 1838; based on Probate Court File #188, he was born in 1830 (Dietz 1976, 58).

29. Marin County Journal, August 13, 1880. An upstanding citizen, Sebastian and "Theopalus" (possibly Teodorico) had arrested an Indian named Jose Antonio, who was accused of beating another Indian to death in 1852.

30. Kelly 1931-1932, Notebook 10, 26b.

31. Marin County Journal, October 2, 1879; Munro-Fraser 1880, 250-254.

32. San Francisco *Argonaut*, May 31, 1879, 3 (the writer signed his name as "Angle");

Marin County Tocsin, August 16, 1879, 3, unsigned.

33. California State Archives, San Quentin Prison Records, #3626. An 1867 newspaper article claimed that Salvador was "by virtue of the law of succession [to be] Chief of that [Nicasio] tribe. He is the son of 'Old Big Head' so well remembered by our old residents" (*Marin County Journal*, March 9, 1867, 3). The term "big head" might have referred to a headdress worn by a religious leader, the precursor of the large headdress worn by dreamers of the Big Head, or Bole-Maru, cult after 1870.

34. *Marin County Journal*, October 2, 1879; Munro-Fraser 1880, 250-254.

35. California State Archives, San Quentin Prison Records #3626. California State Library, Sacramento.

36. Munro-Fraser 1880, 253.

37. Ibid. The author described Rafaela as Salvador's sister, but she was his half-sister.

38. Ibid., 251-252. One hardened reporter wrote, "He comes from a bad lot, his grandfather having been burned alive by the natives for his acts of deviltry, and in his death the county will be rid of a great villain" (*Marin County Tocsin*, September 27, 1879, 3).

39. *Marin County Journal*, October 2, 1879.

40. *Marin County Tocsin*, October 11, 1879, 2-3.

41. Bancroft 1886, vol. 5, 670; Levee 1983 #4, Part 3, unpaginated, "The Mistress of Rancho Bodega" in *The Journal*, Sonoma County Historical Society. See also Parts 1 and 2.

42. Tom Smith's remembrances may not be as reliable as those of Maria Copa, and not necessarily because of his advanced age; according to his descendants, Tom Smith was "teasing" in his interchanges with Isabel Kelly, "testing her gullibility" (as reported by Collier and Thalman in Kelly 2003, xli.)

43. The name Bole-Maru was a combined word from the Hill Patwin and Eastern Pomo tribes.

44. Bean and Vane 1978, 671.

45. Kelly 2003, 234.

46. Du Bois 1939, 111.

47. Rosenus 1999, 219.

48. Petaluma Weekly Journal, April 12, 1856.

49. At the same time the Californios were losing their place of power in the community, H. H. Bancroft was writing his definitive *History of California*, which frequently denigrated the written remembrances of the Spaniards and Mexicans as a "mixture of fact and fancy" (Bancroft 1886, vol. 5, 759.)

50. Dietz 1976, 61-62.

51. Yount 1923, 20.

52. Munro-Fraser 1880, 288. According to Orin Starn, a *San Francisco Chronicle* article in 1850 contained another variant, speaking of the Indians who would disappear "like the dissipating mist in the presence of the morning sun of the Saxon" (Starn 2004, 24).

53. Bell 1927, 313.

54. *Daily Alta*, March 30, 1860; Bancroft 1888, 401. The only other description we have of Marino comes from Dr. Robert C. Thomas, a descendant of Camilo and Cayetana.

Thomas mistakenly believed that Marino was Cayetana's father, which would have made Thomas a descendant of Chief Marin. He claimed that Camilo was about six feet six inches tall and that "Marino wasn't much shorter" (Thomas 1974).

55. Stanger and Brown 1969, 137, 141; Crespi in Galvin 1971, 114.

56. Treutlein 1968, 118.

57. The issue of human skin color is complicated. Color is determined by at least five genes and is subject to natural selection, which means that heritage cannot be determined on the basis of skin color alone.

58. The warehouse can still be seen today; it became the Bolinas Bay Yacht Club in 1970. During the 1950s, the Smith wharves were torn down, and the family house was removed from land that is now the parking lot of the yacht club. The street is still named Smith Brothers.

59. Eugene Buvelot, interview with the author, 2005.

60. Elizabeth Campigli Harlan, interview with Douglas (Dewey) Livingston, 1996.

61. Livingston 1989, 39.

62. The Lipps-Michaels 1919-1920 Survey noted that these healthy residents had no evidence of tuberculosis or trachoma (Lipps-Michaels 1919-1920, 40).

63. Ibid., 40. Stewart's Point was the home of the Kashaya Pomo, and Sebastopol was also traditionally Pomo country. Indians were also living in other southern Sonoma communities, such as Temelec, a former Miwok village; the 2000 U.S. Census listed six Native Americans living there.

64. Ortiz 1993, 11.

65. Eugene Buvelot, personal communication, 2003; Patricia Cummings, personal communication, 2004; Billy quoted in Ortiz 1993, 12. Cummings began her search for her heritage with her grandmother, who was born in Marshall. Unaware that her grandmother was Indian, she had assumed that the "I" after her mother's name in the state census classified her as Italian. Not until she looked at her grandmother's sister's tombstone did she realize that the "I" stood for Indian. She remembered: "I was amazed at the Indian connection. My mother never shared this" (Cummings, personal communication, September-October 2004). She has been able to trace her ancestry back to Carmel Com cha tal, her great-great-grandmother, who was born in Marshall sometime between 1819 and 1838 and who died of pneumonia in 1893.

66. Rosalie Smith Cody, interview with Mary Thames Taylor, August 11, 1910, tape #RSC-1A.

67. Ibid.

68. Du Bois 1939, 114.

69. Kelly 2003, 9.

70. A similar evolution was evident in Copa's mother's name: baptized in 1829 as Juana Evangelista, she became Joan Baptista in the 1880 census. Copa remembered her name as Juana Bauptista.

All of today's registered Coast Miwok and southern Pomo descendants of the Federated

Indians of Graton Rancheria can be traced from 1929 to fewer than twenty ancestors, according to the tribal genealogist, Sylvia Thalman (personal communication, 2004). Unpublished research done by Randall Milliken and independently by the author has traced some of these family trees back into the 1780s through the mission records. It would have been an easier task if the priests had used more variety in the Spanish names they gave to the Indians, since it is impossible to trace the many Juans and Marias accurately. In addition, those descendants whose grandparents and great-grandparents hid their Indian heritage may never be properly identified.

71. Castillo 1998, unpaginated.

72. Greg Sarris, personal communication, 2002.

73. Sarris 2003, 115; Sarris 1994b, 142.

74. Smith in Kelly 2003, 22.

75. Greg Sarris, personal communication, 2006.

76. Greg Sarris, interview with the author, 2002.

77. Otis Parrish, personal communication, December 2004.

78. The photograph was taken by William R. Heick in 1963. Heick also produced the films *Pomo Shaman* (1964) and *Sucking Doctor* (1963). Essie Parrish believed that these healing dances should not be continued after her death. She believed that "another spiritual leader will come but after the death of her descendants" (Eric Wilder, personal communication, November 2004).

79. Greg Sarris, interview with the author, 2002.

80. Sarris 2003.

81. Sarris 2003.

82. Tribal members Eugene Buvelot and Tim Campbell have been active in this organization as president and vice president of the board.

83. Sarris 2003.

REFERENCES

Allardt, G. F. 1841. Map of Corte Madera del Presidio Creek. Mill Valley Public Library.

Altimira, José, and Robert Ernest Cowan. 1853. "Diario de la expedición verificada con objeto de reconocer terranos para la nueva planta de la Misión de N.P.S. Francisco…" MS. June 25-July 6, 1853. The Bancroft Library, University of California, Berkeley.

Alvarado, Juan Bautista. 1874. Letter in Gift, 1875. The Bancroft Library, University of California, Berkeley.

———. 1876. "History of California." 5 volumes. MS. Translated by Earl R. Hewitt.

———. 1982. *Vignettes of Early California: Childhood Reminiscences of Juan Bautista Alvarado.* Translated by John H. R. Polt. San Francisco: Book Club of California.

Amador, José María. 1877. "Memorias sobre la historia de California." MS. Translated by Thomas Savage. Berkeley: The Bancroft Library, University of California, Berkeley.

Ambrose, Stephen. 1996. *Undaunted Courage.* New York: Simon and Schuster.

Anderson, Kat. 1993. In Blackburn and Anderson 1993.

Archives of the Archdiocese of San Francisco, California. *Libro de Bautismos, Libro de Difuntos,* and *Libro de Casamientos* (Books of Baptisms, Deaths, and Marriages) for Missions San Francisco and San Rafael. Referred to in the text as SFB, SFD, SFM, RAB, RAD, and RAM.

Archives of California. See C-A.

Argüello, Luis Antonio. 1992. *The Diary of Captain Luis Antonio Argüello: October 17-November 17, 1821: The Last Spanish Expedition in California.* Translated by Vivian C. Fisher. Series of keepsakes issued for its members by the Friends of the Bancroft Library; no. 40. Berkeley: Friends of the Bancroft Library, University of California, Berkeley.

Arrigoni, Aimee. 2003. *Bay Miwok Readings.* Compiled by the Contra Costa County Historical Society.

Ashcroft, Lionel. [n.d.] Notes accompanying map "Entrance to the Bay of San Francisco, Bays of San Francisco and San Pablo," *U.S. Exploring Expedition Survey Map of the Sacramento River and San Pablo Bay, Lt. Charles Wilkes.* Marin History Museum.

Asisara, Lorenzo. 1877. In Amador 1877.

Ayala, Juan Manuel de. 1775. Journal in Galvin 1971, pp. 77-92.

Balls, Edward K. 1962. *Early Uses of California Plants.* Berkeley: University of California Press.

Bancroft, Hubert Howe. 1886. *History of California, Vols. 1-5.* San Francisco: The History Company.

———. 1888. *California Pastoral, 1769-1848.* San Francisco: The History Company.

Bandini, José. 1828. *A Description of California in 1828*. Translated by Doris Marion Wright. Berkeley: Friends of the Bancroft Library, University of California, Berkeley.

Barbour, Michael [et al.]. 1993. *California's Changing Landscapes: Diversity and Conservation of California Vegetation*. Sacramento: California Native Plant Society.

Barnes, Thomas Charles, Thomas H. Naylor, and Charles W. Polzer. 1981. *Northern New Spain: A Research Guide*. Tucson: University of Arizona Press.

Barrett, S. A. 1908. *The Ethno-geography of the Pomo and Neighboring Indians*. University of California Publications in American Archaeology and Ethnology, vol. 6, no. 1. Berkeley: University of California Press.

————. 1952. "Material Aspects of Pomo Culture." *Bulletin of the Public Museum of the City of Milwaukee,* vol. 20, parts 1 and 2. Milwaukee: Published by order of the Board of Trustees.

Barrett, S. A., and Edward Winslow Gifford. 1933. "Miwok Material Culture." *Bulletin of the Public Museum of the City of Milwaukee,* vol. 2, no. 4. Milwaukee: Published by order of the Board of Trustees.

Beales, John T. 1978. "The Saga of the Rancho Punta de San Quentin." *Genealogy of the Beales Family*. Piedmont, CA: J. T. Beales.

Bean, Lowell John. 1974. "Social Organization." In Heizer 1978.

Bean, Lowell John, ed. 1994. *The Ohlone, Past and Present: Native Americans of the San Francisco Bay Region*. Menlo Park, CA: Ballena Press.

Bean, Lowell John, and D. Theodoratus. 1978. "Western Pomo and Northeastern Pomo." In Heizer 1978.

Bean, Lowell John, and Sylvia Brakke Vane. 1978. "Cults and Their Transformation." In Heizer 1978.

Bean, Walter, and James J. Rawls. 1988. *California: An Interpretive History*. New York: McGraw-Hill.

Bean, Lowell John, and Thomas F. King, eds. 1974. *ANTAP: California Indian Political and Economic Organization*. Ramona, CA: Ballena Press.

Beardsley, Richard K. 1954. *Temporal and Areal Relationships in Central California Archaeology*. 2 vols. Berkeley: University of California Archaeological Survey.

Beck, Warren A., and Ynez D. Haase. 1974. *Historical Atlas of California*. Norman: University of Oklahoma Press.

Becker, Robert H. 1969. *Designs on the Land: Diseños of California Ranchos and Their Makers*. San Francisco: Book Club of California.

Becker, Robert H., and United States District Court (California: Northern District). 1964. *Diseños of California Ranchos: Maps of Thirty-seven Land Grants, 1822-1846, from the Records of the United States District Court, San Francisco*. San Francisco: Book Club of California.

Beebe, Rose Marie, and Robert M. Senkewicz, trans., ed., and anno. [1851] 1996. *The History of Alta California: A Memoir of Mexican California,* by Antonio María Osio. Madison: University of Wisconsin Press.

————. 2001. *Lands of Promise and Despair: Chronicles of Early California, 1535-1846.*

Berkeley: Heyday Books, co-published with Santa Clara University.

Beechey, Frederick William. [1831] 1941. *An Account of a Visit to California, 1826-27.* Introduction by Edith M. Coulter. San Francisco: Grabhorn Press for the Book Club of California.

————. 1855. *Port de San Francisco: levé en 1827 et 1828.* France: Dépôt-général de la Marine.

Beeler, Madison Scott, and California Indian Library Collections. 1993. "An Extension of San Francisco Bay Costanoan?" Berkeley: California Indian Library Collections distributor. Originally from *International Journal of American Linguistics,* vol. 38, no. 1, January 1972, pp. 49-54.

Bell, Horace. 1927. *Reminiscences of a Ranger; or Early Times in Southern California.* Santa Barbara: W. Hebberd.

Bennyhoff, James A., and Richard E. Hughes. 1987. "Shell Bead and Ornament Exchange Networks between California and the Western Great Basin." *Anthropological Papers of the American Museum of Natural History,* vol. 64, part 2. New York: American Museum of Natural History.

Benson, Arlene, and Tom Hoskinson, eds. *Earth and Sky: Papers from the Northridge Conference on Archaeoastronomy.* Thousand Oaks, CA: Slo'w Press.

Bibby, Brian. 1996. *The Fine Art of California Indian Basketry.* Sacramento: Crocker Art Museum in association with Heyday Books.

Bickel, Polly McWhorter. 1976. *Toward a Prehistory of the San Francisco Bay Area: The Archaeology of Sites A1a-328, A1a-13, and A1a-12.* PhD diss., Department of Anthropology, Harvard University.

Bingham, Helen. 1906. *In Tamal Land.* San Francisco: Calkins Publishing House.

Blackburn, Thomas C., and Kat Anderson, eds. 1993. *Before the Wilderness: Environmental Management by Native Californians.* Menlo Park, CA: Ballena Press.

Bojorques, Juan. 1874. "Recuerdos sobre la Historia de California," interview by Thomas Savage. MS. Berkeley: The Bancroft Library, University of California, Berkeley.

Boronda, José Canuto. 1878. "Notas históricas sobre California." C-D 47. MS. Berkeley: The Bancroft Library, University of California, Berkeley.

Boscana, Gerónimo. 1947. "Chinigchinich: A Historical Account of the Origin, Customs, and Traditions of the Indians at the Missionary Establishment of St. Juan Capistrano, Alta-California." In Robinson 1947.

Botta, P. E. [1828] 1952. *Observations on the Inhabitants of California, 1827–1828.* Translated by John Francis Bricca. Los Angeles: Glen Dawson.

Bowman, J. N. 1943. "The Vineyards in Provincial California." *The Wine Review,* April, May, June, and July 1943. Los Angeles.

————. 1947. "The Area of the Mission Lands." MS (carbon typescript). Dec. 3, 1947. The Bancroft Library, University of California, Berkeley.

Brown, Alan K. 1975. "Pomponio's World" and "San Francisco Westerners." *Argonaut,* no. 6, May 1975, San Francisco.

C-A (Archives of California, Hubert Howe Bancroft Collection). 1796-1848. 63 volumes.

Extracts and summaries of Spanish and Mexican documents; originals destroyed by fire in 1906. The Bancroft Library, University of California, Berkeley.

California Digital Library. 2001. "Historical Census Populations of Counties, Places, Towns, and Cities in California, 1850-1990." Online data file generated by Nancy Miller. http://countingcalifornia.cdlib.org/title/histpop.html.

California Federation of Women's Clubs, History and Landmarks Section. 1907. *Historic Facts and Fancies.* San Francisco: Stanley-Taylor Company.

Callaghan, Catherine A. 1970. *Bodega Miwok Dictionary.* Berkeley: University of California Press.

———. 1978. "Lake Miwok." In Heizer 1978.

Camp, Charles Lewis. 1923. "The Chronicles of George C. Yount, California Pioneer of 1826." *California Historical Society Quarterly,* vol. 2, no. 1, pp. 3-66.

Campa, Miguel de la. 1964. In Galvin 1964.

Carlson, Pamela McGuire, and E. Breck Parkman. 1986. "An Exceptional Adaptation: Camillo Ynitia, the Last Headman of the Olompalis." *California History,* December 1986.

Carranco, Lynwood, and Estle Beard. 1981. *Genocide and Vendetta: The Round Valley Wars of Northern California.* Norman: University of Oklahoma Press.

Carrico, Richard L. 1997. "Sociopolitical Aspects of the 1775 Revolt at Mission San Diego de Alcala: An Ethnohistorical Approach." *Journal of San Diego History,* vol. 43, no. 3.

———. 1998. "When Satan Stalked San Diego: Demonology, Diabolism, and the Mission Indians of San Diego." Paper read at the 1998 California Indian Conference, San Francisco State University.

Castillo, Edward. 1978. "The Impact of Euro-American Exploration and Settlement." In Heizer 1978.

———. 1998. "Short Overview of California Indian History." California Native American Heritage Commission. http://ceres.ca.gov/nahc/califindian.html.

Chamisso, Adelbert von. [1816] 1932. "Chamisso's Observations." In Mahr 1932.

Chavez, David. 1976. "The Archaeology of 4-Mrn-170: A Marin County Shellmound." M.A. thesis, San Francisco State University.

Chichinov, Zakhar (Zakahar Tchitchinoff). 1956. *Adventures in California of Zakahar Tchitchinoff, 1818-1828.* Introduction by Arthur Woodward. Microform. Los Angeles: Glen Dawson. The Bancroft Library, University of California, Berkeley.

Choris, Louis Andrevitch. [1816] 1932. "Choris' Description of San Francisco." In Mahr 1932.

Colley, Charles C. 1970. The Missionization of the Coast Miwok Indians of California. *California Historical Society Quarterly,* vol. 49, no. 2, pp. 143-162.

Cook, Sherburne F. 1976. *The Conflict Between the California Indian and White Civilization.* Berkeley: University of California Press.

Crespi, Juan. 1772. Map in Stanger and Brown 1969.

Cuneo, Ana Maria. [n.d.] *Tales of Bodega Bay.* MS. West County Neighbor History Series.

Davis, William Heath. 1967. *Seventy-five Years in California; Recollections and Remarks by One*

Who Visited These Shores in 1831, and Again in 1833, and Except When Absent on Business Was a Resident from 1838 until the End of a Long Life in 1909. Edited by Harold A. Small. Third ed. San Francisco: John Howell Books.

Delgado, James. [n.d.] *Indian Hispanic Contact at Richardson Bay: A Preliminary Study of Documentary Evidence of the Uimen Nation, 1775-1814.* MS. Sausalito, CA: Sausalito Historical Society.

De Ayala, Juan Manuel. See Ayala, Juan Manuel de.

De la Campa, Miguel. See Campa, Miguel de la.

De la Guerra y Noriega, Jose. See Guerra y Noriego, Jose de la.

De la Torre, Estevan. See Torre, Estevan de la.

De Rojas, Lauro Antonio. See Rojas, Lauro Antonio de.

De Torres, Marian Richardson. See Torres, Marian Richardson de.

Dickinson, A. Bray, Roy Graves, Ted Wurm, and Al Graves. 1967. *Narrow Gauge to the Redwoods: The Story of the North Pacific Coast Railroad and San Francisco Bay Paddle-wheel Ferries.* Los Angeles: Trans-Anglo Books.

Dietz, Stephen A. 1976. "Echa Tamal: A Study of Coast Miwok Acculturation." M.A. thesis, Department of Anthropology, California State University, San Francisco.

Donnelly, Florence. 1967. "A Jubilee Observance." *The Penultimate Mission: A Documentary History of San Rafael, Arcangel,* compiled and edited by Francis J. Weber. Hong Kong: Libra Press, 1983. Originally in the *Marin Independent-Journal,* October 14, 1967, Novato, CA.

Du Bois, Cora. 1939. *The 1870 Ghost Dance.* Berkeley: University of California Press.

Duflot de Mofras, Eugene. 1844. *Port de San Francisco dans la haute Californie.* Paris: Arthus Bertrand.

———. 1937. See Wilbur 1937.

Duhaut-Cilly, Auguste Bernard. 1929. "Duhaut-Cilly's Account of California in the Years 1827-28." Translated by Charles Franklin Carter. *California Historical Society Quarterly,* vol. 8, nos. 2-4, pp. 130-166, 214-250, 306-336.

Edwards, Clinton R. 1979. "Indians of Bodega-Tomales Region in California: Early European Contacts." *Indian Historian,* vol. 2, no. 1, January 1969, pp. 12-16.

Edwards, Philip L. 1890. *California in 1837: Diary of Col. Philip L. Edwards.* Sacramento: A. J. Johnson and Co.

Eldredge, Zoeth Skinner. 1912. *The Beginnings of San Francisco: From the Expedition of Anza, 1774, to the City Charter of April 15, 1850.* San Francisco: Z. S. Eldredge.

Elliott, Jeff. 1995. "The Dark Legacy of Nome Cult." *Albion Monitor,* September 2, 1995. http://www.monitor.net/monitor.

Elsasser, Albert B., and Peter T. Rhode. 1996. "Further Notes on California Charmstones." *Archives of California Prehistory, #38.* Salinas, CA: Coyote Press.

Engelhardt, Zephyrin. 1897. *The Franciscans in California.* Harbor Springs, MI: Holy Childhood Indian School.

———. 1908-1915. *The Missions and Missionaries of California.* Microform. San Francisco: J. H. Barry Co. The Bancroft Library, University of California, Berkeley.

Erlandson, Jon M. 1994. *Early Hunter-Gatherers of the California Coast.* New York: Plenum

Press.

Eschmeyer, William N., and Jacqueline Schonewald. 1981. *Identification and Analysis of Fort Mason Osteological Remains, Archaeological Sites SFR-19, 30, and 31.* San Francisco: California Academy of Sciences.

Fairley, Lincoln. 1987. *Mount Tamalpais: A History.* San Francisco: Scottwall Associates.

Farris, Glenn J. 1990. "The Russian Imprint on the Colonization of California." *Archeological and Historical Perspectives on the Spanish Borderlands East: Columbian Consequences,* vol. 1, edited by David Hurst Thomas. Washington, DC: Smithsonian Institution.

———. 1994. *The Story of the Purchase of Fort Ross and Payment for Bodega Bay by the Russian Promyshlennik, Tarakanov.* Private papers in possession of the author.

Farris, Glenn J., trans. and ed. [1826] 1993. "Visit of the Russian Warship Apollo to California in 1822-1823," by Achille Schabelski. *Southern California Quarterly,* vol. 75, no. 1, Spring 1993.

Farris, Glenn J., and D. R. Jones. 2005. "Coches, Calesas and Celesines: Riding High in the California Missions." California Mission Studies Association Conference, Mission San Fernando Rey de España. February 18-20, 2005.

Faulkner, H. P. 1928. "Mariana Torres: An Epic Linking the Old California with the New." *Oakland Tribune,* March 4, 1928.

Fernández, José. 1874. *Cosas de California.* MS. Berkeley: The Bancroft Library, University of California, Berkeley.

Follett, W. I. 1957. "Fish Remains from a Shell Mound in Marin County, California." *American Antiquity,* 23:68-71.

———. 1968. "Fish Remains from Two Submerged Deposits in Tomales Bay, Marin County, California." San Francisco: Occasional Papers of the California Academy of Sciences, no. 67.

———. 1974. "Fish Remains from the Shelter Ridge Sites in Marin County." *Treganza Anthropological Museum Papers,* no. 15. San Francisco: San Francisco State University.

Fredrickson, David A. 1973. "Cultural Diversity in Early Central California: A View from the North Coast Ranges." *Journal of California Anthropology,* vol. 1, no. 1.

Galindo, Jose Eusebio. 1877. "Apuntes para la historia de California," Santa Clara, CA. MS. Berkeley: The Bancroft Library, University of California, Berkeley.

Galindo, Nasario. 1883. "Early Days at Mission Santa Clara: Recollections of Nasario Galindo." Translated by Cristina Alviso Chapman. *California Historical Society Quarterly,* 38:108-111.

Galvin, John, ed. 1964. *A Journal of Exploration, Northward Along the Coast from Monterey in the Year 1775.* San Francisco: John Howell Books.

———, ed. 1971. *The First Spanish Entry into San Francisco Bay, 1775.* San Francisco: John Howell Books.

Garcia, Juan. 1917. "An Oral Account of Life at Mission San Rafael." *Marin Independent-Journal,* August 14 and 21, 1917.

Geiger, Maynard. 1969. *Franciscan Missionaries in Hispanic California, 1769-1848: A Biographical Dictionary.* San Marino, CA: Huntington Library.

Geiger, Maynard, and Clement W. Meighan. 1976. *As the Padres Saw Them: California Indian Life and Customs as Reported by the Franciscan Missionaries, 1813-1815.* Santa Barbara, CA: Santa Barbara Mission Archive Library.

Gerow, Bert A., and Roland W. Force. 1968. *An Analysis of the University Village Complex: With a Reappraisal of Central California Archaeology.* Stanford, CA: Board of Trustees of Leland Stanford Junior University.

Gifford, E. W., and A. L. Kroeber. 1937. *Culture Element Distributions: IV (Pomo).* University of California Publications in American Archaeology and Ethnology, vol. 37, no. 4. Berkeley: University of California Press.

Gift, George Washington. 1875. "Something About California: Being a Description of Its Climate, Health, Wealth, and Resources, Compressed into Small Compass." San Rafael, CA: San Rafael Herald.

Gilliam, Harold. 1962. *Weather of the San Francisco Bay Region.* Berkeley: University of California Press.

Glass, Bill. 2002. "Historical Fact or Urban Legend?" *Novato Historian,* vol. 25, no. 3, September 2002.

Goerke, Betty, ed. 1994. *Uncovering the Past at College of Marin.* Novato, CA: Miwok Archaeological Preserve of Marin.

Goerke, E. B. (Betty), and F. A. Davidson. 1975. "Baked Clay Figurines of Marin County." *Journal of New World Archaeology,* vol. 1, no. 2, pp. 9-24.

Goerke, E. B. (Betty), R. A. Cowan, A. Ramenofsky, and L. Spencer. 1983. "The Pacheco Site (Marin-152)." *Journal of New World Archaeology,* vol. 6, no. 1. Los Angeles: Institute of Archaeology, University of California.

Golovnin, V. M. 1979. *Around the World on the Kamchatka, 1817-1819.* Translated by Ella Lury Wiswell. Honolulu: Hawaiian Historical Society.

González, Michael J. 1998. "The Child of the Wilderness Weeps for the Father of Our Country." In Gutiérrez and Orsi 1998.

Graham, Frank Jr. 2000. "Day of the Condor." *Audubon,* January/February 2000, pp. 46-53.

Gudde, Erwin G. 1969. *California Place Names: The Origin and Etymology of Current Geographical Names.* Berkeley: University of California Press.

Guerra y Noriega, Jose de la. 1878. "Documentos para la historia de California." MS. C-B 59-65. Berkeley: The Bancroft Library, University of California, Berkeley.

Gutiérrez, Ramón A., and Richard J. Orsi, eds. 1998. *Contested Eden: California Before the Gold Rush.* Berkeley: University of California Press.

Guzmán, José María. [1833] 1926. "Guzman's 'Breve noticia.'" *California Historical Society Quarterly,* vol. 5, no. 3, pp. 209-217.

Hackel, Steven W. 1998. "Land, Labor, and Production." In Gutiérrez and Orsi 1998.

———. 2005. *Children of Coyote, Missionaries of Saint Francis: Indian-Spanish Relations in Colonial California, 1769-1850.* Chapel Hill: Published by the University of North Carolina Press for the Omohundro Institute of Early American History and Culture, Williamsburg, VA.

Harlow, Neal. 1950. *The Maps of San Francisco Bay, from the Spanish Discovery in 1769 to the American Occupation.* San Francisco: Book Club of California.

Hartnell, W. E. P. 1839-1840. "William Edward Petty Hartnell diario y borradores de... dos visitas...en 1839-40." MS. Berkeley: The Bancroft Library, University of California, Berkeley.

Hedges, Ken. 1985. "Archaeoastronomical Sites in the Territory of the Kumeyaay Indians of Southern California and Northern Baja California." *Earth and Sky: Papers from the Northridge Conference on Archaeoastronomy,* edited by Arlene Benson and Tom Hoskinson. Thousand Oaks, CA: Slo'w Press, 135-150.

Heizer, Robert F. 1947. *Francis Drake and the California Indians, 1579.* University of California Publications in American Archaeology and Ethnology, vol. 42, no. 3. Berkeley: University of California Press.

————, ed. 1974a. *They Were Only Diggers: A Collection of Articles from California Newspapers, 1851-1866, on Indian and White Relations.* Ramona, CA: Ballena Press.

————, ed. 1974b. *The Destruction of California Indians: A Collection of Documents from the Period 1847 to 1865 in Which Are Described Some of the Things that Happened to Some of the Indians of California.* Santa Barbara, CA: Peregrine Smith.

————, volume ed. 1978. *Handbook of the North American Indians, California,* vol. 8. Washington, DC: Smithsonian Institution.

Heizer, Robert F., and M. A. Whipple. 1971. *The California Indians: A Source Book.* 2nd ed. Berkeley: University of California Press.

Heizer, Robert F., and Albert B. Elsasser. 1980. *The Natural World of the California Indians.* Berkeley: University of California Press.

Hendry, G. W., and J. N. Bowman. Part I ("Marin County") and Part IX ("San Francisco County") from "The Spanish and Mission Adobe and Other Buildings in the Nine San Francisco Bay Counties, 1776 to about 1850." Typescript. Berkeley: The Bancroft Library, University of California, Berkeley.

Hinton, Leanne. 1994. *Flutes of Fire: Essays on California Indian Languages.* Berkeley: Heyday Books.

Hittell, Theodore. 1885, 1897. *History of California.* Vols. 1 and 2; San Francisco: Pacific Press Publishing House and Occidental Publishing Co., 1885. Vols. 3 and 4; San Francisco: N. J. Stone and Company, 1897.

Hudson, Travis, and Craig D. Bates. 1984. "People from the Water: Indian Art and Culture from Russian California." MS. In possession of Betty Goerke.

Huggins, Dorothy H. 1945. "The Pursuit of an Indian Chief." *California Folklore Quarterly,* vol. 4, no. 2, pp. 158-167.

Hurley, Gail. 1995. "Archaeological Research Project in Marin," paper for Anthropology 206 class, College of Marin. In possession of Betty Goerke.

Jackson, Robert H., and Edward Castillo. 1995. *Indians, Franciscans, and Spanish Colonization.* Albuquerque: University of New Mexico Press.

Johnson, Troy. "The Alcatraz Indian Occupation." www.nps.gov/alcatraz/indian.html. Accessed 2006.

Juarez, Cayetano. 1875. *Narrative of Cayetano Juarez.* MS. Berkeley: The Bancroft Library, University of California, Berkeley.

Kasch, Charles. 1947. "The Yokayo Ranchería." *California Historical Society Quarterly,* 26:209-215.

Kelly, Isabel Truesdell. 1931-1932. "Notebook of Interviews with Tom Smith and Maria Copa." In possession of Sylvia Thalman.

———. 1931-1932. Typescript of *Interviews with Tom Smith and Maria Copa.* In possession of Sylvia Thalman.

———. 1978. "Coast Miwok." In Heizer 1978.

———. 2003. *Interviews with Tom Smith and Maria Copa: Isabel Kelly's Ethnographic Notes on the Coast Miwok Indians of Marin and Southern Sonoma Counties, California,* edited by Mary E. T. Collier and Sylvia Barker Thalman. Novato, CA: Miwok Archaeological Preserve of Marin.

King, Chester. 1978. "Protohistoric and Historic Archaeology." In Heizer 1978.

King, Thomas F. 1970. "The Dead at Tiburon: Mortuary Customs and Social Organization on Northern San Francisco Bay." Originally published by the Northwestern California Archaeological Society, with the cooperation of the Society for California Archaeology. Salinas, CA: Coyote Press.

———. 1974. "The Evolution of Status Ascription around San Francisco Bay." *ANTAP: California Indian Political and Economic Organization,* edited by Lowell J. Bean and Thomas F. King. Ramona, CA: Ballena Press.

Khlebnikov, K. T. 1829. *Memoirs of California.* Translated by Anatole G. Mazour. Glendale, CA: Reprinted in *Pacific Historical Review,* vol. 9, no. 3, September 1940.

———. 1990. "The Khlebnikov Archive: Unpublished Journal (1800-1837) and Travel Notes (1820, 1822, and 1824)." Edited by Leonid Shur and translated by John Bisk. Fairbanks: University of Alaska Press.

Kostromitonov, P. 1839. "Notes on the Indians in Upper California." *Ethnographic Observations on the Coast Miwok and Pomo by Contre-admiral F. P. von Wrangell and P. Kostromitonov of the Russian Colony Ross.* Translated by Fred Stross, with ethnographic notes by Robert F. Heizer. Berkeley: Archaeological Research Facility, Department of Anthropology, University of California, Berkeley, 1974.

Kotzebue, Otto von. 1816. Extract from Kotzebue's "Report." In Mahr 1932.

———. 1830. *A New Voyage Round the World, in the Years 1823, 24, 25, and 26.* London: Henry Colburn and Richard Bentley.

Kroeber, Alfred L. 1916. *California Place Names of Indian Origin.* Berkeley: University of California Publications in Archaeology and Ethnology, vol. 12, no. 2, 31-69.

———. 1970. *Handbook of the Indians of California.* Smithsonian Institution, Bureau of American Ethnology, Bulletin 78. Washington, DC: Government Printing Office.

La Pérouse, Jean François de. 1989. *Life in a California Mission: Monterey in 1786.* Berkeley: Heyday Books.

Langsdorff, G. H. von. 1927. *Langsdorff's Narrative of the Rezanov Voyage to Nueva California in 1806.* Larkspur, CA: Private press of T. C. Russell.

—————. 1991. *Larkspur Past and Present: A History and Walking Guide.* Larkspur, CA: Larkspur Heritage Committee. The Bancroft Library, University of California, Berkeley.

Lauff, Charles A. 1916. "Reminiscences of Charles Lauff." Typescript. Published in the *Marin Independent-Journal,* January 25–May 23, 1916. Marin History Museum.

Lawrence, Eleanor, and Cecelia Fitzsimons. 1985. *An Instant Guide to Trees.* New York: Bonanza Books.

Leigh, R. W. 1928. *Dental Pathology of Aboriginal California.* University of California Publications in American Archaeology and Ethnology, vol. 23, no. 10. Berkeley: University of California Press.

Levee, Tish. 1983. "The Mistress of Rancho Bodega." *The Journal.* Sonoma County Historical Society, Santa Rosa, #2, 3, and 4.

Lightfoot, Kent. 2005a. "Archaeology and Indians: Thawing an Icy Relationship." In *News from Native California,* vol. 19, no. 1, Fall 2005.

—————. 2005b. *Indians, Missionaries, and Merchants: The Legacy of Colonial Encounters on the California Frontiers.* Berkeley: University of California Press.

Lillard, Jeremiah B., R. F. Heizer and Franklin Fenenga. 1939. *An Introduction to the Archeology of Central California.* Sacramento Junior College, Department of Anthropology, Bulletin 2. Sacramento, CA: The Board of Education of the Sacramento City Unified School District.

Lipps-Michaels. 1919–1920. *Survey of Landless Nonreservation Indians of California.*

Little, Elbert L. 1980. *The Audubon Society Field Guide to North American Trees, Western Region.* New York: Knopf.

Little, Lucretia. 1967. "The Mystery of Mission San Rafael: Lucretia Hanson Little's Sesqui-Centennial Art History," Resource Guide for Saint Raphael's Parish Docents. Draft of unpublished manuscript located at Mission San Rafael.

—————. 1989–1990. The Bells of Mission San Rafael. In *Marin County Historical Society Magazine,* vol. XV, Nov 1, 1989.

Livingston, Douglas (Dewey). 1989. *Hamlet, 1844-1988.* Point Reyes, CA: National Park Service.

Loeb, Edward M. 1926. *Pomo Folkways.* University of California Publications in American Archaeology and Ethnology, vol. 19, no. 2. Berkeley: University of California Press.

Loughead, Flora Haines, ed. 1915. *Life, Diary, and Letters of Oscar Lovell Shafter: Associate Justice Supreme Court of California, January 1, 1864, to December 31, 1868.* San Francisco: Blair-Murdock.

Luby, Edward M. 1994. "Excavations at East Marin Island (Mrn-611)." *Society for California Archaeology,* 17:105–115.

Mackey, Margaret Gilbert, and Louise Pinkney Sooy. 1932. *Early California Costumes, 1769-1847, and Historic Flags of California.* Stanford, CA: Stanford University Press.

Mahr, August C., editor and translator. 1932. *The Visit of the "Rurik" to San Francisco in 1816.* Stanford, CA: Stanford University Press.

Margolin, Malcolm. 1989. Introduction and commentary in La Pérouse 1989.

————. 1993. *The Way We Lived: California Indian Stories, Songs, and Reminiscences*. Berkeley: Heyday Books.

Marin County Journal. 1869. "Town and Country." April 17, 1869, vol. 9, no. 5, p. 3.

Marin Indepdendent Journal. June 24, 1880-March 9, 1883; December 1897.

Mason, Jack. 1971. *Early Marin*. Written in collaboration with Helen Van Cleave Park. Petaluma, CA: House of Printing.

————. 1975. *The Making of Marin (1850-1975)*. Written in collaboration with Helen Van Cleave Park and under the auspices of the Marin County Historical Society. Inverness, CA: North Shore Books.

Mayfield, David W. 1978. *Ecology of the Pre-Spanish San Francisco Bay Area*. M.A. thesis, San Francisco State University.

Mayfield, Thomas Jefferson. 1993. *Indian Summer: Traditional Life among the Choinumne Indians of California's San Joaquin Valley*. Berkeley: Heyday Books.

McCorkle, Thomas. 1978. "Intergroup Conflict." In Heizer 1978.

McPhee, John. 1994. *Assembling California*. Reprint. New York: Farrar, Straus and Giroux, 1993. New York: Noonday Press.

Meighan, Clement W., and Robert J. Squire. 1953. *Papers on California Archaeology: 19-20.* ("Preliminary Excavation at the Thomas Site, Marin County" [Clement W. Meighan] and "The Manufacture of Flint Implements by the Indians of Northern and Central California" [Robert J. Squire].) Berkeley: University of California Archaeological Survey.

Merck Manual for Healthcare Professionals. http://www.merck.com/mmpe/sec14/ch1941i.html. November 2006.

Merriam, C. Hart. 1907. "Distribution and Classification of the Mewan Stock of California." *American Anthropologist,* new series vol. 9, no. 2, April-June 1907.

————. 1916. "Indian Names in the Tamalpais Region." *California Out-of-Doors.* April 1916.

————. 1955. "California Mission Baptismal Records." *Studies of California Indians,* pp. 188-225. Berkeley: University of California Press.

————. 1968. "Village Names in Twelve California Mission Records." *Reports of the University of California Archaeological Survey,* no. 74. Berkeley: Archaeological Research Facility, Department of Anthropology, University of California, Berkeley.

————, ed. [1910] 1993. *The Dawn of the World: Myths and Weird Tales Told by the Mewan Indians of California*. Nebraska: University of Nebraska Press.

Miller, Robert Ryal. 1995. *Captain Richardson: Mariner, Ranchero, and Founder of San Francisco*. Berkeley: La Loma Press.

Miller, Teresa. 1977. "Identification and Recording of Prehistoric Petroglyphs in Marin and Related Bay Area Counties." M.A. thesis, Department of Anthropology, California State University, San Francisco.

Milliken, Randall. 1995. *A Time of Little Choice: The Disintegration of Tribal Culture in the San Francisco Bay Area, 1769-1810*. Menlo Park, CA: Ballena Press.

————. 1996. *The Founding of Mission Dolores and the End of Tribal Life on the Northern San Francisco Peninsula*. Santa Clara, CA: California Mission Studies Association.

———. 1998. "The Aguastos and Their Neighbors." *Archaeological Investigations at CA-MRN-254,* by David G. Beiling. San Francisco: Holman and Associates.

Milliken, Randall, Lynn M. Riley, and Steven C. Wilson, eds. 1974. *Shelter Hill: Archaeological Investigations at MRN-14, Mill Valley, California.* San Francisco: Treganza Anthropology Museum.

Moratto, Michael J. 1984. *California Archaeology.* Orlando: Academic Press.

Morotto, Michael J., L. M. Riley, and S. C. Wilson, eds. 1974. "Shelter Hill: Archaeology I Investigations at 4-Mrn-14, Mill Valley, California." San Francisco: Treganza Anthropological Museum Papers 15 and MAPOM Papers 2:1–166.

Muir, John. 1938. *John of the Mountains: The Unpublished Journals of John Muir.* Edited by Linnie Marsh Wolfe. Madison: University of Wisconsin Press.

Munro-Fraser, J. P. 1880. *History of Marin County, California.* San Francisco: Alley, Bowen.

Nelson, Nels Christian. 1909. *Shellmounds of the San Francisco Bay Region.* University of California Publications in American Archaeology and Ethnology, vol. 7, no 4, 309–356. Berkeley: University of California Press.

———. 1910. Sausalito Mound #3 (original notes), MS 353. Berkeley: University of California Archaeological Survey.

Ogden, Adele. 1941. *The California Sea Otter Trade, 1784-1848.* University of California Publications in History, vol. 26. Berkeley: University of California Press.

Olmstead, D. L., and Omer C. Stewart. 1978. "Achumawi." In Heizer 1978. Ordaz, Blas. [1821] 1958. "La Última Exploración Española en América." *The Diary of Fr. Blas Ordaz,* with introduction and notes by Donald C. Cutter. Reprinted from *Revista de Indias,* vol. 18, no. 72, April-June 1958.

Ortiz, Beverly R. 1991. *It Will Live Forever: Traditional Yosemite Indian Acorn Preparation.* Berkeley: Heyday Books.

———. 1993. "A Coast Miwok History." *We Are Still Here: The Coast Miwok Exhibit,* edited by Kathleen Smith. Bolinas, CA: Bolinas Museum.

———. 1994. "Chocheño and Rumsen Narratives: A Comparison." *The Ohlone, Past and Present: Native Americans of the San Francisco Bay Region,* edited by Lowell John Bean. Menlo Park, CA: Ballena Press.

———. 2003. "Restoring the Land: The Federated Indians of the Graton Rancheria." *News from Native California,* vol. 16, no. 4, Summer 2003.

Osio, Antonio María. [1851] 1878. *Historia de la California, 1815-1848.* MS. Copied by John J. Doyle Esq., for the Bancroft Library, University of California, Berkeley.

———. [1851] 1996. *The History of Alta California: A Memoir of Mexican California.* Translated, edited, and annotated by Rose Marie Beebe and Robert M. Senkewicz. Madison: University of Wisconsin Press.

Paddison, Joshua, ed. 1999. *A World Transformed: Firsthand Accounts of California before the Gold Rush.* Berkeley: Heyday Books.

Pahl, Gary, ed. 2004. *Mrn17.* Treganza Museum Publication #17. San Francisco: San

Francisco State University.

Palou, Francisco. 1926. *Historical Memoirs of New California.* 4 volumes. Translated and edited by Herbert Eugene Bolton. Berkeley: University of California Press.

Parrish, Otis. 2002. Lecture for the Marin Musuem of the American Indian. November 2002.

Payeras, Mariano. 1995. *Writings of Mariano Payeras.* Translated and edited by Donald C. Cutter. Publications of the Academy of American Franciscan History, Documentary Series, vol. 12. Santa Barbara, CA: Bellerophon Books.

Peacock, Doug. 1996. "Once There Were Bears: The Rise and Fall of the California Grizzly." *California Wild,* vol. 49, no. 3, summer 1996, pp. 8-17. San Francisco: California Academy of Sciences.

Peirce, Henry Augustus. n.d. *Rough Sketch of the Life and Experiences of Henry Augustus Peirce: With Additional Memoranda.* MS. Berkeley: The Bancroft Library, University of California, Berkeley.

Pierce, Richard A., ed. 1972. *Rezanov Reconnoiters California, 1806: A New Translation of Rezanov's Letter, Parts of Lieutenant Khvostov's Log of the Ship Juno, and Dr. Georg von Langsdorff Observations.* San Francisco: Book Club of California.

Pinart, A. L. 1823–1825. Prayer from "Catechism and Prayer in the San Rafael Dialect." MS. Berkeley: The Bancroft Library, University of California, Berkeley.

Pinney, Thomas. 1989. *A History of Wine in America from the Beginnings to Prohibition.* Berkeley: University of California Press

Powers, Stephen. [1877] 1976. *Tribes of California.* Berkeley: University of California Press.

Pratt, Richard Henry. 2003. *Battlefield and Classroom: Four Decades with the American Indian, 1867-1904.* Edited and with an introduction by Robert M. Utley and a foreword by David Wallace Adams. Norman, OK: University of Oklahoma Press.

Provincial State Papers. 1809. *Arguello to Arrillaga.* 12:267. Archives of California. Ransom, Leander. 1873. Map of Corte Madera Creek. Private collection of Mary Alice Deffebach.

Rawls, James J. 1984. *Indians of California: The Changing Image.* Norman: University of Oklahoma Press.

Revere, Joseph Warren. 1872. *Keel and Saddle.* Boston: J. R. Osgood and Company. Located at the Marin County Free Library, California Room, San Rafael, CA.

Richardson, Stephen. 1918. *The Days of the Dons: Reminiscences of California's Oldest Native Son,* edited by James H. Wilkins. Originally in the *San Francisco Bulletin,* April 20-June 8, 1918. California Room, Civic Center Library, San Rafael, CA.

Riddell, Francis A. 1978. "Maidu and Konkow." In Heizer 1978.

Riley, Lynn M. 1979. *Shelter Hill: An Analysis of Faunal Remains and Artifacts from a Marin County Shellmound (04-Mrn-14).* M.S. thesis, San Francisco State University.

Ringgold, Cadwalader. 1851. *A Series of Charts with Sailing Directions.* Washington, DC: J. T. Towers.

Robinson, Alfred. [1846] 1947. "Chinigchinich: A Historical Account of the Origin,

Customs, and Traditions of the Indians at the Missionary Establishment of St. Juan Capistrano, Alta-California," by Geronimo Boscana and translated by Alfred Robinson. *Life in California.* Oakland, CA: Bio-books.

Rojas, Lauro Antonio de. 1938. "California in 1844 as Hartnell Saw It." *California Historical Society Quarterly,* vol. 17, no. 1, pp. 21-27.

Rosen, Daniel Bernard. 1957. *The History of the Presidio of San Francisco during the Spanish Period.* M.A. thesis, Department of History, University of California, Berkeley.

Rosenus, Alan. 1999. *General Vallejo and the Advent of the Americans.* Berkeley: Heyday Books.

Sandels, G. M. Waseurtz af. 1880. *Visit of the King's Orphan to California in 1842-3 from Upham's Notes and S. Jose Pioneer.* MS. Berkeley: The Bancroft Library, University of California, Berkeley.

Sandos, James A. 1998. "Between the Crucifix and Lance: Indian-White Relations in California, 1769-1848." In Gutiérrez and Orsi 1998. Santa Maria, Vicente. [1775] 1971. In Galvin 1971.

Sarris, Greg. 1994a. *Grand Avenue.* New York: Hyperion.

———. 1994b. *Mabel McKay: Weaving the Dream.* Berkeley: University of California Press.

———. 2001. "First Thoughts on Restoration and Notes from a Tribal Chairman." *News from Native California,* vol. 14, no. 3, Spring 2001.

———. 2003. "On Sacred Places." *Bay Nature,* April-June 2003.

SBMR (Santa Barbara Mission Records). Santa Barbara Misison Library, Santa Barbara, CA.

Schabelski, Achille. [1826] 1993. "Visit of the Russian Warship Apollo to California in 1822-1823." Translated and edited by Glenn Farris. *Southern California Quarterly,* vol. 75, no. 1, Spring 1993.

Shafter, Oscar Lovell. 1915. *Life, Diary, and Letters of Oscar Lovell Shafter: Associate Justice Supreme Court of California, January 1, 1864, to December 31, 1868.* Edited by Flora Haines Loughead. San Francisco: Blair-Murdock.

Shanks, Ralph, and Lisa Woo Shanks. 2006. *Indian Baskets of Central California.* Novato, CA: Miwok Archaeological Preserve of Marin and Costaño Books.

Shuford, W. David. 1993. *The Marin County Breeding Bird Atlas: A Distributional and Natural History of Coastal California Birds.* Bolinas, CA: Bushtit Books.

Shur, Leonid A., and James R. Gibson. 1973. "Russian Travel Notes and Journals as Sources for the History of California, 1800-1850." *California Historical Society Quarterly,* vol. 52, no. 1, Spring 1973.

Silliman, Stephen. 2004. *Lost Laborers in Colonial California: Native Americans and the Archaeology of Rancho Petaluma.* Tucson: University of Arizona Press.

Simpson, George. [1850] 1930. *Overland Journey Round the World during the Years 1841 and 1842.* San Francisco: Private press of T. C. Russell.

Slaymaker, Charles. 1977. *The Material Culture of Cotomko'tca: A Coast Miwok Tribelet in Marin County, California.* Novato, CA: Miwok Archaeological Preserve of Marin (MAPOM Papers, 3).

Small, Harold A., ed. 1967. *Seventy-five Years in California: Recollections and Remarks by One*

Who Visited These Shores in 1831, and Again in 1833, and Except When Absent on Business Was a Resident from 1838 until the End of a Long Life in 1909, by William Heath Davis. Third ed. San Francisco: J. Howell Books.

Smilie, Robert S. 1975. *The Sonoma Mission, San Francisco Solano de Sonoma.* Fresno, CA: Valley Publishers.

Snyder, Susan. 2003. *Bear in Mind: The California Grizzly.* Berkeley: Heyday Books.

Stanger, Frank M. 1944. "The Hospice of Mission San Mateo." *California Historical Society Quarterly,* 23:247-258.

Stanger, Frank M., and Alan K. Brown. 1969. *Who Discovered the Golden Gate? The Explorers' Own Accounts, How They Discovered a Hidden Harbor and At Last Found Its Entrance.* San Mateo, CA: San Mateo County Historical Association.

Starn, Orin. 2004. *Ishi's Brain.* New York: W.W. Norton and Co.

Stephens, Laura A., and Cornelia C. Pringle. 1933. *Birds of Marin County.* San Francisco: Audubon Association of the Pacific.

Sullivan, Charles L. 1998. *A Companion to California Wine: An Encyclopedia of Wine and Winemaking from the Mission Period to the Present.* Berkeley: University of California Press.

Susman, Amelia. 1976. "The Round Valley Indians of California: An Unpublished Chapter in Acculturation in Seven (or Eight) American Indian Tribes." *Contributions of the University of California Archaeological Research Facility, No. 31.* Berkeley: University of California, Department of Anthropology.

Tac, Pablo. 1830s. "Indian Life at San Luis Rey." In Beebe and Senkewicz 2001.

Tarakanoff, Vassili Petrovitch. 1953. *Statement of My Captivity Among the Californians.* Translated by Ivan Petroff. Los Angeles: Glen Dawson.

Taylor, Alexander S. 1865a. Letters of the Catholic Missionaries of California from 1772-1849. 8 volumes. Taylor Collection, Chancery Archives, Archdiocese of California, Menlo Park.

———. 1865b. *Daily Alta California,* March 30, 1865.

Taylor, Daniel. [n.d.] *Reminiscences in Marin Peninsula History.* Typescript. San Rafael, CA: Marin County Free Library.

Taylor, Zachary. 1850. *Message from the President of the United States Communicating Information Called for by a Resolution of the Senate of the 17th Instant in Relation to California and New Mexico.* January 24, 1850. Washington, DC: Printed by W. M. Belt.

Tchitchinoff, Zakahar. 1956. *Adventures in California, 1818-1828.* Introduction by Arthur Woodward. Los Angeles: Glen Dawson. The Bancroft Library, University of California, Berkeley.

Teather, Louise. 1986. *Place Names of Marin: Where Did They Come From?* San Francisco: Scottwall Associates.

Teiser, R., and Catherine Harroun. 1983. *Winemaking in California.* New York: McGraw-Hill.

Thomas, David Hurst, ed. 1990. *Archeological and Historical Perspectives on the Spanish Borderlands East: Columbian Consequences,* vol. 1. Washington, DC: Smithsonian Institution.

Thomas, Robert C. 1974. Oral history. Typescript. Interview by Carla Ehat for the Anne T. Kent California Room Oral History Project, Marin County Free Library, San Rafael,

CA.

Torre, Estevan de la. 1877. "Reminiscencias." C-D 163. MS. Berkeley: The Bancroft Library, University of California, Berkeley.

Torres, Marian Richardson de. 1928. "Mariana Torres: An Epic Linking the Old California with the New." *Oakland Tribune*, March 4, 1928.

————. 1928. "Recollections." *Oakland Tribune,* magazine section, March 4, 1928, pp. 4-5.

Tracy, Jack. 1983. *Sausalito, Moments in Time: A Pictorial History of Sausalito's First One Hundred Years, 1850-1950.* Sausalito, CA: Windgate Press.

Treutlein, Theodore E. 1968. *San Francisco Bay: Discovery and Colonization, 1769-1776.* San Francisco: California Historical Society.

Trimble, Robert K. 1936. "Marin County Mexican Land Grants." MS. San Rafael, CA: Marin County Free Library.

Valencia, Antonio. 1830-1831. *Sumaria Contra Felipe Gómez y Roman (Neófito, Misión de San Rafael) y Documentos Relativos: Presidio, San Francisco.* MS. Berkeley: The Bancroft Library, University of California, Berkeley.

Vallejo, José de Jesús. 1875. "Reminiscencias históricas de California." C-D 16. MS. Berkeley: The Bancroft Library, University of California, Berkeley.

Vallejo, Mariano Guadalupe. 1769-1850. *Documentos para la historia de California, 1769-1850.* 36 vols. Berkeley: The Bancroft Library, University of California, Berkeley.

————. Ca. 1832-1889. *Vallejo Family Papers.* MS. Berkeley: The Bancroft Library, University of California, Berkeley.

————. 1850. "Report of the Derivation and Definition of the Names of the Several Counties of California." April 16, 1850. California Senate *Journal*, first session, appendix, p. 530.

————. 1875. *Historical and Personal Memoirs Relating to Alta California [Recuerdos históricos y personales tocantes à la Alta California], 1769-1849.* Translated by Earl R. Hewitt. MS. Berkeley: The Bancroft Library, University of California, Berkeley.

————. [n.d.] "Early Settlements in California" in http://www.cagenweb.com/yuba/hycc-misc.htm.

Wagner, Henry R. 1931. "The Last Spanish Exploration of the Northwest Coast and the Attempt to Colonize Bodega Bay." *California Historical Society Quarterly.* vol. 10, no. 4, pp. [313]-345.

Walker, Dale L. 1999. *Bear Flag Rising: The Conquest of California, 1846.* New York: Tom Doherty Associates.

Wallace, W. J. 1978. "Music and Musical Instruments." In Heizer 1978.

Wallace, William J., and Donald W. Lathrap. 1975. *West Berkeley (CA-Ala-307): A Culturally Stratified Shellmound on the East Shore of San Francisco Bay.* Berkeley: Archaeological Research Facility, Department of Anthropology, University of California, Berkeley.

Watson, Elizabeth Ann. Ca. 1920s. *Sketch of the Life of George C. Yount.* Microform. Berkeley: The Bancroft Library, University of California, Berkeley.

Weber, Francis J., ed. 1979. *Mission Dolores: A Documentary History of San Francisco Mission.*

San Francisco. The Bancroft Library, University of California, Berkeley.

Weber, Francis J., comp. and ed. 1983. *The Penultimate Mission: A Documentary History of San Rafael, Arcangel,* by Florence Donnelly. Originally in the *Marin Independent-Journal,* October 14, 1967, Novato, CA.

Wetmore, Charles A. 1884. *Ampelography of California: A Discussion of Vines Now Known in the States: Together with Comments on their Adaptability to Certain Locations and Uses.* San Francisco: Merchant Pub. Co.

Wilbur, Marguerite Eyer, ed. and trans. 1937. *Duflot de Mofras' Travels on the Pacific Coast.* Santa Ana, CA: Fine Arts Press.

Wilson, Norman L., and Arlean Towne. 1978. "Nisenan." In Heizer 1978.

Wolfe, Linnie Marsh. 1938. *John of the Mountains: The Unpublished Journals of John Muir.* Madison: University of Wisconsin Press.

Wood, Harry O., and N. H. Heck. 1941. "Earthquake History of the United States, Part II." *U.S. Department of Commerce, U.S. Coast and Geodetic Survey, Serial No. 609.* Washington, DC: Government Printing Office.

Wrangell, F. P. von. 1839. "Some Remarks on the Savages on the Northwest Coast of America—The Indians in Upper California." *Ethnographic Observations on the Coast Miwok and Pomo by Contre-admiral F. P. von Wrangell and P. Kostromitonov of the Russian Colony Ross.* Translated by Fred Stross, with ethnographic notes by Robert F. Heizer. Berkeley: Archaeological Research Facility, Department of Anthropology, University of California, Berkeley, 1974.

Yount, George C. [1855] 1923. Quoted in Camp 1923.

Zavalishin, Dmitry. [1864] 1973. "California in 1824." Translated and annotated by James R. Gibson. *Southern California Quarterly*, vol. 55, no. 4, Winter 1973.

NEWSPAPERS

Daily Alta California (San Francisco)
Los Angeles Herald
Marin County Journal
Marin County Tocsin
Marin Independent-Journal (San Rafael)
Mill Valley Herald
Petaluma Argus Courier
Petaluma Weekly Journal and Sonoma County Advertiser
Sausalito News
San Francisco Call-Bulletin
San Francisco Monitor
Santa Clara News
Sonoma County Journal
Sonoma Democrat

PUBLIC DOCUMENTS

"Before the United States Surveyor-General of California, in the matter of the Rancho Corte Madera del Presidio: Testimony and Proceedings." 1876. San Francisco: Francis and Valentine.

C-A. Archives of California, Hubert Howe Bancroft Collection, 1796-1848. 63 volumes. Extracts and summaries of Spanish and Mexican documents; originals destroyed by fire in 1906. Bancroft Library, University of California, Berkeley, California.

California State Archives. 1843. Landgrant Papers, vol. 7, pp. 60-67. Sacramento.

————. 1844. Landgrant Papers, vol. 5, pp. 145-50. Sacramento.

Marin County Coroner's Files. 1850-1887. Marin Civic Center, San Rafael, CA.

Register of Brands. 1828. Archives of California, Hubert Howe Bancroft Collection, 1796-1848, vol. 62, pp. 3-5. The Bancroft Library, University of California, Berkeley.

United States District Court (California: Northern District). 1885. "Diseño del Rancho Corte Madera del Presidio: Marin Co., CA." The Bancroft Library, University of California, Berkeley

United States Land Commission. 1854. Land Case 210 #80, Northern District, Tinicasia, United States District Court, The Bancroft Library, University of California, Berkeley.

————. 1854. Land Case #183, Northern District, Corte Madera del Presidio, United States District Court, The Bancroft Library, University of California, Berkeley.

————. 1855. Land Case 404 #684, Northern District, Nicasio or ex-Mission San Rafael, United States District Court, The Bancroft Library, University of California, Berkeley.

MISSION REGISTER REFERENCES

RAB. San Rafael Mission baptisms. *Libro de Bautismos.* Archives of the Archdiocese of San Francisco, California.

RAD. San Rafael Mission deaths. *Libro de Difuntos.* Archives of the Archdiocese of San Francisco, California.

RAM. San Rafael Mission marriages. *Libro de Casamientos.* Archives of the Archdiocese of San Francisco, California.

SBMA. Santa Barbara Mission Archives, Santa Barbara Mission Archives Library, Santa Barbara, California.

SBMR. Santa Barbara Mission Records, Santa Barbara Mission Archives Library, Santa Barbara, California.

SFB. San Francisco Mission (Mission Dolores) baptisms. *Libro de Bautismos.* Archives of the Archdiocese of San Francisco, California.

SFD. San Francisco Mission (Mission Dolores) deaths. *Libro de Difuntos.* Archives of the Archdiocese of San Francisco, California.

SFM. San Francisco Misison (Mission Dolores) marriages. *Libro de Casamientos.* Archives of the Archdiocese of San Francisco, California.

INDEX

Grimes 101
Grindstone Rancheria 101
Gualinlela 237
Guaulen 46, 70, 75, 111, 228, 236
Guaulenes 180
Guequistabal: see Nicasio (namesake) 140
Güillito 101
Guiluc 78, 89-90, 93
Gutierrez, José de Jesús María 131-132

Habasto 222
Halleck Creek 115, 184; figure 29b
hallucinogens 24
Hamilton City 101
Hamlet 192
Harlan, Elizabeth Campigli 191
Hartnell, W. E. P. 156-158
hawks 23
Healdsburg 88, 89, 122, 192, 197
healing 24, 197; see also doctors, medicine
herbs 4
Herodotus 107
Herrera, Cañada de 157
Herrera, José (Corporal) 74, 89-91, 93, 105,
    242
Hicks Mountain 115
Híjar, José María 138
Hittell, Theodore 138
Ho koo e koo Trail 180
hoipu 27-28
Hopland 186
Huchiun 40-41, 56, 242
Hueñux: see Camilo
Huggins, Dorothy H. xv
Huicmuse: see Marino
Huimen ix, 10, 12, 35, 41-42, 46-47, 48, 66,
    70, 72-73, 74, 75, 85, 86, 111, 228; figure
    22b
hukuiko 180, 257
hunting 29, 30

Ignacio 14, 180
Ignacio Valley 157
incarceration (of neophytes) 64, 66
Indian Grinding Rock State Park 227
infanticide 20
initiation 20

invitation strings 227
Íollo 74, 92, 237; figure 7
Isabel 161
Ishi 19

Jacinto 48, 49, 57, 111, 228
Jacobo 62
Jacome 86, 147
Jaume, Luís (Father) 119
Jausos 41
Jauyomi/Gualomi 78
Jayme, Luis 250
jewelry, figures 11b, 11d
Jimeno, Casarín (Manuel) 170, 172, 174, 177-
    178, 255
Joaquin 130
Jobochea: see Rafael
Jones, Farrington 234
Jorge 130, 145
José María 73, 83, 84, 85, 86, 147, 236, 251
Juan Antonio: see Quilajuque
Juan de Dios 79
Juana ix, 56, 57, 66, 67, 83-85, 87, 120, 124,
    125, 130, 135, 146, 150-151; figure 27c
Juanita: see Juana
Juarez, Cayetano 122, 166
Juliana 67
Juluio 46
Justina 67, 86
Justino 79, 85-86, 236, 251

Kainamako
Kearny, S. W. (General) 168
Kelly, Isabel xvi, 24
Kentfield 157
Khlebnikov, K. T. 59
Khlebnikov, N. K. 92
Kidd Creek 183
kidnapping of Indian children 145, 146
King, Tom 15
Kintín: see Quintino 108
Knight's Landing 101
Kostromitonov, P. 133-134, 209
Kotzebue, Otto von 30, 50, 53, 62, 63, 92,
    110, 120
Kroeber, Alfred xv
Kule Loklo 198, 227; figure 32b

Miller Valley 141

Milliken, Randall xii

Miranda, Juan 157

Mission Dolores: see Mission San Francisco de Asís

Mission La Purísima Concepción 82

Mission Pass 227

mission records x, xi, xii, xvi, 56, 68, 78, 148, 152, 162, 194, 211–212; figures 25, 26a, 26b, 27a, 27b, 27c, 27d

Mission San Antonio 61

Mission San Buenaventura 94

Mission San Carlos Borromeo 50, 54, 80, 83, 117, 118

Mission San Diego 61, 118, 119, 250

Mission San Francisco de Asís 1, 3, 10, 44–70, 61, 67, 71, 72, 85, 87, 93, 94, 96, 121, 124, 194, 213, 235; figures 8, 22b

Mission San Francisco de Solano 89, 93–94, 131, 136, 139, 144, 146, 213

Mission San Gabriel 118, 125

Mission San Jose 51, 59, 62, 71, 72, 73, 80, 81, 93, 94, 96, 112, 118, 161, 165, 194, 213, 233, 254; figure 17c

Mission San Juan Bautista 149

Mission San Luis Rey 84

Mission San Miguel 61

Mission San Rafael 66, 71–94, 100, 103, 120, 121–124, 127, 128–147, 158, 160–161, 210, 211–212, 213; figures 28a, 28b

Mission Santa Clara 50, 55, 67, 96, 112, 131, 136

Mission Santa Cruz 61, 81, 69, 118

Mission Santa Inés 73

Mission Soledad 118, 161

mission system (origins) 45

missions, attacks on: see resistance; crops 81–82; deaths 67, 151, 250; distribution of property to Indians 128, 137, 141–142, 156–159, 168–178; food at 58, 228; housing at 49, 50, 76; life after leaving 124; reasons for entering 47; treatment of women 50; unrest at 60–64

Miwok Archaeological Preserve of Marin xii, 198

Miwok, Bay 36, 48

Miwok, Bodega 133, 208

Miwok, Lake 99, 102, 151, 167

Miwok, Sierra 148

Mohave 32

moieties 225

Molina 246

Molina, José Santos 130–131, 135–136

Monico 162–163

Monzaga, Edward, figure 30

Monzaga, Joseph, figure 30

Moraga, Gabriel 74

Moreno, Rafael de Jesús (Father) 247

mortars 30

Morton Springs 257

Mottiqui: see Marina

Mount Burdell 67

Mount Diablo 25, 26, 27; figure 3b

Mount Konocti 25

Mount Lassen 101

Mount St. Helena 25, 26, 102

Mount Tamalpais 25, 26, 75, 179, 180; figure 3a

mountains 25

Murphy, Hugh J. (Chief Justice) 181

Murphy, Timothy 157, 159, 161, 167, 168, 174, 175

museums (European) 226

music 23, 59–60, 79; see also song

Mutuc 41

Naique ix, 12, 14, 75

Nanaguani ix, 72, 75, 249

Napa 180

Native Alaskans 7, 74

natural world of the Coast Miwok 1–9

Nelson, Nels 11, 13

Nemenciana 233, 236

Nemenciano: see Telemele

Nepomuceno, Juana 236

Nerea 83, 86

Nereo 12, 83, 86, 146, 236

Neri; see Nereo

Nestor 245

nets 29

New Albion 91

Nicasio 3, 81, 86, 88, 115, 140–141, 142, 149, 151, 152, 162, 170–178, 180, 189, 190, 215, 224, 228; figure 29b

Nicasio (namesake) 140

San Diego Mission: see Mission San Diego
San Fernando College 129
San Francisco Bay (formation of) 162–163
San Francisco Mission: see Mission San Francisco de Asís
San Geronimo 157, 165, 257
San Jose Mission: see Mission San Jose
San Mateo 125
San Pablo 145, 161
San Pedro 157
San Pedro Alcantara 77
San Pedro, Rancho de 113
San Quentin Point 107–108, 141, 157, 215
San Quentin Prison (name of) ix
San Rafael Creek 72
San Rafael Hill 75, 110
San Rafael Mission: see Mission San Rafael
San Rafael 11, 46, 80, 88, 141, 155, 179, 192, 195, 215, 228
San Ramon 165
San Vicente, Agustín Fernandez de 245
Sánchez, José (Sgt.) 74, 88, 98, 123
sandstone 13
Santa Clara Mission: see Mission Santa Clara
Santa Cruz Mission: see Mission Santa Cruz
Santa Eulalia (rancho) 125
Santa Margarita (rancho) 157
Santa María, Vicente (Father) 36–39, 40–41, 42, 51, 191, 226
Santa Rosa 145, 192, 195
Santa Rosa plain 100
Santiago 88
Sarría, Vicente de (Father) 69, 73, 81, 93
Sarris, Greg ix–x, xii, 196–199
Satan 54–55, 119
Satiyomi 143
Sausalito 11, 14, 46, 85, 162, 163, 215, 222
Savalishin 81
Schabelski, Achille 53, 90, 92
Schelikov, Achille 91–92
Scolastica: see Escolastica
scratching sticks 21
sea lions 6
seals 6
Sebastian ix, 140, 170, 172, 173–174, 176, 185
Sebastopol 192, 196
secret societies 23, 26

secularization 128, 137–142, 170
Serra, Junipero (Father) 119
Severa 103
Severo 102–103
sex 29
Shanks, Lisa xii
Shanks, Ralph xii
shell mounds 7, 11, 12, 13, 162
shellfish 7, 75, 192
shells 75
shipwrecks 190
Shishmarev 53
si'ika 185
Sierra Miwok: see Miwok, Sierra
Silva Island 14
Simpson, George (Sir) 161
Sloat, J. D. 168
smallpox 151–152
Smith, Bill (William) ix, 182, 187, 191, 196
Smith Brothers Fishery, figure 31
Smith, Carrie 188
Smith, Grant 182
Smith, Kathleen xii, 182, 183
Smith, Stephen 187, 191
Smith, Stephen Jr. 183
Smith, Tom ix, xvi, 3, 5, 6, 7, 18, 20, 24, 149, 152, 182, 187, 188, 193, 196, 197, 199, 236; figure 17b
Smith, Verna xii
soapstone 13
Solá, Pablo Vicente (Governor) 52, 71, 88, 95
Solano, Chief 139, 143, 144–145, 147, 163, 180, 240
Solano County (name of) 180
Solano (tribe) 164
Soledad 116
solstices 26; figure 4b
song 24, 32, 59, 60, 193; see also ceremonies, dance
Sonoma 65, 81, 180
Sonoma, Chief 126, 245
Sonoma Creek 228
Sonoma Mission: see Mission San Francisco de Solano
Sonoma Mountain 25, 67
Sonoma (tribe) 143
Sotoatijeium: see Juana

ABOUT THE AUTHOR

Photo by Marvin Collins

Betty Goerke has been teaching anthropology and archaeology at the College of Marin for over thirty years. She has done archaeological fieldwork in California, Colorado, Greece, Holland, Kenya, and India; has authored books and articles; and has produced several videotapes, including *Archaeology: Questioning the Past*. She lives with her husband in Mill Valley, California.

Since its founding in 1974, Heyday Books has occupied a unique niche in the publishing world, specializing in books that foster an understanding of the history, literature, art, environment, social issues, and culture of California and the West. We are a 501(c)(3) nonprofit organization based in Berkeley, California, serving a wide range of people and audiences.

We thank the following for their help in launching and supporting Heyday's California Indian Publishing Program:

Anthony Andreas, Jr.; Barona Band of Mission Indians; Fred & Barbara Jean Berensmeier; Black Oak Casino; Buena Vista Rancheria; California Indian Legal Services; Candelaria Fund; Columbia Foundation; Colusa Indian Community Council; Lawrence E. Crooks; Patricia A. Dixon; Elk Valley Rancheria; Federated Indians of Graton; Marion E. Greene; Hopland Band of Pomo Indians; LEF Foundation; Middletown Rancheria Tribal Council; Morongo Band of Mission Indians; National Endowment for the Arts; Pacific Legacy, Inc. San Francisco Foundation; Sandy Cold Shapero; Sierra Native American Council; Ernest & June Siva; Tomioka Family (In memory of Taeko Tomioka); Tom White; Harold and Alma White Memorial Fund

For more information about Heyday Institute, our publications and programs, please visit our website at www.heydaybooks.com.